HOSPITALITY SUPERVISION AND LEADERSHIP

LEVEL 3

David Foskett
Patricia Paskins
Gary Farrelly
Ketharanathan Vasanthan
Lindsay Steele

Orders: please contact Bookpoint Ltd, 130 Milton Park, Abingdon, Oxon OX14 4SB. Telephone: (44) 01235 827720. Fax: (44) 01235 400454. Lines are open from 9.00 to 5.00, Monday to Saturday, with a 24-hour message answering service. You can also order through our website www.hoddereducation.co.uk

If you have any comments to make about this, or any of our other titles, please send them to educationenquiries@hodder.co.uk

British Library Cataloguing in Publication Data

A catalogue record for this title is available from the British Library

ISBN: 978 1 471 84752 3

This edition published 2015.

Impression number   10 9 8 7 6 5 4 3 2 1

Year   2015, 2016, 2017, 2018

Copyright © 2015 David Foskett, Patricia Paskins, Gary Farrelly, Ketharanathan Vasanthan, Lindsay Steele

All rights reserved. No part of this publication may be reproduced or transmitted in any form or by any means, electronic or mechanical, including photocopy, recording, or any information storage and retrieval system, without permission in writing from the publisher or under licence from the Copyright Licensing Agency Limited. Further details of such licences (for reprographic reproduction) may be obtained from the Copyright Licensing Agency Limited, of Saffron House, 6–10 Kirby Street, London EC1N 8TS.

Hachette UK's policy is to use papers that are natural, renewable and recyclable products and made from wood grown in sustainable forests. The logging and manufacturing processes are expected to conform to the environmental regulations of the country of origin.

Typeset by Helvetica Neue Lt Std 45 Light by Aptara, Inc.

Printed in Great Britain for Hodder Education, an Hachette UK Company, 338 Euston Road, London NW1 3BH.

CONTENTS

The Level 3 NVQ Diploma in Hospitality Supervision and Leadership

How to use this book

CHAPTER 1 — 401
Set objectives and provide support for team members — 1
Communicating the team's objectives and purpose to team members — 1
Developing plans showing how team objectives will be met — 4
Monitoring and evaluating progress and recognising individual team achievement — 7

CHAPTER 2 — 402
Develop productive working relationships with colleagues — 10
The benefits of working with colleagues — 10
Establishing working relationships with colleagues — 12
Working in a professional and respectful manner — 17
Work-related difficulties and solutions — 21

CHAPTER 3 — 403
Contribute to the control of resources — 24
Identifying resources — 24
Using resources — 32

CHAPTER 4 — 404
Maintain health, hygiene, safety and security in the working environment — 39
Supervising health, hygiene, safety and security — 39
Dealing with emergencies — 53
Assessing risk — 64

CHAPTER 5 — 405
Lead the team to improve customer service — 77
Introduction — 77
Planning and organising the work of a team — 80

CHAPTER 6
Supervise functions — 88
Planning and preparing for a function — 89
At the end of the function — 98

CHAPTER 7
Supervise food service — 103
Planning for food service — 103
Preparing for food service — 109
Delivering food service — 113

CHAPTER 8	Supervise drink services	117
	Introduction	117
	Delivering drinks services	123

CHAPTER 9	Supervise housekeeping operations	128
	Supervising housekeeping operations	131
	Understanding the requirements of housekeeping operations	142
	Understanding how to supervise housekeeping operations	146
	Monitoring and reviewing housekeeping services	148

CHAPTER 10	Supervise reception services	155
	The role of the reception department	157
	Reception supervisor's duties	160

CHAPTER 11	Supervise reservations and booking services	166
	The reservations and booking service	166
	Organisational standards and policies	174
	Monitoring and reviewing procedures	180

CHAPTER 12	Contribute to promoting hospitality products and services	188
	Promotional activities	188
	Planning promotional activities	192
	Carrying out promotional activities	200

CHAPTER 13	Supervise linen services	204
	The linen service	204
	Planning and supervising the service	205

CHAPTER 14	Monitor and solve customer service problems	220
	How to resolve immediate customer service problems	220
	How to prevent repeated customer service problems	224

CHAPTER 15	Improve the customer relationship	229
	Communication	229
	Meeting expectations	231

CHAPTER 16	Support learning and development within own area of responsibility	236
	Learning and development	236
	Providing advice	237

CHAPTER 17	Supervise the use of technological equipment in hospitality services	240
	Introduction	
	Introducing new technologies	243

CHAPTER 18 426	Supervise practices for handling payments	252
	Handling payments	253
	Payment security	255
CHAPTER 19	Contribute to the selection of staff for activities	261
	Identifying staffing needs and planning	261
	Recruitment and selection process	262
	Staffing requirements and selection procedures	264
CHAPTER 20	Lead and manage meetings	272
	Introduction	272
	Carrying out the meeting	274
	After the meeting	276
CHAPTER 21 432.	Employment rights and responsibilities	229
	Employer and employee rights and responsibilities and organisational procedures	280
	Factors affecting your organisation and occupation	284
	Glossary	**289**
	Index	**293**
	Picture credits	**296**

The Level 3 NVQ Diploma in Hospitality Supervision and Leadership

The Level 3 NVQ Diploma in Hospitality Supervision and Leadership is designed to help you to progress to a more senior role within the hospitality industry. It allows you to broaden your existing knowledge and gain important leadership and management skills. It is a competency-based qualification; this means it assesses your ability to do your job (either in the workplace or in a realistic working environment). The qualification is also part of the Hospitality Supervision and Leadership apprenticeship (see below).

To achieve the Level 3 NVQ Diploma in Hospitality Supervision and Leadership you must achieve 37 credits in total. 23 credits must come from Mandatory Group A; at least 4 credits should come from Optional Group B; and the remaining 10 credits should come from Optional Groups B or C. The units and credit values are listed in the table below.

Unit title	Credit value
Mandatory Group A	
Set objectives and provide support for team members	5
Develop working relationships with colleagues	3
Contribute to the control of resources	4
Maintain the health, hygiene, safety and security of the working environment	4
Lead a team to improve customer service	7
Optional Group B	
Supervise food production operations	4
Supervise functions	5
Supervise food service	4
Supervise drink services	4
Supervise housekeeping operations	4
Supervise portering and concierge services	4
Supervise reception services	5
Supervise reservations and booking services	5
Optional Group C	
Contribute to promoting hospitality products and services	5
Contribute to the development of recipes and menus	4
Supervise off-site food delivery service	4
Supervised cellar and drink storage operations	5
Manage the receipt, storage or dispatch of goods	3
Supervise the wine store/cellar and dispense counter	5

Unit title	Credit value
Optional Group C	
Supervise vending service	5
Supervise linen services	4
Monitor and solve customer service problems	6
Improve the customer relationship	7
Support learning and development within own area of responsibility	5
Supervise the use of technological equipment in hospitality services	4
Supervise practices for handling payments	4
Contribute to the development of a wine list	5
Manage the environmental impact of work activities	5
Contribute to the selection of staff for activities	5
Ensure food safety practices are followed in the preparation and serving of food and drink	5
Lead and manage meetings	4
Employment rights and responsibilities in the hospitality, leisure, travel and tourism sector	2

The assessment process

Your assessor will first carry out an initial assessment to help you to decide which units to complete, identify any prior learning you have completed, any training you may need, and to agree an assessment plan with you. This assessment plan will include details of when and where you will be assessed and who will assess you. It will also include details of what evidence you will produce. There are many different types of suitable evidence, and the types of evidence you collect will vary depending on your job role. Your assessor will help you to identify what might be suitable, but evidence is likely to include some of the following:

Observation

This is likely to be the most common form of evidence. Your assessor will observe your performance at work.

Products of work

This includes real documents or products created as part of your work role – for example, staff rotas, accident reports, requisition sheets, menu plans, meeting minutes.

Witness testimony

This is a useful form of evidence, as your assessor may not always be present to observe your performance. There are two types of witness testimony:
- a witness testimony from a colleague, customer or supplier. This will be used alongside other forms of evidence towards your assessment
- an expert witness testimony from a line manager or other person who it has been agreed by your awarding organisation has sufficient experience or knowledge to be able to judge your competence

Candidate statement/report

This is a clear, written description of something you have done. You will need to cross-reference this to the units, learning outcomes and assessment criteria it covers. You can write about something you have done in the past, but it will need to be recent enough for the assessor to be able to infer that you are still able to complete the task.

Professional discussion

This is one or a series of planned in-depth discussions between you and your assessor about what you have done and when and how you did it. This type of evidence can also be used to supplement the other types of evidence listed above.

Evidence of knowledge and understanding

As well as assessing **performance evidence** (what you are able to do) by the methods listed above, some learning outcomes and assessment criteria assess what you **understand**. Evidence to assess your understanding may include:
- **questioning** – oral or written questions that assess knowledge and understanding
- projects, case studies and reflective accounts
- **professional discussion** – see above; professional discussion can be used to assess knowledge and understanding as well as performance
- **inferring knowledge and understanding from performance** – sometimes your assessor will be able to infer that you know and understand something from observing your performance or examining work products or witness testimonies.

Hospitality Supervision and Leadership apprenticeships

If you are working towards a Hospitality Supervision and Leadership apprenticeship, in addition to the Level 3 NVQ Diploma in Hospitality Supervision and Leadership you will also need to complete the Level 3 Award in Hospitality Supervision and Leadership Principles as your knowledge qualification or Technical Certificate (as well recognised English and Maths qualifications).

The Level 3 Award in Hospitality Supervision and Leadership Principles includes three units:
- Unit 1 Principles of leading a team in the Hospitality industry
- Unit 2 Supervision of Operations in the Hospitality industry
- Unit 3 Principles of Supervising Customer Service Performance in Hospitality Leisure Travel and Tourism

Units 1 and 2 are assessed by an online multiple-choice test.

Unit 3 can either be assessed by an externally set and marked short-answer test or an online multiple-choice test.

While Accredited Prior Learning (APL) cannot be transferred from the Level 3 NVQ Diploma in Hospitality Supervision and Leadership to the Level 3 Award in Hospitality Supervision and Leadership Principles, there are some core units in the NVQ qualification that touch upon outcomes within the Award. Refer to chapters in this book for details of content that is relevant to the Level 3 Award in Hospitality Supervision and Leadership Principles.

How to use this book

This book has been specially designed to help you master the skills and knowledge you need when building your evidence portfolio for the Level 3 NVQ Diploma in Hospitality Supervision and Leadership, or when working towards your Hospitality Supervision and Leadership apprenticeship.

Each chapter covers a different unit of the qualification; all of the mandatory Group A units are covered and 16 optional units from Groups B and C are included.

Chapters cover all of the underpinning knowledge you will need for the unit and clearly signpost to

All of the important **key words** are explained, to help you to understand exactly what you need to be able to do and understand.

Evidence boxes appear throughout each chapter and give you advice and guidance on the types of evidence that may be suitable for inclusion in your portfolio. Each of these evidence suggestions is clearly signposted to the assessment criteria to which they are relevant, to help you and your assessor to track and monitor your assessment progress.

Take it further boxes guide you to sources of other useful information that may also help you when building your evidence portfolio.

Knowledge check questions at the end of each chapter help you to check your knowledge and prepare for assessment, particularly when preparing for professional discussions or questioning. If you are an apprentice, they may also be useful when helping you to prepare for assessment of the Hospitality Leadership and Supervision Principles technical certificate.

The **Evidence checklist** at the end of each chapter summarises all of the assessment criteria and where you might find information to help you meet them.

Hospitality Supervision and Leadership Dynamic Learning Teaching and Learning Resources

Hospitality Supervision and Leadership Level 3 Teaching and Learning Resources provide further tailor-made support to help you to build your evidence portfolio.

For each unit you will find:
- a **unit overview** – a tutorial summarising the key underpinning knowledge for the unit. These are useful summaries for you to refer to as you prepare for assessment.
- **performance assessment activities** – these provide further suggestions for how you might demonstrate evidence for the performance assessment criteria. Each activity includes a clear explanation of what assessment criteria are asking you to do and provides suggestions for suitable evidence. The assessment criteria the activity is relevant to are clearly marked, so you can track progress through the unit and the qualification.
- **sample assignments** – to support you with generating knowledge and understanding assessment evidence. Assignments may cover a single assessment criterion or multiple criteria, and may be split into several smaller activities. They include activities such as writing reports or accounts, suggestions for professional discussions to have with your assessor, or series of questions to answer.

- **useful forms and templates** – while you're likely to be able to use many of the documents used as part of your work role and which meet the requirements and practices of your organisation, some useful templates and example documents are provided for reference.
- **automatically marked practise tests** – these are specifically designed to help with preparation for assessment of the Level 3 Award in Hospitality Supervision and Leadership Principles Technical Certificate for those completing the Hospitality Supervision and Leadership apprenticeship. For non-apprentice learners, these may also be useful for testing knowledge and understanding and for assessment preparation. Tests are marked automatically and feedback is given to both you and your assessor, to help you to identify where you may need further support with knowledge and understanding prior to assessment.

Find out more and sign up for free trials – visit:
www.hoddereducation.co.uk/dynamiclearning

CHAPTER 1

Set objectives and provide support for team members

This chapter will give you the information you need to develop and support team members through objective setting. Working in the hospitality industry is all about team work and it is essential to work together with set objectives to produce the desired result.

Learning objectives

On completion of this chapter, you should:
1 Be able to communicate a team's purpose and objectives to the team members.
2 Be able to develop a plan with team members showing how team objectives will be met.
3 Be able to support team members, identifying opportunities and providing support.
4 Be able to monitor and evaluate progress and recognise individual and team achievement.

The NVQ Level 3 in Hospitality Supervision and Leadership allows you to demonstrate your team-building skills. You will be required to provide evidence from your workplace on what you do and what you know. Throughout this chapter there are suggestions showing the assessment criteria and the evidence you might gather to meet them. There is also an Evidence Checklist at the end of the chapter. However, these are just a guide and are not exhaustive; there will be many other examples of evidence as you go about your daily duties.

Communicating the team's objectives and purpose to team members

1.1 The purpose of a team

The purpose of creating teams is to provide a working framework that has the ability to increase employees' participation in planning, problem solving and decision making to better achieve the aims and objectives of the organisation and to increase customer service. Much more can be achieved by teams than by individuals.

> **Evidence 1**
>
> **1.1**
>
> What is the purpose of your team?
>
> Use information from team meetings, emails and team briefings to help you write a personal statement about the purpose of your team and your involvement in it. Alternatively, you could have a professional discussion with your assessor about the purpose of your team and its aims and objectives. This discussion may be recorded for internal and external verification purposes.

Increased participation promotes:
- better understanding of decisions
- more support for and participation in implementation plans
- increased contribution to problem solving and decision making
- more ownership of decision processes and changes.

1.2 2.4 Setting objectives

An **objective** is a statement which describes what an individual, team or organisation is hoping to achieve. The supervisor or manager must get the objectives right to support the team members. Badly formulated objectives will lead the individuals and the team in the wrong direction, often creating confusion.

Team members have to be given clear objectives to successfully achieve their targets. The objectives must be realistic and support each individual team member. Achievable and realistic objectives engage and motivate individuals. Ensure that all members of the team agree that the objectives laid down can be achieved.

SMART objectives

SMART is an acronym which has been accredited to both Peter Drucker (1955) and George T. Doran (1981). It is now in common use among managers, who use SMART to set objectives within an appraisal and performance management system.

Objectives are SMART if they are: **S**pecific, **M**easurable, **A**chievable, **R**ealistic and **T**imely (time-bound).
- **Specific:** outline in a clear statement precisely what is required.
- **Measurable:** include a measure to enable you to monitor progress and to know when the objective has been achieved.
- **Achievable:** objectives can be designed to be challenging, but it is very important that failure is not built into objectives. Employees and managers should agree to the objectives to ensure commitment to them.
- **Realistic:** focus on outcomes rather than the means of achieving them.
- **Timely** (or time bound)**:** agree the date by which the outcome must be achieved.

To help set specific objectives, state:
- What is the team or individual going to do, and for whom?
- How will this be done and what strategies will be used?
- Why is this important to do?
- Is (or are) the objective or objectives understood by the team?
- Are you using action verbs to state the objectives?
- Who in the team is going to be responsible for what, and do you need anyone else to be involved?
- Where this will happen?
- When do you want it completed?
- What needs to happen?
- Is (or are) the outcome or outcomes clear?
- Will these objectives lead to the desired outcomes to help and promote the business?

> **Key terms**
>
> **Objective** – what you are trying to achieve
>
> **SMART objectives** – objectives that are Specific, Measurable, Achievable, Realistic and Time-bound

> **Evidence 2**
>
> **1.2** **2.4**
>
> You need to demonstrate that you can set both team objectives and personal work objectives with members of your team that are SMART (Specific, Measurable, Achievable, Realistic and Time-bound). Possible evidence that you are able to do this could include:
> - A list of team members, with SMART objectives attached and an explanation of how these support the business
> - A written list of team objectives
> - Target setting – this should include details of how these will be achieved and should be signed by team members
> - Team meeting minutes
> - Daily briefings
> - Appraisal forms
> - Individual targets

1.3 Communicating the team's purpose and objectives to its members

When communicating the team's purpose and objectives to team members, it is important to be specific, describing the result that is desired in a way that is detailed, focused and well-defined.

Figure 1.1 It is important to clearly communicate what the team's objectives are

The acronym KISS – Keep It Short and Simple – can be used in a business environment, and applies to both verbal and written communication. The basic principle of this is:
- use fewer words
- use shorter words
- use pictures, graphs or charts where possible.

Evidence 3

1.3

You need to be able to show that you can communicate the purpose of your team and the team's objectives to team members. Possible evidence to support this could include:

- team meeting minutes
- team briefings
- job descriptions
- department policies.

You should keep copies of team minutes and briefings in your portfolio of evidence, together with job descriptions and departmental policies (if these are not confidential). It is also useful to obtain copies of witness testimonies by your line manager or observation records from your assessor.

This approach can be used to ensure that you communicate effectively. Remember always to use:

- the right language for the occasion
- the right medium (this could be verbal communication, or it might be emails and letters).

This can help you to get your message across exactly how you want it to be received.

To reduce the potential for misinterpretation or confusion:

- maintain eye contact
- observe body language.

When listing your team's objectives and individual objectives, use action verbs – for example:

- analyse
- apply
- change
- create
- determine
- differentiate
- identify
- perform.

Avoid jargon words and phrases which are or can be misleading or ambiguous, such as:

- 'be aware of'
- 'have an awareness of'
- 'be prepared for a variety of.'

Developing plans showing how team objectives will be met

2.1 2.2 Discussing how team objectives will be met and ensuring team members participate in the planning process

When setting objectives with individuals and the team, remember that the objectives may seem intimidating to them. Often it is best to sit down with them and explain how they can be met. Demonstrate your support and confidence in them. Make sure all the team understands the team's objectives as well as the objectives of the organisation; and that they clearly understand their own roles and responsibilities in being able to achieve these objectives.

Team members must be encouraged to participate in planning of objectives, through brainstorming sessions, individual meetings and suggestion boxes. Brainstorming in an unthreatening environment can encourage creative thinking and can lead to the development of constructive ideas when planning aims and objectives.

When planning how team objectives will be met, allow people to respond, listen to what is being said to you and be prepared to discuss issues. Don't allow individual team members to dominate team meetings and convince other team members that their opinion is right. Remember, you may be outvoted by your team: accept it; a collective decision is more powerful and more likely to work than decisions imposed by the team leader.

2.3 Meeting objectives

Achievable objectives

Objectives, once set, must be achievable; they can be challenging but not unachievable. Set realistic objectives for your team. An objective is achievable if:
- You know that it is able to be measured.
- Others have already successfully achieved the objective.
- The resources are in place for them to be achievable.
- All limitations have been assessed.

Setting objectives that are unachievable is poor leadership and will lessen motivation. People react to this by applying little or no energy or enthusiasm because they see the objectives as futile and impossible. Equally, setting objectives at too low a level can be just as dispiriting.

Recognise that by stating that an objective is achievable, you are making a commitment to provide a level of resources, staff, money and time, without which the objective will not be achievable. This implies that in changed circumstances the objective would no longer be SMART for the individual, team or organisation.

Realistic objectives

Setting realistic objectives does not mean that they need to be easy. They can challenge the individuals and the team who have to deliver the objectives. To be challenging, it must mean that there is a high chance of success. When setting realistic objectives, you must take into account all your resources: skill, money available (the budget), equipment and time. You need to know:
- Is the objective achievable?
- Who is going to do it – an individual or a whole team?
- Do your staff have the skills to deliver the objective? (For example, if the restaurant wants to gain a Michelin star, do the chefs have the skills and are the resources available to upgrade the restaurant?)
- Who is responsible for what?

Managers and supervisors must avoid:
- setting objectives which aren't specific
- having no system, procedure or method in place to track and record the behaviour or action on which the objective is focused
- setting unachievable objectives
- setting unrealistic objectives
- not having the time frames for the achievement of the objectives
- setting an unachievable and unrealistic time frame
- failing to remember that situations change and therefore individuals and teams need to return to the objectives to renegotiate when situations make them less certain to achieve them or even impossible to achieve them.

> **Evidence 4**
>
> **2.1** **2.2**
>
> As a supervisor, you need to ensure team members participate in the planning process and think creatively about how team objectives will be met. Organise a creative workshop in which you and your team discuss and plan how you will meet your objectives. Evidence could include:
> - observation of the creative workshop by your assessor/witness
> - minutes of the planning meeting.

> **Evidence 5**
>
> **2.3**
>
> You need to develop plans to meet team objectives with your team. This should include making sure all the resources (staff, skills, equipment, money) are in place to achieve the objectives, knowing who is going to do what and when and having a system in place to track and record actions. Make these plans available for evidence – they should list team objectives.

5

3.1 3.2 3.3 3.4 Supporting team members, identifying opportunities and providing support

It is important for supervisors to identify opportunities or difficulties that team members may face and to give support to the team at all times when dealing with these challenges or opportunities.

Discuss with the team if they are facing any difficulties. Examples of common difficulties that may be faced in the hospitality industry include:
- how to overcome staff shortages
- how to cover for staff sickness
- how to deal with an unexpected booking which has not been recorded
- how to cope with a delayed flight with large numbers of upset travellers and how to book them in efficiently and provide for their needs.

In addition to these work-related difficulties, the supervisor may have to give emotional support to a team when some members are going through a difficult time personally or socially.

Supporting team members is not all about difficulties. It is also about providing support in looking for opportunities. This can be supporting the team to enter culinary competitions or attending industry events such as wine tastings. It may also include opportunities to gain additional qualifications and, when members want to move on to gain further experience, supporting them in their applications.

Evidence 6
3.1 3.2 3.3

If a member of your team is facing a difficulty or challenge, discuss this with them and provide them with appropriate advice and support to help them overcome these difficulties. Possible evidence for your portfolio could include:
- appraisal forms
- individual team member meetings (notes)
- team members' endorsement of your actions
- minutes of team meetings
- team briefing notes
- other evidenced documentation of how you deal with individual staff.

Evidence 7
3.1 3.2 3.4

For a member of your team who has a particular opportunity, discuss this opportunity with them and provide them with appropriate advice and support to make the most of their opportunity. Possible evidence for your portfolio could include:
- appraisal forms
- individual team member meetings (notes)
- team members' endorsement of your actions
- minutes of team meetings
- team briefing notes
- list of identified opportunities for each member of staff
- list of advice given
- outcomes of identified opportunities.

Monitoring and evaluating progress and recognising individual and team achievement

4.1 Monitoring and evaluating team activities and progress

In order to be able to **monitor** and **evaluate** progress, it is important that objectives are measurable and time-bound.

Measurable objectives

Ensuring that objectives are measurable is hugely important because it means that evidence is available from a system, method or procedure which has tracked and recorded the behaviour or action on which the objective is focused. This will enable you to know that the objective has been achieved.

When discussing with team members how team objectives will be met, consider:
- How will I know that the change has occurred?
- Can the measurements be obtained?

If it can't be measured now, the chances are that it won't be possible to measure in the future either.

Examples of measurable objectives are: 'The team is asked to achieve a 2% increase in gross profit sales'; or 'The housekeeping team is asked to increase productivity by asking each room assistant to clean an additional bedroom'.

Timely (or time-bound) objectives

Equally, it is important to have a deadline, date or time for delivering the objective or objectives to allow you to monitor and evaluate progress. Will the activity be accomplished or completed on time? A deadline creates urgency, prompts action and focuses the mind of those who are accountable for the commitments that they have made through the objectives. Not setting a deadline can reduce the motivation of the team or individual.

Always ask the question: Can the objective be delivered within the deadlines which have been established, taking into account all other competing demands which may cause delay?

Examples of measurable and time-bound objectives against which progress can be monitored include: 'The team is to achieve a 2% increase in gross profit sales within a six-month period'; or 'The housekeeping team is asked to increase productivity by asking each room assistant to clean an additional bedroom each hour'.

> **Key terms**
>
> **Monitor** – check, control, keep a record
>
> **Evaluate** – find or judge the value

> **Evidence 8**
>
> **4.1**
>
> You need to be able to monitor and evaluate individual and team activities and progress. Possible evidence to demonstrate this could include:
> - appraisal forms
> - observation of team review meetings
> - customer feedback sheets.

4.2 Recognising achievement of objectives

It is extremely important to recognise when a team has performed well and achieved its objectives. This in turn will help to increase staff members' motivation and their commitment to the team. The team may be awarded an annual bonus; individuals in the team may be singled out for a special achievement, for example, providing excellent customer service as revealed by a customer satisfaction survey. The individual employee may be awarded employee of the month and may be given a cash voucher as a reward.

> **Evidence 9**
>
> **4.2**
>
> You need to demonstrate that you provide recognition when individual and team objectives have been achieved. Possible evidence could include:
> - project appraisal forms
> - a list of rewards
> - promotion interviews.

Figure 1.2 A cash voucher or bonus may be given as a reward for a particular achievement

Knowledge check

1. What is an objective?
2. What does SMART stand for?
3. Why is SMART important in the planning process?
4. Why must your objective setting be achievable?
5. Give an example of a team objective in a:
   a. hotel restaurant
   b. reception area
   c. housekeeping area
   d. bar.
6. Why is it important to set deadlines?

Evidence checklist		
Assessment criteria		**Possible evidence**
1.1	Describe the purpose of a team	Evidence activity 1
1.2	Set team objectives with its members which are SMART (Specific, Measurable, Achievable, Realistic and Time-bound)	Evidence activity 2
1.3	Communicate the team's purpose and objectives to its members	Evidence activity 3
2.1	Discuss with team members how team objectives will be met	Evidence activity 4
2.2	Ensure team members participate in the planning process and think creatively	Evidence activity 4
2.3	Develop plans to meet team objectives	Evidence activity 5
2.4	Set SMART personal work objectives with team members	Evidence activity 2
3.1	Identify opportunities and difficulties faced by team members	Evidence activity 6 Evidence activity 7
3.2	Discuss identified opportunities and difficulties with team members	Evidence activity 6 Evidence activity 7
3.3	Provide advice and support to team members to overcome identified difficulties and challenges	Evidence activity 6
3.4	Provide advice and support to team members to make the most of identified opportunities	Evidence activity 7
4.1	Monitor and evaluate individual and team activities and progress	Evidence activity 8
4.2	Provide recognition when individual and team objectives have been achieved	Evidence activity 9

Set objectives and provide support for team members

9

CHAPTER 2

Develop working relationships with colleagues

This chapter is about how you develop productive working relationships with your colleagues within your own work environment, organisation and within other organisations so that they support and deliver your work and the work of the overall organisation.

> **Learning objectives**
>
> On completion of this chapter, you should:
> 1 Understand the benefits of working with colleagues.
> 2 Be able to establish working relationships with colleagues.
> 3 Be able to act in a professional and respectful manner when working with colleagues.
> 4 Be able to communicate with colleagues.
> 5 Be able to identify potential work-related difficulties and explore solutions.

In this chapter you are required to gather evidence of how you build and develop working relationships with colleagues. The Evidence Checklist at the end of this chapter lists the learning objectives and assessment criteria of your qualification and the types of evidence you could supply related to each criterion. Use this as a guide and, depending on where you are working, you will be able to find more examples of evidence.

The benefits of working with colleagues

1.1 The benefits of productive working relationships

The supervisor is responsible for developing good teamwork and helps to maintain good relationships within the team. As individuals working within an organisation, we can achieve very little, but working within a group we are able to achieve a great deal more. Those managing/supervising within the hospitality industry must develop effective teams in order to achieve the high standard of work that is required to satisfy both the organisation's management and the customers' demands.

Each member of a team must regard themselves as being part of that team. They must interact with one another and perceive themselves as part of the group. Each must share the purpose of the team. This will help build trust and support and will, in turn, result in an effective performance. Co-operation is important in order for the work to be carried out.

The characteristics of a good team

A good team will have the following characteristics:
- The objectives and goals of team should be clear and understood by everyone. Individuals need to fully understand what is expected of them and how to achieve their own personal goals.
- Everyone needs to understand what their responsibilities are, as well as the responsibilities of others and the team as a whole. There needs to be a culture where everyone is working together as a whole team.
- There needs to be good communication from team leaders, supervisors and managers, as well as good communication between team members and with those from other departments or teams. Communication channels must remain open and discussion must be positive and supportive.
- There will be people working at different levels with a good mix of skills. These skills should be used in harmony with each other; there should be a culture of 'skills sharing' and teaching new skills to less experienced colleagues.
- A good team will have members with mutual respect and trust for each other and an appreciation of each other's skills and what each person has to offer, contributing to the overall success of the team.
- There should be team spirit, with the mutual goal of striving towards success and moving the whole team forward to achieve excellence.

Figure 2.1 Staff working together as a team. Team members should understand their own responsibilities and those of others.

Benefits of team development

Selecting and shaping teams is very important and requires management skills. Matching each individual's talent to the task or job is an important consideration. A good, well-developed team will be able to do the following:

- create useful ideas
- analyse problems effectively
- get things done
- communicate with each other
- respond to good leadership
- evaluate logically
- perform skilled operations with technical precision and ability
- understand and manage the control system.

> **Evidence 1**
>
> **1.1**
>
> Write a report describing your experience of the benefits of developing productive working relationships with your colleagues at work. You may wish to include some of the following supporting evidence:
> - team meetings
> - targeted objectives being met in the team
> - team sales figures
> - customer feedback
> - testimonials from staff and managers.

Establishing working relationships with colleagues

2.1 Colleagues in your own and other organisations

Colleagues are any people you are expected to work with; this includes people in a similar position to you, as well as those in other positions. It may include people within your team or department (for example, other chefs in your brigade), others in your organisation (for example, the housekeeping team if you work in the reception team), or those who work in other organisations with whom you work (for example, suppliers).

Staffing within the hospitality industry is often very structured, with clear levels of management and defined job roles. However, job titles and roles may differ slightly from organisation to organisation. The person completing the supervision role may be known by their colleagues as the head chef, sous chef, chef de partie, kitchen supervisor, housekeeper, restaurant supervisor, reception supervisor or some other job title. The kitchen supervisor, for example, will be responsible to the catering manager; while in hotels and restaurants, a chef de partie will be responsible to the head chef. Some may be supervising a specific area of the kitchen or have specific supervisory tasks such as overseeing food safety. In a commercial catering role, they may supervise a section or sections of the food production system. Generally the head chef will have both managerial and supervisory skills and he/she will determine kitchen policies.

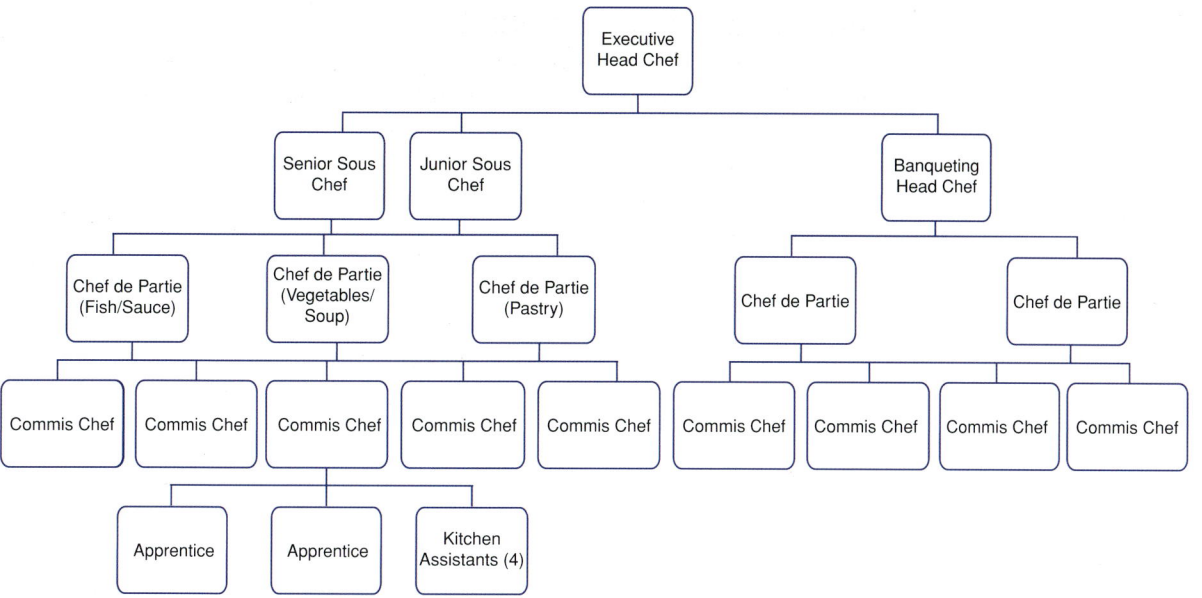

Figure 2.2 An example of staffing structure for a medium-sized hotel kitchen

The role of the supervisor

The supervision role is a very important one in the hospitality industry. Supervisors tend to be placed where the actual day-to-day work is being completed and so have an excellent understanding of the working area and the procedures within it. However, in addition to this, they often complete some management tasks and procedures, as well as communicate frequently with those at management levels. This puts them in a valuable and unique position to be able to liaise between the different employee levels easily. Those working on more practical and everyday tasks such as in a kitchen often feel more confident and comfortable communicating with the supervisor they see and work with every day than they would with someone in a more senior position.

The exact details of the job will vary according to the different areas of the industry and the size of the various units, but the supervisory role is essentially that of an overseer. It involves three functions:

1 **Technical function** – the supervisor needs to be able to actually do the job themselves and do it well, and to impart these skills to others in the team.
2 **Administrative function** – the administrative function includes the allocation of duties. It may also include the writing of reports.
3 **Social function** – the supervisor needs to motivate the staff in the team. This means keeping them interested and keen to achieve and progress. Supervisors often take responsibility for staff training and the recording of training. Training may be delivered by supervisors themselves or they may organise others to complete it where more specialist knowledge is needed.

Evidence 2

2.1

Who are your colleagues, both within your own and in the other organisations you work with? Possible evidence for your portfolio to show this could include:

- testimonials from colleagues
- organisational charts
- competitor staffing analysis charts.

2.2 Agreeing roles and responsibilities

The primary role of the supervisor is to ensure that a group of people work together to achieve the goals set by the business, managing physical and human resources to achieve customer service goals. This requires planning, organising, staffing, directing and controlling. On a daily basis, the supervisor is the person who ensures everything runs as smoothly as possible and that all the necessary tasks are allocated logically among the available staff, so the job gets done. Those within the hospitality industry tend to work within very tight deadlines and time constraints, yet the demands of customer expectations and requirements must still be met. The supervisor is there to ensure this happens and that targets for individuals, the team and the wider organisation are met. One of the key aspects of the supervisor's administrative function is to agree the roles and responsibilities of people within their team.

Forecasting and planning

Before making plans and agreeing roles and responsibilities for their team, it is necessary for the supervisor to look ahead, to foresee possible and probable outcomes and to allow for them. For example, if a supervisor knows that their assistant will not be in work the next day, they will need to look ahead and plan accordingly. This may involve agreeing different roles and responsibilities for some people. When deciding on responsibilities, they may need to consider, for example, how many meals need to be prepared, how many staff will be needed and which staff will be needed and at what times.

Job descriptions

A team member's job description will give an overview of the job and the duties and responsibilities that come with it. When an organisation writes a job description for new members of staff, they often include the key duties and responsibilities of the job. However, job descriptions often do not include specific details for every task a team member will complete as part of their role, and generally only outline key duties and responsibilities. Job descriptions often include clauses which state that staff may be expected to carry out other duties discussed with their line manager, and it is the supervisor's role to discuss these responsibilities with their staff.

JOB DESCRIPTION

Title of job: Restaurant waiter

Purpose of job: To provide a quality food and beverage service to meet our customers' expectations and to enhance and maintain the reputation of the company.

Reporting to: Restaurant supervisor

Skills, experience and qualifications required:
- Good communication, presentation, time management and social skills
- One year's similar experience
- Wine knowledge useful but not essential as training will be given
- Current Food Handler's Certificate desirable but full training will be provided

Main duties:
- Preparation of the restaurant area ready for service in accordance with the establishment daily duties list.
- Service of food and beverages to customers in accordance with the service specification.
- Ensuring correct charges are made and payment received.
- Clearing of restaurant area in accordance with service specification.
- Ensuring compliance with control procedures for equipment and other stock.
- Following correct health and safety procedures to ensure welfare of both staff and customers.
- Explaining to customers the content, preparation and presentation of all menu and beverage items, and promoting sales through positive selling techniques.
- Additional food and beverage service duties as required in order to meet business demands.

Training requirements
- Induction and company policy as contained in the Staff Handbook
- Menu and beverage list content and updates as required
- Customer care programme
- Basic food hygiene
- Basic fire training at induction and further training every six months
- Basic health and safety at induction and full COSHH every six months
- Manual handling at induction

Performance measures
- Customer feedback
- Management feedback
- Regular knowledge test on foods, wine and other services offered
- Six-monthly appraisals with restaurant supervisor

Figure 2.3 A job description for a restaurant waiter. Notice how it includes the main tasks of the role, but not every specific task.

Allocating tasks based on the team's skills

Maintaining the success of the team and developing it further demands constant attention. The individual members of a group will never become a team unless effort is made to ensure that the differing personalities are able to relate to one another, communicate with each other and value the contribution each employee or team member makes. The team leader or supervisor needs to identify the strengths and weaknesses of each individual team member, to allocate responsibilities according to team members' abilities, and to develop ways to help to overcome any weaknesses there may be to ensure the team works effectively together. For example, they need to consider some of the following questions. Do members of the team possess the required skills for the tasks they have been asked to complete? Is one member of the team better at some tasks than someone else? The supervisor may need to plan for any additional training sessions that may be needed so that staff can undertake their responsibilities.

Commanding

Hospitality is often a disciplined and time-constrained operation. The supervisor needs to give instructions to staff about:
- How specific tasks need to be completed.
- Exactly what needs to be done.
- When each process needs to be completed and individual items need to be ready.

The successful supervisor is able to give instructions effectively, having made decisions and established the basic priorities. They need to communicate this to their teams. This may be done using various methods, including duty rotas, briefings, meetings or training sessions.

Co-ordinating

Co-ordinating is a skill required to get all of the tasks completed to come together at the time required and for staff to co-operate and work together in harmony. To achieve this, the supervisor has to be interested in the staff, deal with their queries, listen to their problems and be helpful. They also need to maintain good relationships with other areas and departments. Good service is dependent on effective co-ordination.

Delegation

By giving a certain amount of responsibility to others, the supervisor can be more effective. The supervisor needs to be able to judge the person capable of responsibility before any delegation can take place. But then, having recognised the abilities of an employee, the supervisor who wants to develop the potential of those under his or her supervision must allow the person entrusted with the job to get on with it.

Motivating the team

A supervisor must motivate his/her team by striving to make their work interesting, challenging and demanding. People must know what is expected of them and what the standards are. Rewards should be linked to effort and results. All of these factors must also work towards fulfilling:
- the needs of the organisation
- the expectations of team members.

For the supervisor to manage his/her staff effectively, it is important to get to know them well, understand their needs and aspirations and attempt to help them achieve their personal aims. Although not everyone is capable of or wants significant amounts of responsibility, the supervisor still needs to motivate those who are less ambitious. Most people are prepared to work to improve their standard of living or status, but getting satisfaction from the work they do is also a motivating factor. The supervisor must be aware of why people work and how different people achieve job satisfaction and then be able to act on this knowledge. Involving staff in decision making and planning, and making them aware that they are valued goes a long way in achieving this. Opportunities must be made to extend their abilities and learn new skills. Everyone should be kept fully occupied and the working environment must be conducive to producing their best work.

If a supervisor is able to manage the team by co-ordinating its members' aims with the corporate objectives – by reconciling their personal aspirations with the organisation's need to operate profitably – this supervisor will manage a successful team and, in addition, will enhance their own reputation.

> **Evidence 3**
> **2.2**
> You need to be able to demonstrate that you can agree the roles and responsibilities for colleagues. Possible evidence to demonstrate that you have agreed the roles and responsibilities for people within your team could include:
> - team meeting minutes
> - job descriptions
> - signed worksheets.

Working in a professional and respectful manner

3.1 Professional behaviour

The supervisor as a team leader has a strong influence on their team or brigade. The supervisor is expected to set examples that have to be followed. They need to work with the team, often under pressure, and sometimes deal with conflict, personality clashes, changes and stress. The supervisor has to adopt a range of strategies and styles of working in order to build loyalty, drive, innovation, commitment and trust in team members. In doing this, it is important that they demonstrate professional behaviour at all times.

Characteristics of leadership

Certain leadership qualities are needed to enable the supervisor to carry out the role effectively and professionally. A good supervisor is someone who is:
- a good team member who can lead by example
- open to new ideas and can initiate new ideas
- fair
- well informed and knowledgeable
- well organised and able to organise others
- a good communicator and mediator
- motivational and able to inspire
- consistent and reliable
- an effective planner
- a good decision maker
- understanding and approachable
- supportive and respectful to the rest of the team
- able to establish policies and procedures
- aware of current legislation
- able to work under pressure
- able to co-operate well at different levels
- able to command loyalty and respect.

The good supervisor will need to develop excellent 'people skills' – building trust and earning respect from those they are supervising. They need to be someone who is approachable, with good listening skills, who can be spoken to with complete confidentiality and can identify and deal with problems, conflict and unrest that may occur in their area. The effective supervisor is always proactive, sets the standards and leads the team by good example.

Leadership and supervisory styles

Staff must be encouraged and motivated to follow required procedures. This can be done in a positive way by offering incentives or rewards, or a more disciplinary approach may sometimes be necessary. Both methods can be effective and can be used by supervisors to achieve their required goals. Leadership style is the way in which the functions of leadership are carried out – the way in which the supervisor typically behaves towards members of the team. There are many dimensions to leadership and many possible ways of describing leadership style. These are:

- **Dictatorial** – a supervisor who is autocratic and can often be oppressive and overbearing.
- **Bureaucratic** – a supervisor who follows official procedure and can be considered 'office bound'. The bureaucrat sticks to the rules and operates best within a hierarchical system.
- **Benevolent** – a kind, passionate, humane, kind hearted, good, unselfish and charitable supervisor.
- **Charismatic** – a supervisor with personality and special charm who inspires loyalty and enthusiasm from the team.
- **Consultative** – the consultative supervisor discusses issues with the team through team or individual meetings.
- **Participative** – a supervisor who gets involved with the team, taking part in activities and issues and making an active contribution to the success or failure of the team.
- **Unitary** – the supervisor unites the team, bringing them together as a whole unit.
- **Delegative** – the delegative supervisor entrusts others in the team to make decisions, assigning responsibility or authority to others.
- **Autocratic** – this is where the supervisor holds onto power and all the interactions within the team move towards the supervisor. The supervisor makes all the decisions and has all the authority.
- **Democratic** – the team has a say in decision making. The supervisor shares the decision making with the team. The supervisor is very much part of the team.
- **Laissez-faire** – this style is where the supervisor observes that members of the group are working well on their own and leaves them 'to get on with it'. The supervisor passes power to the team members, allows them freedom of action, does not interfere but is available for help if needed.

The supervisor should be able to obtain the best from the team they have responsibility for. They also need to completely satisfy the management of the establishment that an effective job is being done.

Ethical issues

The supervisor needs to treat everyone in the team with equality and fairness and ensure there is no discrimination within the team, especially on grounds of gender, race, religion and beliefs, sexual orientation and disability.

A supervisor must be consistent when handling staff, avoiding favouritism and perceived inequity. Such inequity can arise from the amount of training or performance counselling given, from the promotion of certain employees and from the way in which shifts are allocated. Supervisors should engage in conversations with all staff, not just a selected few, and should not single out some staff for special attention. Ethical treatment of staff is fair treatment of staff. A good supervisor will gain respect if they are ethical.

Take it further

The hospitality industry is becoming more diverse and, for this reason, the team must celebrate and welcome diversity and embrace equal opportunities. The free movement of labour within the European Union, for example, has meant that large numbers of people from different cultures now work together in the hospitality industry. Diversity can contribute positively to the development of the team, bringing to it a range of skills and ideas from different cultures. Diversity recognises that people are different. It includes not only cultural and ethnic differences, but differences in gender, age, disability and sexual orientation, background, personality and work style. Effective working relationships should harness such differences to improve creativity and innovation and be based on the belief that groups of people who bring different perspectives will find better solutions to problems than groups of people who are the same.

Confidentiality

Confidentiality is an important issue for the supervisor. Employees or customers may wish to take the supervisor into their confidence and should be able to trust that confidentiality will be maintained. Confidentiality and security of information and data are a legal requirement under the Data Protection Act 1988.

Ensuring the welfare of colleagues

The supervisor must ensure all the necessary tasks are allocated logically among the available staff, so the job gets done. This must be done with the welfare of the workforce in mind, avoiding too much stress or pressure on individuals. The supervisor plays a very important part in making the environment as safe and as pleasant to spend time and work in as possible. A good working environment tends to be valued by employees and this will be reflected in their attitudes to work and the quality of work they produce. Good working conditions and environments also contribute to staff loyalty and a lower staff turnover.

Adherence to legislation

Hospitality workplaces are governed by significant amounts of legislation and the supervisor needs to have good knowledge of this and also know where to find out about the details they are not fully sure of. A good knowledge of relevant legal matters allows the supervisor to apply this to the working area, ensuring that areas, equipment and procedures meet legal requirements. They will also use their knowledge of legal requirements as part of staff training.

Evidence 4
3.1

You need to be able to explain how to display and demonstrate behaviour that shows professionalism. This could include:
- line manager testimonials
- customer feedback
- recorded interviews
- written evidence
- a copy of your organisation's policy on professional behaviour
- a self-reflection statement
- your appraisal form.

Communicating with colleagues

In the hospitality industry, most jobs have some communication component and successful communication is vital to building successful working relationships. As a supervisor/manager, the emphasis is on achieving results through the team, and communication is the key to this. A great deal of the supervisor's time will be taken up with communicating with large numbers of people. The supervisor will use their communication skills to lead and motivate others so the required goals are met. It would be very difficult, if not impossible, to supervise others if you were not a good communicator. Effective communication is at the heart of good supervision and leadership and effort should be put into communicating well at all times.

Figure 2.4 Effective and appropriate is a key skill for a supervisor

4.1 Communicating information to others clearly and concisely

In order to convey orders, instructions and information, the supervisor should possess a positive attitude to those with whom they need to communicate. The ability to convey orders and instructions in a manner that is acceptable to the recipient is dependent not only on the words but on the emphasis given to the words, the tone of voice, the time selected to give them and on who is present when they are given. This is a skill that supervisors need to develop. Instructions and orders can be given with authority without being dictatorial.

Breakdowns in communication occur when the intent of a communication is not translated into the effect – your colleague does not do what you have asked them to do because they misinterpreted what you said or the manner in which you said it. Such breakdowns affect staff and team relationships and individuals' attitudes towards and views of each other.

By communicating clearly and concisely so that the person or people you are communicating with understand and respond accordingly, you can begin to change the culture of the working environment. Effective communication has a positive effect: staff begin to respect each other; they listen more carefully to each other, with positive expectations, hearing the constructive intent and responding to it.

In order to ensure that information is communicated clearly when communicating verbally, supervisors should:
- Speak clearly, with good pronunciation and sufficient volume.
- Try not to speak too fast, especially when speaking to someone whose first language is not English.
- Be specific about the task you want someone to complete or the information they need to understand.
- Check whether the person or people can hear you clearly.
- Check that they understand what is being said and what needs to be done.
- Respond appropriately to any questions the team ask you.

Similar principles apply to information you communicate in writing. It is important that you write clearly so that others understand your meaning.

4.2 Receiving and clarifying information

When receiving information from others:
- Concentrate on what is being said.
- Think about what is being said.
- Show interest in the person speaking to you.
- Acknowledge what is being said.
- If necessary, ask questions to confirm what is being said, what you need to do or if you do not understand.
- Clarify in your own words what the person is asking you to do.

Work-related difficulties and solutions

5.1 Potential work-related difficulties and conflicts of interest

Difficulties and conflicts of interest can arise between individuals and teams, especially when bidding for resources and with budget constraints. These can relate to staffing issues, equipment and staff development budgets. Conflicts of interest often arise between different departments within an organisation.

Evidence 5
4.1 **4.2**

You need to be able to identify how to pass information to others clearly and concisely. Possible evidence to demonstrate this includes:
- written information sheets
- recorded staff briefings.

You will also need to be able to explain how to receive and clarify your own understanding of information that is given to you. Possible evidence includes:
- copies of emails
- management meeting briefing notes.

Evidence 6
5.1

You need to be able to identify potential work-related difficulties and conflicts of interest. Possible evidence could include:
- minutes of health and safety meetings
- maintenance records
- records of staff meetings.

Additional evidence can be gained through a professional conversation with the assessor and/or a report on managing conflicts in the workplace by the candidate.

A conflict with the manager or with a colleague can easily get entangled with issues about work and status, both of which can make it difficult to approach the problem in a rational and professional way. One of the skills of the supervisor is the ability to identify conflict so that plans can be put in place to minimise it. The following are just some of the points that should be borne in mind:

- Conflict arises where there are already strained relationships and personality clashes between members of the team.
- Conflict often occurs when the team is understaffed and under pressure, especially over a long period. Pressure can also come from, for example, restaurant reviews and guides when a chef is seeking a Michelin star or other special accolade.
- Conflicts damage working relationships and upset the team and this will eventually show up in the finished product.

The supervisor must also be aware of any conflict that may be going on around them in less obvious places. Covert conflicts (those that take place in secret) can be very harmful. Although this type of conflict is often difficult to detect, it will undermine the team's performance. Many conflicts start with misunderstandings or a small upset that grows and escalates out of all proportion.

5.2 Resolving difficulties

The supervisor needs to anticipate possible problems and build up a good team ethic to overcome problems. This means that work needs to be allocated according to each individual's ability.

Resolving potential difficulties can be a particularly demanding task for the supervisor. This can be done through acting as an arbitrator for the various individuals or teams in conflict, discussing the issues with them and talking to reach a compromise. It is important to demonstrate empathy with all parties and not to take sides, but come to a resolution that all parties agree on.

Evidence 7
5.2

You need to be able to explain how to resolve any potential difficulties in your organisation. Possible examples of evidence might include:
- recorded conversations
- question and answer sessions
- case study evidence.

Knowledge check

1. Describe how you would improve communication within your team.
2. State the qualities that would confirm to you that a group of people were demonstrating good teamwork practices.
3. List six positive types of behaviour from team members that would enhance the performance of the team.
4. As a supervisor, what are the ways you could demonstrate to your team that everyone is being treated fairly and with equality?
5. List the various tasks you would delegate to your team.
6. Why is it important to give feedback to your team?
7. State the various ways in which you motivate your team.
8. If you are having difficulties in developing a positive working relationship with one or two team members, what do you consider you need to do to achieve a positive outcome?

Evidence checklist		
Assessment criteria		**Possible evidence**
1.1	Describe the benefits of productive working relationships	Evidence activity 1
2.1	Identify colleagues within own and other organisations	Evidence activity 2
2.2	Agree the roles and responsibilities for colleagues	Evidence activity 3
3.1	Explain how to display behaviour that shows professionalism	Evidence activity 4
4.1	Identify information to others clearly and concisely	Evidence activity 5
4.2	Explain how to receive and clarify own understanding of information	Evidence activity 5
5.1	Identify potential work-related difficulties and conflicts of interest	Evidence activity 6
5.2	Explain how to resolve identified potential difficulties	Evidence activity 7

CHAPTER 3

Contribute to the control of resources

This chapter is about making sure that you and the staff you are responsible for use resources effectively and efficiently, without unnecessary waste. It covers obtaining supplies, checking equipment, monitoring the use of resources and keeping records.

> **Learning objectives**
>
> On completion of this chapter, you should:
> 1 Be able to contribute to the control of resources.
> 2 Understand factors affecting the use of resources.
> 3 Understand how to contribute to the control of resources.

The NVQ Level 3 in Hospitality Supervision and Leadership is based on what you do in your working area and working day. It is therefore necessary for you to provide evidence of what you do and how you do it. Throughout the chapter there are suggestions showing the assessment criteria of your qualification, and the types of evidence you could supply related to each criterion. These are also summarised in the Evidence Checklist at the end of the chapter. Just use these as a guide; you will probably be able to find more examples of evidence within your workplace.

Identifying and ordering resources

1.1 2.1 Identifying the resources you need

> **Key term**
>
> **Resource** – a product, person, money by an item used by an organisation or individual to function efficiently

All departments will need different **resources** to perform their specific roles within a business. It is important that these resources are identified, obtained, used and managed to ensure the business runs efficiently and profitably. Businesses and departments within a business will use a number of or even all of the following resources:

- **Staff** – the most important resource any business has is their staff. As supervisor you may have a number of staff working for you to produce your products and meet your targets.
- **Supplies** – these are items that are needed for your staff to perform and complete their jobs within the organisation. For example, a chef needs food to prepare and cook for customers and a housekeeper needs cleaning materials, linen and toiletries to prepare a room for a new guest. These can also be reusable supplies that are held by the business, such as plates, glasses and cutlery.

- **Equipment** – the equipment needed for each department will differ. However, equipment such as ovens, refrigerators and food processors in the kitchen and coffee machines in the café can be essential for the day-to-day smooth running of the department. A supervisor may need to identify more equipment to be used when planning for new business or functions.
- **Time** – time is a resource that needs to be managed well to ensure tasks and objectives are met. A supervisor is expected to manage their time and the time of their staff effectively, by applying the optimum number of staff, equipment and supplies needed to complete the task on time. For example, a hotel may have to strip a room down from breakfast and prepare it for a wedding in three to four hours. A supervisor will delegate the tasks and have the equipment and supplies in place to ensure they are completed in time.
- **Finance** – for any business to survive, it needs to make money to pay the bills and the wages of the staff working for the company. These are just the basic finances for the business to survive. For a business to be successful and grow, it needs to make a profit. The business as a whole will have a business plan and each department will have a budget to work within to ensure it does not overspend and the financial targets are met. All resources within the business will be governed within this financial plan. A well-run business will have procedures in place to monitor the money being spent in each department and the stock being held.
- **Energy** – energy such as gas and electricity is used by all organisations and is not usually the responsibility of each department to manage within their budgets. Energy can be extremely expensive, however, and is often not used correctly and wasted. For instance, just leaving lights on in rooms or ovens left on when they are not being used can greatly increase a business's energy bill. It is important that staff are trained to understand the importance of saving energy in the workplace and supervisors manage this resource to ensure the business is not losing money unnecessarily.

Figure 3.1 As a supervisor you should make sure there is adequate equipment for the smooth running of your department

Availability of resources

Identifying and having the correct resources available at the correct time is essential for the smooth running of any business. If a function in a hotel has a special menu, it is the head chef's or supervisor's job to ensure the chefs preparing the meal have the correct ingredients, equipment, staff and time to have it ready on time. It is also important that there is a contingency plan in place if anything should go wrong such as shortage of staff, missing ingredients or equipment breaking down. If these resources are not available on time, it may result in staff not being able to complete the tasks on time. This could result in unsatisfied customers and have a negative effect on the business.

Checking the availability of resources

To ensure that resources are available to each department, businesses often have systems and procedures in place to check that there is enough stock, equipment and staff available for each department to function efficiently.

- **Stock checks** – may be done regularly to see what is in stock and what is needed for the future needs of the business. These could include a daily fresh food stock check or weekly dry stores check in the kitchen or regular checks to see if there are enough plates, cutlery and glasses for future functions.
- **Equipment lists or inventories** – each department should keep an inventory of its equipment. This inventory should also include the number of items, the safety checks and service records and where each piece of equipment is kept or positioned in the department. Large organisations may have equipment they store and only use for special events or functions. Small organisations may not have an inventory of their equipment; however it is important that they have regular checks to ensure the equipment is safe and in good working order.
- **Staff rotas** – it is important that every business has the correct number of staff available to suit the demands of the day. All departments will have days when they are busier than others. It is important that the staff rota reflects that level of business, so more staff are available at these busy times. The staff rota also allows the supervisor to manage their staff's days off, holidays, training and make changes when staff are off sick.

> **Evidence 1**
> **1.1** **2.1**
> Locate or list all of the resources your department uses and highlight all of the resources you use in your role.

2.10 2.11 Ordering supplies

The responsibility for ordering supplies can differ in all organisations. In some organisations, it is the responsibility of the head of department to identify the suppliers they would like to use. Restrictions on what can be purchased by each department and member of staff can also be made by some organisations. This helps the company monitor what is being purchased and limits the number of people authorised to order supplies.

Suppliers may also be chosen for other reasons such as ethical and environmental reasons. They may be specialist suppliers that stock high quality and niche products. The senior management may have a preference for which suppliers are used. They may offer larger discounts or better payment terms on their products. Small and privately owned businesses may choose to use smaller and more specialist suppliers.

Types of supplier

- **Manufacturer** – organisations may buy directly from the supplier. These products may include large equipment such as ovens, mixing machines and dishwashers for the kitchen, and furniture and beds for hotel rooms.

- **Wholesaler and distributor** – purchases of large quantities of resources from different organisations and suppliers such as meat, fish, beverages and dry goods. They often have sales teams that can advise on new products and promotions. They take the order and deliver the order directly to the business, with delivery often for free or as long as your order is over their minimum spend.
- **Nominated suppliers** – larger companies may have nominated suppliers that they must use. Some companies even have purchase order numbers that must be given to the supplier with each purchase, so the company has a record of all orders.
- **Cash-and-carry and markets** – some smaller hospitality businesses may choose to buy their products from cash-and-carries, as they need them. These are premises that you can walk around and take the products you need and buy at a discounted rate. Markets can also be used to buy meat, fish, fruit and vegetables in bulk and at a discounted rate. These suppliers do not deliver, so it would be the responsibility of the organisation to take the stock back to the business.
- **Retail outlets** – these are high street shops and supermarkets that may have limited special offers that are cheaper than the wholesaler. They allow the business to buy smaller quantities and additional supplies if there is a shortage. Electrical and small equipment such as blenders and domestic microwaves should not be purchased for commercial businesses, as they do not have the capacity or power of commercial equipment and could be a health and safety risk if they are used.
- **Specialist suppliers** – these may specialise in fine wines, stationery and specialist fine foods. These suppliers will be very knowledgeable about their products; however they may only be able to obtain and supply small quantities of their products. This is not always suitable for larger organisations.
- **Local suppliers** – some organisations may prefer to purchase their products from local suppliers, to support their local community. Some chefs like to name the local business or producer on their menu, which shows the provenance and traceability of their ingredients.

> **Evidence 2**
> 2.10 2.11
>
> Identify the suppliers your department or college uses, with the products they supply. Name the department or people responsible for ordering resources within your organisation or college.

1.2 3.4 2.7 2.8 2.9 Obtaining additional resources – budgets and spending limits

Financial **budgets** and targets are often made in advance and do not make allowances for busy periods and additional business that may have been booked later in the year. If more resources are needed, the supervisor managing the budget may have to use surplus money available from quieter months. If it is necessary to go beyond the spending limits of the department, management approval will have to be sought to acquire more money. This will often involve making a case as to why it is needed and why they are exceeding the financial budget set for that department. It is extremely important that all supervisors work within their agreed spending limits to ensure their department and organisation remain profitable and competitive in the market.

> **Key term**
>
> **Budget** – an estimate of the amount of money, resources or revenue that can be used over a set period of time

> **Evidence 3**
> 1.2 3.4
>
> Produce a flow chart to show your organisation's procedures for ordering step by step.

> **Evidence 4**
>
> **2.7** **2.8** **2.9**
>
> With your line manager, discuss and document your organisation's procedures for your department's spending limits and the process of obtaining management approval for additional resources beyond your spending limits.

Figure 3.2 As a supervisor you should think about the spending requirements of your department

> **Evidence 5**
>
> **2.2**
>
> Use a stock sheet to show the resources you use within your department.

1.5 2.2 2.3 Checking the suitability of resources

It is important that the resources needed within each department meet the needs of the business and are fit-for-purpose. These checks can be carried out during formal stock checks or just a visual check to see if the resources available are of the correct quality and quantity required. The expectations of a customer in a fine dining restaurant may require the chef to source specialist ingredients for the menu and the headwaiter may need fine glass and china for each of the courses during the restaurant service. In all businesses, supervisors and staff should be able to assess the quality of the resources and products being used and know when to remove damaged and poor quality products when needed. Most organisations will make a record of any waste or damaged goods so it can be accounted for in the budget.

> **Evidence 6**
>
> **1.5** **2.3**
>
> Record a discussion with the person responsible for ordering in your department about how the quality, quantity and suitability of resources are selected.

1.5 1.6 3.6 3.10 Storing and maintaining resources

Storing resources

Resources can be stored and collected by each department from one central store, which gives a business better control over the amount of resources being used by each department. A central store prevents members of staff walking in and taking stores whenever they want and usually requires each department to have an order or requisition list for the store manager to issue them with what they require. In large organisations, the store manager may also be responsible for ordering some of the resources, like dry stores, doing stock checks and checking deliveries from suppliers.

In some organisations each department may have their own stores and be responsible for maintaining their own stocks. Having separate stores for each department makes it easier for each department due to the store being easier for their staff to access; however it makes it harder to manage the amount of stock being used. For instance, there may be strict controls on certain products the customers can have which is linked to the department's budget. If staff have direct access to the stores, these rules may be overlooked and, in turn, the financial targets may not be met.

Ordering resources

Depending on the organisation's size and structure, a central purchasing officer may be responsible for ordering, receipt, control and issuing resources to each department. This gives the organisation more control of the suppliers they use and the quantities they buy. It can also give them more power to gain larger discounts and payment plans. A centralised purchasing office would be suitable for the day-to-day resources that do not change. These would include cleaning materials, linen and toiletries for the housekeeping departments. The purchasing officer could also manage some dry stores. However the head chef may be responsible for ordering, receiving and managing their own stock, due to the requirement of specialist ingredients and differing sizes and cuts of meat, fish and vegetables for their menus and functions.

Checking the quality and quantity of resources

When resources are delivered it is essential that they are checked to ensure they meet the quality and quantity required by the organisation.

Standard delivery checks

The delivery van should be visually checked for cleanliness and the temperature checked regularly, especially for food deliveries.
- All deliveries should be accompanied by a delivery note, invoice or receipt for cash on delivery items.
- The quantity should be checked. Does the number of boxes and items match the original order and the supplier's invoice?
- The packaging should be checked for damage as this could affect the quality of resources being delivered.
- High-risk goods, such as cooked and raw meat and fish, should be temperature checked on (see page 31 for correct temperatures) delivery to meet the company and HACCP requirements.
- The quality of the items should be checked against standards and specifications required by the organisation.
- Equipment and fragile items should be checked for damage.

Invoice checking, delivery notes and credit notes

Documentation for the goods being delivered such as invoices, delivery notes and credit notes are very important as they represent a legal agreement between you and your supplier that the goods were received and that they were of the quality and quantity you required. An invoice follows certain legal requirements. If an invoice is not sent, the supplier will send a delivery note. This is almost the same as the invoice; however it only shows the details of the goods being delivered. It does not ask for payment.

Evidence 7

1.6 3.6 3.10

Take pictures of your stores and describe how the resources are organised and how they are handled and issued to staff members.

After all of the delivery checks on the goods have been made, the delivery note should be signed to say that you are satisfied with the goods and accept the delivery. If any damage is discovered after this, it is often difficult to return the goods unless the damage was difficult to see at the time of delivery; for example, damaged goods at the bottom of a box or mouldy biscuits in a sealed tin.

Company name

Invoice
123 Main Street
London
NW1 3BH
Phone: 0000 000 0000

TO:
Joe Bloggs
135 Main street
London
NW1 3BH

INVOICE

INVOICE #137
DATE: 13/04/2015
GST # 55-444-333

Description	Units	Price per unit	Amount
Adult bicycle	1	118.50	118.50
Adult unicycle	1	88.50	88.50
Children's tricycle	3	46.35	139.05

Figure 3.3 An example of what an invoice might look like

If any goods are damaged or not of the quality or delivery temperature required by the organisation, this should be written on the delivery note and the goods returned and replaced immediately. If the goods are not replaced for any reason and the supplier, which makes reference to the invoice concerned and discounts the value of the good, should issue credit note returned.

It is a legal requirement that an invoice must have:
- the full name of the invoicing company (e.g. Smith's Dry Stores Ltd)
- the name and address of the business being invoiced (e.g. The Restaurant, 144 High Road, Bishop, KJ2 8TV).

Methods and types of storage

Depending on the type of resource, different types of storage should be used. These include chilling, freezing and storing at room temperature. The time and temperature food goods should be stored at are a legal requirement and HACCP systems are used to monitor and demonstrate that the goods being stored are kept within these legal limits.

Frozen storage

Frozen goods should be stored at or below −18°C. Frozen goods can be stored in the freezer for the time specified by the manufacturer or supplier. Organisations may have different time periods allowed for fresh food that has been individually wrapped and frozen. Good practice is one month from the date it was delivered. HACCP requires regular temperature records and use-by dates should be checked regularly. Any issues with the freezer and temperature should be reported immediately.

Chilled storage

Chilled goods include fresh food and drinks. Chilled goods should be stored in a refrigerated unit between 3 and 5°C. Fresh food should be stored for the time specified by the manufacturer or supplier. High-risk fresh food wrapped and stored on the premises should be stored for three to five days depending on the food type and size. HACCP requires that refrigerator temperatures should be taken two times per day. Any issues with the refrigerator and temperature should be reported immediately.

Room temperature storage

Resources stored at room temperature include stationery, crockery and glassware. Food such as fruit, vegetables and dry foods can also be stored at room temperature. Room temperature storage for dry foods should ideally be in a clean, dark, dry and well-ventilated room between 16 and 18°C. Dry foods should be stored in sealed containers raised off the floor, preferably in stainless steel containers, to protect the food from spoilage, pests and other forms of contamination. These conditions will also prevent other resources being damaged during long-term storage.

Specialist storage

Some expensive resources such as cigars and wines may have to be stored at specific temperatures and humidified conditions, for example, to prevent cigars from drying out. Chemicals and cleaning materials should be stored safely away from food preparation areas in a locked metal cabinet to keep them safe and inaccessible to people who are not trained to use them. It also prevents the risk of misuse, fire and cross-contamination. Hazardous chemicals are regulated under Control of Substances Hazardous to Health (COSHH) regulations. Advice can also be sought from the Fire Authorities, the Health and Safety Executive and Environmental Health Officers.

Security of resources

Keep all resources free from damage, contamination and theft. Delivered goods should not be left unattended and should be stored immediately after delivery. They should not be left in loading bays, corridors or on the floor in any part of the building and should be taken to a suitable storage area and stored securely under lock and key if possible. Only authorised staff should be allowed access to these goods when required.

> **Key term**
>
> **Maintain** – to keep something at the same level.

1.3 1.4 Dealing with problems when obtaining resources

There are times when there are problems obtaining some resources. This could be simply when the product is out of stock. In this case, other suppliers may be able to obtain these products for you or you may be able to obtain the product from a local supplier or retailer. If a product is a specialist product or ingredient, it may not be available due to short supply or seasonal restrictions. In this case, advice should be sought from other members of the team and suppliers to source a suitable alternative. This can be an issue when using smaller manufacturers and specialist products and suppliers.

> **Evidence 8**
>
> **1.3 1.4**
>
> Identify a resource you use in your role and explain what you would do if you could not obtain that resource.

Using resources

`1.6` `1.7` `1.9` `3.4` `3.9` Efficient and effective use of resources

To ensure efficient and effective use of resources, it is essential that staff are trained to use these resources correctly and they are not wasted so the financial targets and business objectives are met. It is important that a supervisor monitors the resources being used within their department to ensure that they are being used as efficiently as possible and identify any issues, so they can be rectified quickly.

All departments should be aware of the budgets and costs in their department. These costs include staff costs, energy and equipment costs and especially any products used within the department such as perishable foods in the kitchen and cleaning and toiletries in the housekeeping department.

Efficient monitoring would include monitoring waste, such as food waste due to poor storage, incorrect preparation and cooking methods. Other issues could include monitoring the misuse or incorrect measurement of cleaning materials, which could result in areas not being cleaned to required standards; lights and equipment being left on for too long; and staff not being managed well or not given sufficient work to do during their shift.

`1.8` `2.4` `3.5` `1.10` Monitoring resource use

Depending on the department and the type of resource, there are a number of ways they can be monitored efficiently. These include:

Food and beverage

- **Customer satisfaction surveys** – these can be used to identify issues and areas that need to be improved and areas of good practice.
- **Stock control and turnover** – these can be used to monitor the use of specific products and resources which can be measured against usage and financial targets. It also ensures that produce is being used in the correct manner, using a first-in, first-out system, which means that the older produce should be moved forward and used first. Then the new **stock** should be used after.
- **Financial results and targets** – these can be used to see if you are working within financial limits and budgets. This will help to highlight areas where there may be over spending and allow time to get this area under control.
- **Waste management** – keeping records of waste and understanding where products and produce are being wasted can help to introduce training, systems and procedures that may help to reduce or eliminate this waste.
- **Staff assessment** – staff should be asked if they are happy with the products they are using and if there is any need for a change of products or for staff training to make the best of these products. Staff are often in direct contact with the customers and because of this, they will often be the first to hear of any problems or issues with the products or service being offered.

Evidence 9
`1.7` `1.9` `3.4` `3.9`

Design a poster that could be used to highlight how one of the products you use can be used more efficiently and effectively. Use your organisation's policies to guide you.

Key terms

Stock – purchased products and items being stored on the premises before being used

Stock control – the process of managing products and items stored on the premises to ensure there are enough to meet the demands of the business and stay within the budget

Equipment

It is important to monitor equipment and to know if it is working efficiently and doing the work it is designed for. This can be monitored by:

- **Asking the staff using the equipment** – staff that use the equipment will know how efficient it is, if it is reliable and if it does the job it was brought in to do. They will also be able to give the advantages and disadvantages of the equipment and offer any advice on how it could be improved or replaced with a more efficient piece of equipment, if necessary.
- **Record of the usage of the equipment** – this can monitor any equipment that is not being used and pieces of equipment that are being used more often or misused. These records can also be used to identify the reliability of each piece of equipment, by checking it against the repair manual.
- **Accident book** – this will monitor and identify pieces of equipment that have caused harm to members of staff. This equipment can then be adapted or replaced to make it safe for the staff to use. Equipment that causes any injury to staff should be removed from use immediately.
- **Repair manual** – the repair manual should show the repairs that have been carried out on each piece of equipment in the building. These records can also be used to identify and monitor old or inefficient pieces of equipment that may be becoming too expensive to maintain and could be replaced with a new and more efficient piece of equipment.
- **Computer system failure** – all computer systems within the organisation should be monitored to show how often they are not functional. These shutdowns can be a huge drain on resources, due to information not being immediately available to staff which may result in a loss of business and a loss of data and the staff's time.
- **Assessment of energy use** – the efficiency of equipment can be monitored against the manufacturer's information on the equipment and devices can be fitted to show the energy each piece of equipment uses.

Evidence 10
1.8 2.4 3.5 1.10

Produce a PowerPoint presentation that shows how the resources you use in your area are or can be monitored against normal consumption levels. Use any documentation you use at work to illustrate this.

Key terms

Standards – a set level of attainment, quality and service

Monitoring – a method of supervising or measuring a process, product or service

3.1 3.2 Health and safety when using resources

In any industry, accidents can happen and hotels and restaurants can be particularly dangerous places to work due to the equipment and conditions found in kitchens, restaurants and other hospitality departments. Slips, trips and falls account for most of the major injuries in the workplace. Manual handling also accounts for the second highest number of injuries in the workplace. This is due to heavy loads being lifted or moved incorrectly, which can causes serious back pain, sprains and strains. The Health and Safety Executive deals with health and safety issues in the workplace; for more information, visit their website: www.hse.gov.uk.

Water and cleaning materials are widely used throughout the hospitality industry in kitchens, restaurants, bars and housekeeping departments. All of the staff in these departments use many different products for washing and cleaning rooms, equipment and other products. Using these products regularly and having constantly wet hands can cause medical conditions such as dermatitis. In cases like this, as a supervisor it would be your responsibility to minimise your staff's exposure to these products, by introducing equipment such as dishwashers and protective gloves to prevent them from hand washing products and utensils.

As a supervisor, it is important that you are aware of any hazards or dangers your staff may encounter within their job. This could be physical danger such as wet floors, hot or dangerous equipment. It could also include dangers such as dealing with angry and aggressive customers and colleagues that may cause them mental or emotional harm. In your role as a supervisor, it is your responsibility to reduce and protect your staff from these issues to the best of your ability.

Risk assessments

Risk assessments are a way of identifying and cataloguing dangers and risks within your department that may cause your staff harm. After identifying a risk, you have a duty of care to inform the management and staff of the risk and to make a reasonable attempt to reduce this risk to your staff. This can be done by physically fixing the problem, implementing safety measures to avoid any issues or giving additional training to your staff to understand the risks and safe procedures to prevent any accidents. This could be as simple as plates and chairs being stacked too high, so the stacks are reduced in height to prevent them from falling on someone; or the guards of mixers and slicers being checked regularly to ensure the safety of the chefs using them. These measures also show due diligence that every effort has been made to identify potential hazards to keep the staff safe from injury.

Evidence 11
3.1 3.2

Take pictures of all the health and safety posters and documents used in your department and list underneath each picture the resources you use that may be linked to these.

For a resource you use, describe how you lift and move it safely to make sure you avoid injury.

3.3 Environmental considerations

All resources have an impact on our environment. During its manufacture, the materials and the way in which a product is produced can have a great impact on the environment. The way the product is packaged, shipped and delivered to its customers can also affect its impact on the environment. Even the way in which the product is used and disposed of can cause damage to the environment.

Many hospitality businesses are choosing to be more environmentally friendly in the way they operate their business and in the products they choose to use. Simply choosing products that are more natural and biodegradable can help the environment. Choosing products that are produced more locally can help to reduce the miles which the produce has to travel. This also reduces the company's carbon footprint. The way in which the product is used and disposed of can also help, by using the product more sparingly, more than once and by recycling it when it is finished with. Water and energy also need to be used wisely, as they use fossil fuels and water supplies that are becoming scarcer and may cause further environmental issues in the future.

> **Evidence 12**
> 3.3
> Write 500 words on how the resources you use can impact on the environment.

3.4 3.7 3.8 Waste control and recycling

Controlling the amount of waste an organisation produces is not only a financial drain, it also adds pressure to the staff's time as more councils expect businesses to sort and recycle their waste. Some councils are now charging for the bags being used for food and general waste, which adds further costs to the amount of waste a company produces. Systems should be put in place to ensure that waste is kept to a minimum and as much waste as possible is **recycled**. Food waste can be reduced by purchasing pre-portioned products and finding further uses for food trimmings and offcuts, for example, soups and stocks. Training can also help staff understand how to reduce waste.

> **Key term**
> Recycling – to re-use old or waste products and turn them into other products

> **Evidence 13**
> 3.4 3.7 3.8
> In a chart format, show your organisation's waste management system (ask your line manager to help if needed). Then make recommendations on how this could be improved to keep waste to a minimum.

Figure 3.4 Supervisors should advise staff on how to recycle and reduce waste

3.12 Computerised stock control systems

Computerised purchasing and stock control software is becoming more widely used in hospitality organisations as it can give an up-to-date record of resources that are in stock and information on how much is being used. In some cases, it can give the current prices and spend for individual resources, departments and the overall spend in a specific time.

The advantages of a computerised stock control system are:
- Levels of resources in stock can be easily accessed, and these computerised records can be used to manually check that the computerised records are correct.
- Pre-set stock levels can be set to show when stock needs to be reordered.
- Prices and finance levels can be checked whenever needed.
- The quantities of each item can be tracked to show how much is being used and who is using it.
- Any signs of fraud or theft can be identified quickly.

A computerised stock control system can be a valuable asset to any organisation; however it is only as good as the information that is put into it. Some stock control software can be very time consuming and difficult to keep up to date. It has to be backed up regularly and often has a paper-based system running alongside it to ensure no information is lost if the system breaks down.

Evidence 14
3.12

Ask the person responsible for using your computerised ordering system what its advantages are and record their answers. If you do not use one, explain how this could benefit your organisation.

2.5 Cost control

The cost of resources can change depending on the type and the time of year. The cost of food can change greatly from season to season. When a certain food is in season it is generally cheaper than imported produce from overseas. The prices of resources such as cleaning materials, stationery, china and glass can also differ greatly from supplier to supplier. A supervisor should always be aware of differing prices of their products from other suppliers so that they can negotiate better deals with their current suppliers or even move to a more competitive supplier, if agreed by their organisation or purchasing officer.

Evidence 15
2.5

Use a copy of an invoice to show the cost of resources used in your area.

1.11 3.11 Improving use of resources

As a supervisor it is your responsibility to monitor, maintain and make recommendations to improve the efficient and effective use of all of the resources under your supervision. This could include making recommendations to your line manager or even senior management, depending on the size of your organisation and the importance of the recommendation being made. It is important that any supervisor understands their company's organisational structure and who they should approach for different issues within their department. For staff issues they may have to report to their human resources manager. For other resources and equipment they may have to report to the purchasing manager or house manager.

It is important that a supervisor keeps their management team up to date on any issues that may affect the business and make recommendations on how the departments can be run more efficiently by reducing costs, staffing levels and enhancing the customer's experience. Depending of the organisation's size and structure, recommendations may be passed on in a number of ways. In some organisations they may be simply passed on verbally to the line manager. However, in other organisations a written recommendation in the form of a business case or formal presentation may be needed to get the approval of senior management.

Evidence 16
1.11 3.11

Using the PowerPoint presentation produced for Evidence 10 for monitoring the use of resources, make recommendations for how these resources can be used and improved.

Knowledge check

1. List all of the resources that are used in the area for which you are responsible.
2. You should always try to keep to the budget you have been allocated. Why is this important?
3. Describe what you would do if you did need to spend more money than your agreed spending limit.
4. List the suppliers that your organisation uses regularly.
5. Who in your workplace is responsible for ordering supplies?
6. What is your organisation's policy/procedure for controlling waste?
7. Do you recycle any waste? If so, what is the procedure for this?
8. State five advantages of using a computerised stock control system. Why are computerised systems better than other stock control systems?

Evidence checklist		
Assessment criteria		**Possible evidence**
1.1	Identify the resources needed from those available	Evidence activity 1
1.2	Follow organisational procedures for obtaining additional resources	Evidence activity 3
1.3	Follow organisational procedures when dealing with any problems in obtaining resources	Evidence activity 8
1.4	Update relevant people within the organisation when dealing with any problems in obtaining resources	Evidence activity 8
1.5	Determine the quality, quantity and suitability of resources needing to be used	Evidence activity 6
1.6	Ensure that equipment and materials are correctly stored and maintained	Evidence activity 7
1.7	Encourage colleagues to make efficient use of resources	Evidence activity 9
1.8	Monitor the use of resources in your own area of responsibility	Evidence activity 10
1.9	Contribute to the effective and efficient use of resources in line with organisational and legal requirements	Evidence activity 9
1.10	Maintain accurate records about resources in line with organisational requirements	Evidence activity 10
1.11	Propose ways of making better use of resources following organisational requirements	Evidence activity 16
2.1	Identify the resources that are used in your own area of responsibility	Evidence activity 1
2.2	Explain how to check the resources that are required for the work that needs to be carried out	Evidence activity 5
2.3	Explain how to ensure resources are suitable for the work that needs to be carried out	Evidence activity 6
2.4	Describe normal consumption levels for resources in own area of responsibility	Evidence activity 10
2.5	Identify the approximate costs of the resources used in own area of responsibility	Evidence activity 15
2.6	Explain how resource costs affect the organisation's financial targets	Evidence activity
2.7	Explain the importance of working within agreed spending limits	Evidence activity 4
2.8	Describe the procedures that need to be followed when it is necessary to go beyond agreed spending limits	Evidence activity 4
2.9	Explain the importance of getting management approval when needing to go beyond agreed spending limits	Evidence activity 4

Contribute to the control of resources

Evidence checklist		
Assessment criteria		**Possible evidence**
2.10	Identify the organisation's regular suppliers	Evidence activity 2
2.11	Identify who within the organisation is responsible for ordering supplies	Evidence activity 2
3.1	Describe the appropriate lifting and handling methods and techniques for moving resources in own area of responsibility	Evidence activity 11
3.2	Describe the health and safety requirements for the resources used in own area of responsibility	Evidence activity 11
3.3	Explain the environmental impact some resources can have on the environment	Evidence activity 12
3.4	Describe the organisation's policies and procedures for: ● obtaining resources ● using resources ● controlling waste ● recycling	Evidence activity 3 Evidence activity 9 Evidence activity 14
3.5	Explain how to monitor the use of resources	Evidence activity 10
3.6	Outline how resources should be stored	Evidence activity 7
3.7	Explain the importance of keeping waste to a minimum	Evidence activity 13
3.8	Explain how to keep waste to a minimum	Evidence activity 13
3.9	Explain how to encourage efficient use of resources to benefit the organisation and the environment	Evidence activity 9
3.10	Explain how to ensure resources are handled and stored in line with organisational requirements	Evidence activity 7
3.11	Explain how to present recommendations to improve the use of resources	Evidence activity 16
3.12	Explain the advantages of using computerised stock control systems	Evidence activity 14

CHAPTER 4

Maintain the health, hygiene, safety and security of the working environment

This chapter will provide information about maintaining health, hygiene, safety and security standards relevant to your areas of responsibility. The maintenance of high standards in these places is essential to protect staff, visitors and customers from harm, injury or ill health when in your working areas.

Learning objectives

On completion of this chapter, you should:
1 Be able to maintain the health, safety, hygiene and security of the working environment.
2 Understand the importance of maintaining the health, safety, hygiene and security of the working environment.
3 Understand how to maintain the health, safety, hygiene and security of the working environment.

The NVQ Level 3 in Hospitality Supervision and Leadership is based on what you do in your working area and working day. It is therefore necessary for you to provide evidence of what you do and how you do it. Throughout the chapter there are suggestions showing the assessment criteria of your qualification and the types of evidence you could supply related to each criterion. These are also summarised in the Evidence Checklist at the end of the chapter. Just use these as a guide; you will probably be able to find more examples of evidence within your workplace.

Supervising health, hygiene, safety and security

Many employees in hospitality areas have a supervisory role built into their job specification and responsibilities. Sous chefs, team leaders, restaurant, reception, bar and housekeeping supervisors, and others, may all be responsible for supervising health, safety, hygiene and security within the workplace, making others aware of risks and remaining compliant with the correct procedures. It is important to plan and supervise the daily work and to train employees in good practice to ensure that they adopt a healthy, safe and secure way of working and achieve consistently high standards to comply with all legal requirements. As part of their supervising role, they may also liaise with management or business owners and keep them informed about the day-to-day running of the business.

> **Key term**
>
> **Health and Safety Executive (HSE)** – the national independent watchdog for work-related health, safety and illness. It acts in the public interest to reduce work-related death and serious injury across Great Britain's workplaces; www.hse.gov.uk.

2.1 Setting and enforcing laws and regulations

The Health and Safety Executive (HSE)

The Health and Safety Commission, responsible for health and safety law and standards and for consulting with professional bodies, has now merged with the **Health and Safety Executive (HSE)**. The HSE regulates health and safety law in industry and public areas. The merged organisations operate under the name of the Health and Safety Executive.

Local authorities

The HSE gives local authorities delegated power to regulate health and safety law in premises such as retail shops, offices, catering services, restaurants, hotels, etc. An environmental health officer is employed by the local authority.

Authorised officers

Health, safety, hygiene and security law is enforced by:
- Health and safety inspectors from the HSE.
- Environmental Health Officers (EHOs) and technical officers from local authorities.
- Fire officers: in the majority of premises, local fire and rescue authorities are responsible for enforcing fire safety
- For factories, farms and hospitals, the enforcing officer is a health and safety inspector from the HSE.
- Trading Standards Officers (TSOs) act on behalf of consumers and businesses to advise and enforce laws on the way goods and services are sold. They usually work for local authorities, advising on consumer law, conducting inspections, dealing with offences and investigating complaints.
- For shops, restaurants and leisure centres, the enforcing officer is the local EHO. Fire officers can visit all these premises for the purposes of enforcing the law on fire safety and fire precautions.
- Compliance of data protection legislation is regulated and enforced by the Information Commissioner's Office, which also has guidance relating to the Act: see their website at https://ico.org.uk/.

Enforcement

Inspections of premises can be carried out by HSE inspectors or Environmental Health Officers, Fire Officers or Trading Standards Officers.

Inspectors have a number of powers including the right of entry to premises, to serve legal notices requiring improvement work to be done and prohibiting work procedures, processes and the use of work equipment. Inspectors may:
- Enter premises at any reasonable time.
- Take a police officer or an authorised person or equipment to help with the investigation.
- Make necessary examinations and inspections.
- Take samples, measurements, photographs or recordings.
- Take possession of and detain/dismantle any article or substance for examination or to ensure that no one tampers with it.
- Require any person to give information to assist with any examination or investigation.
- Require documents to be inspected or copied.
- Require that assistance and facilities be made available to allow full investigation.

- Remove anything which the inspector believes could cause danger or serious injury.
- Serve notices (see below).
- Close the business, part of the business or a procedure immediately.

The supervisor's role

The supervisor is likely to be asked to accompany an inspector during an inspection of their area. The supervisor will need to answer any questions the inspector may have and make the necessary paperwork and records available for inspection. The inspector may also discuss any improvements needed with the supervisor.

Improvement notices

If the inspector thinks there is a contravention of legislation, for example, with health and safety or food safety legislation, an **improvement notice** may be served on the person responsible, stating the details of the contravention. The notice also requires the person responsible to remedy the contravention within a fixed time. The person responsible is the director, manager or supervisor in charge of the premises at the time of the inspection.

The notice must state:
- that a contravention exists
- the details of the law contravened
- the inspector's reasons for his or her opinion
- that the person responsible must arrange to remedy the contravention
- the time given for the remedy to be carried out. This must not be less than 21 days.

If a person fails to comply with an improvement notice, he or she commits a criminal offence.

> **Key term**
>
> **Improvement notice** – issued by an inspector if he/she thinks there is a contravention of legislation. It states the details of the contravention and requires the person responsible to remedy it within a fixed time.

Prohibition notices

If an inspector believes that work activities have a serious risk of 'personal injury', a **prohibition notice** may be served on the person in charge of the work activity. This will prevent further work being carried out in the premises or area deemed to be dangerous. This would also apply if an EHO thought there was imminent risk of food poisoning if a food business remained open. The notice must:
- State that, in the inspector's opinion, there is a risk of serious personal injury or illness.
- Identify the matters which create the risk.
- Give reasons why the inspector believes there to have been a contravention of the laws governing the business.
- Direct that the activities stated in the notice must not be carried on, by or under the control of the person served with the notice, unless the matters associated with the risk have been rectified.

Serving this notice would mean immediate closure of the business for three days, during which time the inspector must apply to magistrates for an Emergency Prohibition Order to keep the premises closed. Notices/orders must be displayed in a visible place on the premises. The owner of the business must apply for a Certificate of Satisfaction before they can re-open.

> **Key term**
>
> **Prohibition notice** – issued if an inspector believes that work activities involve a serious risk of 'personal injury' or lead to an incidence, such as food poisoning. This will prevent further work being carried out in the premises or area deemed to be dangerous.

2.2 Implications of non-compliance

Fines and penalties for non-compliance by employers

- Magistrates' courts can impose fines of up to £5,000 for each offence, a six-month prison sentence, or both.
- For serious offences such as knowingly selling food dangerous to health or knowingly making employees use dangerous equipment, magistrates could impose fines of up to £20,000 and/or six months' imprisonment.
- In a Crown Court, unlimited fines can be imposed and/or two years' imprisonment.

Fines and penalties for non-compliance by employees

If it can be proved that an incident or injury was caused by the negligence or wrong-doing of an employee or that the employee intentionally did not comply with the employers' procedures, it could result in:

- fines imposed appropriate to the offence
- compensation payments to an affected or injured person
- up to two years' imprisonment
- dismissal from employment.

2.3 Legislation relating to health and safety, hygiene and security

It is important that supervisors are well aware and remain up to date with health, safety, hygiene and security matters and with the relevant legislation that applies to their industry, establishment and the people working within it. **Legislation** is updated periodically to deal with modern working procedures and equipment, but the main acts are outlined below.

Aims of legislation

- To secure the health, safety and welfare of people at work.
- To provide regulations and approved codes of practice that set the standards of health, safety hygiene and security.
- To establish the minimum requirements for different areas of the workplace.
- To control the storage and use of dangerous substances such as explosive, **corrosive**, highly flammable or otherwise dangerous materials.
- To protect people other than employees who may be in the area, for example, guests, customers, contractors, suppliers and others against any risks within the area.

> **Key terms**
>
> **Legislation** – as required by law.
>
> **Corrosive** – something that causes the deterioration or eating away, usually of metal. Acid is an example of something that would be described as corrosive.

- To protect the personal information and data of individuals.
- To serve customers with safe food and drinks that will not cause ill health or injure them in any way.
- To provide relevant and useful information about allergens in foods being supplied.

Health and Safety at Work Act (1974)

The legislation dealing with workplace Health and Safety in England, Wales and Scotland is the Health and Safety at Work Act 1974. Similar provision is covered in Northern Ireland under the Health and Safety at Work (Northern Ireland) Order 1978.

The Act is mostly about establishing and maintaining good health and safety practice for employees in the workplace. The Act sets out the requirements that employers must comply with all parts of the Act in keeping employees and others on the premises safe as far as reasonably possible.

It also requires that employees work in a safe way that does not endanger themselves and others. They must comply with health and safety procedures introduced by their employers and report any defect or problem that could affect health and safety. There was a review and updates were made to the Act in 1994.

Workplace (Health, Safety and Welfare) Regulations 1992

These regulations are also in place to ensure the safety and well-being of employees within their working environment. The act covers such things as suitable working premises, staff hygiene facilities, heating, ventilation and lighting.

Unless there are fewer than five employees, the regulations require employers to conduct **risk assessments** of all areas and procedures and ensure safe ways of working. The outcomes of risk assessments must be fully recorded and available for inspection. Employers will need to keep premises and equipment in safe working order and provide/maintain personal protective equipment for employees. All of this must be recorded and updated within the risk assessment records. However, even if there are fewer than five employees, the employer still has a responsibility for their health, safety and welfare.

Other significant health and safety regulations are explained below.

Management of Health and Safety at Work Regulations 1999

Where an employer has five or more employees there must be a written health and safety policy in place that is issued to every member of staff. This will outline the responsibilities of the employer and employee in relation to health and safety. They must also be given relevant health and safety information. This could be in the form of training packs, leaflets, posters, DVDs and stickers, all of which are available from the HSE.

> **Key term**
>
> **Risk assessments** – these require the employer to evaluate risks to employees' health and safety from any workplace hazards. The employer needs to consider what in the working area could cause injury or harm and if the hazards could be eliminated; and if not, which preventive or protective measures can be put in place to control the risks.

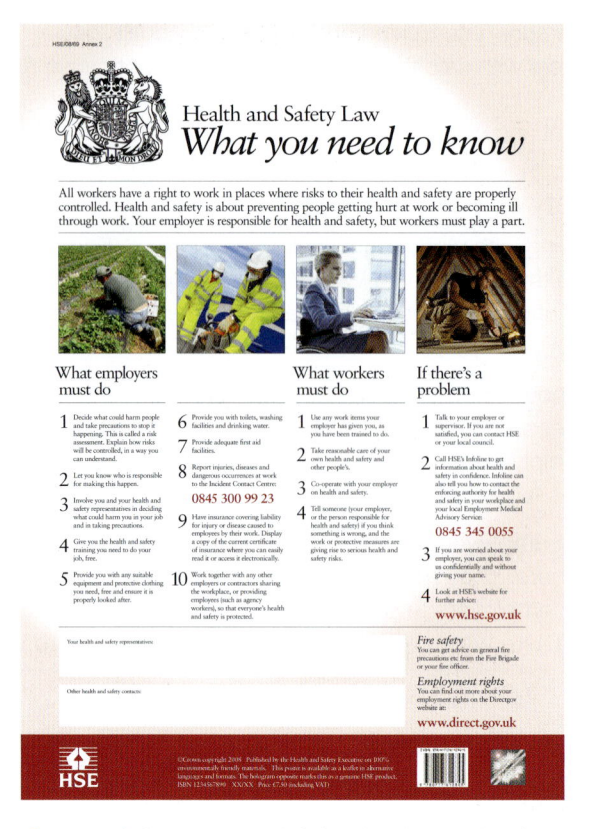

Figure 4.1 A poster explaining health and safety law.

Personal Protective Equipment at Work Regulations 1992

These regulations require employers to assess the need for and provide suitable personal protective equipment (PPE), and/or clothing at work. In a hospitality environment this may include chefs' uniforms and items for cleaning tasks such as rubber gloves, goggles and masks. Employers must keep these items clean, in good condition and provide suitable storage for them. Employees must use them correctly and report any defects or shortages.

Manual Handling Operations Regulations 1992

These regulations are in place to protect employees from injury or accident when required to lift or move heavy or awkwardly shaped items. A risk assessment must be completed, employees trained in correct manual handling techniques and lifting or moving equipment provided where appropriate.

Provision and Use of Work Equipment Regulations 1998 (PUWER)

Work equipment covers items such as electronic equipment, housekeeping equipment, slicers, ovens, fryers, knives and many more. These regulations place duties on employers to ensure that work equipment is suitable for its intended use, is maintained in efficient working order and in good repair and that adequate information, instruction and training on the use and maintenance of the equipment and any associated hazards is given to employees. Work equipment that poses a specific risk must be used only by designated people who have received relevant training. Requirements cover dangerous machinery parts, protection against certain hazards (such as falling objects, ejected components, overheating and entrapment). Also covered is the provision of certain stop and emergency cut-out controls, isolation from energy sources, stability lighting, markings and warnings.

Control of Substances Hazardous to Health (COSHH) Regulations 2002

Under the Control of Substances Hazardous to Health Regulations (COSHH) 2002, risk assessments must be completed by employers of all hazardous chemicals and substances that employees may be exposed to at work, their safe use and disposal. Each chemical must be given a risk rating that is recorded and employees given relevant information and training on the chemicals they will be using.

Some examples of chemical substances found in hospitality areas are:
- cleaning chemicals – alkalis and acids
- detergents, sanitisers, descalers, degreasers and polishes
- chemicals associated with silver cleaning and burnishing
- pest control chemicals, insecticides and rodenticides.

Evidence 1

1.1 **1.2** **1.8** **2.4** **2.7** **2.9** **2.11** **2.12** **2.13** **3.1** **3.3** **3.4** **3.7**

Prepare a list of all chemicals and substances used in your area: do you have data sheets for all of them? (Remember things such as photocopier toner.) If not, download them or ask the supplier for them.

Are the chemicals you use the safest and most ecologically friendly available or could they be replaced with something else? Are they the most economical option? Make a chart of each chemical used and add the above information to present to your manager.

The Reporting of Injuries, Diseases, and Dangerous Occurrences Regulations (RIDDOR) 1995, updated October 2013

This is the law that requires employers, and/or the person with responsibility for health and safety within a workplace, to report and keep records of any:
- work-related fatal accidents
- work-related disease
- accidents and injury resulting in the employee being off work for three days or more
- dangerous workplace events (including 'near-miss' occurrences)
- major injuries, loss of limbs or eyesight.

The 2013 changes simplify the reporting procedures and provide shorter lists of the incidents/diseases that need to be reported but most requirements remain broadly unchanged.

Take it further

Accidents and incidents under RIDDOR need to be reported. This can be done by contacting the HSE by telephone on 0845 300 9923 or by completing the RIDDOR form on their website: www.hse.gov.uk/riddor. This must be done within three days.

Fire Precautions (Workplace) Regulations and Orders

The main regulations are:
- The Fire Precautions (Workplace) Regulations 1997, updated with the Regulatory Reform (Fire Safety) Order 2005 covering general fire safety in England and Wales.
- Part 3 of the Fire (Scotland) Act 2005, supported by the Fire Safety (Scotland) Regulations 2006.

These state that premises with five or more employees must have a written fire risk assessment with details of the appropriate fire safety precautions in place. These may include:
- provision of emergency exit routes and doors
- 'Fire Exit' signs, and emergency lighting to cover the exit routes where necessary
- fire-fighting equipment, fire alarms and where necessary fire detectors
- fire training for employees in fire safety following the written risk assessment
- production of an emergency plan and enough trained people and equipment to carry out the plan
- equipment such as fire extinguishers, alarm systems and emergency doors being regularly maintained and faults rectified as soon as possible
- employers' planning, organising, controlling, monitoring and reviewing the measures taken to protect employees and others from fire.

The Electricity at Work Regulations 1989

These regulations state that all pieces of electrical equipment used in the workplace should be checked every 12 months by a qualified electrician and this must be recorded (this is called **PAT testing**). It is also recommended that a supervisor or other responsible person check these items on a regular basis. All equipment should be included in the health and safety risk assessment and staff must have training in the safe use of the equipment.

> **Key term**
>
> **PAT testing** – portable appliance testing; yearly testing of electrical equipment by a qualified electrician.

Data Protection Act 1998

The Data Protection Act controls how personal information is used by organisations, employers, employees or government departments. Everyone responsible for using data has to follow strict rules called 'data protection principles'. You must not disclose personal details about any member of staff or customer to someone else without their permission. This includes telephone numbers and addresses. You must make sure that any information in your possession is:
- used fairly and lawfully
- used for limited, specifically stated purposes
- accurate and used in a way that is adequate, relevant and not excessive
- not kept for longer than is necessary
- compliant with an individual's data protection rights
- kept safe and secure and not transferred outside the UK without adequate protection.

There is stronger legal protection for more sensitive information, such as ethnic background, political opinions, religious beliefs, health, sexual health and criminal records.

There have been updates to data protection **legislation** since 1998, including Section 56 in December 2014, which prevents employers from requiring people to provide certain records as a condition of employment except where the record is required by law or is justified in the public interest.

The Food Safety Act 1990

The 1990 Act covers the selling of food and drinks to ensure they meet food safety requirements. Where this is not the case, it makes enforcement powers available to recognised officials. The Act provides the foundation for all subsequent food safety legislation.

Food Safety (General Food Hygiene) Regulations 1995

These established further food safety rules including the need to identify hazards in food, to establish a process to identify hazards at different stages of food production and a requirement for monitored food safety controls.

In 2006, revised legislation enhanced the existing Acts and regulations though most of the actual regulations remained the same. The main differences in the laws introduced in 2006 were to strengthen existing legislation and provide a framework for EU legislation to be enforced in England (with similar requirements for Wales, Scotland and Northern Ireland). The new legislation included the requirement to have an approved food safety management procedure in place, with up-to-date permanent records available, including staff training and supervision records. All records must be reviewed and monitored regularly, especially if there is a change in procedures.

Food Allergens Legislation – EU Food Information for Consumers Regulation 1169/2011

From 13 December 2014 this legislation requires all food businesses to provide allergy information on food sold unpackaged in restaurants and other catering outlets such as takeaways, deli counters, bakeries and salad/sandwich bars. There will also be changes to existing legislation on labelling allergenic ingredients in pre-packed foods. The legislation has highlighted 14 of the main allergen ingredients that must appear on information. There is a wide range of guidance on this from the Food Standards Agency: www.food.gov.uk.

Some other relevant regulations that apply to the workplace:
- Lifting Operations and Lifting Equipment Regulations 1998 (LOLER)
- Noise at Work Regulations 1989
- The Health and Safety (First Aid) Regulations 1981
- Health and Safety (Display Screen Equipment) Regulations 1992
- Equality Act 2010
- Race Relations Act 1977
- Asylum and Immigration Act 1996
- Sex Discrimination Act 1975
- Human Rights Act 1988
- Licensing Act 1964
- Working Time Regulations 1998
- National Minimum Wage Act 1998
- Disability Discrimination Act 1995.

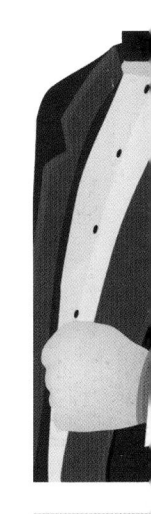

Sources of support for supervisors of health, safety, hygiene and security

Supervisors should have a good knowledge of health and safety matters and of the related legislation that affects them, but there are a number of helpful sources where they can find health and safety information, including:

- workplace HR departments and health and safety representatives
- Health and Safety Executive (HSE); there is a wealth of information on their website, some of it specific to hospitality: www.hse.gov.uk
- 'Safer Food, Better Business' (available from the Food Standards Agency)
- Environmental Health Officers
- Food Standards Agency: www.food.gov.uk
- fire safety officers: www.gov.uk/workplace-fire-safety-your-responsibilities
- product manufacturers and the literature and learning materials they produce
- various health and safety publications and chef/hospitality textbooks
- trade unions.

> **Key terms**
>
> **Contravention** – violation or failure to comply with requirements.
>
> **Monitoring** – observing and checking that a procedure or practice is working properly.

Approved Codes of Practice

The Health and Safety Executive can endorse practical guidance books for employers and employees to help them to comply with the regulations and duties which apply to them. The advice is issued as a Code of Practice. If the Health and Safety Executive approves these standards, they can bear the title 'Approved Code of Practice'.

Approved Codes of Practice have a special place in legislation. They are not law but a failure to observe any part of an Approved Code of Practice may be admissible in criminal court proceedings as evidence about a related alleged **contravention** of workplace legislation. If the advice in the Approved Code of Practice has not been followed, then it is up to the defendant to prove that they have satisfactorily complied with the requirement in some other way.

> **Take it further**
>
> There are large amounts of useful information for hospitality businesses on the Food Standards Agency website and on the HSE website. Many people are not aware of this information and how useful it could be to them. Take a look at one or both of the sites and make a list of the information that could be useful to your working area and others.

Industry Guides

The Industry Guide to Good Hygiene Practice gives advice (in plain, easy-to-understand English) to food businesses on how to comply with food safety law. Most industries have similar guides and while the guides have no legal force, food authorities must give it due consideration when they enforce the regulations. It is the intention that industry guides will help business owners and managers understand and use the information to meet legal obligations and to ensure food safety. Printed industry guides are available from Her Majesty's Stationery Office (HMSO) or can be downloaded from www.food.gov.uk/about-us/publications/industrypublications.

> **Contacts**
>
> Make sure that you know who your workplace health and safety representative is and how they can be contacted. It is also important to know the whereabouts or have the contact details of designated first aiders. If there is someone in charge of security arrangements you should also know how to contact them.

> **Take it further**
>
> Examples of approved codes of practice:
> - Management of Health and Safety at Work
> - Workplace Health, Safety and Welfare
> - Control of Substances Hazardous to Health
> - Safe Use of Work Equipment
> - Safe Use of Lighting Equipment
> - First Aid at Work

2.4 Organisational procedures

Every employer will have organisational procedures in place that are suitable for the business, the premises and the work being carried out. This is particularly important for areas of health, safety, hygiene and security so procedures are completed properly and employees and others remain in safe, hygienic and secure areas. The procedures adopted need to be discussed and agreed and the supervisor is likely to be involved in these initial discussions. All organisational procedures must be recorded and fully updated when changes are necessary. It is, of course, essential that where staff are directly affected or protected by organisational procedures, they must be made fully aware of those procedures and reminder sessions should take place to ensure that everyone remains aware.

Areas likely to be covered would be procedures for:
- safe methods of completing everyday work and particular tasks
- safe storage, handling, cooking and serving of food
- dealing with incidents, accidents and injury
- first aid provision
- fire and evacuation (including practising these)
- safe use of chemicals and equipment
- use of PPE and protective clothing
- lifting and correct storage of certain items
- security risks, threats and emergencies.

There will also be others, depending on the individual business and work being carried out.

Employers' responsibilities to their employees

Every employer has a duty of care for their employees as far as is reasonably practicable. In hospitality this means:
- Providing and maintaining work areas, accommodation and systems of work that are safe and without risk to health.
- Making sure that storage areas and transporting of items such as food and equipment are safe and will not cause injury or risk to health.
- There is information, instruction, training and supervision necessary to ensure the health, safety and welfare of employees at work.

- Maintaining the premises and building to make sure they are safe and pose no risk to health.
- Maintaining entrances and exits to the workplace and access to work areas that are safe and without risk to personal safety and security.
- Providing a clean and safe environment and safe working procedures.
- Provision of rest and welfare facilities to take breaks and also toilet, hand-washing and storage for personal items such as outdoor clothing and bags.
- Providing and maintaining the required personal protective equipment (and clothing).
- Where appropriate, providing occupational health care for employees.

Employers must provide a written statement about:
- the general policy towards employees' health and safety at work
- the organisation and arrangements for carrying out that policy (risk assessment).

2.5 The supervisor's responsibilities in health, safety, hygiene and security

The responsibility of supervisors and others concerned with health, safety, hygiene and security is to ensure that the relevant policies and standards planned for the workplace are upheld. The supervisor also has the responsibility to deal with possible workplace risks and any accidents that may occur in order to safeguard all who are working, using or visiting the area. This must be done promptly following legal and organisational procedures to protect staff, visitors and customers.

Legal responsibilities

Everyone in the workplace has a responsibility for health, safety, hygiene and security. Legislation makes it clear that employers are responsible for the well-being of their employees when at work and, as a supervisor, you need to make sure that you are aware of the relevant legislation and the workplace policies and procedures.

Regular meetings and discussion with the person in overall charge of health, safety, hygiene and security for the workplace will help to ensure that there is the required compliance with procedures that need to be applied to the workplace and a full understanding of what is already in place. As a supervisor, you will be working close to where day-to-day procedures are carried out, so you are in a very good position to form an understanding of how well these are working.

Monitoring

The supervisor's role includes regular monitoring of the working area and ensuring that procedures are sufficient to control any possible risks to the health, safety, hygiene and security of those working in the area. (For more information on how to monitor the working area, see below.)

Duties of employees

Every employee has a duty to take reasonable care of their own safety and that of other people who may be affected by what they do or fail to do when carrying out their work. Employees must co-operate with the employer to enable the employer to comply with the necessary requirements. Employees must also remain vigilant and report anything they think could be a health, safety, hygiene or security hazard or could cause injury.

If an employee feels that their employer is not complying with regulations for health, safety, hygiene and security, they should in the first instance discuss their concerns with a supervisor or manager. If their concern is unresolved, they should contact the HSE or the Environmental Health Officer at the local authority who can then investigate the problem.

2.6 Keeping staff and colleagues informed

Supervisors, along with management, need to ensure that all staff (both permanent and temporary) are well informed about health, safety, hygiene and security matters and that their knowledge is regularly updated to remain effective. Training and instruction will help to reduce the risk of accidents and to help staff work efficiently and safely. They need to take part in good initial and ongoing training in all matters relating to work areas and procedures. Regular reminder, consolidation and update sessions will keep their knowledge current and help to reinforce the importance of health, safety, hygiene and security as part of every working day.

Staff training should be planned, monitored and fully recorded. These records must be kept and made easily available for inspection purposes and to ensure that all staff have completed the training. Good record keeping will also assist with future planning of training for each staff member. It is important to remember that training also needs to be completed with temporary and agency staff and those on work placement. Problems arising with any employee failing to comply with health, safety, hygiene and security standards should be identified and prompt, appropriate action taken.

Staff will also need to be supervised and mentored at a level relevant to their work, knowledge and experience. This is especially important for new or young employees.

Evidence 2

1.1 1.2 1.3 1.4 2.5 3.1 3.8

Collect or make a list of all health, safety, hygiene and security staff training that has taken place in your area. List both formal and informal training and make sure that all of the training that has been completed is dated and recorded correctly.

Evidence 3

1.2

Collect the information you give to staff or details of where you tell them to look for it. Provide a list of pictures or information/posters used.

2.7 Communicating with employees

Those working in hospitality areas may be given information and made aware of health, safety, hygiene and security related to their employment by:
- initial information and training at induction
- taking part in formal training courses which may be linked to a qualification
- online training courses and learning packages
- direct supervision and mentoring
- visiting trainers covering specific knowledge areas
- information given at staff briefing at the start and end of their working day and at shift handover briefings
- team meetings to discuss health, safety, hygiene and security matters
- use of posters, leaflets, film clips and noticeboard information
- training given by equipment and systems companies
- directing to websites with relevant information
- local libraries and employment centres
- seeking advice from supervisors, managers or HR departments.

Figure 4.2 Direct supervision and mentoring is one of the ways a supervisor should give information on health, safety and security

The information given at staff handover sessions and briefings is particularly useful because a handover will involve staff from both shifts who may not meet at other times. It is an opportunity to share ideas and concerns and to discuss these with the supervisor, who can then make suggestions, find solutions or make management aware of issues arising. It is also a time when problems and ideas are fresh in the minds of employees who may have forgotten by the next shift.

Evidence

1.3

Possible evidence could include:
- induction and new employee training records
- COSHH data sheets and where they can be found by staff
- information and training on workplace security policy and procedures
- supervisor job description.

> **Evidence 4**
>
> `1.1` `1.2` `1.3` `1.4` `1.8` `1.9` `2.6` `2.7` `2.9` `2.11` `2.12` `2.13` `3.1` `3.4` `3.7`
>
> In your usual work areas, look around to see where there is information on health, safety, hygiene and security for staff. Where it is in the form of a poster or sticker, are employees in the area actually taking notice of them? Are they in good condition and easy to read? Does everyone understand them (consider where English is not the first language)? Could these be improved on with different items? Ask staff if they are aware of the various items of information available for them and where they can be found. If there are negative answers, run a short training session on this and record it. Report your findings to management/the health and safety representative.

> **Evidence 5**
>
> `1.1` `1.2` `1.3` `1.4` `1.5` `1.8` `1.9` `2.1` `2.2` `2.4` `2.6` `2.7` `2.11` `2.12` `2.13` `3.8` `3.9`
>
> Find details of how you communicate risk assessment, HACCP information or other areas concerning health, safety, hygiene and security to the staff. How can you tell if your communication has been effective, and how could you tell if improvements have taken place because of what you have communicated to staff? Pass on your findings to management in a suitable written or electronic format.

Dealing with emergencies

`2.9` `2.11` `3.12` Emergency procedures

Reporting hazards

All staff should be aware that if they see a hazard in the work area that could cause an accident, they should:

- Make the hazard safe, as long as it can be done without risking personal safety.
- Report the hazard to a supervisor or manager as soon as possible, making sure no one enters the area without being aware of the danger.
- Warn others if there is a hazard that cannot immediately be made safe, block the route past the hazard and use a sign such as a bright yellow wet floor sign.

Safety and hazard signs

Signs are an effective way of informing people of a hazard. These generally take the following forms:

- Prohibition signs – **red**, for example, 'no smoking'.
- Fire-fighting signs – **red**, for example, with white symbols or writing such as a 'fire hose reel').
- Warning signs – **yellow**, for example, 'caution – hot surface'.
- Hazard warning signs – **yellow**, for example, 'corrosive substance'.
- Mandatory signs – **blue**, for example, 'protective gloves must be worn'. A solid blue circle with a white picture or writing gives a reminder of something you must do such as 'shut the door'.
- Emergency/escape and first aid signs – **green** with a white picture or writing, for example, emergency sign for escape or first aid.

When using chemicals that could harm you, signs that highlight the following information may be displayed on the container:

- corrosive – could burn your skin
- toxic – may cause serious harm if swallowed
- irritant – may cause itching or a rash if in contact with skin
- oxidising/flammable – easily flammable liquids that can catch fire and burn.

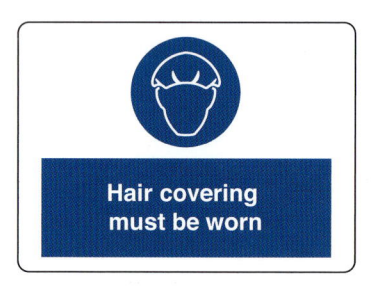

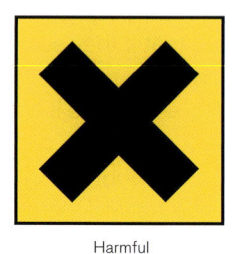

Figure 4.3 Some of the most common safety and hazard signs

Dealing with accidents

Even with good working procedures and practices in place, workplace accidents can still occur.

The main causes of accidents are unsafe actions, unsafe conditions or a combination of both.

If an accident occurs it must be always be dealt with promptly and in line with the organisation's operational procedures. It must be properly recorded on an accident form which is then stored in a file or on a suitable electronic system. Managers or health and safety officials must be kept aware of accidents that occur and any serious accidents must be formally reported to a central authority (see RIDDOR on page 45).

Full name of injured person:			
Occupation:		Supervisor:	
Time of accident:	Date of accident:	Time of report:	Date of report:
Name of injury or condition:			
Details of hospitalisation:			
Extent of injury (after medical attention):			
Place of accident or dangerous occurrence:			
Injured person's evidence of what happened (include equipment/items and/or other persons):			
Witness evidence (1):		Witness evidence (2):	
Supervisor's recommendations:			
Date:		Supervisor's signature:	

Figure 4.4 An example of an accident recording form

2.8 First aid

When people at work suffer injuries or fall ill, it is important that they receive immediate attention and that in serious cases, medical help is sought. The arrangements for providing first aid in the workplace are set out in the Health and Safety (First Aid) Regulations 1981 and there is detailed advice available on the HSE website.

As a minimum, a workplace must provide:
- a suitably stocked first aid kit
- an appointed and named person in charge of first aid arrangements
- easy-to-understand information with details of first aid arrangements.

First aid procedures need to be considered as part of the risk assessment procedures.

Where risks are considered minimal, an **appointed person** may take charge of first aid arrangements such as looking after first aid boxes and facilities, and calling the emergency services if needed. This person is not necessarily required to have any formal training, though training is available for this role.

However, for most hospitality workplaces an appropriate number of trained first aiders will be needed. These are people who have been trained by a recognised training provider in first aid at work or emergency first aid at work. The training provider will complete the training and arrange for awarding the relevant certificates of competence, which need to be updated as specified. The trained first aider will take charge of and apply the first aid requirements of an individual, as well as helping to assess if further treatment is needed. They may also arrange the calling of emergency services and manage the situation until they arrive.

As a minimum, a first aid box should contain:
- a card giving general first aid guidance including basic emergency procedures
- individually wrapped sterile, adhesive, waterproof dressings of various sizes
- 25g cotton wool packs
- safety pins of various sizes
- two triangular bandages
- two sterile eye pads, with attachment
- four medium-sized sterile unmedicated dressings
- two large sterile unmedicated dressings
- two extra-large sterile unmedicated dressings
- disposable rubber gloves
- scissors.

Do not supply any medication or antiseptic creams because the injured person may have a reaction to these.

First aid boxes must be easily identifiable and accessible in the work area. They should be in the charge of a responsible person, checked and refilled when necessary.

Large establishments may have an on-site nurse and a suitably equipped first aid/medical room.

Evidence 6
1.1 1.2 1.3 1.4 1.6 1.7 1.9 2.6 2.7 2.11 3.5 3.8

Identify how new staff in your area are informed about the first aid and accident procedures. Is this recorded and how often are the training records updated? Consider producing a leaflet or poster to remind staff of the correct accident reporting procedure and a checklist or chart to be used by the person checking and replenishing the first aid boxes.

Have you identified any improvements necessary to accident forms, accident and first aid procedures? If so, pass this on in a written format to the relevant person. Keep copies of meeting notes for informing staff of accident and illness reporting procedures.

Fire safety

All employers have a duty for the safety of their employees in the event of a fire. The Regulatory Reform Fire Safety Order 2005 places a greater focus on fire prevention. It places responsibility for the fire safety of the occupants of premises on a defined responsible person, usually the employer. The responsible person must:

- Make sure that the fire precautions, where reasonably practicable, ensure the safety of all employees and others in the building.
- Make an assessment of the risk of and from fire and put suitable precautions and safety measures in place. Like other risk assessments, this must be recorded, regularly updated and be available for inspection. Special consideration must be given to dangerous chemicals or substances, and the risks that these pose if a fire occurs.
- Put in place reviews for preventative and protective measures.

Fire safety requires constant vigilance to reduce the risk of a fire by adopting safe working methods and providing frequent staff training and information. Risk is reduced in the event of a fire by the provision of detection and alarm systems. The alarm systems must be regularly tested and there must be well practised emergency and evacuation procedures that take place regularly. These must be both recorded and available for inspection in the risk assessments.

Fire precautions

- Identified hazards must be removed or reduced as far as is reasonable. All persons must be protected from the risk of fire.
- All escape routes must be safe and used effectively.
- Means for fighting fires must be available on the premises.
- Means of detecting a fire and giving warning in case of fire must be available.
- Arrangements must be in place for planned action to be taken in the event of a fire on the premises, including the instruction and training of employees.
- All precautions provided must be installed and maintained by a competent person.

The fire and rescue authorities will inspect premises and ensure adequate fire precautions are in place. They will also wish to be satisfied that the risk assessment has been completed, is comprehensive, relevant and up to date.

For a fire to start, three things are needed:
1 A source of ignition (heat)
2 Fuel
3 Oxygen.

If any one of these is missing, a fire cannot start. Taking steps to avoid the three coming together will therefore reduce the chances of a fire occurring.

Methods of extinguishing fires concentrate on cooling or depriving the fire of oxygen such as an extinguisher that uses foam or powder to exclude oxygen.

Once a fire starts, it can spread very quickly from one source of fuel to another. As it grows, the amount of heat it gives off will increase and this can cause other fuels to self-ignite.

Fire detection and fire warning

There needs to be effective means of detecting any outbreak of fire and for warning people in your workplace quickly enough so that they can escape to a safe place before the fire makes escape routes unusable.

An electrical fire warning system with manually operated call points is likely to be the minimum needed. In unoccupied areas, where a fire could start and develop, thereby blocking escape routes, it is likely that automatic fire detection will also be necessary.

Lighting of escape routes

All escape routes, including external ones, must have sufficient lighting for people to see their way out safely. These need to be included on the fire risk assessment.

Means of fighting fire

There needs to be effective fire-fighting equipment in place for employees to use, without exposing themselves to danger. The equipment must be suitable to the risks and appropriate staff will need training and instruction in its proper use.

In small premises, having one or two portable extinguishers in an appropriate location may be all that is required. In larger or more complex premises, a greater number of portable extinguishers, strategically sited throughout the premises, are likely to be the minimum requirement and some areas may be fitted with sprinkler systems. Various means of fighting fire may need to be considered and these are shown in Figure 4.5.

KNOW YOUR FIRE EXTINGUISHER COLOUR CODE

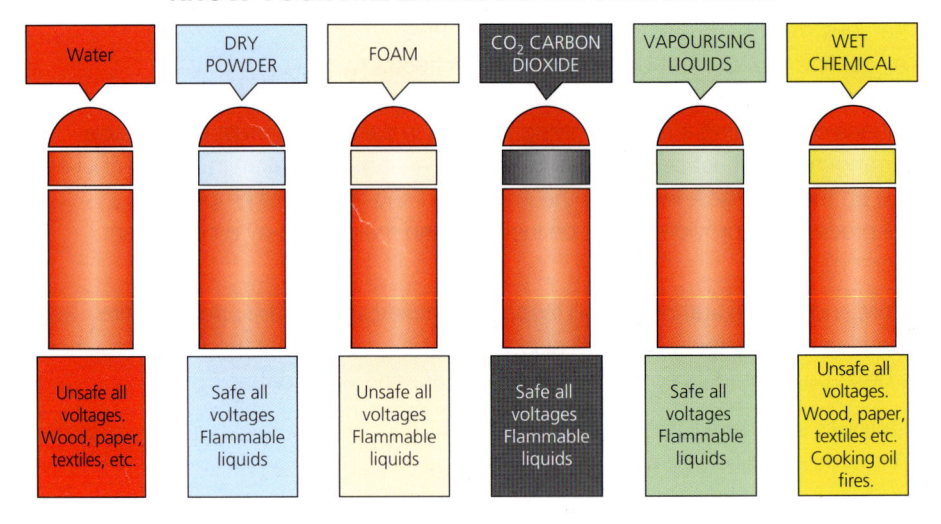

Water	Dry Powder	Foam	CO_2 Carbon Dioxide	Vapourising Liquids	Wet Chemical
Unsafe all voltages. Wood, paper, textiles, etc.	Safe all voltages Flammable liquids	Unsafe all voltages Flammable liquids	Safe all voltages Flammable liquids	Safe all voltages Flammable liquids	Unsafe all voltages. Wood, paper, textiles etc. Cooking oil fires.

Figure 4.5 The six types of fire extinguisher and their uses

Portable fire extinguishers enable suitably trained people to tackle a fire in its early stages, if they can do so without putting themselves in danger. When you are deciding on the types of extinguisher to provide, you should always get suitable advice from extinguisher manufacturers or fire prevention authorities. Consideration needs to be given to the nature of the materials, surfaces and substances likely to be found in your workplace.

Oil and deep fat fryer fires

These can cause very serious fires and burn fiercely once alight. None of the standard fire extinguishers should be used on these fires and it would be very dangerous to do so. The only fire extinguisher to use is called 'wet chemical' and has a yellow band across the front.

Alternatively for small fat and oil fires, a fire blanket can be used. This will exclude oxygen from the fire and it will start to diminish. When using a fire blanket, always wrap the top of the blanket round the hands first.

Reporting of maintenance issues

All working areas will need planned and regular maintenance if they are to achieve the required standards of health, safety, hygiene and security, and it is part of the supervisor's role to ensure that this is done. Many hospitality areas are in use over long hours throughout the day, and in busy public areas wear and tear of walls, floor coverings, furniture and furnishings will be inevitable. However, lack of maintenance, replacement and repair can also have a serious impact on health, safety, hygiene and security. Consider the following issues:

- Worn carpets and other flooring can cause slips, trips and falls.
- Broken or sharp edges on fittings or equipment such as a glass display unit could cause injury and splinters of glass in food.
- Faulty lighting can lead to accidents.
- Faulty ventilation can make certain work areas very hot and a build-up of steam can make floors slippery.
- Damaged electrical equipment and cables can cause electric shock or burns.
- Flaking paint, cracks in walls, ceilings and loose plaster can fall into and contaminate food.
- Damage or wear around windows and doors could allow pests to enter the building and could be a security hazard.
- Faulty equipment can cause personal injury.
- Malfunctioning equipment can cause hygiene hazards, for example, refrigerators running at the wrong temperature.
- Security systems that are not working leave the premises and staff vulnerable to security breaches.

With maintenance issues a proactive approach is always best: plan for care and maintenance before something goes wrong. A planned weekly maintenance check can highlight what will need attention or replacement so this can be done before problems occur. Ultimately this will be less costly than emergency maintenance and replacement. The maintenance report should be sent to your line manager, with findings clearly identified.

However, there will be occasions when emergency or urgent maintenance is needed. Be sure of the procedure that you need to follow to report the issue, the paperwork or electronic systems you need to use and who may need copies.

Be aware of any maintenance issue causing health, safety, hygiene and security dangers or lack of legal compliance. It may be necessary to halt a procedure or close an area until the maintenance is complete. For example, if the water supply was cut off, a restaurant would have to close.

Workplace security

Workplace security is important to ensure the safety of employees and everyone else using the premises, as well as the actual premises and their contents and fittings. Standards must remain high within working areas and customer areas and all staff must be aware of contingency measures to be used in the case of a security problem or breach of security. Any incident or breach of security that you are aware of must be recorded and reported to the appropriate person immediately, in line with your workplace operational procedure.

> **Fire safety**
> Do not attempt to extinguish fires or ask anyone else to do so unless they have been properly trained in procedures and the use of extinguishers/fire blankets. Never put yourself or others in additional danger.

Security measures are necessary to protect against the following problems:

- **Personal injury** involving staff or customers must be avoided and measures such as risk assessments should be in place to help prevent personal injury occurring. Premises that are in good repair, with well-lit and well-signed areas, along with staff working with care, following correct procedures, will all help to prevent personal injury.
- **Personal assault** can unfortunately happen to customers and staff and although it is often a physical assault, verbal assault can be distressing too. All assault must be taken seriously and good, effective security personnel and strict security systems can reduce the likelihood of this happening, allowing incidents to be dealt with quickly. All incidents of assault should be recorded, forwarded to the appropriate person or department and stored.
- **Theft** can place an unnecessary financial strain on a hospitality business. Theft may be by staff or customers and can include: food and drinks, equipment, furnishings, guest items such as towels and bathrobes and, of course, money. Theft may also occur with staff and customers' property. Vigilance, good staff training and effective security measures may all help to reduce incidences of theft.
- **Fraud** is becoming increasingly sophisticated and well planned. Fewer transactions now occur with cash so fraud from that area has reduced. However, staff who handle cash still need to be vigilant against the possibility of counterfeit cash. Although credit cards are considered to be safer, there has been a significant increase in credit card fraud and other electronic fraud methods. Staff need to remain alert and report anything suspicious or unusual. They must also remain aware of possible theft of credit cards.
- **Vandalism** may cover a wide range of damaging acts to the building and its finishes, furniture, equipment and furnishings. It may also be the deliberate starting of a fire, flooding or graffiti. Once again, staff need to remain observant and vigilant and report anything suspicious or unusual they may notice.
- **Terrorism** has become an increasing concern and is a very serious security risk. Terrorism can be presented through phone calls, emails, texts, suspect letters and packages, abandoned luggage or a threat in person. Having a contingency plan for such events will help staff to deal with the situation calmly. This may be leaving the building, alerting security, calling the police or following other workplace procedures.

The supervisor's role

Supervisors must inform and train all employees to remain vigilant with security matters and immediately report anything they think may be a breach of security.

All staff must be trained in the use of the company's security procedures and induction may be a good time to do this, followed by frequent updates. Everyone must observe and use security measures put in place by the employer properly. These may include:

- employee ID and swipe cards, along with always wearing the workplace identification badge
- correct use of locks and security key pads
- CCTV cameras placed at strategic places inside and outside the building
- safes and secure boxes or drawers for cash and valuable items
- passwords and security codes used as appropriate
- staffed security/reception desks.

Large amounts of cash may be handled by staff in hospitality establishments and this could be vulnerable to theft, fraud or misuse. Encourage regular removal of cash to safes or to finance personnel, regular collection of cash by security companies and also encourage the use of debit/credit cards or loyalty cards so less cash is handled.

One main entrance for customers using the building will help to reduce security concerns. Doormen, reception and greeting staff in place can help to identify who is on the premises. Having customers' contact details also helps to identify occupants of the building.

Employee entrances need to be secure with staff using electronic ID cards, security staff at the entrance or both. Any visitor or contractor should have a record of their expected visit or an appointment, they should be required to sign in and out, have a visitor pass and be accompanied by a member of staff.

Delivery entrances also need to be secure, kept locked when not actually in use and observed when open for use. With regard to stock of food, drinks and other consumables, good stock control methods and secure storage should help to reduce loss and theft. However, if discrepancies do occur, these should be investigated to establish when and how the loss occurred, then measures should be put in place to avoid it happening again.

Items lost, damaged or discarded should be recorded, giving details of why and how any damage happened, what the items are and what subsequent steps have been taken. Similar records should be kept for a customer's lost item. If property is found after the customer has left, record the time it was found, what it is and where it has been stored for safe keeping. If the person who lost an item is known to the establishment, steps should be taken to contact them and inform them about the lost item.

Evidence 7
1.6

Deal with risks and accidents promptly following organisational and legal requirements for safeguarding customers and staff.

Possible evidence could include:
- accident reports
- reporting of concerns to management
- staff briefing or handover meeting notes
- staff training sessions
- equipment working order checklists
- allergies policy.

Evidence 8
1.7

Follow organisational procedures when recording or reporting risks and any health, safety, hygiene and security action taken.

Possible evidence could include:
- accident forms
- meeting notes for informing staff of accident and illness reporting procedure
- temperature charts (refrigerators and hot food)
- security report.

Take it further

New, increasingly sophisticated systems for security of premises, property and people appear all the time. Research some of these systems and consider which of them could be used in your workplace.

2.10 Evacuation procedures

Be sure that you fully understand the procedure for evacuation of the building in case of fire or any other emergency such as explosion or bomb alert. It is important too that everyone working in your area understands the procedure and knows exactly what to do. Include this in initial training and induction. Regular evacuation procedure practices will ensure that staff remain aware of the workplace standards and procedures for evacuation. If an evacuation practice of the building does not work properly or efficiently it is important that this is reported to the appropriate person so that changes can be made.

> **Evidence 9**
>
> 1.1 | 1.2 | 1.3 | 1.4 | 1.5
> 2.4 | 2.5 | 2.6 | 2.7 | 2.9
> 2.10 | 2.13 | 3.11 | 3.12
>
> Find the risk assessments and other relevant information for emergency procedures and evacuation in your workplace and highlight any parts of it that describe your role in this. How are staff informed of the procedures? Add to it how well you think this worked last time it was practised – could anything be improved or added when evacuating your area?

The usual workplace procedure for evacuation on hearing the alarm is:

1. Switch off any appliances such as gas stoves; this may be possible by using a single cut-off switch. Leave the building by the designated escape route.
2. Assist any customers or guests to leave the building if they are in your work area.
3. Go to the designated assembly point; the supervisor may then complete a check that all staff are present.
4. Remain at the assembly point until instructed that it is safe to re-enter the building.

2.11 3.1 3.2 3.3 Recording and storing information

Information and records relating to health, safety, hygiene and security may need to be made available to a wide number of people and departments within the establishment and other organisations for a number of reasons. These include auditing, dealing with disputes or legal matters, ensuring compliance with legislation, allowing for planning and for day-to-day running of the business. Always be certain that it is within your authority to pass on information and take great care that no employee personal information is disclosed.

Table 4.1 Information to be recorded and members of staff likely to require such information

Those within the organisation who may need information	Information and records required
Managers within the immediate working areas	Records of formal and informal staff training
Executive/head chefs	Certificates of training and competence
Executive/head housekeepers	Accident and incident reports and RIDDOR reports
Estates, premises and maintenance managers	Staff handbooks
Front office managers	Reported staff sickness and injury
Restaurant managers	Equipment maintenance and repair documentation
Food and beverage managers	Records of staff PPE and where specific items are used
Banqueting managers	Employer's liability insurance
Stores managers	Evacuation and emergency procedure
Security managers	First aid procedures and record of trained first aiders
Company auditors	Health and Safety Risk Assessments
Health and safety representatives/managers	COSHH documentation
First aid personnel	HACCP policy and documentation
Human resources departments	Copies of inspection reports
Trades union representatives	Contact details of suppliers and contractors
Finance departments	Deep cleaning/specialist cleaning records
IT and technology departments	Pest control audits
Relevant people at other establishments but within the organisation	Contact details of staff and recruitment agencies
	Lists of health, safety, hygiene and security posters, letters and information

As well as making necessary information available to relevant people within your own organisation, it is sometimes necessary to provide information and documentation to those outside of the workplace. As seen on pages 40–41, certain authorities have the right to enter your premises and complete inspections. Documents and paperwork will be required to support and assist with their inspection and it is the supervisor who often makes these available. The authorities or individuals involved and the documentation they may need are as follows.

Table 4.2 Types of information that may be required for external purposes

Those outside of the organisation who may need information	Information and records required
Environmental Health Officers Fire and rescue authorities Health and Safety Executive inspectors Trading Standards inspectors Police or other law enforcement officers Emergency services External auditors	Employer liability insurance documentation Certificates of training and competence Accident and incident reports and RIDDOR reports Copies of previous inspection reports and actions Fire Risk Assessments Evacuation and emergency procedures First aid procedures and record of trained first aiders Health and Safety Risk Assessments COSHH documentation and data sheets HACCP policy and related documentation Induction and training records Staff personnel records (where authorised to do this) Staff working rotas and absence records CCTV recordings Servicing and repair of equipment documents Contact details for suppliers of goods/services

2.12 2.13 Making recommendations

As the supervisor is the person overseeing the daily operations in the business, it is your responsibility to keep management and anyone involved in policy making for the business well informed of matters regarding health, safety, hygiene and security and of any ongoing problems that need management attention. Improvements to existing procedures may be suggested and recommended to management by the supervisor. The supervisor may also suggest changes in processes, procedures and staffing levels and make recommendations regarding equipment and maintenance. This important communication should be a planned, regular and ongoing occurrence.

A supervisor can keep management informed and updated by:
- attending meetings and making health, safety, hygiene and security an agenda item with time-bound action points
- sending a weekly/monthly report
- written incident reports
- regular emails or letters outlining current situations and any changes
- giving verbal information (preferably followed by a written account).

Evidence 10

1.8

Possible evidence could include:
- minutes of meetings
- emails
- notes of training or information sessions with staff
- copy of questions asked of staff
- statement of successfully giving information to non-English speakers.

Evidence 11

1.9

Possible evidence could include:
- letters, memos, emails to management
- EHO or HSE reports
- minutes of meetings and notes of one-to-one discussions
- new or suggested stickers
- information posters in staff areas.

Assessing risks

3.4 Potential hazards

Workplace accidents

An accident is an:
- unplanned and uncontrolled event
- event that causes injury, damage or loss
- event that could lead to an accident or near-miss accident

There are a number of reasons why accidents may occur.

Human factors and errors

The ability (or lack of ability) to recognise hazards and risks, lack of skills, general attitude to safety such as taking short cuts, insufficient care taken, tiredness, use of alcohol or drugs.

Occupational factors

This means exposure to possible hazards in the workplace specific to the occupation. A chef may risk cuts or burns, a room service waiter may suffer back strain from carrying heavy trays all day.

Environmental factors

This refers to the working environment such as poor lighting, poor air quality and excessive temperatures in the workplace. It may also refer to the time allowed to carry out certain jobs and the pressure of the work environment.

Organisational factors

The organisation or establishment could affect the safety of staff. For example:
- the safety standards of the organisation
- safety precautions
- enforcing/encouraging of precautions and standards by the employer
- the effectiveness of communication between work colleagues and the employer
- the amount of training individuals have received, advice, mentoring and supervision.

The causes of accidents

Accidents happen in many ways. The three main causes are:
1. Unsafe actions.
2. Unsafe conditions.
3. A combination of unsafe actions and unsafe conditions.

Examples of unsafe acts in hospitality premises

Below are some examples of unsafe acts that can occur in hospitality premises:
- Unsafe equipment, using sharp or mechanical equipment without guards.
- Walking on wet or greasy floors.
- Hazards on the floor that could cause a trip or fall.
- Carrying saucepans of hot liquid or oil.
- Carrying sharp or dangerous objects.
- Using damaged equipment.
- Lifting heavy loads in an incorrect way.
- Not wearing the advised protective clothing.
- Using unsafe methods when using chemicals.
- Inadequate maintenance of work equipment.
- Working in poor environmental conditions such as low lighting, bad ventilation or extreme temperatures, high humidity, poorly designed buildings.
- Unhygienic working environments.
- Poor work systems in place.
- Actions leading to entrapment of clothing, hair, hands etc. in machines.

Accidents will occur in the workplace if health and safety are not taken seriously and there is no culture of safety in the workplace. There will be a low risk of accidents in an organisation that has an effective health and safety policy, a strong safety culture and a real commitment from management and employees.

3.5 3.6 Monitoring the working area

To limit risks, monitoring should take place on a regular basis, as well as when the supervisor feels that some extra checks may be beneficial. Monitoring may include daily working practices, new procedures, special events or changes to usual practices; use of equipment, staff uniforms and use of PPE; compliance with security measures; and checking that correct hygiene procedures are taking place. Any significant deficiencies highlighted by monitoring checks should be recorded, discussed with management or other relevant people and actions put in place as appropriate.

Evidence 12

1.4

Check that colleagues follow the health, hygiene, safety and security procedures in your own area of responsibility

Possible evidence could include:
- Copies of records of any health and safety checks, temperatures, hygiene, security procedures, equipment checks
- Records of discussions of how you monitor this in your area.

Evidence 13

1.5

Monitor your own area of responsibility for risks to health, safety, hygiene and security.

Possible evidence could include copies of any paperwork relating to use of:
- risk assessment, HACCP
- equipment faults reports
- hygiene checks
- problems with security
- staff sickness records
- accident report entries
- record of fire evacuation exercises
- cleaning schedule
- pest audits
- staff training records.

Evidence 14

1.1 1.2 1.3 1.5 1.7 1.9 2.4 2.6 2.7 2.9 2.10 2.11 3.1 3.2 3.5 3.6 3.7 3.8 3.10 3.11 3.12

Locate the forms and documents you use in your area relating to health, safety, hygiene and security matters. Where you have fully completed forms and documents relating to health, safety, hygiene and security, these could be used as evidence for some of the learning objectives in this chapter but make sure that you remove any personal or sensitive data from items you may use as evidence.

2.11 3.7 3.8 Assessing risk (risk assessment)

Assessing risk and producing a formal risk assessment is the key to effective health and safety in the workplace and this is a legal requirement when there are five or more employees. Risk assessment is a careful examination of anything in the workplace that could cause harm or injury to people, so that the necessary safeguarding precautions can be put in place to prevent harm.

Five steps to assessing risk

The five steps to assessing risk and producing a risk assessment are outlined below. There is more detail on the HSE website and also a template to assist in producing a risk assessment.

1 Identify the hazards – the things that could cause harm

Assess your work areas, equipment and procedures and decide what could cause harm. Involving the staff who work in the area could be very useful as they may have noticed things that are not immediately obvious to others.

Check equipment manufacturers' instructions or data sheets for chemicals as they can be very helpful in identifying hazards and putting in place the necessary precautions. Checking previous accident and ill-health records can also help to identify hazards.

2 Decide who might be harmed and how

For each hazard, be clear about who could possibly be harmed. It is not necessary to name everyone but it is helpful to identify groups of people such as those spending time in cold storage rooms or those moving deliveries. Remember those with different needs such as new and young workers, migrant workers and people with disabilities. Also consider visitors, contractors, maintenance workers who may not be in the workplace all the time and customers/guests. Record the type of injury or ill health that might occur to people in the specific areas.

3 Evaluate the risk and decide if existing precautions are adequate or if more are needed

Having identified the hazards, decisions need to be taken about what actions are necessary. The law requires that everything 'reasonably practicable' is done to prevent harm.

Consider the controls already in place and how the work is organised. Decide if this is the best practice (advice is available on HSE website). Consider if more could be done to achieve best practice. For example, could the hazard be eliminated altogether? If not, how could it be controlled so that harm is unlikely?

Consider applying the following to each hazard:
- Try a less risky option.
- Prevent access to the hazard.
- Organise work to reduce exposure to the hazard.
- Issue personal protective equipment.
- Provide appropriate welfare facilities such as first aid and washing and changing facilities.

Remember to involve those working in the area so that what is proposed will work in practice and will not introduce new hazards or difficulties.

4 Record the findings and implement them

Recording the results of the risk assessment and sharing them with others will formalise the decisions. Keep the recording and written account clear and simple so everyone understands it.

When preparing the written risk assessment, make sure the following is done:
- a thorough check is made
- who might be affected is fully considered

- all the obvious hazards are dealt with, accounting for all those who could be involved
- the precautions are reasonable and workable, and the remaining risk is low.

5 Regularly review the risk assessment and revise it as necessary

Areas, equipment and procedures are subject to change. A new menu, new procedures or a new piece of equipment could lead to new risks so reviews of the risk assessment must be updated regularly. This can easily be forgotten so set dates through the year for risk assessment reviews when any changes can be considered and the risk assessment amended. Also consider any new or changed hazard/risk pointed out by staff and consider the risk assessment alongside changes such as a new piece of equipment, so updates occur immediately.

Considering the risks

The prevention of accidents and incidents in hospitality establishments must be given careful attention. Therefore it is essential to analyse each situation and decide on the action to be taken. The hazards/risks will fall into one of the following categories.

1. **Minimal risk** – safe conditions with safety measures in place.
2. **Some risk** – acceptable amounts of risk; however, attention must be given to ensure safety measures operate.
3. **Significant risk** – where safety measures are not fully in operation (also includes food most likely to cause food poisoning). Requires immediate action.
4. **Dangerous risk** – processes and operation of equipment to stop immediately. The system or equipment to be completely checked and recommendations made for improvement.

When producing a risk assessment, risks are sometimes categorised as high, medium, low or no risk. Or the risks may be given a number, with 3 as high, 2 as medium, 1 as low and 0 insignificant.

The risk assessment must be recorded, kept available and in a safe place. It needs to remain a 'live document'; this means that it should be regularly updated and changes made as appropriate. Regular updates must be planned and recorded. The health and safety risk assessment will also be kept in the establishment's records – part of **due diligence**.

The purpose of the exercise of assessing the possibility of risks and hazards is to prevent accidents. First, it is necessary to monitor the situation, and to have regular and random checks to see that the standards set are being complied with. However, should an incident occur, it is essential that an investigation is made as to the cause or causes and any defects in the system remedied at once. Immediate action is required to prevent further accidents. All personnel need to be trained to be actively aware of the possible hazards and risks and to take positive action to prevent accidents occurring.

Reporting back

Reviews and updates to risk assessments must be planned and occur regularly. The actual frequency will depend on:
- the working areas and the risks they pose
- problems highlighted in previous assessments
- company policy and procedures.

> **Key term**
>
> **Due diligence** – when a person or organisation who may be subject to legal proceedings can establish a defence to show that they have taken 'all reasonable precautions and exercised due diligence' to proceed in the correct way to avoid committing an offence.

All proposed changes to risk assessment need to be reported to department heads/management or business owners and this could be done by:
- written report or letter
- email
- sending the amended report with a covering letter
- presenting the changes at a meeting
- a 'walk round' the areas covered by the assessment, followed by a written report.

When proposed amendments to risk assessments are reported back, it also presents opportunities for the supervisor to make recommendations for improvement in health, safety, hygiene and security in the area. This would be particularly effective in a meeting or presentation session and during 'walk-round' monitoring.

Hazard Analysis Critical Control Point (HACCP)

Hazard Analysis Critical Control Point (HACCP) is a familiar term in hospitality and food-related businesses. HACCP is an internationally recognised **food safety management system** that identifies stages in any process and identifies hazards that could occur, i.e. what could go wrong, when, where, how.

- **Hazard analysis** – considering all hazards or potential hazards in the food production process or business.
- **Critical control point** – the points or stages in a process where something could go wrong if the hazards were not controlled.

HACCP considers seven stages:
1. Identify the **hazards.**
2. Identify the **critical control points** (the points at which something could go wrong if not controlled).
3. Set **critical limits**. These are the maximum limits within a process that will be allowable to keep food safe, for example all cooked chickens are tested and the temperature must be no less than 75°C.
4. **Monitoring**. This is checking that the procedures are working as intended.
5. **Corrective action** is what is put in place as a correction if something is going wrong.
6. To prove that the HACCP system is operating properly, **verification** takes place.
7. **Documentation** is the keeping of all the paperwork and records relevant to the HACCP system.

> **Key terms**
>
> **HACCP** – an internationally recognised food safety management system that identifies stages in any process and identifies hazards that could occur, i.e. what could go wrong, when, where, how.
>
> **Food safety management system** – having this in place is a requirement for all food businesses. The system must be based on the principles of HACCP and be available for inspection.

> **Key terms**
>
> **Critical control points** – the stages in food production where any possible hazards need to be controlled.
>
> **Critical limits** – the actual limits within a process to keep food safe. They must be absolute and measurable. For example, food being kept not for service must never fall below 63°C.

Supervisors tend to be very much involved with the HACCP system as they are working in the areas where the procedures are taking place. The system needs to be regularly updated for it to work properly and changes need to be made when there are changes in procedures.

Documents and records are kept that show the system is working and for due diligence purposes. They will also be inspected at an EHO inspection. A wide range of documents are used as part of the HACCP system. These include:

- staff training records (include level of training, dates and topics covered)
- list of suppliers – **traceability**
- records of reported staff illnesses and work-related accidents
- temperature control records for refrigerators, freezers, display and serving equipment, cooked food
- delivery temperatures
- equipment maintenance records
- **calibration** of food temperature probes
- pest control **audits**
- cleaning schedules.

Key terms

Traceability – having information and records to be able to trace something back to its source. For example, being able to trace eggs back to the farm where they were laid.

Entrapment – getting trapped, for example, clothing or hair trapped in machinery, or a person completely trapped in an area or equipment.

Audit – a complete and careful inspection and examination of how a system or business is operating.

Calibration – the setting or correcting of a measuring device, usually by matching it to a set standard. For example, testing a food temperature probe by placing in boiling water.

Evidence 15

1.1 | 1.5 | 1.6 | 2.1 | 2.2 | 2.4 | 2.5 | 2.11 | 2.12 | 3.1 | 3.2 | 3.3 | 3.4 | 3.6 | 3.8 | 3.11

Copy the risk assessment or HACCP documentation that applies to your area. These could include:

- hazard reports, temperature records, staff sickness records (remove any personal data), maintenance reports, pest audit certificates
- documents relating to faulty equipment, maintenance required or any other problems
- completed accident reports (remove any personal data).

You could present this a record of documentation stored electronically.

3.9 The limits of the supervisor's authority

While the supervisor will have the knowledge and authority to deal with a number of issues relating to risks and hazards, it is important to remain aware that there are some limits to what they can authorise or deal with and authorisation, advice and assistance may need to be sought from a manager, health and safety representative or security officer.

Examples may be:
- when equipment or a procedure does not comply with legal requirements
- authorising expenditure for repairs to the building
- decisions to change cleaning chemicals or equipment used in the area
- serious concerns about the honesty of a staff member
- a serious pest problem in the building
- an outbreak of food poisoning
- a serious injury to a member of staff or a customer.

3.10 Dealing with faults with equipment

Hospitality areas will have a wide range of different types of equipment essential for particular areas or tasks. As mentioned, equipment should be subject to planned maintenance and checks to ensure that it is in best working order and reduce the incidence of failure and emergency repair. It is, however, inevitable that equipment will occasionally develop faults and break down. When this happens:

- Make staff aware of when they should stop using the equipment (for example, an item with a worn electrical flex).
- Place a clear sign telling others not to use the item and switch off/unplug as necessary.
- Isolate the item if still considered a possible danger.
- For items such as faulty refrigerators and freezers, food may need to be transferred to other refrigerators and freezers.
- Consider if working procedures need to be temporarily changed.
- Contact the repair contractor as soon as possible.
- If an area needs to be closed because of the faulty item, inform the manager.
- If necessary, consider hiring some suitable emergency equipment.
- Keep a written record of the breakdown and subsequent repairs.

3.11 Contingency planning

This means planning for the possibility of any health, safety, hygiene or security problems occurring and having plans in place to overcome or deal with the problems. Staff should also be fully aware of contingency plans so that, when needed, the plan can be put into action quickly. An example would be a staff entrance door normally operated with an electronic card not working, so a member of security staff would need to stand by the insecure door to check the identity of staff entering the building. A well managed establishment takes health, safety, hygiene and security issues seriously because doing so allows for a professionally run business, as well as being compliant with the law on such issues. Health, safety, hygiene and security as applied to a hospitality business link closely with each other and remain of great importance to the running of a successful business.

Take it further

Health and Safety Executive www.hse.gov.uk

Food Standards Agency www.food.gov.uk

Fire Safety www.gov.uk/workplace-fire-safety-your-responsibilities

Data Protection https://ico.org.uk/

Chartered Institute of Environmental Health (CIEH) www.cieh.org

Royal Society of Public Health (RSPH) www.rsph.org.uk

Institute of Occupational Safety and Health (IOSH) www.iosh.co.uk

Knowledge check

1. Suggest five ways that a supervisor could pass on health, safety, hygiene and security information to staff in their area.
2. a) Which law is in place to protect employees who deal with potentially dangerous chemicals?
   b) What items of PPE would you supply to an employee cleaning a bar area which has some broken glass when beer line cleaners?
3. If an employee had an accident in your work area causing them to need five days off work, where would this be reported and how would you do this?
4. In your work area, what is meant by monitoring? Give three examples of the monitoring you may carry out.
5. What is meant by PAT testing? Suggest three items in your area that may be subject to this testing.
6. a) In your working area suggest three types of information that needs to be recorded.
   b) Why do these records need to be kept?
7. Under the Data Protection Act 1998, what are three pieces of information that you must not disclose to others?
8. What are the five main stages used when conducting a risk assessment? How many employees need to be employed in the business for a risk assessment to be needed?
9. Suggest five measures you could take to keep your premises and working areas safe and secure.
10. What do the letters HACCP stand for and how would HACCP be used in a hospitality business?
11. Suggest five items of information that need to be listed on an accident reporting form and five items that need to be in a work area first aid box.
12. What are the three elements needed for an accidental fire to start? Which fire extinguisher could be used on:
    a) a deep fat fryer fire?
    b) an electrical equipment fire?
    c) a wastepaper basket fire?
    d) a flammable liquids fire?

Assignment

Make a list of all the employees in your area and produce a plan for all of the training they will need in matters concerning health, safety, hygiene and security.

State how this training will be completed (formal and informal) and how you will record that the training has taken place. Will a certificate be issued? Where will you keep these records and do you need to give the information to anyone else?

Make a plan of when the training will need to be renewed or updated for each person.

This will also cover 1.1, 1.2, 1.3, 1.4, 2.2, 2.4, 2.5, 2.9, 2.10, 3.12.

Evidence checklist		
Assessment criteria		**Possible evidence**
1.1	Obtain information on the health, safety, hygiene and security procedures in your own area of responsibility	Locate the forms and documents you use in your area relating to these matters. Copies of completed documents are good.
1.2	Ensure colleagues have relevant information on the health, hygiene, safety and security in your own area of responsibility	Collect the information you give to staff or details of where you tell them to look for it. Provide a list of pictures or information/posters used.
1.3	Inform colleagues about the importance of following health, hygiene, safety and security procedures	Induction and new employee training records. COSHH data sheets and where they can be found by staff. Information and training on workplace security policy and procedure. Supervisor job description.
1.4	Check that colleagues follow the health, hygiene, safety and security procedures in your own area of responsibility	Copies of records of any health and safety checks, temperatures, hygiene, security procedures, equipment checks. Recording or discussion of how you monitor this in your area.
1.5	Monitor own area of responsibility for risks to health, safety, hygiene and security	Copies of any paperwork relating to use of risk assessment, HACCP, equipment faults reports, hygiene checks, problems with security, staff sickness records, accident report entries, record of fire evacuation exercises, cleaning schedule, pest audit. Staff training record
1.6	Deal with risks and accidents promptly following organisational and legal requirements for safeguarding customers and staff	Accident reports Reporting of concerns to management Staff briefing or handover meeting notes Equipment working order checklists Allergies policy
1.7	Follow organisational procedures when recording or reporting risks and any health, safety, hygiene and security action taken	Accident forms Meeting notes for informing staff of accident and illness reporting procedure Temperature charts (refrigerators and hot food) Security report
1.8	Pass on information about how health, safety, hygiene and security procedures are working	Minutes of meetings Emails Notes of training or information sessions with staff Copy of questions asked of staff Statement of successfully giving information to non-English speakers

Maintain the health, hygiene, safety and security of the working environment

Evidence checklist

Assessment criteria		Possible evidence
1.9	Recommend improvements for health, safety, hygiene and security procedures	Letters, memos, emails to management EHO or HSE reports Minutes of meetings and notes of one-to-one discussions New or suggested stickers or information posters in staff area
2.1	Identify the statutory authorities that enforce the health, hygiene and safety laws and regulations	Evidence activity 5 Evidence activity 15
2.2	Explain the implications of breaking the law on health, hygiene and safety for individuals and the organisation	Evidence activity 5 Evidence activity 15 Assignment
2.3	Describe the main areas of health, hygiene and safety laws and regulations for own area of responsibility	Evidence activity 9 Evidence activity 13 Evidence activity 15 HACCP documentation, Health and Safety poster, chemical data sheets.
2.4	Describe the organisation's health, hygiene, safety and security procedures for own area of responsibility	Evidence activity 1 Evidence activity 5 Evidence activity 9 Evidence activity 14 Evidence activity 15 Assignment
2.5	Describe own responsibilities for health, hygiene, safety, and security	Evidence activity 2 Evidence activity 9 Evidence activity 15 Assignment
2.6	Explain the importance of making sure permanent and temporary staff are aware of relevant procedures	Evidence activity 4 Evidence activity 5 Evidence activity 6 Evidence activity 9 Evidence activity 14
2.7	Explain how to communicate with colleagues on issues relating to health, hygiene, safety, and security	Evidence activity 4 Evidence activity 5 Evidence activity 6 Evidence activity 9 Evidence activity 1
2.8	Identify the person responsible in the organisation for first aid, health, hygiene, safety and security and their responsibilities	**Text to follow**

Evidence checklist		
Assessment criteria		**Possible evidence**
2.9	Explain the organisation's emergency procedures	Evidence activity 1 Evidence activity 4 Evidence activity 9 Evidence activity 14 Assignment
2.10	Describe the evacuation procedures that relate to own area of responsibility	Evidence activity 9 Evidence activity 14 Assignment
2.11	Describe the procedures that should be followed when recording and storing information about health, hygiene, safety and security	Evidence activity 1 Evidence activity 4 Evidence activity 5 Evidence activity 6 Evidence activity 14
2.12	Describe the procedures that should be followed when making recommendations about health, hygiene, safety and security	Evidence activity 1 Evidence activity 4 Evidence activity 5 Evidence activity 15
2.13	Identify who to make recommendations to regarding health, hygiene, safety and security	Evidence activity 1 Evidence activity 4 Evidence activity 5 Evidence activity 9
3.1	Describe the appropriate lifting and handling methods and techniques for moving resources in own area of responsibility	Evidence activity 1 Evidence activity 2 Evidence activity 4 Evidence activity 14 Evidence activity 15
3.2	Describe the health and safety requirements for the resources used in own area of responsibility	Evidence activity 14 Evidence activity 15
3.3	Explain the environmental impact some resources can have on the environment	Evidence activity 1 Evidence activity 15
3.4	Describe the organisation's policies and procedures for: • obtaining resources • using resources • controlling waste • recycling	Evidence activity 1 Evidence activity 4 Evidence activity 15
3.5	Explain how to monitor the use of resources	Evidence activity 6 Evidence activity 14

Evidence checklist		
Assessment criteria		**Possible evidence**
3.6	Outline how resources should be stored	Evidence activity 14 Evidence activity 15
3.7	Explain the importance of keeping waste to a minimum	Evidence activity 1 Evidence activity 4 Evidence activity 14
3.8	Explain how to keep waste to a minimum	Evidence activity 2 Evidence activity 5 Evidence activity 6 Evidence activity 14 Evidence activity 15
3.9	Explain how to encourage efficient use of resources to benefit the organisation and the environment	Evidence activity 5
3.10	Explain how to ensure resources are handled and stored in line with organisational requirements	Evidence activity 14
3.11	Explain how to present recommendations to improve the use of resources	Evidence activity 9 Evidence activity 14 Evidence activity 15
3.12	Explain the advantages of using computerised stock control systems	Evidence activity 9 Evidence activity 14 Assignment

CHAPTER 5

Lead a team to improve customer service

This chapter is about combining your organisation and staffing resources to improve overall customer service. It is about leading by example – being enthusiastic about customer service and it is important to support, guide and encourage your team to improve their customer service delivery.

Learning objectives

On completion of this chapter, you should:
1. Be able to plan and organise the work of a team.
2. Be able to provide support for team members.
3. Be able to review performance of team members.
4. Understand how to lead a team to improve customer service.

Introduction

1.1 4.2 Meeting organisational objectives

Customer service is not something that can be completed in one day, one training session or one meeting. The company **customer service charter** (a promise on what kind of service an organisation delivers, so that a customer knows what to expect) needs to be trained, practised and reinforced continually throughout the **employee cycle**. Every type of hospitality sector needs to keep their customers satisfied and to keep them returning in order to be successful and this cannot be achieved by one individual. Recruiting positive, cheerful, well presented people is the first step to success, followed by an effective induction, on going **in-house training** and performance monitoring. It is key to establish a measurement of success, clearly outlining areas for improvement for your team. Working on this together will increase the team's commitment to achieving the goals set out.

The objective of your team is to continually strive to deliver effective customer service and to achieve this, a group of individuals must be brought together for the common task. The ability to facilitate team work starts with the supervisor. They must role model all the behaviours expected of the team. They need to consistently treat all team members with courtesy and respect. Teams will not trust a leader who is erratic, unpredictable and emotional; they need to be able to trust that their supervisor will listen, help, support and share information vital to the team's success.

Key terms

Customer service charter – a promise on what kind of service an organisation delivers so that a customer knows what to expect

Employee cycle – the stages that every employee goes through, from the time they start working for an organisation to the time they leave

In-house training – any training that is happening at the organisation and could be delivered by the employees themselves

Figure 5.1 A good supervisor will encourage staff to work together to provide good customer service

Evidence 1

Explain how:
- your performance, and
- the performance of your team

can affect the achievement of organisational objectives.

What would happen if you didn't improve your customer service performance? How would this affect the members of your team and your organisation?

4.3 Failing to improve customer service

If the factors above are not in place and the customer service provision is inadequate, the organisation can lose:

- Possible customers – if a new customer is introduced to a business by rude or incompetent staff, they are likely to leave before spending any money.
- Loyal customers – even customers with a strong rapport with a business will not return if they are continually treated poorly.
- Future customers – customers who have had bad experiences with a business will tell their colleagues, friends and families. All those people will have a negative opinion of the business before ever visiting it.
- Future employees – people will not seek to work at a business with a poor reputation as they want to be in a workplace they are proud to be a part of.
- Current employees – if staff are continually dealing with complaints and problems, they will become demotivated and want to leave.

Ultimately all this equates to a loss in profit and an organisation operating like this will not be able to invest in the development or retention of its staff. It may even close.

The following chapter will further describe how to motivate your people to care for customers.

1.2 4.1 The roles and responsibilities of team members

Employee induction

Effectively orienting new customer service employees to their roles is critical in ensuring their understanding of the company's expectations and how they should perform from the very beginning. A properly planned and executed **induction** will prevent the new employee feeling frustrated, shorten the time they require for learning the role and lower levels of **staff turnover**. The employee's first impressions and interactions within the team should be a positive and professional example for the new employee to follow.

Key terms

Induction – a procedure for welcoming new employees and preparing them for their roles

Staff turnover – the rate at which employees join and leave an organisation

Preparation

Before the employee's first day, the following should be prepared:

- A clear and specific job description.
- A training plan covering at least the new starter's first two weeks and outlining when the training will be undertaken.
- Access to the department's operations manual and standard operating procedures (either online or in written format).
- One member of the team should be assigned as a buddy for the new starter to shadow for the first two weeks and go to with questions after that; this person should be a role model who will exhibit the behaviours and perform as the new starter is needed to.
- The new starter's workstation should be clean and ready; if possible their uniform should be organised and any required IT/email access set up.
- A copy of the company's policies including Health and Safety procedures.
- Some written explanation of the company's organisational chart/hierarchy and how the new starter fits in.
- Instructions on what to do in the case of an emergency.

A new starter checklist can be used as a tool to remind supervisors and managers what is required and ensure preparations are in place consistently for each new starter.

> **Evidence 2**
>
> 1.2 4.1
>
> Prepare a new starter checklist.

The employee's first few weeks

A new starter will be anxious starting a new job so it is important to try to create a comfortable and welcoming atmosphere. The employee should be collected from the entrance and welcomed by their new buddy on their first day. Information overload should be avoided but this period will include:

- Introductions to the team, the supervisor and any other key people.
- Discussion or presentation of the company's customer service charter, including any mission or vision statements.
- An explanation of benefits and opportunities available to the new starter.
- A review of all the information that has been prepared for them in advance.
- Their job description, as this is a tool of communication and an opportunity to inform the new starter exactly what tasks and duties are expected of them. It may also include a person specification which may outline the required behaviours.
- Scheduled performance evaluation meetings to discuss their progress and obtain the new starter's feedback and overall first impressions. Any concerns need to be addressed at these meetings.

Planning and organising the work of a team

1.3 1.5 4.7 Involving and motivating the team

The benefits of involving team members in decisions when planning and organising work are clear. Overall levels of **morale**, motivation to improve customer service levels and satisfaction in their jobs will be higher because team members will feel valued and be significant contributors to the success of the work. When people feel valued, their commitment and effort will increase. Team members will be able to make decisions that their supervisors will approve of as they will have been involved in the development of the department's customer service direction and have accurate information. Team members will also feel a stronger sense of responsibility for the decisions they make and work harder to correct mistakes. If decisions were made by management, the team member is more likely to blame the management to the customer when things go wrong.

The outcome is more time for the supervisor to contribute to the success of the department in other areas but some investment on the part of the supervisor is needed to achieve all this. They will need to invest more time in team members at the beginning of the process; they will need to show forgiveness when mistakes are made to prevent the fostering of a blame culture; and mostly they will need to trust their team members to do their jobs. The supervisor will also need to ensure that the tools, resources and support necessary are in place in order to allow the team's success.

> **Key term**
>
> **Morale** – the ability of a group to maintain a positive attitude and motivation

1.4 4.4 Taking account of customer service skills and the organisation's objectives

To ensure your team's work is in line with the goals of the organisation, the first step to planning the workload is to confirm and clarify what is required with the manager. By doing this, you will prevent any misunderstandings and future problems. Identify the priorities and activities that are most critical to the success of the team and be aware of the resources available. Before allocating work, perform a short analysis of your team that covers the following:

- Their individual skills, including technical ability and their ability to build rapport with customers.
- Their knowledge of the standard operating procedures and the hospitality product, for example, menus, wines, opening times.
- Their understanding of the priorities and critical activities; for example, if a customer asks a team member where the toilets are when the team member is polishing glasses, do they understand that it is more important to assist the guest than to finish polishing the glasses?
- Their experience in the different tasks required of their roles. A team member assigned to a task that they have never been trained in before is likely to result in failure and feelings of resentment. New starters should be paired with their buddies.
- Check that the workload that has been allocated to them already is fair. For example, imagine one of your highest performing team members is a student and their exams are approaching. By assigning them less work now to allow them time to study, they are more likely to return after their exams committed and loyal than if they were given no consideration.

- Ensure that you provide fair opportunity for the development of the whole team. Don't continually allocate the most challenging duties to the same few team members because they have a proven track record of doing it successfully. This may cause resentment from the team members being prevented from developing and cause problems when the high performers leave the company.
- After taking all this into consideration, spread the workload fairly and deliver a thorough briefing to your team, including the expected level of performance. Include questions to check their understanding and encourage them to ask questions if they need clarification.

> **Evidence 3**
> 1.3 1.5 2.2 2.3 2.4 4.5
>
> Work with your team to create a presentation for your manager on the team's ideas for improving the levels of customer service within your team. Include:
> - What each team member will contribute (for recognition).
> - How you will support them to succeed.
> - What the benefit will be to the customer.
> - What the cost will be to the organisation.
> - What the benefit will be to the organisation.

> **Evidence 4**
> 1.4 4.4
>
> Using a one-week rota that you have written, outline the reasons for organising the workload in this way.

2.1 2.2 2.3 2.4 4.5 4.6 Supporting the team

When a plan has been decided in this way, a supervisor must communicate it to the team openly and clearly, including the reasons behind all decisions. They must give the team an opportunity to ask questions to clarify their understanding and respond to any feedback that the team gives. The supervisor is also responsible for showing recognition to those that stick to the plan and encouraging those that don't to return to the plan.

It is not enough to provide a job description and personal specification at the start of a team members' employment and expect them to continually strive to improve their levels of customer service delivery. A supervisor must regularly role model commitment to the company customer service charter.

Briefings
Pre-service briefings are an excellent opportunity to discuss as a team how their customer service can be improved and, by having this discussion before each service, the customer service objectives are fresh in the minds of all team members. A good briefing will also include what the supervisor will be doing throughout service and who to go to if a team member needs help.

Debriefings
By holding a debriefing after service, you are providing your team members with a voice which shows respect, reinforces **group coherence** and increases morale. The supervisor needs to act as a facilitator, ensuring a safe environment for the discussion and that all comments made by team members are constructive. It serves as an opportunity to reflect on team and individual performance. The debriefing must include how well the team met the objectives outlined in the briefing, how individuals performed using specific examples and an opportunity for each member of the team to give input. The supervisor must act on any agreed actions to improve service so as to be seen to follow through with what they promise to do.

Team meetings
By holding regularly scheduled team meetings, your team will understand that you want communication with them. Try not to cancel or reschedule these meetings or they may feel that they are unimportant to you. Your team will feel more like a part

> **Key term**
>
> **Group coherence** – a shared mental and/or emotional state of mind that allows a group to work well together

of the company if they hear news and developments from you rather than rumours. Arrange the agenda so that there is plenty of time for your points and for the team to give feedback. If you are asked a question that you need to follow up on, make sure that you have the answer or an update ready for the next meeting so the team feel like they are your priority.

Use these meetings to complete customer service activities with your team to ensure they understand their part in delivering high customer service standards.

Figure 5.2 Team meetings can help staff feel more part of the company

Evidence 5
2.1 **3.2**

Ask your teams what qualities and skills are needed to work in customer service. The discussion needs to be no more than five or ten minutes' long and the results can be put into a poster and displayed in back of house areas as a visual reminder. The following are some skills that your team should come up with:

- **Patience** – team members need to have patience with each other, other internal teams and customers, especially when they are under pressure.
- **Adaptability** – surprises happen frequently in hospitality and little goes as planned without changes. For excellent customer service, team members need to adapt accordingly and with a smile and positive attitude.
- **Effective communicators** – team members need to smile in a genuine way, welcoming customers like they are friends but not go too far. They need to be able to 'read' people and change their communication style to match them.
- **Resilience** – if a team member makes a mistake, they need to correct it, learn from it and move on, sometimes very quickly during a busy service. They cannot let the mistake affect their confidence as this will result in further mistakes in the service.
- **Integrity** – they need to see problems and queries through to their resolution and customers will appreciate a team member who is honest with them.
- **Enthusiasm** – team members need a willingness to learn, to help their colleagues and to take pride in the service they deliver.
- **Time management** – getting the customers what they want in an acceptable time frame can be daunting in a busy service – the ability to prioritise is key.

Evidence 6
1.1 **2.3** **4.6**

Ask each member of your team to write a short SWOT analysis on the team by answering the following questions.
- Strengths – what do they do well?
- Weaknesses – what can they improve in?
- Opportunities – what opportunities are available to help individuals and the team succeed?
- Threats – what threatens the success of the team?

Ensure that the exercise is anonymous to encourage the teams to be honest and frank in the feedback they provide. Use this feedback to evaluate your own performance as a supervisor. This task can be repeated every three to six months to monitor for changes and new opportunities.

3.1 3.2 3.3 4.6 4.7 Reviewing and improving performance

Good performance management is not only about when a team member does something wrong; it covers all aspects of the contributions team members make to the goals of their teams and company. It ensures everyone in the organisation knows what the business is trying to achieve, their roles in helping to achieve the goals, the skills and knowledge required, the standards of performance required, how they can develop their performance, how they are doing at the moment and what to do about it when there are problems.

This can all be achieved with regular dialogue between supervisors and their team members. Supervisors should have regular informal meetings or one-to-one meetings about how the team member is doing, development points and any concerns. All the information can be passed on to the manager to form records and establish a development plan for the employee.

Most businesses will have review processes in place to set goals for team members. Where possible, make the goals SMART – Specific, Measurable, Attainable, Realistic, Timely – and focus on the goals rather than the specific way to do things. This allows team members to feel important with increased autonomy and gain experience and career development. (For more information on this see Chapter 1.)

Evidence 7
3.2

Read aloud a letter of complaint with your team and start a discussion on how the problem could have been prevented, including what systems/procedures could be changed in order to ensure the problem is not repeated. Be careful to remove any names of team members when reading the letter as the objective is not to create blame but to learn. Similarly, compliment letters can be read to allow recognition and celebration of excellent performance and praise or reward given.

Specific

Measurable

Achievable

Realistic

Timely

Figure 5.3 SMART goals definitions

Constructive feedback

Constructive feedback is when a team member will be informed of a gap between the skills and knowledge they have now and the standard desired by the supervisor. Without effective feedback, the team member may never become aware that the gap exists. By helping the team member to recognise their strengths and weaknesses they can work to achieve the desired standards.

The Johari Window is a theory commonly used when developing self-awareness. It consists of four perspectives:
- What an individual knows about themselves and others also know – an 'open area'.
- What is known by others but is unknown to the individual – a 'blind area'.
- What an individual knows about themselves that others do not know – a 'hidden area'.
- What is unknown by the individual and unknown by others – an 'unknown area'.

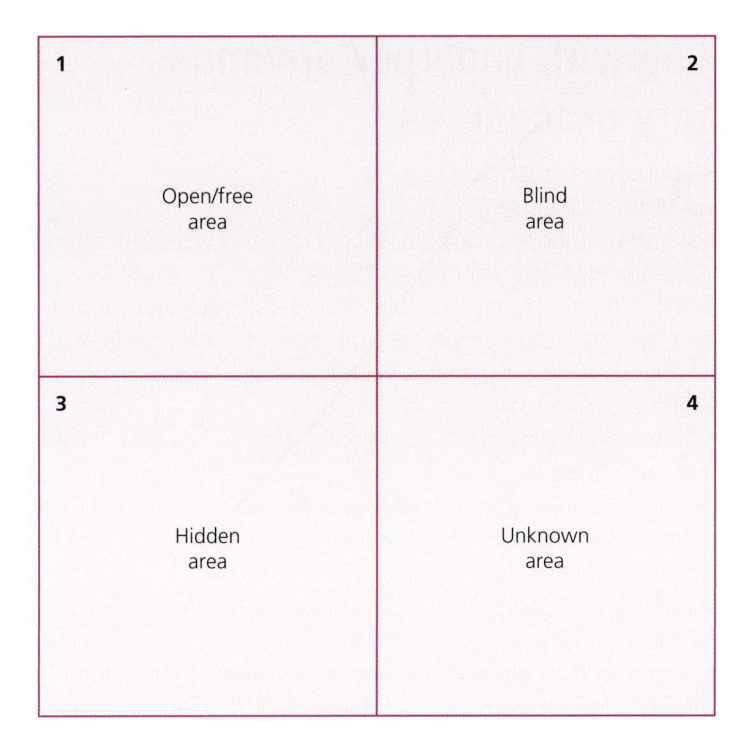

1 Open/free area	**2** Blind area
3 Hidden area	**4** Unknown area

Figure 5.4 The Johari Window

The four 'window panes' of the Johari Window can increase and decrease in size. An employee who has just joined an organisation will have a much smaller 'open area' in a team, as much less is known about them than the rest of the group. The 'open area' is the most productive perspective for a team to work in as it encourages and reinforces group cohesion and reduces miscommunication and mistrust.

- The 'open area' of an employee can be increased through team-building activities and other regular interactions between the team, the individual and the supervisor.
- The 'blind area' is when an employee is oblivious to an issue about themselves. This area can be reduced by careful feedback between the supervisor and employee. Different people have different tolerance levels for sensitive feedback so the supervisor must adjust their approach accordingly. Always point out that reducing the 'blind area' can benefit the employee's career by developing them personally and professionally.
- The 'hidden area' could be fears, emotions, agendas or private information that an employee does not want to reveal. The goal would be to reduce this area as much as possible through disclosure but this must not be forced. A supervisor could decrease the 'hidden area' in their teams by asking careful questions.
- The 'unknown area' is typically larger in younger, inexperienced employees. It refers to the natural abilities that an individual has not discovered that they have. To reduce the 'unknown area', supervisors can encourage their teams to try new things.

Evidence 8

1.5 **2.4** **3.1** **3.2** **3.3** **4.6** **4.7**

Use the Johari Window model to create a self-assessment. Consider how you work with your team and draw the 'window panes' size in accordance.

Repeat the exercise for each individual team member.

Use the diagrams to plan the development needs of your team, including activities to increase the 'open area' within your team and to shrink the levels of 'hidden' areas, which team members may require feedback on their 'blind areas', and ways you can support employees in self-discovery.

Repeat the exercise after a period of three to six months and evaluate the change in size of any 'window panes'.

4.8 Dealing with underperformance: disciplinary procedures

How to address underperformance:
- Identify the performance issue.
- Record specific performance problems using a range of witnesses from different levels to be able to review different perspectives.
- Determine whether the problem is due to a misunderstanding in expectations, due to a temporary issue in the team member's personal life, or from a lack of training.
- Consider options to address the issues such as mentoring, coaching, training or a change in work responsibilities.
- Don't make personal judgements or comments. Keep focused on the actions or behaviour that are incorrect.
- Keep your manager fully informed of the issues and any action you are taking.
- Consult with Human Resources and review your company policy prior to speaking with the team member.
- Determine what the consequences will be if the employee fails to resolve the performance issue.
- Choose a time and a place where you will be uninterrupted to have the conversation with the team member; do not avoid the issue as it will only escalate.
- When talking with the team member, remove any emotional language and acknowledge the person's experience and position.
- Clearly state the problem and be objective and factual, ensuring your tone is calm and even tempered.
- Agree actions that the team member is going to take, including any support that will be required and sign a document with the details.
- Schedule meetings to review the team member's progress and make it clear that the team member can come to you if they need any further support or have any questions.

If issues continue then the disciplinary procedures should be initiated.

> **Evidence 9**
> **4.8**
> Describe your organisation's disciplinary procedure policy.

Knowledge check

1. Clearly describe how to handle an underperforming employee.
2. Why are training plans for new employees important?
3. Explain what a supervisor can do to motivate their team.
4. How does one employee's excellent performance affect the organisation?
5. How does one employee's poor performance affect the organisation?

Evidence checklist		
Assessment criteria		**Possible evidence**
1.1	Treat team members with respect at all times	Evidence activity 6
1.2	Agree with team members their role in delivering effective customer service	Evidence activity 2
1.3	Involve team members in planning and organising their customer service work	Evidence activity 3
1.4	Allocate work which takes full account of team members' customer service skills and the objectives of the organisation	Evidence activity 4
1.5	Motivate team members to work together to raise their customer service performance	Evidence activity 3 Evidence activity 8
2.1	Check that team members understand what they have to do to improve their work with customers and why that is important	Evidence activity 5
2.2	Check with team members what support they feel they may need throughout this process	Evidence activity 3
2.3	Provide team members with support and direction when they need help	Evidence activity 3 Evidence activity 6
2.4	Encourage team members to work together to improve customer service	Evidence activity 3 Evidence activity 8
3.1	Provide sensitive feedback to team members about their customer service performance	Evidence activity 8
3.2	Encourage team members to discuss their customer service performance	Evidence activity 5 Evidence activity 7 Evidence activity 8
3.3	Discuss sensitively with team members action they need to take to continue to improve their customer service performance	Evidence activity 8
4.1	Describe the roles and responsibilities of team members and where the team members fit in the overall structure of the organisation	Evidence activity 2
4.2	Explain how team and individual performance can affect the achievement of organisational objectives	Evidence activity 1
4.3	Explain the implications of failure to improve customer service for the team members and the organisation	Evidence activity 1
4.4	Describe how to plan work activities	Evidence activity 4
4.5	Explain how to present plans to others to gain understanding and commitment	Evidence activity 3
4.6	Explain how to facilitate meetings to encourage frank and open discussion	Evidence activity 6 Evidence activity 8
4.7	Explain how to involve and motivate staff to encourage teamwork	Evidence activity 8
4.8	Describe how to recognise and deal sensitively with issues of underperformance	Evidence activity 9

In addition to the generation of evidence suggested throughout the chapter, the following may be used as part of your evidence:
- Job descriptions
- Personal specifications
- Organisational hierarchy map
- Agendas and minutes from team meetings
- Employees' personal development plans, appraisals, reviews
- Photographs of team activities
- Photographs of examples of when teams have made extra effort (birthday plates)
- Disciplinary procedure policy from your organisation
- Training plans.

CHAPTER 6

Supervise functions

This chapter is about supervising a function such as a banquet, corporate entertainment event, reception or conference. It covers the preparation, running and closing of the event, as well as activities such as briefing the staff, monitoring the event, clearing up and debriefing staff after the event is over.

> **Learning objectives**
>
> On completion of this chapter, you should:
> 1. Be able to supervise functions.
> 2. Understand how to plan functions.
> 3. Understand how to supervise functions.

3.2 Functions

A function can be described as the service of food and drink at a specific time and place, for a given number of people, at a known price. Examples of hospitality functions include:
- **social functions** – weddings, anniversaries, dinner dances
- **business functions** – conferences, meetings, working lunches, working dinners
- **social and business functions** – corporate entertaining.

Sometimes functions are called banquets; however the word banquet is normally used to describe a large, formal occasion.

The variety of function events ranges from simply providing bar facilities in a conference reception area before a meeting, to a more formal occasion catering for perhaps 1,500 to 2,000 people. Many establishments concentrate and market themselves as specialist function caterers. The function business may be the company's sole business; on the other hand, it may be part of the product range – for example, in a hotel, you may well find rooms, restaurants, conference facilities and banqueting.

The type of function facilities found in an establishment will also depend on the market for which it is catering. Function catering is found in the commercial and public sector of the hospitality industry. The types of function suites and variety of functions on offer in all establishments will often differ considerably.

The financial policy will also determine the different types of functions and different menus on offer, as well as their pricing structure. Gross profit margins in function catering tend to be higher than those achieved in hotel restaurants and coffee shops. An average gross profit percentage of 65–75 per cent is usually required in function catering, depending on the type of establishment, types of customers, level of service and so on.

Figure 6.1 A wedding is an example of a social function

Marketing considerations

The marketing policy of a function establishment will focus on the market the business aims to capture, and how best to promote the special characteristics of the establishment. A manager must be constantly aware of the types of products and services on offer in the marketplace. Every consideration must be given to customers' needs and matching these needs to the establishment's facilities. Every organisation needs to advertise and promote its functions and there are a number of ways in which an organisation can promote the business. For more information on promoting products and services, see Chapter 12.

Evidence 1

3.2

List the variety of products and services that your establishment offers. How do these products and services support the functions you offer? Are there any other products or services you might need to support other types of function?

Planning and preparing for a function

Planning and preparing for a function in advance is essential to ensure that everything runs smoothly and customer requirements are met.

1.2 2.5 Information required

A considerable amount of information is needed in advance of a function to help in the planning process. This includes:
- number of guests (to assess the size of the venue needed)
- price per head or cover
- menu requirements
- drinks required
- types of menu
- any specific customer requirements (e.g. specific dietary requirements)
- budget.

This information allows the manager to assess the resource requirements, for example, staffing, linen, food and drink, and equipment.

Evidence 2

1.2 **2.5**

Collect examples of the following documents and include them in your portfolio:
- An example of a list of customer requirements.
- The organisation's staffing policy for functions.
- Outline of a budget for a function.
- Details of types of venues, capacity and resources. Also include details on specific food and drink requirements, IT, additional staffing and entertainment to support a variety of functions.

Key term

Function sheet – A sheet recording all of the customer requirements for a specific functions

Customers are usually invited for a detailed view of the venue; in some establishments this will include a menu tasting. During the menu tasting, the customer is encouraged to discuss their requirements; usually the food and beverage manager will gather this information. The customer will also be advised of the different options available. For example:
- different room layouts
- choice of menu (including any vegetarian or allergy requirements)
- order of service
- flowers
- cloakroom requirements
- technical requirements (overhead projectors, public address system etc.).

1.11 1.12 3.15 3.16 Record keeping

The customer requirements are then summarised on a **function sheet** and divided into departmental responsibilities. The function sheet may be issued to the customer one week before the function. Ideally, function sheets should be colour-coded for each department. The date for confirmation of the final catering numbers is noted on the function sheet.

Name of Establishment		
Function number		
Name and address of client		
Telephone number		
Email		
Date of function		
Time of function		
Type of function	Lunch	Dinner
	Cocktail Reception	Buffet
Copes to be sent to	Kitchen	Function office
	Reception	Accounts
	Cloakroom	
Price per head		
Special requirements, including specialist staffing requirements		
Menu	Wines	
	Reception	Table wines
Menu printing details		
Table place cards		
Flowers		
Toastmaster		
Other requirements (including special IT or public address system)		

Figure 6.2 An example of a function sheet

Other records relating to functions may include:
- telephone enquiry
- bookings diary
- hire contract
- function sheet
- internal function sheet
- invoice
- feedback form
- weekly report
- thankyou letter.

Information may be presented in different ways, either formally or informally. Information relating to a client's function must be professionally presented, accurate and reflect the company's image.

All information relating to the needs of the customers must be recorded throughout the booking process using appropriate documentation, for example, a hire contract or function sheet.

1.5 2.7 3.4 3.7 3.8 3.10 Equipment and resources

The type of equipment and resources needed will be dependent on the function and the type of service on offer. For example, most seated functions use plate service; silver service is rarely used today but buffet service is common, especially for finger buffets, including cocktail parties. You will need to consider the types of crockery, cutlery and glassware, and food and beverages you will need. You also need to consider staff, linen, equipment and furniture requirements.

Seating plans and arrangements

The event manager has to consider the requirements of the customer. It is important to discuss with the customer exactly how they want the tables and set up arranged. This includes what shapes they want the tables to be (e.g. round, square, rectangle, horseshoe); and how the tables are to be identified (either by numbers, letters, place names, towns, cities etc.). The tables must be easily identifiable for ease of service and most importantly for the guests.

The siting of the seating plan is very important; it must be placed in a key position either at the entrance or in another strategic position. The events team must have a copy for reference.

Table plans

These are designed for guests so that they are able to easily identify where they are required to sit. Names may be listed alphabetically with their table number or there may be a list of tables with the guest names attached to them. Whichever system is used, they must be double checked by the customer for accuracy.

The layout of the tables

This has to be down to the customer requirements according to the type of event, the size and shape of the room, the facilities available and the numbers expected. Some examples include sprig, horseshoe and circles.

Evidence 3

1.11 1.12 3.15 3.16

What are your organisation's procedures for record keeping for functions? What types of records do you keep, how are they stored and who has access to them? How do you share records with the relevant people in your team? Discuss these questions with your assessor.

Include copies of the following documents in your portfolio:
- function sheets
- sample risk assessments
- client details
- marketing history
- customer preferences
- supplier records

It is important for ease of service that the food service staff can move easily around the tables. Usually functions are clothed with white linen; occasionally coloured linen is used, especially if the event is themed. There are many establishments where the tables are not clothed, usually in private estates, palaces and diplomatic residences. This is because the tables are highly polished.

It is important that you check that all equipment is working well in advance of the function; any broken equipment may need to be replaced or repaired. It is important that you know who in your organisation is responsible for storing equipment, and to whom you should report any faults, loss or damages.

Costs and resources

Resources for each department must be deployed and used effectively in order to maximise profitability. All revenue earned and costs are summarised on a weekly basis in the form of a weekly cost breakdown report. This is then passed onto the control office, manager or director. Expenditure for each function is usually controlled on a daily basis. The head chef must be aware of the total food expenditure target for each function. All costs must be controlled through the careful management of resources. Staffing needs to be kept to a minimum without compromising quality.

The importance of timing

The accurate timing of functions is vital, for the following reasons:
- Each department needs time to prepare for the function. Some departments will require more time than others. For example, the kitchen needs the most time to prepare the menu, while a technician requires only a few minutes to prepare the video playback machine.
- The timing of deliveries is most important as late deliveries can cause severe problems for the kitchen. It is also important that deliveries meet the required specification.
- In high quality banqueting houses, much of the service and presentation are finished at the last minute.
- Any delays in the function will result in hourly paid staff being paid extra time, thus pushing up costs.
- Timing can affect the smooth running of the function and whether it is possible to turn the room around in enough time for a second function (e.g. lunch then dinner).

Evidence 4
1.5 **2.7** **3.4**
- How do you make sure you have all of the resources and equipment you need for a function? Discuss with your assessor how you manage resources for functions in your organisation. Include a resources list and audit in your portfolio – consider staffing, equipment, materials and their availability.
- What do you need to consider when arranging food and beverages for functions?

Evidence 5
3.8 **3.10**

Include copies of completed equipment inspection sheets in your portfolio. Who in your organisation is responsible for storing equipment for functions? To whom should you report any loss or damage? You may wish to include a copy of your departmental policy relating to loss, damage and storage of equipment in your portfolio.

Atmosphere

Creating the right atmosphere for a function is also important to its success. Lighting, décor, props, themes and music can all have an impact on the atmosphere. As a supervisor you need to be able to ensure you set the correct atmosphere using these resources and are able to adjust it as necessary.

`1.3` `2.13` `2.14` `3.3` Staffing

Function staff roles and responsibilities

Many establishments who specialise in events and functions have a dedicated team whose responsibility it is to market, sell, co-ordinate and set up functions, making sure the event runs smoothly and to the expectations of the customer. Smaller establishments will use staff who also have responsibilities for the other areas.

Event companies usually have a core staff team who are permanent and use casual staff regularly, depending on the size of the event or events. Often this is known as the shamrock approach, as illustrated in the diagram below.

> **Evidence 6**
> `3.7`
> Include details of atmosphere adjustments (e.g. lighting, décor, props and themes) on the function sheet for a function and include a copy in your portfolio. Discuss with your assessor how you might adjust the atmosphere for a function.

Core permanent staff

Contractors   Casual staff

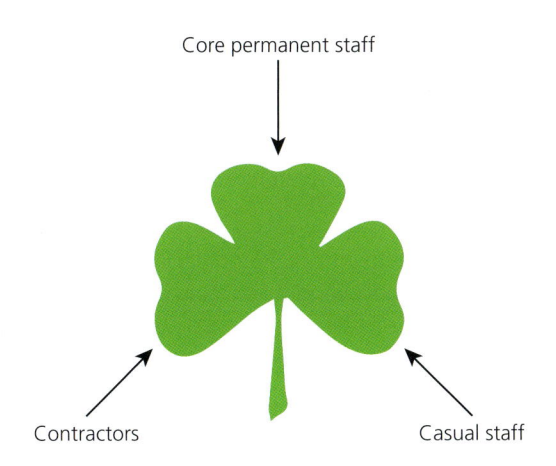

Figure 6.3 The shamrock approach

Roles include:
- **Event manager:** the event manager may also be known as the conference or banqueting manager. Their duties include administration, meeting customers and building a relationship with the customer. They are responsible for communication with other departments through the function sheet and co-ordinating the whole process. The range of activities an event manager has to cover include marketing, sales, administration, special requirements (flowers, entertainment, photography, IT equipment), seating plans, place cards, menu cards, cloakrooms, parking, security, rooms for VIPs, toastmaster and signage.
- **Sales manager:** the sales manager is the person who has to sell the venues and events. They make contact with present and future customers to secure sales in the future.
- **Administration office staff:** these staff members support the events manager and the events team. They maintain all customer records and requirements, including customer history, and communicate with all relevant departments. They take all enquiries and book appointments with the events manager.
- **Operations function staff:** responsible for the event set up and functioning.
- **Function head waiter:** in charge of the set up and organisation of the room or venue and manages the front-of-house team.

> **Key term**
>
> **Contractor** – the company or companies required to carry out specialist work who are brought in by an event company.

- **Dispense manager:** responsible for stocking and control of all drinks for the event. Makes sure the bar is well stocked. Responsible for cash and the security of cash.
- **Function sommelier:** responsible for the service of wines for the event, working closely with the dispense bar to co-ordinate the flow of drinks service.
- **Casual staff:** casual staff will be the front-of-house staff, food servers, cloakroom attendants, doormen etc. They may also include kitchen porters and additional kitchen assistants. These members of staff are usually supplied by an agency; however, large event establishments generally have their own pool of casual staff.
- You may also employ **contractors** offering specialist services such as entertainment, marquees, dance floors, tables and chairs, toilets etc. As a supervisor, it is important that you appoint the appropriate contractors and that it is clear what is expected of them.

Briefing staff and allocating responsibilities: internal communication procedures

Internal communication is especially important within any organisation. Information needs to be broken down and allocated to the appropriate departments, and it is vital that there is two-way communication between departments. This information must be accurate and well presented so that staff are able to understand clearly what is expected of them.

Staff are required to familiarise themselves with function sheets, identifying any special requirements that are needed by the organiser. It is also important for staff to be given a full briefing so that they understand exactly what is required of them and to reconfirm the function details.

Frequent meetings are essential to inform staff of forthcoming events and the expected working hours for the following week. Any changes to the function must be communicated to all those concerned immediately.

Often, more detailed and user-friendly internal function sheets are compiled so that the key people are aware of customer requirements. Internal function sheets should be given to the relevant staff at least one week in advance of the function. It is then up to each department to assess its own responsibilities and needs relating to the event, so that the work can be planned in advance. These sheets will determine the amount of staff required for the function and how much linen, crockery, glassware etc., are required. All instructions should be in detail, leaving nothing to chance or guesswork.

Such decisions will have to be made taking account of the price the customer is paying and the overall budget. Final attendance numbers should be confirmed with the client at least 48 hours before the event.

As a supervisor, it is important that you consider the skills of your staff and allocate roles and responsibilities accordingly. You may need to give training or hire specialist staff for certain tasks.

> **Evidence 7**
>
> **1.3** **2.13**
>
> Carry out a training and skills audit on your team to work out which skills and knowledge they have and what you may need to develop.
>
> Hold a skills updating workshop for your team.
>
> Possible evidence to include in your portfolio might include:
> - training and skills audit
> - copies of staff appraisals
> - notes/observation record from a skills updating workshop.

> **Evidence 8**
>
> **2.14**
>
> Devise a scoring sheet to help you identify which contractor is most appropriate for a function you have supervised. Include in your evidence portfolio copies of meeting minutes from any contractor tender meetings you hold.

Evidence 9
1.7 **3.3**

Include copies of the following in your portfolio:
- duty rotas
- briefing notes from staff briefings
- copies of function documents.

Discuss with your assessor how you decide on allocation of responsibilities.

1.7 3.1 3.12 3.13 Customer care and communicating with the customer/function organiser

It is important to look after customers/guests, from the initial enquiry through to the event and follow up afterwards. Customer care is about caring for the guest. It is important that the client feels that they are being looked after and that they can feel at ease. The function must be executed as planned, in line with the client's needs. Remember when supervising to put the guest/customer first: make them feel special; make them feel comfortable; make them feel important.

Information, in the first instance, should be given to the first point of customer contact (i.e. the event organiser, the food and beverage manager or the conference and function organiser). This is essential to ensure that the customer's needs are being met. At a later stage, more specialist information may be gathered by the individual department heads, using various means of communication, for example, telephone, email, fax or face-to-face meetings.

Always keep the guests/customers informed. Show empathy and be able to discuss the function or event from their point of view. Remember, emotional factors surround the products that people buy. Customer satisfaction comes from the way people are treated. Customers/guests are buying the total event/function package. Excellent customer care and service will make you stand above the competition, winning customers/guests and keeping them loyal.

When a customer/guest comes into contact with you or your staff, you are representing the company: your image and the style and treatment of customers must promote the company brand. As a supervisor, it is likely to be your responsibility to train staff in aspects of customer care for functions. This could include:
- identifying the right staff for events/functions who know how to care for the customer
- knowing and understanding what customers want and what they may ask for
- knowing the product, the menu and beverages.

All staff must know:
- What the company stands for.
- What behaviour the company values highly.
- That all guarantees must be honoured.

Good communication within the organisation assists in the development of customer care. Customer care for functions/events is a team game – all staff must work to the same aim and understand customers.

Customer care
For more information on customer care, see Chapter 14.

Evidence 10
1.7 3.1 3.12 3.13

Discuss your organisation's customer care policy with your assessor. Why is it important to communicate with the organiser of the function?

Include the following in your portfolio to demonstrate how you liaise with people throughout the function, and how you communicate information about the function with customers:
- minutes of briefing meetings with staff
- copies of function documents covering customer requirements
- copies of letters and emails to customers
- brochures and leaflets.

Evidence 11
1.7 2.6 2.8

Write a list of examples of specific requirements a customer may have. These could include specific food and drink requirements, entertainment or IT needs, colour schemes etc.

Include copies of your organisation's policy for delivering special requirements in your portfolio. This may include menus for those with special diets, allergy information, or information on access to the function venue for wheelchairs.

1.7 2.6 2.8 Dealing with special requirements

In small establishments, the services on offer can be tailored to the needs of the customer. Some customers may have specific requirements, for example:
- Specific dietary needs that must be catered for (e.g. food allergies – the chef must consider these allergies and waiting staff must be informed of the contents of the dishes).
- It is important that, if wheelchair access is required, it is made available.
- Certain age groups (for example, children or older people) may have specific dietary or other requirements.

Where it is difficult to accommodate certain special requirements, the customer should be given alternatives where possible.

1.6 1.10 2.1 3.9 3.14 Health, safety and legal requirements

All functions must be planned within the legal framework. Consideration must be given to the welfare of staff and all staff working at a function need to be trained in health, safety and hygiene; this includes any casual staff who should have received a health and safety induction. Employees must understand the fire regulations and evacuation procedures. Training is particularly important in risk assessment, handling dangerous equipment and handling of chemical products.

Companies also have a legal responsibility to the customer – for example, the customer needs to be aware of the maximum number of guests permitted in the building due to fire regulations and similarly, whether or not a licence extension or evacuation procedure in the event of a fire or bomb threat are in place.

Legal requirements

For more information on legal requirements, including health and safety requirements and evacuation procedures that affect functions, refer to Chapter 4.

2.2 Food safety measures

You must ensure that the kitchen has followed all of the correct hazard analysis and critical control procedures and all the records are in place.

Evidence 12
1.6　1.10　2.1　3.9　3.14

Produce a health and safety leaflet for the customer's attention that outlines the health and safety and legal requirements affecting the function. Include details of:
- the fire/emergency evacuation procedure and policy for the venue
- health and safety and other relevant legislation
- the organisation's health and safety policy
- information on crowd control and access to the venue.

Produce a checklist that can be used to ensure the function complies with relevant legislation and organisational standards.

Food safety
For more information on food safety measures, including food safety management systems and risk assessment, see Chapter 4.

Evidence 13
2.2

Write a report on the food safety measures that have been put in place for a function.

1.4　2.3　2.4　2.10　2.11　2.12 Inspecting the venue and risk assessment

Assessing risk and producing a formal risk assessment is the key to effective health and safety. Before a function, it is essential that you inspect the venue, not only to ensure that all preparations are in order and meet customer requirements, but also to ensure measures are in place to protect the safety of staff and guests. A careful examination of anything that could cause harm or injury to people, so that the necessary safeguards can be put in place to prevent harm, is important. Ensure risk assessments have been carried out on equipment, including any specialist equipment on hire for the event. The outcomes of risk assessments must be fully recorded and available for inspection.

It is also important to consider the impact the function may have on the environment and the public. For example, how can you minimise noise disruption to people living nearby? Do you have plans in place to dispose of waste correctly?

Risk assessment
For information on how to carry out a risk assessment and recording information relating to risk assessment, see Chapter 4.

Evidence 14
1.4　2.3　2.4　2.10　2.11　2.12

1. Write an impact report for a function that explains:
   - How you have assessed the impact the function is likely to have on others.
   - Why it is important to assess the impact of the function on others.
   - Measures you have put in place to minimise the impact.
2. Include photographic evidence from your venue inspection which shows you have checked the venue to ensure it is prepared as agreed.
3. Include a copy of a risk assessment for a function in your portfolio and discuss with your assessor how you carried out the risk assessment.

Evidence 15
1.1 | 1.7 | 1.8 | 3.5

Include an observation record in your portfolio which shows you are able to monitor functions to ensure everything is running to plan. Make sure your assessor observes you checking on staff, resources and timings etc. Include copies of a function sheet, progress sheet and departmental communication sheet in your portfolio to support your evidence.

Evidence 16
1.9 | 2.9 | 3.6

1. List the activities and problems that could potentially occur at a function and explain how to solve them quickly so they do not affect the customer experience. What contingency plans could you put in place to prevent these problems from occurring?
2. Write a report for a function, detailing any problems that arose and how you dealt with them.

Evidence 17
3.11

Include details of your organisation's complaints procedure and customer service policy in your portfolio.

1.7 | 1.8 | 3.5 Monitoring the function

Defined standards of performance must be monitored and measured. You need to monitor success in terms of your promises to customers. Measuring the right things helps staff to clearly understand what is important. As a supervisor, it is your role to monitor the function to ensure everything is going to plan, customer requirements are being met and any unexpected situations are dealt with effectively.

1.9 | 2.9 | 3.6 | 3.11 Dealing with problems and complaints

Occasionally managers have to make changes based on unavoidable or unforeseen situations. During the function you may find, for example, that you have a number of guests/customers who have an allergy but who have not informed you beforehand of their dietary requirements. Contingency plans should be developed to anticipate potential problems and to minimise the risk of disruption to a function, should any unexpected problems occur. These plans should be communicated clearly to function staff.

Encourage customers to complain on the spot if they are unhappy with any aspect of the function. They should be encouraged to inform a member of staff. This allows the supervisor to act immediately. Treat any guest/customer who complains well; turn a negative into a positive. Show them empathy, use appropriate body language, show concern and sympathise. Always apologise. If you treat the customer well, you will make them feel important and they will become your ambassador.

Always listen, take notes if necessary, ask questions to clarify detail. Always provide feedback and inform them what you propose to do. If the company or venue is at fault, offer compensation and get their agreement. When you get closure, make sure they are happy and satisfied with the result. (Remember, on the odd occasion, this may not happen as the guest/customer may be asking for the impossible.)

Customer complaints

96 per cent of dissatisfied customers do not go back and complain, but they do tell between 7 and 11 other people how bad your establishment is on service.

13 per cent will tell at least 20 other people.

90 per cent will never return to your establishment.

At the end of the function

Customer feedback

At the end of the function, it is essential to gain feedback from the client to ensure that, if the client was not satisfied, a follow-up letter apologising or offering some compensation can be sent. This client evaluation should then be passed onto the staff. Some companies will contact the client one to three days after the function to obtain constructive feedback, using a standard evaluation form for them to fill in.

Well organised functions that give customer satisfaction can not only be profitable, but may also lead to repeat business.

Costs

A final calculation of the costs incurred by each department needs to be done to check the efficiency of the budget management. Invoices are then raised.

Knowledge check

1 List the different types of functions.
2 Consider the amount of information required in advance of a function to assist the planning process. Draw up a list of such information.
3 Complete a function sheet for an event.
4 Explain what is meant by the following terms:
   a) core permanent staff
   b) casual staff
   c) contractors
5 Define the importance of good communication in event/function planning.
6 What special requirements have to be considered when running a function by law?
7 Briefly describe how you should deal with complaints.

Evidence checklist

Assessment criteria		Possible evidence	Evidence activity
1.1	Supervise functions	• Observation by assessor • Written reports	Evidence activity 1
1.2	Plan procedures to ensure that requirements are met and contingencies are developed	• Policy documents, action plans • Assessor questioning	Evidence activity 2
1.3	Ensure staff have the skills, knowledge and resources needed to carry out their responsibilities	• Skills audit • Resources review and audit	Evidence activity 7
1.4	Inspect the function venue to ensure that it is prepared as agreed	• Report on function venue • Leaflets • Photographic evidence	Evidence activity 14
1.5	Ensure that the equipment and materials needed for the function are available to the staff that will use them	• Equipment list and audit	Evidence activity 4
1.6	Communicate relevant health and safety and legal requirements to customers	• Health and safety policy • Minutes of briefing meeting with staff	Evidence activity 12
1.7	Liaise with relevant people throughout the function to ensure that the arrangements meet customer requirements	• Minutes of briefing meetings with staff • Copies of function documents covering customer requirements	Evidence activity 9 Evidence activity 10 Evidence activity 11 Evidence activity 15
1.8	Monitor the function to ensure that it is running to plan	• Assessor observation of check on staff, resources, timings etc.	Evidence activity 15
1.9	Deal with any problems that threaten to disrupt operations	• Function report detailing any problems or possible problems and how they are dealt with	Evidence activity 16

Evidence checklist

Assessment criteria		Possible evidence	Evidence activity
1.10	Ensure the function and all associated activities comply with relevant legislation and the organisation's standards	• Check and report on all food safety and health and safety procedures • Compile a checklist	Evidence activity 12
1.11	Record all relevant information in a suitable format	• Copies of all function sheets placed in a portfolio of evidence	Evidence activity 3
1.12	Make records available to the relevant people	• Place all relevant records in a portfolio	Evidence activity 3
2.1	Describe the health and safety and other legal requirements that affect the function and need to be communicated to the customer	• List all health and safety legal requirements that affect the function • Produce a health and safety leaflet for the customers' attention	Evidence activity 12
2.2	Describe the food safety measures that need to be employed	• Questioning by assessor • Report on food safety procedures	Evidence activity 13
2.3	Explain the importance of assessing the impact that the function is likely to have on others	• Questioning by assessor • Impact report	Evidence activity 14
2.4	Explain how to assess and minimise the impact the function is going to have on others	• Questioning by assessor • Report on minimising impact	Evidence activity 14
2.5	Identify the variety of information required to plan different types of functions, including: • customer-specific requirements • staffing • budget • venue capacity • other specifications	• Example of a list of customer requirements • Staffing policy for functions • Outline of budget for a function • Details of types of venues, capacity and resources • These would include evidence on specific food and drink requirements, IT, additional staffing and entertainment	Evidence activity 2
2.6	Identify the types of specific requirements customers may have	• List examples: these may include specific food and drink requirements, entertainment, IT, colour schemes etc.	Evidence activity 11
2.7	Identify the factors that need to be considered in arranging food and beverages for the function	• List the resources and their availability: staffing, crockery, china, linen, glassware, materials	Evidence activity 4
2.8	Explain how to deal with special requirements for different client groups, including: • children • older people • people with disabilities	• Questioning by assessor • Written policy on delivering special requirements: diets, allergy information, access for wheelchairs	Evidence activity 11

Evidence checklist			
Assessment criteria		**Possible evidence**	**Evidence activity**
2.9	Explain the importance of anticipating problems that may occur at functions	• Questioning by assessor • List of activities and problems that may occur and how to solve them quickly so they do not affect the customer experience	Evidence activity 16
2.10	Explain how to inspect a venue to ensure preparations are in order	• Questioning by assessor • Inspection report	Evidence activity 14
2.11	Explain how to carry out a risk assessment of the venue	• Copy of a risk assessment on file • Explanation of how to complete a risk assessment • Questioning by assessor	Evidence activity 14
2.12	Describe what to do with the information relating to the risk assessment of the venue	• Risk assessment procedure document placed in portfolio	Evidence activity 14
2.13	Explain how to ensure that staff have the required skills, knowledge and resources to carry out their responsibilities	• Training and skills audit • Staff appraisals, skills updating workshops • Questioning by assessor	Evidence activity 7
2.14	Identify how to ensure appropriate appointment of contractors in own area of responsibility	• Copies of meeting minutes of contractor tender meetings • Copies of scoring, sheets in file • Questioning by assessor	Evidence activity 8
3.1	Describe the organisation's customer care policy	• Assessor questioning	Evidence activity 10
3.2	Explain how to ensure the organisation of products and services support a variety of functions	• Assessor questioning • Mapping exercise: products and services against a variety of the establishment's functions	Evidence activity 1
3.3	Explain how to ensure effective management of staff for the function, including: • allocation of responsibilities • briefing • supervision	• Duty rotas • Briefing minutes • Assessor questioning	Evidence activity 9
3.4	Explain how to manage resources available for a function	• Reports • Assessor questioning	Evidence activity 4
3.5	Explain how to monitor a function and ensure it goes to plan	• Function sheet • Progress sheet • Departmental communication sheet • Assessor questioning • Observation	Evidence activity 15
3.6	Describe how to deal with problems that may occur	• Contingency plans for functions • Report on how problems are dealt with	Evidence activity 16

Evidence checklist				
Assessment criteria		**Possible evidence**	**Evidence activity**
3.7	Describe how to adjust the atmosphere of functions	• Assessor questioning • Function sheet with atmosphere adjustments, e.g., lighting, décor, props, themes	Evidence activity 6
3.8	Describe how to inspect equipment used during functions	• Equipment inspection sheets completed • Assessor questioning • Observation	Evidence activity 5
3.9	Describe how to evacuate premises safely in the event of an emergency	• Fire evacuation procedures policy • Assessor questioning	Evidence activity 12
3.10	Identify who is responsible for storing equipment and reporting loss or damage	• Departmental policies • Assessor questioning	Evidence activity 5
3.11	Explain how to respond to requests and complaints	• Complaints procedure • Customer service requirement policy • Assessor questioning	Evidence activity 17
3.12	Describe how information about the function should be communicated to customers	• Letters to customers • Brochures, leaflets, emails	Evidence activity 10
3.13	Explain the importance of communicating with the organiser of the function	• Assessor questioning • Function policy procedures	Evidence activity 10
3.14	Describe the legal requirements that cover the clearing of a venue	• Assessor questioning • Outline health and safety legislation, crowd control, access	Evidence activity 12
3.15	Describe the types of records that should be maintained for functions	• Samples of risk assessment, client details, marketing history, customer preferences, supplier records, assessor questioning	Evidence activity 3
3.16	Describe the organisation's procedures in relation to record keeping for functions		Evidence activity 3

CHAPTER 7

Supervise food service

This chapter is about how to plan your staffing levels and prepare resources to deliver excellent food service. You need to provide your team with all the information and equipment needed in order for them to be successful in their roles. It is about being able to prepare and communicate plans effectively.

Learning objectives

On completion of this chapter, you should:
1. Be able to supervise food service.
2. Understand how to plan food service.
3. Understand how to supervise food service.

Planning for food service

3.4 Types of food service methods

There are countless types of food service outlets, each with their own style. The large majority will use one of the following types of food service method:
- **Plated** – the customer is served at a laid table; this is the most common style of service in restaurants.
- **Silver** – the customer is served food by a waiter from a dish using a spoon and fork.
- **Family** – the dishes are placed in the centre of the table and customers serve themselves.
- **Banqueting** – a table of customers are served plated food simultaneously.
- **Butler** – a waiter will present a dish of food from which the customer will serve themselves.
- **Buffet** – the customer will go to the table of food and serve themselves.
- **Carvery** – the customer will go to the table of food and a waiter or chef will serve them (normally by carving a joint of meat).
- **Take away** – the customer will order, pay and collect their food from a counter.
- **Delivery** – food is delivered to the customer's home after they have ordered over the phone or online.
- **Trolley** – food is served from a trolley, for example, on a train, plane or in hospital.

The potential differences in work processes can be dependent on innumerable factors such as the type, size, customer expectations and location of the organisation. However, some duties for a supervisor of food service are consistent throughout all organisations.

103

1.1 1.2 3.1 3.2 3.3 Legal responsibilities

It is the responsibility of the supervisor to maintain records of food management systems in order to allow an organisation to prove due diligence if required. Food management systems are the actions that an organisation will take to reduce and eliminate, where possible, risk or hazard to its staff, customers and any other visitors. They are required to do this by law. In order to comply with legislation, a supervisor must prevent their working environment from causing food to become dangerous, customers being sold food unfit for consumption and customers being served food that does not meet their expectations through being misled or given false information.

The following are the main pieces of legislation that will affect your food service operations:
- Food Safety Act 1990
- Food Safety (General Food Hygiene) Regulations 1995
- Food Allergens Legislation – EU Food Information for Consumers Regulation 1169/2011.

A supervisor must ensure that their teams have the knowledge and ability to work within the guidelines of these laws by executing the following:
- New team members must have a thorough induction.
- All team members are trained on the standards outlined in the operations manual.
- All supervisors must attend regular refresher training to make certain that their own knowledge is up to date.
- Teams are given access to relevant information through Standards of Practice documents or visual displays.
- Training is repeated regularly to prevent it being forgotten.
- Team members are monitored after training to confirm that the skills have been learned.
- If there are indicators that a team member is not following procedures, then further training or performance measures should be arranged.
- All training records are thorough and up to date.

Key terms

Due diligence – the reasonable steps taken to avoid committing an offence

Operations manual – a document that describes in detail the procedures that an organisation uses to deliver services

Performance measures – the process of collecting, reviewing and taking action on information regarding the performance of an individual

All breaches of legislation, including all the details of any incident, need to be reported to security or department heads, management or business owners and this could be done by writing a written report or letter or sending an email.

It is important to keep a thorough written record to refer to. When proposed opportunities for improvements in food safety are implemented, the supervisor must evaluate their effectiveness through 'walk-round' monitoring and spot checks. More guidance is available from your manager, your human resources department or at the Food Standards Agency website, www.food.gov.uk.

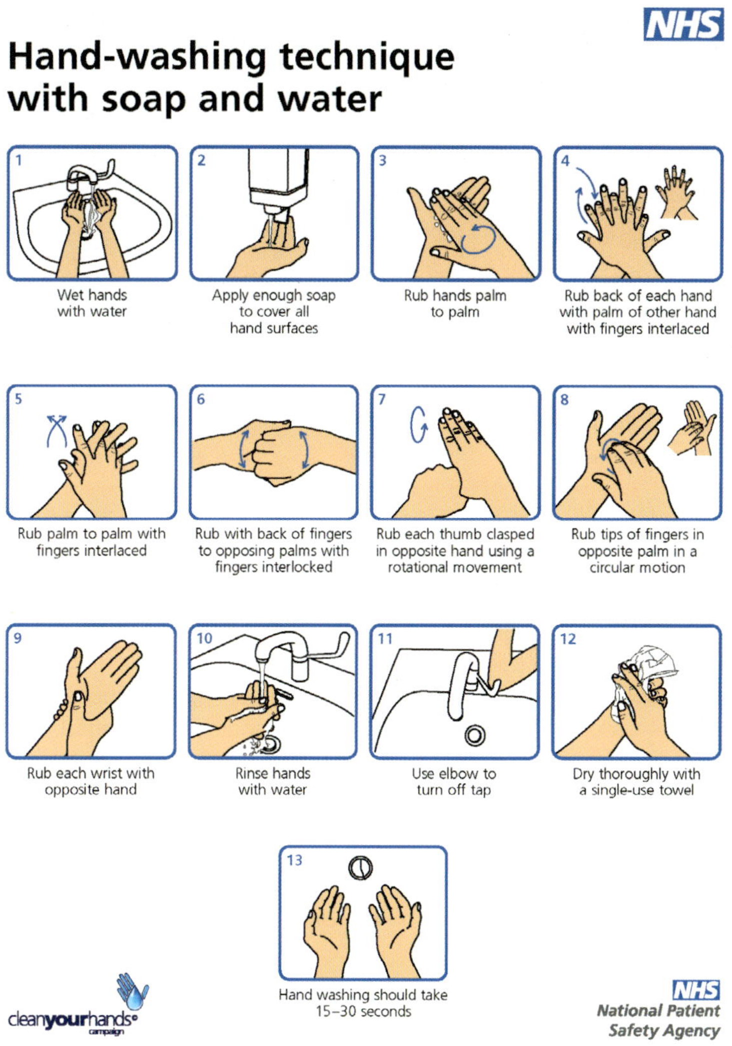

Hand-washing technique with soap and water

NHS

1. Wet hands with water
2. Apply enough soap to cover all hand surfaces
3. Rub hands palm to palm
4. Rub back of each hand with palm of other hand with fingers interlaced
5. Rub palm to palm with fingers interlaced
6. Rub with back of fingers to opposing palms with fingers interlocked
7. Rub each thumb clasped in opposite hand using a rotational movement
8. Rub tips of fingers in opposite palm in a circular motion
9. Rub each wrist with opposite hand
10. Rinse hands with water
11. Use elbow to turn off tap
12. Dry thoroughly with a single-use towel
13. Hand washing should take 15–30 seconds

cleanyourhands campaign

NHS National Patient Safety Agency

Figure 7.1 Posters can help remind staff of health and safety requirements

Individual Training Record for [INSERT COMPANY NAME]

Employee:		Date:	
Position:		Line Manager:	
Department:		Trainer	

Area of Training	Employee signature	Trainer signature	comments
[INSERT TRAINING]			
[INSERT TRAINING]			
[INSERT TRAINING]			
[INSERT TRAINING]			
[INSERT TRAINING]			
[INSERT TRAINING]			
[INSERT TRAINING]			

Figure 7.2 A sample training record

Supervise food service

105

> **Take it further**
>
> For the latest information on food safety procedures, visit the Food Standards Agency website, www.food.gov.uk.

For more details and other legislation that affects your food service work, see Chapter 4, 'Maintain the health, hygiene, safety and security of the working environment'.

> **Evidence 1**
>
> `1.1` `1.2` `3.1` `3.2` `3.3`
>
> Possible evidence relating to your legal responsibilities in relation to food safety procedures, regulations and codes of practice could include:
> - food safety training records
> - organisational food safety policy
> - photographs of food safety resources – SOPs, posters, temperature records, policies, notices
> - expert witness statements.

`1.9` `2.1` `2.3` `3.5` `3.6` Who is involved?

The diagram below outlines a simplified version of all of the roles needed to deliver excellent food service. Roles can vary considerably from outlet to outlet, but the following information can help to assist understanding of how the success of each is dependent on the success of the others. Not all are food service related.

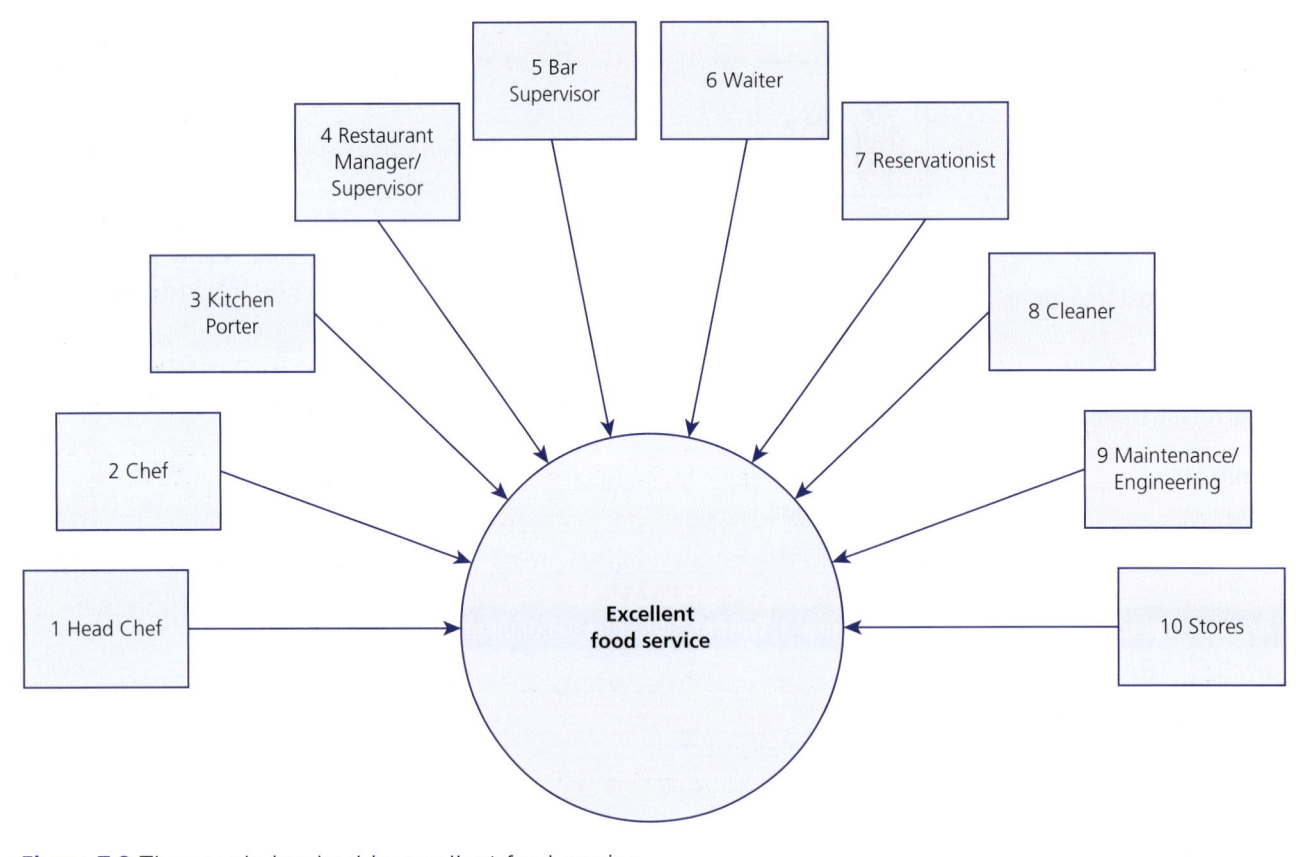

Figure 7.3 The people involved in excellent food service

1. Head chef – management of food production, sourcing produce, menu development, staff training, rotas.
2. Chef – food production, stock control.

3. Kitchen porter – basic food preparation, washing up, kitchen cleaning.
4. Restaurant manager/supervisor – setting the standards for service, staff training, rotas, checking mise en place.
5. Bar supervisor – stock control, menu development, preparing drinks.
6. Waiter – setting the restaurant and tables, taking orders, serving food and beverages, mise en place, cleaning.
7. Reservationist – taking bookings through the phone or online, including special requests.
8. Cleaner – restaurant and toilet cleaning.
9. Maintenance – general care and repairs of all equipment required.
10. Stores – ordering, purchasing and liaising with suppliers.

Examples of more specialist jobs that a supervisor may encounter include cashier, sommelier, pastry chef, security personnel and hostess.

A supervisor is required to communicate with these people when organising the food service. When interacting with colleagues at any level, it is important to be courteous and polite, as it shows respect.

> **Key term**
>
> **Mise en place** – translates from French as 'put in place' and is a term used in the hospitality industry to describe the preparations needed for service

Table 7.1 Job titles and responsibilities of key roles in the hospitality industry

Job title	Role and responsibilities
Head chef	To confirm menu details and set appropriate prices. To address food problems such as customer complaints.
Chef	For orders, food production and to confirm ingredients of dishes.
Kitchen porter	To maintain the cleanliness and equipment of back of house areas.
Bar supervisor	Wine, cocktails and drinks menu development. To manage beverage stock levels. For the bar team rota. To assist in any issues with beverages.
Waiter	To communicate availability to work when writing the rota. To work to the best of their ability while following organisational procedures and comply with relevant legislation during food service. To communicate with customers and colleagues in a professional and hospitable manner. To complete their work as per the supervisor's instructions.
Reservationist	To communicate with customers in a professional and hospitable manner when taking reservations. To communicate all relevant information regarding bookings (such as birthdays and special diets) to the team.
Cleaner	To maintain cleanliness of equipment, the restaurant and toilets to the highest standards.
Maintenance	To repair any reported fault promptly and to a high quality.
Stores	To source reasonably priced and high quality products. To maintain good working relations with valuable suppliers.

Through liaising with these people, a supervisor can obtain the resources needed to organise the food service. For example:
1. Equipment ready for use – maintenance, kitchen porter.
2. Correct levels of stock prepared – head chef, bar supervisor, stores, waiter.
3. Restaurant set ready for service – cleaner, waiter.
4. Customer special requests and dietary requirements – reservationist.
5. Food – head chef, chef.

An issue in one of these areas can cause a wave of problems, but it is important to be supportive and patient when issues arise as then others are more likely to be patient when you are experiencing problems.

For example: 'That's not my problem'

A reservationist forgot to put details of a birthday cake request in the booking information for a table of four. On the evening of the dinner, the customer queried with the waiter when the cake would be presented. The waiter passed this query to the supervisor who asked the head chef. It was at this point the mistake was realised.

Scenario A
Action – The head chef says he cannot help. 'That's not my problem.'

Result – The customer is informed and a complaint is made.

Scenario B
Action – The head chef adapts a dessert with birthday candles and writes 'Happy Birthday' in chocolate on the plate.

Result – The birthday girl is delighted and impressed. She posts photographs on social media sites and her friends are also impressed and become regular customers of the restaurant.

> **Evidence 2**
> 1.9 2.1 2.3 3.5 3.6
>
> Explain three scenarios (from your experience or in theory) where one department has depended on the performance of another to deliver excellent food service.

2.2 2.4 2.7 3.11 Allocating duties when planning the rota

List all the tasks or duties required to prepare for food service and sort them into **chronological order**. This will support efficiency and prevent having to repeat tasks. For example, you would not hoover the floor before wiping the tables as, when wiping the tables, you may knock crumbs onto the floor. Use this information to plan what duties each shift will perform on the rota.

Use or create templates of the required staffing levels for each type of service that the organisation provides.

For example, a buffet lunch service for 20 people will need the following staff:
- 1 × supervisor
- 1 × behind the bar
- 2 × serving trays of drinks and top ups
- 2 × behind the buffet to assist customers
- 2 × to clear plates and glasses.

The rota should clearly indicate the tasks and duties to be completed and the member of staff responsible for them. Collect the following information before allocating shifts.

> **Key term**
>
> **Chronological order** – a record of events starting with the earliest and following the order in which they occurred

Organisation information
- Opening hours and days
- The times in which orders are taken for food and drinks
- Average time for customers to have lunch
- Average time for customer to have dinner
- Number of customers per service in previous weeks
- Any unusual occurrences, e.g. special offers, VIPs, speeches, etc.

Staff information
- Availability
- Skills and experience
- Training required
- Performance issues
- Preferences.

Enter the information and communicate to your team in a timely manner. Your team will appreciate as much notice as possible for their working hours in order for them to be able to arrange their personal lives.

	Monday 1st June	Tuesday 2nd June	Wednesday 3rd June	Thursday 4th June	Friday 5th June	Saturday 6th June	Sunday 7th June
Manager	Rose	Rose	Rose	John	John	Stuart	Alex
Reception	Stacey	Stacey	Stacey	Stacey	Stacey	Paul	Paul
	Alex	Alex	Mary	Mary	Alex	Alex	Alex
	Zoe	Zoe	Zoe	Seth	Seth	Seth	Zoe
Bar	Andrew	Andrew	Mike	Mike	Andrew	Andrew	Mike
	Paul	Paul	Paul	Jane	Paul	Paul	Jane
				Sarah	Sarah	Sarah	Sarah
Wait staff	Roger	Shirley	Shirley	Roger	Roger	Roger	Roger
	Harriet	Harriet	Harriet	Rachel	Rachel	Rachel	Rachel
	Zoe	Zoe	David	David	Zoe	Zoe	Zoe
				Joanne	Joanne	Joanne	Joanne
Kitchen	Jim	Jim	Simon	Jim	Jim	Simon	Jim
	Lesley	Sharon	Lesley	Lesley	Lesley	Sharon	Sharon
	Emma	Emma	Rebecca	Rebecca	Rebecca	Rebecca	Emma
	John	John	Gemma	Gemma	Gemma	John	John
Cleaner	Jane	Jane	Jane	Jane	Jane	Mark	Mark
	Richard	Richard	Richard	Richard	Jenny	Jenny	Jenny

Figure 7.4 Staff rota

Top tips

1. Remember to make notes of differences in service levels monthly and for annual events. For example, an organisation will be much busier at Christmas.
2. Assign a 'buddy', a more experienced team member who role-models desired qualities, to look after new starters.
3. By matching staff to their preferred working times, you are more likely to reduce turnover.
4. If team members' requests cannot be met, then explain to them clearly the reasons why.
5. Consider the development/training that your team requires and be sure to make time for it during quieter periods.

Evidence 3
2.2 2.4 2.7

Prepare one list of tasks, one staffing template and one rota and explain the reasons for your decisions.

Preparing for food service

1.3 1.6 Maintenance report

It is the responsibility of the supervisor to report any faults in the environment or equipment within their work areas. It is good practice to incorporate a maintenance report for the 'walk round' monitoring in order to keep track of the progress of multiple maintenance issues.

R & M Equipment/ Vendor History Form				
Equipment Name _____			Model no. _____	
Brand _____			Serial no. _____	
Purchased from _____			Purchase date _____	
Warranty period–Parts _____			Warranty–Labour _____	
Primary service vendor _____			Alt. service co. _____	

Service date	Equipment issue	Serviced by	Cost and invoice no.	Notes

Figure 7.5 Sample maintenance report

Include the following information:
- equipment description
- location of equipment
- supervisor's name
- date reported
- who fault was reported to
- details of fault
- details of agreed action
- completion date.

For more details, see Chapter 4, 'Maintain health, hygiene, safety and security of the working environment' and the section on reporting of maintenance issues.

1.5 Daily/weekly/monthly/yearly checklist

To ensure food safety compliance and customer satisfaction, implement a daily/weekly/monthly/yearly cleaning checklist and schedule times to assess whether the tasks are being completed. A checklist including space to complete the listed information can help to achieve this and should include the following information:
- details of task
- frequency required
- name of person responsible
- date completed.

Daily	Weekly	Monthly	Annually
✓ Make beds	✓ Water plants	✓ Wipe down doors	✓ Launder curtains
✓ Wash sheets	✓ Wash door knobs	✓ Wash all railings	✓ Clean carpets
✓ Wash towels	✓ Clean mirrors	✓ Flip matresses	✓ Wash windows
✓ Wash dishes	✓ Dust ceiling fans	✓ Wash rubbish bins	
✓ Scrub kitchen sink	✓ Dust lamps	✓ Dust air vents	
✓ Vacuum carpets	✓ Dust picture frames		
✓ Wash floors	✓ Polish silver		

Figure 7.6 Sample daily, weekly, monthly and yearly cleaning checklists

Evidence 4
1.6 **1.3**
- Collect or create a maintenance report form.
- Collect or create a cleaning checklist.

1.4 Stock check

It is the duty of the supervisor to ensure that there is sufficient stock for service. To manage stock levels, it is good practice to implement a **par level** system. To find the minimum levels of stock required, answer the following questions:

1. How long is the required time between ordering?
2. What is the average usage rate of the required time?
3. How long does it take the supplier to deliver?

For example:

A restaurant sells an average of ten bottles of champagne per week.

A wine order is placed every two weeks.

Once an order has been placed, it is delivered within 48 hours.

The supervisor should have 25 bottles of champagne as a par stock level; 20 bottles to cover the expected sales; and 5 bottles as a safety stock or buffer.

Key term
Par level – the minimum quantity of a stock item that an organisation must have stored on the premises

Evidence 5
1.4

Work out the par level required for one item of stock (from your experience or in theory).

Supervise food service

1.7 | 1.8 | 2.5 | 2.8 | 3.9 | 3.10 | 3.16 Pre-service preparation

For smooth service and to prevent disruptions in the food service, use a list of things you can do to be well prepared before the customers arrive. Complete each action as close to opening time as possible, but leave enough time to deliver a thorough briefing to your team. Below are some examples of things to consider.

Check:
- the booking diary for the number of reservations and that the tables have been set accordingly
- that all allocated tasks have been completed
- that the room has been set up correctly with furniture positioned correctly
- all the equipment on the tables is present, clean and polished
- there are sufficient levels of stock
- the lights are switched on and no bulbs need replacing
- there are no other health and safety risks such as tripping hazards
- the kitchen has been provided with all the plates and other equipment they require
- the menus and signs are well presented and the details are correct
- the waiters' stations and back-of-house equipment are set up (e.g. coffee pots, sugar, cups etc.).

Team briefings are a two-way form of communication. They provide staff with the opportunity to ask questions and clarify any points they may be unsure about. Treat all questions with courtesy, as something that may seem obvious to you may not be to an inexperienced person. It is better that the team feel that they can communicate openly and clarify concerns than they guess and provide incorrect information to customers, especially when it comes to allergens and other legislation that they need to comply with. Face-to-face communication with your team is not always easy; many managers struggle to find the time to bring the team together but it is a supervisor's responsibility to provide all the information that the team needs and to check they understand their part in the processes. It is also a great opportunity to solicit honest feedback from your team – as they are working with customers directly, they often have ideas on how to improve things. Always be calm and even tempered, even when you hear things you don't like, as it is important to make your team feel that it is safe to be candid. It is not professional to shout or bring your emotions into a team meeting. Brief the team on the following:
- the menu
- any specials
- any pre-ordered special dietary requirements
- VIPs, birthdays or other special occasions
- the plan of where they will be working
- health and safety information such as fire procedures
- any new team members, to allow the team to support them
- a **refresher training** topic such as excellent customer service.

Question your team on what you have discussed to check their understanding.

> **Key terms**
>
> **Team briefing** – a short face-to-face meeting between supervisors and their teams where information can be given and questions asked
>
> **Refresher training** – training intended to reinforce previously acquired knowledge and skills (such as fire training procedures or food hygiene)

> **Evidence 6**
> 1.7 | 1.8 | 2.5 | 2.8 | 3.9 | 3.10
> - Create a checklist of what to check before food service.
> - Provide a witness statement from a team member who has attended a briefing you delivered.

Delivering food service

During service a supervisor's role is to monitor the work of their team and only assist when required. It is a common mistake for some supervisors to believe that they are being useful and helpful by performing tasks themselves; however, this has a number of consequences. Team members will not get the opportunity to develop their skills and will become demotivated when they are not learning anything. They will believe that their supervisor does not trust them and that when the supervisor is not there, things will go wrong. Instead, during service, a supervisor must perform a 'walk around' inspection to monitor and ensure the team are delivering the food service as per the procedures and standards they have been briefed on.

1.5 1.10 1.11 3.7 3.16 Observation checklist

To ensure this happens, use an observation checklist with all the duties of one team member during service and tick or cross whether they complete their duties as expected. Also include the behavioural standards expected such as the way that the team member interacts with customers and whether their attitude is welcoming. This approach will focus you on the details of your team's performance and can be used as evidence to refer to in their performance reviews. Observations should be carried out more frequently at the beginning of a team member's career. Remember especially to recognise high performance, as well as to correct staff members when they don't quite get it right.

Table 7.2 Example of an observation checklist

Date:	Name of supervisor:	Name of employee:	
Did the employee welcome the guest in a genuine and hospitable manner?			Yes
Did the employee explain the specials of the day?			Yes
Did the employee serve the drinks in a reasonable amount of time?			No
Comments	The bar was experiencing unusually large volumes of orders		

1.12 2.6 3.8 3.13 3.14 Dealing with difficult situations

No matter how effective you are at preparing, difficult situations will always arise. Create a contingency plan to help you tackle problems when things go wrong. You can utilise your risk assessment skills learned in Chapter 4. Using your experience and feedback from colleagues at all levels, make a list of the potential problems that are at risk of happening during food service and rate them from 1 (can often be ignored) to 10 (being the most severe impact). Next, rate them according to their probability of occurring from 1 (not likely to happen) to 10 (highly likely to happen). Plot them on a grid to identify which potential problems should be prioritised.

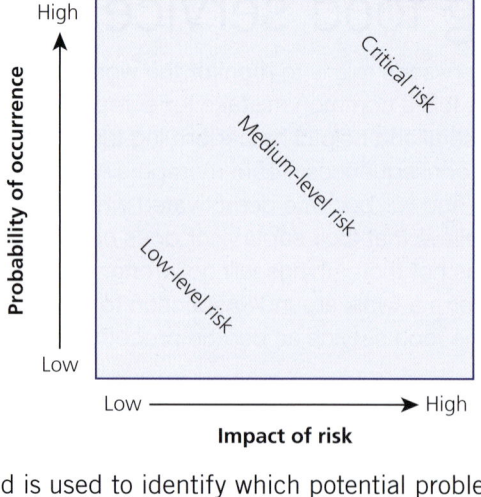

Figure 7.7 A risk grid is used to identify which potential problems should be prioritised.

The goal of a contingency plan is to keep the food service going. Keep it as simple as possible and incorporate the plan into training whenever possible. Approval of any people in authority must be sought before implementing the plan and it must be communicated to all who are involved. Answering the following questions will help you to create an effective plan.
- What are the opportunities to reduce the risk of this problem from happening? A measure to manage the risk may reduce it but often it can't eliminate the risk altogether.
- What are the options? Identify what potential actions you could take and use the decision-making methods described in Chapter 14, 'Monitor and solve customer service problems', to select the best.
- What specifically will trigger the implementation of the plan?
- What kind of resources will the plan need to be successful and whose approval will need to be gained? Use the earlier role descriptions to identify which colleagues are involved.

For example:

Risk – the coffee machine in the banqueting department breaks down.

Impact – customer complaints, loss of reputation, loss of revenue through voids and repeat business.

Probability – medium to unlikely depending on the age and condition of the equipment.

Measures to take to reduce risk – regular assessments of equipment by the maintenance department.

In spite of the regular maintenance checks, the coffee machine breaks down anyway.

Contingency plan – report the issue to the duty engineer and ascertain the time it will take to fix. If the length of time is sufficient to impact the food service negatively, consider these options:
1. Inform and offer the customer an alternative such as instant coffee or tea.
2. Contact the food and beverage department to request to use their facilities.

Be sure to add the details to the maintenance report to monitor and to make certain the equipment is repaired.

1.13 3.15 Review

If the contingency plan is used, be sure to conduct an assessment of the results. Gather feedback from colleagues at all levels who were involved to evaluate if and where improvements can be made. Present your findings to your manager at the appropriate time such as a weekly meeting. In your report include answers to the following:

1. How successful was your contingency plan?
2. Did the plan fix the whole problem or just the symptoms? In the case of our example, providing an alternative only temporarily fixed the issue. It may be that a new coffee machine is needed which would require the approval of a person in authority.
3. Consider what decisions were made when dealing with the problem. Could they have been better?
4. Could another solution have solved the issue more successfully?

Evidence 7
1.5 3.12 2.6

- Create an observation checklist of your own duties and use it to evaluate your own performance during one service.
- Do the same for the staff in your team and use it to monitor their performance and communications with customers.
- Create one contingency plan for your area of work using the described approach.

Evidence 8
1.11 1.12 1.13 3.14 3.15 3.16

Collect a witness statement from your manager from a time they have observed you solve a good service problem effectively.

Evidence 9
3.4 3.7 3.11

Collect standards operating procedures for food service from your company and highlight the key points.

Knowledge check

1. Name five types of food service methods.
2. What legal responsibilities does a supervisor of food service have?
3. What legal responsibilities does a team member of food service have?
4. Name three things a supervisor must consider when setting the par stock level.
5. List all the departments needed to deliver food service at your place of work.
6. Name four things to consider when writing a rota.
7. What methods can a supervisor use to ensure that their working environment is ready for food service?

Evidence checklist		
Assessment criteria		**Possible evidence**
1.1	Obtain up-to-date information about food safety procedures	Evidence activity 1
1.2	Check that staff have the skills, knowledge and resources to carry out their responsibilities	Evidence activity 1
1.3	Check that service equipment is ready for use and located correctly	Evidence activity 4
1.4	Ensure service areas are stocked in preparation for service	Evidence activity 5
1.5	Ensure that procedures for clearing, cleaning and stocking service areas are followed correctly	Evidence activity 7
1.6	Ensure the environment meets customer requirements	Evidence activity 4

Evidence checklist		
Assessment criteria		**Possible evidence**
1.7	Ensure any special customer areas are arranged as agreed	Evidence activity 6
1.8	Carry out preparations in sufficient time to allow an effective service to be provided	Evidence activity 6
1.9	Liaise with relevant people and departments to ensure effective delivery of the service	Evidence activity 2
1.10	Monitor staff conduct and communications with customers	Evidence activity 7
1.11	Confirm that communication with customers by all staff takes place in a manner that is likely to promote goodwill and understanding	Evidence activity 8
1.12	Deal with problems that may affect the standard of food service	Evidence activity 8
1.13	Feedback on the effectiveness of procedures in own area of responsibility to the appropriate person in the organisation	Evidence activity 8
2.1	Identify the appropriate person to liaise with when organising the food service	Evidence activity 2
2.2	Explain how to identify trends in levels of demand which influence staffing requirements	Evidence activity 3
2.3	Explain how to identify and obtain the resources needed for food service	Evidence activity 2
2.4	Explain how to organise staff depending on service requirements	Evidence activity 3
2.5	Explain how to communicate operational procedures to staff	Evidence activity 6
2.6	Explain how to develop contingency plans	Evidence activity 7
2.7	Explain how to ensure staff receive the correct training to support their responsibilities	Evidence activity 3
2.8	Explain how to check that equipment is ready for use	Evidence activity 6
3.1	Identify industry-specific regulations and codes of practice that need to be followed	Evidence activity 1
3.2	Explain how to obtain information on regulations and codes of practice to ensure procedures are kept up to date	Evidence activity 1
3.3	Explain how to identify, deal with and report breaches of legislation, regulations and codes of practice	Evidence activity 1
3.4	Describe the organisation's procedures and standards for food service and customer service	Evidence activity 9
3.5	Explain how food service operations integrate with other activities and departments in the organisation	Evidence activity 2
3.6	Explain how the roles and responsibilities of individuals within own department affect the food service	Evidence activity 2
3.7	Describe how staff should communicate with customers and conduct themselves in the food service area	Evidence activity 9
3.8	Describe what to do in the event of equipment failure	Evidence activity 7
3.9	Identify the information about food service that customers may need	Evidence activity 6
3.10	Identify how the information should be presented	Evidence activity 6
3.11	Explain how to prioritise tasks to regulate the time available	Evidence activity 7
3.12	Explain how to ensure that staff follow procedures and standards	Evidence activity 7
3.13	Describe how to correct and report failures according to organisational standards and procedures	Evidence activity 7
3.14	Identify the appropriate person to consult in the event of food service problems	Evidence activity 8
3.15	Evaluate potential solutions to problems that may occur in food service	Evidence activity 8
3.16	Explain how to minimise disruptions to the food service	Evidence activity 8

CHAPTER 8

Supervise drinks services

This chapter is about how to plan your staffing levels and preparing resources to deliver excellent drinks services. You need to provide your team with all the information and equipment needed in order to be successful in their roles. This includes how they must comply with the rules and regulations outlined in Licensing and Weights and Measures legislation. Also you and your team must understand how to serve alcohol responsibly.

Learning objectives
On completion of this chapter, you should:
1 Be able to supervise drinks services.
2 Understand the requirements that need to be met when supervising drinks services.
3 Understand how to supervise drinks services.

Introduction

Drinks service is a short way to describe an extensive range of activities, products and services. In some areas professionals can study for years to become expert (wines). This chapter will provide a general overview of the responsibilities of a supervisor and how they connect with other areas of the organisation.

3.2 Products and services

Types of drinks service outlets include:
- restaurants
- hotels
- wine bars
- cocktail bars
- pubs
- self-service outlets
- cafes
- temporary outlets (such as at concerts or festivals).

Types of products include:
- non-alcoholic beverages
- wine
- beer
- cider

- spirits
- liqueurs
- fortified wines
- cocktails.

3.4 3.5 Roles and responsibilities of staff

All drinks service staff need to know how to prepare the drinks on offer, in what type of glass, where the ingredients should be stored before consumption (at room temperature or in a fridge etc.) and the price of the drinks. They need to be aware of legislation and how they must comply with it. Drinks service staff need all the personality characteristics of any other person in a front-of-house role and specifically the confidence to deal with challenging (and sometimes drunk) customers.

Job roles in drinks service can be at entry level, supervisor or manager, and can be in any of the following areas, each of which requires specialist knowledge and information:

1 **Bar** – changing barrels and kegs
2 **Sommelier or wine waiter** – grape varieties, countries and flavours of wine
3 **Dispense bar** – knowledge of drinks service for events
4 **Mixologist or cocktail waiter** – cocktail flair and recipes
5 **Room service** – building layout

> **Evidence 1**
> 1.4 3.2 3.4 3.5
> - Collect a job description for your role and one for a member of your team.
> - Collect a drinks menu from your workplace.

1.1 1.2 1.3 1.4 1.6 3.3 3.12 Planning drinks services

Training staff

A supervisor must ensure that their teams have the knowledge and ability to perform their roles successfully by executing the following:
- New team members have a thorough induction.
- All team members are trained on the standards outlined in the operations manual.
- All supervisors must attend regular refresher training to make certain that their own knowledge is up to date.
- Teams are given access to relevant information through Standards of Practice documents or visual displays.
- Training is repeated regularly to prevent it being forgotten.
- Team members are monitored after training to confirm that the skills have been learned.
- If there are indicators that a team member is not following procedures then further training or performance measures should be arranged.
- All training records are thorough and up to date.

Liaising with colleagues

A drinks service supervisor may be required to communicate with various people within and outside the organisation when organising the drinks service. When interacting with colleagues at any level it is important to be courteous and polite as it shows respect.

Table 8.1 Liaising with colleagues

Colleagues you may liaise with	Reason
Bar team	To arrange the rota and training in preparing for service, how to serve drinks and complying with the legislation involved with their roles
Suppliers	To seek and order high quality products at competitive prices
Restaurant manager	To confirm any requirements that may be out of the ordinary from the day-to-day running of the department, such as events or promotions
Chef	To liaise regarding any food being offered in the bar area such as canapés and matching wines with food
Cleaner	To maintain high standards of cleanliness and presentation in the bar area
Maintenance	To carry out any repairs of equipment required
Stores	To arrange for the delivery and storage of stock required for service including any unusual conditions required such as temperature

Requisition forms

A requisition form is a formal request for stock from the stores. It helps the stores to keep track of their stock levels and also provides evidence of who has requisitioned items. There is normally a list of staff who have the authority to requisition and this protects the organisation from losing stock either through mistakes or theft.

Photographs of standards

A useful tool in maintaining high standards in the drinks service area is the use of clear labelling and training photographs in the operations manual. By labelling the shelves with the item and the quantity required, inexperienced team members would know what to restock and where; labels would also assist them in finding 'assist them in finding' items ordered much faster.

Figure 8.1 Labelled shelved can help staff know what to restock and where

By having photographs of how the bar should be set up displayed in back of house, your staff can copy them to safeguard consistency in the presentation of the bar area. Comparing the photograph to the current set up will highlight items missing and aid the restocking procedure.

Figure 8.2 Photos are useful for showing how the bar should be set up

Drinks specifications

Similarly, drinks specification sheets can support the consistency in quality and presentation of drinks served by your team. The specifications should include the following information:
- equipment required such as glass, cocktail shaker, juice squeezer, muddle stick etc.
- ingredients required including any garnish
- recipe or method of making including the **correct measures of alcohol**
- a photograph of the final presentation.

Figure 8.3 Supervisors should make sure that the team has the right equipment

Don't forget to inform your teams of the consequences of not serving the measures of alcohol outlined in your specifications!

Managing use of resources

For advice on how to plan best use of your resources and team through peak and off-peak times, refer to Chapter 7: Supervise food service.

1.7 2.1 2.2 2.3 2.4 The law

Licences

In England and Wales, there are four licensing objectives:
1. The prevention of crime and disorder
2. The protection of public safety
3. The prevention of public nuisance
4. The protection of children from harm.

The types of organisations that need a premises licence to sell or supply alcohol on a permanent basis include:
- pubs and bars
- cinemas
- theatres
- nightclubs
- late-opening cafes
- takeaways
- village and community halls
- supermarkets.

Temporary permission can be sought by applying for a temporary event notice through your local council. Every premises that sells or supplies alcohol needs to have a designated premises supervisor (DPS) who holds a personal licence. Not everyone working at the premises is required to hold a personal licence.

The Licensing Act 2003

The Licensing Act 2003 (Mandatory Licensing Conditions) Order 2010 outlines certain conditions on the permission to sell or supply alcohol and these are as follows:
- An age verification policy is enforced at the premises.
- Irresponsible promotions are banned.
- Alcohol is never dispensed directly into customers' mouths.
- Tap water is provided free of charge.
- Smaller measures of alcohol are available and this information is provided to customers in printed format such as a menu/price list.
- Alcohol must not be sold below the cost of duty plus VAT (added in 2014).

Alcohol can only be bought by, bought for, or consumed by customers who are over the age of 18. It is an offence to supply alcohol to a customer who is under 18. However, 16 and 17 year olds can drink beer, lager, wine or cider bought for them by a parent or guardian who is over 18 when they are eating a table meal.

Evidence 2

1.1 1.2 1.3 1.6 3.3

Collect the following items:
- a drinks specification
- a photograph of your workspace set up ready for customers
- a copy of training records from a member of your team.

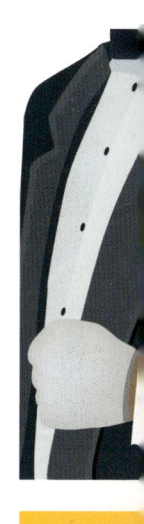

The Licensing Act 2003 brought changes to the traditional permitted hours to sell alcohol and the drinking-up time. It is now possible for premises to obtain a licence to sell alcohol for up to 24 hours, but a supervisor must still make sure that the following does not happen:

a) The premises carries on or attempts to carry on a licensable activity on or from the premises other than what has been authorised in their licence.

b) Staff knowingly allow a licensable activity that is not authorised in their licence to occur.

Other activities included that require a licence are regulated entertainment such as live music or DJ performances, the provision of late night refreshment and gambling.

Alcohol can be served to hotel residents past the permitted serving times outlined in the licence without an extension. A one-hour extension to the permitted serving times can be applied for where patrons are having a table meal.

Weights and measures

The Weight and Measures Act 1985 states that alcoholic drinks must be served in specified quantities. If a customer asks for a drink without specifying the size, for example, a 'glass of wine', they should be informed of the smaller measures that are available.

Units of measurement must be millilitres or litres with the exception of draught beer and cider or milk, which may be served in pint or half-pint measures.

1. Still wine must be served in 125 ml, 175 ml, or multiples of 125 ml and 175 ml.
2. Fortified wine e.g. port or sherry must be served in 50 ml, 70 ml, or multiples of 50 ml or 70 ml.
3. Gin, rum, vodka and whisky must be served in either 25 ml or multiples of 25 ml, or 35 ml or multiples of 35 ml but not both on the same premises.

Where there is a combination of three or more liquids (e.g. in a cocktail), the weights and measures rules do not apply.

Price lists

Customers must be fully informed about goods prior to their purchase. A menu should clearly state accurate product descriptions, including alcoholic strengths, the price (inclusive of VAT) and the quantities in which they are served. When a brand is listed, the drink served must be prepared with that brand. For example, other brands cannot be served when a customer orders a Bacardi and Coke.

Breaches of legislation

Anyone who works (paid or unpaid) at any premises with the authority to sell alcohol, the holder of a premises licence and the designated premises supervisor could all be prosecuted and fined for the following breaches of legislation:

1. Sale of alcohol to a drunk person.
2. Obtaining alcohol for a drunk person.
3. Unaccompanied children under 16 in premises primarily used for the sale of alcohol.
4. Unaccompanied children under 16 in premises that sell alcohol between midnight and 5am.
5. Supply of alcohol to children.
6. Purchase and consumption of alcohol by children.
7. Also for permitting the misuse of drugs to take place.

Prosecution could result in the premises licence being withdrawn, which risks the loss of jobs as a hospitality organisation would struggle to be profitable without being able to sell alcohol.

The following authorities are responsible for the enforcement of this legislation:
- police
- local fire and rescue
- the local licensing authority
- environmental health authority
- planning authority
- local trading standards.

You can seek advice and support from any of these on how your organisation can best comply with the standards.

1.5 3.1 2.6 Preparing drinks services

Use a pre-service checklist to make sure that all the necessary tasks allocated to staff have been completed before service starts. Include the following questions:
1. Do all bars have enough stock for service?
2. Is the stock at the correct temperature for serving (for example, white wine chilled)?
3. Do all bars have enough glasses for service?
4. Is all the required equipment working?
5. Is the bar clean and neatly presented?
6. Are the guest seating areas clean and neatly presented?
7. Are the toilets clean (if applicable)?
8. Are the menus correct, neat and clean?
9. Are all signs displaying correct information?
10. Are all the lights working?

Estimate and include the appropriate time to start your checks whilst leaving enough time to brief your staff thoroughly.

> **Take it further**
> More information on licensing legislation is available at www.legislation.gov.uk.

> **Evidence 3**
> 1.5 3.1
> Create a pre-service checklist specific to your place of work.

Delivering drinks services

1.9 3.9 3.13 3.14 Alcohol misuse

You, your staff and your organisation have an ethical and legal duty to serve alcohol responsibly. It is an offence to 'over serve', but more importantly you must keep people safe. There are more risks involved for the business than the customer who is drunk. Drunk customers are more difficult to deal with as there is normally disorder (spillages, breakages, vomit, etc.) and therefore more cost to maintain the premises. Aggressive and violent incidents may occur which could increase turnover as people do not like to work in that type of environment. The organisation's licence is at risk if there are continuous breaches of legislation.

Drunk customers are vulnerable as they are more at risk of being attacked or having an accident; if they chose to drive, they could kill themselves or an innocent bystander. Long-term misuse of alcohol will result in serious health problems such as liver disease.

3.10 Contingency planning

When planning your team's drinks service, consider using the contingency planning methods outlined in Chapter 7, 'Supervise food service', to explore what action you can take to reduce the risks of alcohol misuse. For example:

1. A security team could be employed to deal with unruly drunk customers and fights.
2. Implement 'good practice policies' such as not serving shots and not allowing double orders when last orders are called.
3. Train your staff to stop serving customers as soon as they show signs of intoxication, and make sure they know that you will support their decision to stop serving.
4. Train your staff on your organisation's age verification policy.
5. Keep records of staff who have been trained and use tests to check their understanding.
6. Call last orders in plenty of time.
7. A member of staff can be allocated at the exit to the premise at the end of service to ensure customers leave quietly and do not disturb local residents.
8. Develop a relationship with a taxi company that will collect your drunk customers.

1.10 2.5 3.6 3.7 Monitoring

Use an incident and refusal diary to record any arguments, fights or other disturbances. This can be monitored for repeated problems, and details can be provided to the police, if required. Thorough records are useful in any legal action that may take place. This book can also be used to record when service was refused after checking a customer's age identification. All this information proves that your organisation is responsible.

1.8 3.8 3.11 3.15 3.16 3.17 Action to take when there are problems

If a member or members of your team are particularly busy, or if some staff do not have the particular skills or knowledge to deal with certain problems, it may be necessary to reallocate tasks to other members of your team who have more time or the skills and knowledge to carry out tasks more effectively.

Identifying the symptoms early

You can tell a customer is becoming drunk if they:
- slur their speech
- are unsteady and stumble
- become louder and obnoxious.

Refusal of service

Any refusal to serve a drunk customer should be done politely and respectfully. Try to identify the signs of intoxication as early you can. Tell them that you are sorry but they can no longer be served as it is against the law and they are welcome to return another time. Be calm and patient as it may take time for them to understand; you may need to repeat yourself several times. Look for friends in their group who may assist you in the situation. Keep your colleagues, security and your manager informed of the situation and call the police if the customer becomes verbally threatening or aggressive.

Have a plan of what you or a member of staff should do if an incident escalates, which may include calling the police. Make sure it is communicated to everyone who might be involved. Get advice from the police on what this should be, if needed.

Evidence 4
1.74 2.1 2.2 2.5

Collect a copy of your company's service of drinks and alcohol policy and highlight key points.

Evidence 5
2.4 3.6

Collect a copy of an 'incident or refusal' report.

Evidence 6
2.6 3.1

Collect a copy of the standards of practice or operations manual for your department

Assignment 1
3.13 3.14 3.15 3.16 3.17

Create a feedback questionnaire on the drinks service delivered in your department. Survey the following stakeholders to produce an accurate depiction of the service provided;

1. Customers
2. Team members
3. Managers

Repeat the survey at regular intervals such as monthly meetings

Assignment 2
3.8 3.9 3.10 3.11 3.12

Use feedback from your customers, team and managers to create a table of common problems. For each issue enter suggested contingencies to tackle the problem.

Assignment 3
3.13 3.14 3.15 3.16 3.17

Use the knowledge you have gained in this chapter to create a short training session for your team including the following;

1. The importance of an effective drinks service
2. The consequences of alcohol misuse
3. Best practice for the refusal of alcohol service
4. Effective communication with customers under the influence of alcohol
5. How to deal with difficult situations and challenging customers
6. The consequences of not following legislation

Collect a copy of the tools you create and the attendance record

Key terms

Dispense bar – an area that dispenses beverages to staff to be served in another outlet

Intoxication – to lose control of behaviour or faculties, especially through alcohol or drugs

Age verification policy – the organisational procedures set out to ensure that staff check the age of those that they serve alcohol to ensure they are over 18

Knowledge check

1. Name three authorities that you can contact for advice on licensing legislation.
2. What are the potential consequences of alcohol misuse to the organisation?
3. What are the potential consequences of alcohol misuse to the customer?

Evidence checklist		
Assessment criteria		**Possible evidence**
1.1	Ensure staff have the skills, knowledge and resources to carry out their responsibilities	Evidence activity 2
1.2	Agree procedures for staff to follow when preparing and restocking the drinks service area	Evidence activity 2
1.3	Ensure that the attractiveness and comfort of drinking areas meet customer needs and expectations	Evidence activity 2
1.4	Liaise with other relevant people and departments to ensure the delivery of an effective drinks service	Evidence activity 1
1.5	Carry out preparations in good time to allow the scheduled drinks service to be provided	Evidence activity 3
1.6	Ensure specified standards and procedures for the service of products are maintained	Evidence activity 2
1.7	Ensure the drinks service complies with social responsibility practices and relevant legislation	Evidence 4
1.8	Confirm that communication with customers by all staff takes place in a manner that is appropriate to them and the situation	Assignment 2
1.9	Maintain the comfort and well-being of other customers and local residents when carrying out activities	Assignment 3
1.10	Deal with any problems promptly and effectively when monitoring drinks service areas	Assignment 3
2.1	State where to find information about licensing legislation	Evidence 4
2.2	Describe the basic legal requirements that affect the drinks service and how to implement these in relation to: • permitted hours • closing time • licences • residents and non-residents • diners and non-diners • young persons, service and employment • right to eject and duty to refuse service • gaming, betting and lotteries • public entertainment • weights and measures • price lists, notices and payment for drinks • drugs • trades descriptions and consumer protection laws	Evidence 4
2.3	Explain the implications of failing to implement basic legal requirements	Assignment 3

Evidence checklist		
Assessment criteria		**Possible evidence**
2.4	Explain how to identify and correct deviations from legislation and industry-specific regulations	Evidence activity 5
2.5	Describe the organisation's policies and procedures that are relevant to the drinks service	Evidence activity 4
2.6	Describe the various procedures that need to be followed for the preparation of the drinks service area, including those relating to: • clearing • stocking products • equipment	Evidence activity 6
3.1	Explain how to supervise the preparation of the drinks service area so that the service meets organisational requirements and is done in time	Evidence activity 3
3.2	Describe the range of products in own area of responsibility	Evidence activity 1
3.3	Explain how to prepare and serve the range of products in own area of responsibility	Evidence activity 2
3.4	Explain the roles and responsibilities of people in own area of responsibility and in other parts of the organisation as relevant to the drinks service	Evidence activity 1
3.5	Describe the skills and knowledge staff need to carry out their responsibilities effectively	Evidence activity 1
3.6	Compare different methods of monitoring the drinks service area effectively	Evidence activity 5
3.7	Explain how to monitor and supervise staff practice in order to maintain standards	Assignment 1
3.8	Explain what action needs to be taken when preparation and delivery standards are not met	Assignment 2
3.9	Explain how to identify and address the problems that can affect the drinks service and the preparation of areas	Assignment 2
3.10	Explain how to develop contingency plans to reduce the impact of drinks service problems	Assignment 2
3.11	Explain how to reallocate work to different members of staff to reduce the impact of service problems	Assignment 2
3.12	Describe how to vary practice according to: • quiet periods • busy periods • delivery of service to customers with special requirements	Assignment 2
3.13	Explain how an effective drinks service affects profitability and customer satisfaction	Assignment 3
3.14	Describe the possible consequences of alcohol misuse	Assignment 3
3.15	Describe best practice in the refusal of service	Assignment 3
3.16	Explain how to communicate and deal effectively with the range of customer groups (including those who are experiencing the effects of alcohol)	Assignment 3
3.17	Explain the importance of effective communication	Assignment 3

CHAPTER 9

Supervise housekeeping operations

This chapter covers the competence that hospitality supervisors require to maintain and improve the housekeeping service. It deals with the preparation, supervision and review of the service, involving the planning of equipment and supplies, preparing staff rotas, briefing staff and collecting customer feedback.

Learning objectives

On completion of this chapter, you should:
1. Be able to supervise housekeeping operations.
2. Understand the requirements of housekeeping operations.
3. Understand how to supervise housekeeping operations.
4. Understand the importance of monitoring and reviewing housekeeping services.

3.1 3.4 The roles and responsibilities of the housekeeping service

Efficient and well run housekeeping services are essential to a successful hospitality business or operation. Good housekeeping standards can create positive impressions in almost any part of the building and housekeeping departments are usually responsible for the largest volume of area in the establishment. Housekeeping teams usually have responsibility for the cleanliness and servicing of all guest rooms/suites, public areas, conference areas, lounges, corridors, lifts, staff areas and offices. However, kitchens, restaurants and some bar areas are traditionally cleaned by the staff working within them. Because of this wide area of responsibility, housekeeping may be the largest department of an organisation in terms of staffing.

A positive first impression and attractive areas that are clean, tidy and hygienic all help to reflect on how the whole establishment is managed. Commitment to excellent standards of housekeeping will ensure clean, hygienic and well cared for premises. **Customer/guest surveys** consistently confirm that cleanliness and housekeeping standards rate highly in a visitor's overall satisfaction with their visit and influence whether they are likely to return. Good housekeeping standards can also provide pleasant working conditions for staff.

> **Key term**
>
> **Customer/guest surveys** – a way of getting feedback from guests about their opinions of the service they received. They could be verbal questions at reception, a questionnaire in the room or a telephone/email survey.

An efficient, well run housekeeping team which has received good initial training, as well as ongoing training and staff development, will have an impact on the economic success of the business. A housekeeping team that remains focused on customer care and the importance of providing a high quality service will enhance the guest experience and the profile of the business. A successful, well motivated business is likely to make more profit but the satisfaction that staff achieve when the job is 'well done' is also important.

The main role of a housekeeping supervisor is to ensure that all of the areas within their responsibility are clean, well cared for and presented to the establishment's and customers' expectations. It is an important position because the supervisor works closely with the housekeeping team and is likely to be checking that work completed is of the required standard.

Customers/guests should rightly expect all rooms and public areas to be clean, tidy and hygienic. As a minimum, rooms should be:
- freshly prepared with no evidence of the previous occupant
- have furniture, fixtures and fittings of the expected quality and in a good state of repair
- equipped with items that are safe for use.

In non-profit-making establishments, housekeeping is just as important and needs to be managed in similar ways, though the actual work being completed may affect the housekeeping services. For example, housekeeping services in a hospital must also consider the important area of infection control.

Figure 9.1 Housekeeping supervisors work closely with housekeeping staff to ensure that tasks are completed to the required standard

Housekeeping departments will differ in their structure, depending on the requirements of the organisation and establishment, but a typical structure may be as shown in Table 9.1.

Table 9.1 Housekeeping department structure

Job title	Role and responsibilities
Executive head housekeeper	A senior executive role usually in a large, luxury establishment. The position would carry overall responsibility for all housekeeping operations, possibly policy making, financial and budget control. May have overall responsibility for housekeeping over a group of properties.
Head housekeeper – may report to an executive head housekeeper or another person in a senior position	A management role with responsibility for all housekeeping services within the establishment. A head housekeeper may have control of budgets and responsibility for recruiting and managing staff, as well as organising training.
Assistant head housekeeper	Assists and deputises for the head housekeeper and covers when the head housekeeper is away.
Housekeeping supervisor	Works with housekeeping staff on the day-to-day and occasional housekeeping tasks. Ensures work is running smoothly. They report to the head housekeeper or assistant head housekeeper. Involved in delivering staff training and briefings and producing staff rotas. May order supplies.
Senior housekeeping assistant	May assist with some supervisory tasks and tasks such as issuing materials and equipment. May assist and mentor new staff.
Housekeeping assistants	Any of a wide range of housekeeping tasks as allocated by the supervisor. These may be the same each day or may vary.
Housekeeping porters and those with specific tasks	Unloading deliveries, moving equipment, use of heavier cleaning equipment such as floor-scrubbing equipment. Tasks such as cleaning lifts, stairways and corridors. These staff may work on a night shift.

Evidence 1
2.6 3.4 3.9

Prepare an organisational chart for your own department stating what the main responsibilities are for each role. Who prepares the work rotas and how is work allocated? Discuss this with your assessor and keep it in your portfolio.

Key term

Handover session – this usually refers to areas where staff work shifts to cover the required hours; for example, 6am–2.30 pm and 2.30 pm–10pm. Time would be allocated in the middle for a team meeting all together so one shift can fully hand over to the next.

3.5 Integrating with other departments

Because of the large physical areas covered by housekeeping, it is essential that there is effective communication between housekeeping teams and other departments to ensure that a high standard of service is maintained at all times. Communication may occur through regular meetings, updates and **handover sessions**, or may arise due to increased demands, extra requirements or problems.

Housekeeping teams often work within other departments, sometimes working together to provide the required service. Good communication, understanding and flexibility are essential for all concerned. For example, if housekeeping staff wish to clean a lounge used as a function room but the event is running late, it will be necessary to leave that room for later and complete some work elsewhere. Integration and communication between reception, florists, porters, room service, concierge plus many others are essential for the overall smooth running of the establishment.

Increasingly housekeeping teams communicate with each other, their supervisor and with other departments by use of electronic devices. For example, a housekeeping supervisor may use an electronic system to communicate to reception that a room has been serviced and is ready to re-sell.

Supervising housekeeping operations

1.1 Schedule housekeeping procedures to ensure standards are maintained

Housekeeping services need to cover a wide range of tasks to the required standards, within the time allowed and at specific times of the day. The supervisor needs to have a thorough understanding of:
- the areas they are responsible for and the tasks to be completed
- the levels and types of cleaning required
- the frequency of cleaning needed for specific areas and items
- cleaning methods and processes to be used
- chemicals and equipment to be used
- health, safety and hygiene requirements
- any special finishes or items and how these must be dealt with (e.g. marble, French polished items, chandeliers or antiques)
- the staff available, the hours for which they are employed and any arrangements with staff agencies
- housekeeping budgets.

Careful **scheduling** is a very important part of housekeeping to ensure that all tasks are completed properly and at the time required.
- Lobbies and reception areas can be cleaned overnight or early morning when they are least busy, but will probably need some further attention through the day to maintain standards.
- Guest rooms and suites will probably be serviced when the guests have left them for the day. When guests have checked out of their accommodation, it is important that the area is serviced promptly so the rooms can be reallocated. If rooms are not ready for re-sale, the establishment could lose income.

> **Key term**
>
> **Scheduling** – this is a plan of procedure, usually written, to establish time allowed for each item or process.

In most housekeeping departments there will be time allocations for particular tasks to be completed and areas to be serviced. However, this is not as simple as taking a square metre measurement of an area and allocating someone to clean it within a specific time. Measurement of areas can provide a useful guide but it will also be necessary to consider:

- What is in the area: a bathroom will take longer to clean than a lobby area by a lift.
- Heavily used areas such as cloakroom/toilet areas by a busy banqueting suite will need frequent cleaning and checks.
- Special cleaning processes and techniques that may be needed.
- Whether the area is occupied or not, for example, the guest staying over or departing.

It is essential that the supervisor has a good understanding of the areas to be serviced by housekeeping teams, the specific tasks that need completing and exactly how and when these need to be done. The requirements then need to be communicated fully to housekeeping teams and their actual work supervised so standards are consistent and maintained.

Time allocations are often used for specific areas. For example, a standard double room with a bathroom: 25 minutes; a small suite: 45 minutes; lobby and reception area: 30 minutes; and staff toilets and changing rooms: 50 minutes. Obviously these times would vary according to the size of area, the fittings and finishes used and standards and levels of cleanliness required. Other establishments may use a points system; for example, each double room with bathroom would carry 5 points; a corridor area 3 points; a conference room 6 points. Each member of staff would be allocated a set number of points to complete within their shift.

Initially, someone will need to establish the time allocation or points system and this is usually done by a head housekeeper or supervisor (or occasionally an outside contractor) observing the tasks actually being completed and allocating times or points to them. These may need to be flexible to allow for the 'unexpected', for example, a guest having a party in his suite the night before checking out and leaving the suite needing extra attention. Within a 'chain' or group of businesses, time allocations for housekeeping tasks may be set centrally and used across the whole group.

The manager/supervisor will also need to schedule for levels of busyness and how this may affect demands on housekeeping services. A busy banqueting season in December may mean all rooms are occupied over the weekend; or a holiday hotel in a popular area may expect to be fully booked through the summer months. However, January and February may be quieter and with lower occupancy rates.

1.2 1.3 3.9 4.9 Allocating housekeeping duties to staff

Housekeeping is often the area requiring the greatest numbers of staff. These may be:
- full- or part-time housekeeping staff employed directly by the establishment
- casual staff who will work at busy times for an agreed number of hours
- agency staff employed by a staffing agency and paid by them.

Housekeeping staff are likely to work on shifts to cover the times when housekeeping provision is needed. These shifts may follow a regular pattern such as 6am to 3pm, with alternate weekends off, or a less regular pattern to cover hours required. Some staff work on a 'rolling shift' pattern of five days working and two days off, or four long days (usually 12 hours or more) then three days off. Because a large number of part-time staff are employed in housekeeping, it is necessary to be aware of their exact working agreements. They may, for example, need to finish work in time to collect children from school.

Allocation of specific staff to various tasks needs to be carefully considered and will depend on:
- the skills and experience they already have
- specific specialist training they may have completed
- the hours and times they are contracted for
- the routine and non-routine work that needs to be completed
- any **mentoring** or close supervision needed, as may be the case with a new staff member.

> **Key term**
>
> **Mentoring** – an experienced person assists another in developing specific skills and knowledge, and provides support while learning the job.

For efficiency reasons and to allow for the smooth running of the department, some staff may always work in their own area. For example, a staff member may be allocated 12 rooms to service each day on a specific floor. The advantage of this is that the operative becomes familiar with and builds pride and ownership of their own area. The work is likely to be completed efficiently but remember that cover is still necessary for days off, sickness and holidays and work completed must still be of a high standard.

Other staff may be moved around different areas as the workload requires. This may be less efficient as the operative may be unfamiliar with the area and less sure of what needs to be done. However, with good supervision in place it can provide for a flexible team familiar with a number of tasks in different areas.

Once all the information is assembled about the tasks that need to be completed and the staff available to complete them, working rotas can then be drawn up. A staff rota needs to be planned but will always remain a live document to cover sudden increases or changes in business, staff sickness or other unplanned events. When producing rotas make sure they are done fairly, taking some staff preferences into account. For example, some staff are keen to have occasional weekends off and others may prefer working at the weekend; however it is important to make clear that for the sake of fairness preferences cannot always be met. Where working hours and days are significantly changed week to week, try to produce rotas far enough ahead to allow staff enough time to plan their other commitments.

1.3 3.10 Briefing staff

All staff, whether permanent employees or not, will need regular briefing on:
- **Procedure** – how things are done at the establishment, to ensure a consistently high standard. Even staff with considerable previous experience need to attend briefings to ensure that their knowledge is up to date and that they are aware of any changes in procedure.
- **Work routines** – every establishment will have work routines and standard ways of completing tasks. These are known as *standard operational procedures* and all staff must be fully aware of them and what is required. This information can be given through induction, training and briefings.

- **Standards of behaviour** – housekeeping staff will come into contact with customers/guests and once again there are likely to be standard procedures for accepted behaviour. Politeness at all times is, of course, essential but extra briefing may be given on phrases used to greet guests, how to deal with questions or complaints or standard procedures for entering guest rooms.
- **Communication** – excellent communication is essential, especially as housekeeping staff work across a wide range of areas and within other departments. Briefing on expected standards of communication with guests and other staff is essential.

Because different people learn and remember things in different ways, it is important that the ways you complete training and briefings are varied in content. Increasingly, those working in housekeeping roles come from a wide variety of backgrounds and frequently English is not their first language. Therefore, choosing the correct briefing method is even more important, to ensure that the instruction and training given are fully understood, whether written, visual or verbal. The variety of methods used may include:

- **Verbal instruction** – being told how to do something.
- **Written instructions** – being given instructions in writing on computer screens, whiteboards, flipcharts, leaflets, tick-lists or forms, posters or a cleaning schedule.
- **Demonstrations** – actually being shown how to complete a task.
- **Diagrams** – drawings, pictures maps, etc. These are very useful when the spoken or written instruction is not fully understood.

All supervisors should be appropriately trained in the necessary procedures, especially those concerning communication skills, equal opportunities and equality and diversity.

Figure 9.2 Supervisors should be able to communicate clearly with their team

1.4 4.4 Staff skills, knowledge and resources

To ensure that standards remain high, staff must be provided with the skills, knowledge and resources they need to complete their work effectively.

This can be achieved through thorough induction, initial and ongoing training, briefings, handover sessions, mentoring and supervision. A commitment to all of these methods will help to make staff feel valued and supported in their work and provides an understanding of what is expected from them.

- Make sure all team members understand the importance of their role and the housekeeping service in general.
- Remember their names and greet them by name when you see them. Encourage staff to greet each other, staff from other areas, as well as guests they may encounter.
- Provide functional, well fitting and good quality uniforms.
- Make sure they always have the correct equipment and materials to complete their job properly.
- Value work completed and offer praise where it is deserved. Employee recognition and award schemes can be useful.
- Take staff concerns or issues seriously, especially when concerning poor working relationships within the team.
- Keep team members well informed of changes to department structure, procedures, changes to equipment or chemicals or anything that could affect their work.
- Make sure that staff understand the opportunities and possible promotion that may be available to them. Encourage further training and gaining of qualifications, where possible offering the necessary support to enable this.

4.3 Staff training

Staff training is of absolute importance to achieve and maintain the required standards. All staff should complete an induction programme and in large establishments this may be conducted for a group of new employees. Induction programmes will vary between various establishments to cover their differing needs, but the most usual topics for new housekeeping staff include information about:

- the company and its structure
- key people within the organisation
- human resources services, including pay and pension details
- appraisal procedures
- training that will be required as an employee – mandatory training and additional training
- fire evacuation, health, safety and hygiene procedures
- security procedures and dealing with security concerns
- signing in and out of the building
- uniform and name badges and how these must be worn
- safe use of equipment, machinery and chemicals.

The majority of staff training may be completed by the supervisor, possibly with parts completed by others from specialist areas, such as health and safety representatives or fire officers. It is advisable to have a training record for each member of staff to show that training is up to date and to provide a reminder of anything that needs updating. Certain mandatory training needs to be completed very soon after the start of employment; for example, fire evacuation or safe chemical handling. Other aspects of training may be completed while working with a more experienced member of staff or with the assistance of a mentor. However, when the training is completed, remember to record it on the training record.

Note: It is important for all employees to keep their work-related knowledge current and relevant and it is likely that there will be planned and formal update training for staff. However, updates and changes can also be communicated through briefings, meetings or by alerting staff to new information, signs and posters that may affect them and their work.

Evidence 2

1.3 1.4 1.5 2.3 2.6
2.8 3.1 3.5 3.6 4.3

Develop an induction training topics list that you would complete with new members of staff, including those mentioned above and any other requirements your organisation may have that specifically affect housekeeping teams. Consider the learning needs of the staff and use suitable explanations, pictures/diagrams, suggestions for demonstrations or other items to ensure your staff fully understand the requirements.

Sample training record

Employees Name ....
Department ....
Supervisor ....

	Training completion date	Required update training date	Employee's signature and date	Supervisor's signature and date
Full company INDUCTION TRAINING				
Mandatory Training				
Manual handling				
Health and safety procedure				
Emergency evacuation				
Security procedures				
COSHH training				
Fire procedure training				
Safety procedures				
Use of PPE including protective gloves				
Use of warning signs				
Disposal of used chemicals				
Disposal of waste – colour-coded bags				
Disposal of broken glass				
Cleaning procedure				
Use of cleaning schedules				
Dusting and vacuum cleaning				
Stripping and making beds				
Cleaning bathrooms				
Removal and replacement of linen				
Cleaning glass and mirrors				
Cleaning special surfaces and finishes				
Replacement of complimentary items and toiletries				
Final checking procedure				
Reporting problems				
Broken items				
Missing items				
Electrical or electronic faults				
Drainage or plumbing faults				
Items requiring a special clean e.g. stained curtains or carpet				
Damage to fittings, furniture/furnishings				

Figure 9.3 Sample training record for housekeeping staff

1.5 2.8 Housekeeping procedures

All establishments will have housekeeping procedures to ensure that standards are maintained, work is completed efficiently and with health, safety and security in mind. The actual procedures should be thoroughly covered during induction and ongoing staff training, but special consideration should be given to:
- Fire and emergency evacuation procedure.
- Health and safety, especially when using chemicals, lifting heavy or awkward items, use of protective clothing and placement of warning signs.
- COSHH training for handling and disposal of various chemicals.

Sample cleaning schedule for a bathroom

Bathroom - Room number ………

Cleaned by (sign):	Date:		Checked by (sign):
Tick	Task	Procedure	Materials/equipment
	Remove used towels, bathmats, facecloths. (Unless reuse is requested)	Unused or items for reuse – towels folded with long edges in and placed on rails. Hand towels on top of bath towels facecloths folded on basin and bathmat in half on edge of bath. Used items in laundry bag.	Laundry bags
	Clean toilet and surround	Toilet – flushed, shake on powder cleaner. Clean inside bowl with toilet brush. Use blue cloth and sanitiser to clean seat lid and outside of toilet including pipes and fittings, surrounding wall. Dry with blue paper roll. Close toilet lid	(S4) toilet cleaner *green* (S8) sanitiser *blue* Blue cloth Blue paper roll
	Clean bidet	Rinse inside bowl with warm water. Use blue cloth and sanitiser to clean bowl and outside of bidet including pipes, chrome fittings and surrounding wall. Dry with blue paper roll.	(S8) sanitiser *blue* Blue cloth Blue paper roll
	Clean bath	Rinse bath with hot water. Use a pink cloth and cleaning liquid to clean all parts thoroughly. Clean shower screen and all chrome fittings including soap dish (remember the underside). Dry with blue paper roll. Wash and dry the bath side panel.	(S12) liquid cleaner *pink* Pink cloth Blue paper roll
	Clean basin	Rinse basin with hot water. Use a pink cloth and cleaning liquid to clean all parts thoroughly not forgetting all chrome fittings and overflow. Clean underneath the basin and clean the pedestal stand. Clean toilet roll holders. Rinse and dry with blue paper roll.	(S12) liquid cleaner *pink* Pink cloth Blue paper roll
	Mirrors and glass	Use glass cleaning liquid and dry green cloth	(S 01) glass cleaning liquid *clear* dry green cloth
	Glasses	Remove used glasses. Replace with fresh glasses that have been cleaned in the dishwasher	Clean glasses
	Cabinets and doors	Door tops wiped with damp cloth. Use a damp white cloth to clean cabinet/door fronts/sides. Dry thoroughly.	White cloth Blue paper roll
	Replace toilet rolls	Two on toilet roll holders, ends folded in to a point resting on top of the roll. One spare roll in cabinet wrapped in tissue paper.	Toilet rolls
	Replace complementary toiletries	Bath soap, hand soap, shampoo x 2, conditioner x 2, lotion x 2, toothbrush/toothpaste sets x 2, shower caps x 2	Bath soap, hand soap, 2 shampoo, 2 conditioner, 2 lotion, 2 toothbrush/toothpaste sets, 2, shower caps, 2 cotton wool
	Clean floor	Mop the floor using a little cleaning liquid, hot water and cotton head mop. Rinse and leave as dry as possible.	Mop S12) liquid cleaner *pink*
	Complete final check, checking slowly around the bathroom in a clockwise motion. Leave the door open ready for the supervisor check.		

Figure 9.4 Sample cleaning schedule for a bathroom

137

- Hygiene – using different colour-coded cloths for different areas will help to avoid cross-contamination; using the prescribed disinfectants and other chemicals will help to ensure that cleaning is effective; clean uniforms, correct hand washing and use of protective gloves are also essential to a hygienic environment.

Cleaning procedures need to be planned and every employee needs to work to the same plans to ensure consistency of standards. The cleaning plans are often referred to as a **cleaning schedule**. This is a list of procedures for a specific area, usually appearing in the order in which they will be completed.

Types of cleaning

Not everything needs to be cleaned with the same frequency and different terms are used to describe frequency of cleaning. This is illustrated in Table 9.2.

Table 9.2 Types of cleaning

Type of cleaning	When it is done	Examples
Frequent, planned cleaning	Cleaned at intervals throughout the day	Toilet areas, busy entrances, changing rooms/shower areas
Daily cleaning	Cleaned to schedule every day or more frequently if needed	Guest rooms and suites Public areas
Periodic cleaning	Pre-planned cleaning, not needed every day but could be weekly, monthly or even annually	Windows, curtains, carpets, high cornices, chandeliers
Deep cleaning	A very thorough and in-depth cleaning procedure that usually takes the area out of use until it is completed	Spa or swimming pools Kitchen areas
Emergency cleaning	Cleaning after an unplanned event such as a spillage or water leak	Almost anywhere in the building
Cleaning on request	Cleaning completed when it is asked for	Guest rooms where they did not wish their room to be cleaned at the standard times, e.g. Do Not Disturb sign Other cleaning requests for a variety of reasons

Evidence 3

1.1 1.2 1.3 1.4 1.5 1.7 1.10 3.3 3.5 3.6 3.9 3.10 4.9

Make a chart listing all the areas/items you supervise and if they need daily cleaning, periodic cleaning, deep cleaning or frequent cleaning. Would any of this work be given to a contractor or agency? Would any additional staff training be needed to cover *periodic* or *deep cleaning* and how would you arrange for this training to take place?

1.6 Changes that may affect the service

Occasionally it is essential to make changes that may affect the housekeeping service; these changes may be temporary or more permanent changes. It is essential that all staff are informed of any changes and, where possible, be told of the reasons for the changes. Where the changes directly affect guest/customer expectations, they too must be kept fully informed and offered suitable alternatives where possible.

Activity

Because of a 'flu epidemic, a significant number of housekeeping staff have reported in sick. It is necessary to reschedule the remaining staff to cover the most essential areas first and some tasks will be completed later when some agency staff can be arranged. What procedure will you put in place to inform:

a) staff (including those in other departments), and
b) guests and conference delegates

about the changes that may affect the service?

1.7 3.6 3.7 3.8 Problems that may arise with the housekeeping service

Housekeeping can be a complex operation to run and inevitably there can be problems that may occur from time to time. When problems occur that may affect the housekeeping services, they must be carefully managed to avoid unnecessary disruption or a possible fall in standards of housekeeping provision. Even if disruption was unavoidable, an apology and explanation to guests will tend to ease the situation. However, it is not always part of the supervisor's role to find solutions or make difficult decisions and in certain situations they may not have the authority to deal with larger problems. These would need to be referred to a higher authority, usually part of the management team.

Activity 1

3.8

An assistant housekeeping manager more senior than you appears to be behaving unprofessionally. This includes sexist and racist comments about staff and repeating what has been heard in guest rooms. Why might you feel that it is outside the limits of your own authority to deal with this yourself? What could you do about it?

Some examples of possible problems and solutions are shown in Table 9.3.

Table 9.3 Example of problems faced by housekeeping departments and possible actions

Possible problems faced by housekeeping departments	Possible actions
Staffing problems The work is physically demanding and often relatively low-paid. The hours required may be considered undesirable. Staff shortages for a variety of reasons	Make sure that staff feel valued. This could be a simple thank you for good work completed or staff recognition awards, incentive and bonus schemes. Organise rotas in a fair way and, where possible, with some consistency and consideration for other commitments staff may have. Make sure staff are paid on time, this includes overtime payments. Discuss staff shortage problems with management; consider use of agency or casual staff at busy times.
Lack of communication between the team and with other departments Poor morale and motivation	Emphasise the importance of good communication and make this a regular part of staff briefings and training. Consider ways to motivate staff and keep them interested in the work they do.
Shortage of equipment and materials or poor quality equipment and materials	There must always be enough good quality equipment and materials for staff to be able to do the job well. If supplies are a problem, this needs to be discussed with management. This may also be done in writing or by email.
Faulty cleaning equipment	Make sure that equipment is checked and serviced regularly to avoid faults and breakdown.
Staff with poor verbal and written English skills	Speak clearly so that if English is not their first language, staff have a better chance of understanding. Encourage them to hold conversations with you. Suggest local English language courses.
Problems with services such as power cuts or water supply cuts Emergency evacuation and security alerts	These are likely to be completely unavoidable, however, contingency plans should be in place to minimise disruption as much as possible in such events. As long as staff and guests are kept fully informed of the situation and as much assistance as possible is given to try to avoid inconvenience, people are usually fairly understanding. Returning to normal service as quickly as possible will be appreciated.
Late deliveries of cleaning materials or linen from the laundry	Keep adequate stock of materials and buy from a reliable supplier who can guarantee prompt delivery. Do not let the levels of clean linen get too low and use what is available first in areas where rooms need to be re-let.
Rudeness from guests or angry guests Complaints	As a supervisor, you can often defuse the problem by listening to the full story from the member of staff then speaking calmly to the guest to resolve the issue.

Activity 2

3.7

At a review meeting it has been brought to the attention of staff that in customer feedback questionnaires there is a recurring complaint about towels not being replaced in bathrooms. You think this may be partly due to laundry deliveries arriving late. Draw up a list of action points the supervisors could work on to solve the problem.

1.8 1.9 1.10 2.7 4.7 4.8 4.10 Feedback on housekeeping services from staff and guests

Because housekeeping staff may be in direct contact with guests during completion of their work, they are often the first to hear positive or negative feedback about the services provided. It is important that staff are fully aware that they should pass this information to their supervisor promptly so that action can be taken where necessary. Staff should also be encouraged to discuss any concerns they themselves may have about the services being provided and staff briefing sessions are a good time to discuss these concerns.

Feedback from customers is extremely useful in determining whether or not what you are providing meets or even exceeds customer expectation.

The most usual way is to request that customers/guests complete a survey or questionnaire at some point during their stay or before departure. Feedback may also be from:
- telephone or email surveys to guests after their departure
- letters, cards or emails from guests
- comments or reports to reception at checkout
- the increasing use of social media review sites such as TripAdvisor, Expedia and Hotels.com.

Management will then need to decide the best way of using this useful information. When there are recurring comments, especially if they are negative, they need to be taken very seriously and appropriate actions planned and taken. When it is a formal complaint, the complaint needs to be investigated, then the person contacted with an apology and an explanation of what will be done to put the matter right. This could include a discount or complimentary items at a future stay. Social media sites also have a reply section where an explanation can be given for the complaint received.

Actions taken to avoid future complaints could involve changes in procedure, making sure expectations and promises are met and, inevitably, additional staff training may be necessary.

When using information and data from guests or staff, remember that it is essential and a legal requirement to keep any personal details confidential.

> **Complaints**
>
> Complaints and negative feedback can be used to improve the service you provide. Share the comments with management and with housekeeping staff and devise ways to make changes and get things right.

Managers and supervisors must remain aware that improvement is always possible and ways to improve services should constantly be reviewed and sought. However, remember that this should not just be a task for supervisors and managers; the actual staff completing housekeeping tasks will often come up with the best ideas for improvement because they are working in the actual areas where improvements may be made. They are likely to suggest practical measures, no matter how small, to provide a better service for guests. This is one of the reasons why staff briefings and good communication with staff are essential.

Understanding the requirements of housekeeping operations

2.2 2.5 Legislation

There are a number of areas of legislation that could affect housekeeping services. It is important for the supervisor to be aware of this legislation and understand it to ensure that all housekeeping procedures and activities remain within the law. They must also be aware of any changes and updates made to relevant legislation. Changes and updates to legislation do happen occasionally and the impact of changes must be regularly reviewed. This is of great importance to ensure that the housekeeping procedures comply with legal requirements. Always make sure that such changes are shared with the whole team where this affects their work.

The main items of legislation affecting housekeeping are as follows (more detail on these can be found in other chapters and on various websites):
- Health and Safety at Work Act (1974)
- Management of Health and Safety at Work Regulations 1999
- Personal Protective Equipment at Work Regulations 1992
- Manual Handling Operations Regulations 1992
- Provision and Use of Work Equipment Regulations 1998 (PUWER)
- Control of Substances Hazardous to Health (COSHH) 2002
- Workplace (Health, Safety and Welfare) Regulations 1992
- The Reporting of Injuries, Diseases, and Dangerous Occurrences Regulations (RIDDOR) 1995 (updated October 2013)
- Fire Precautions (Workplace) Regulations 1997
- The Electricity at Work Regulations 1989
- Lifting Operations and Lifting Equipment Regulations 1998 (LOLER)
- Noise at Work Regulations 1989
- The Health and Safety (First Aid) Regulations 1981
- Data Protection Act 1988
- Sale of Goods and Services Act 1982
- Health and Safety (Display Screen Equipment) Regulations 1992
- Equality Act 2010
- Race Relations Act 1977
- Asylum and Immigration Act 1996
- Sex Discrimination Act 1975
- Human Rights Act 1988
- Licencing Act 1964
- Working Time Regulations 1998
- National Minimum Wage Act 1998
- Equality Act 2010
- Disability Discrimination Act 1995.

2.1 2.3 Health and safety responsibilities

Responsibilities for health and safety within the housekeeping department and the whole establishment must be taken very seriously to ensure a duty of care for staff, visitors, guests and anyone else who may be present in the building. Maintaining high standards of health and safety provision and having these recorded and regularly updated is also a legal requirement.

Evidence 4
1.8 1.9 1.10 2.6 2.7
2.9 2.10 4.7 4.8 4.9
4.10

Collect a selection of customer/guest surveys and record your findings – both positive and negative. Identify any negative comments that appear twice or more and make some suggestions for solutions to the problems. What measures could you take to ensure that customer/guest comments remain confidential?

Activity 3
1.6

You have noticed that another supervisor has a list pinned to a notice board with all the names, addresses and phone numbers of the housekeeping staff in her team.

What is wrong with doing this and to which legislation does it relate?

What could you suggest to make sure that all supervisors were up to date with current legislation and the implications it may have on housekeeping teams?

All housekeeping procedures and tasks must be completed, with health and safety matters given high priority. All housekeeping staff must be made aware of the importance of health and safety procedures and partake in ongoing training to enable them to work to high standards of health and safety, as well as complying with legal responsibilities.

A breach of health and safety legislation could have a serious impact on:
- **Customers** – they could be injured or harmed in some way. They could take legal action against the establishment, would be unlikely to return and very damaging publicity could also result.
- **Staff** – staff should expect to remain safe and healthy while carrying out their work. They must receive the necessary training to enable them to work safely and carry out their employment effectively. Staff who are injured or become unwell in the course of their work may take legal action against their employer. This may involve significant costs and compensation to be paid. Injured employees may also need time away from work to recover.
- **The organisation** – the organisation has legal obligations under health and safety legislation to ensure the safety of staff, guests and everyone else using the building. Breaches in compliance to the legislation can result in illness, injury, compensation claims, warnings, fines, court cases, negative publicity and possibly even closure of the business.

Aims of health and safety legislation
- To secure the health, safety and welfare of people at work.
- Providing regulations and approved codes of practice which set the standards of health, safety and welfare.
- To establish the health and safety requirements for different areas of the workplace.
- To protect people other than employees who may be in the area, for example, guests, customers, contractors, suppliers and others, against any health and safety risks within the workplace.
- To control the keeping and use of dangerous substances such as explosive, corrosive, highly flammable or otherwise dangerous materials.

Evidence 5
1.4 1.5 2.1 2.2 2.3 4.3

1. Collect COSHH data sheets for the main chemicals/cleaning materials used in your area. List any health and safety information given to staff. Do they know where to find information on health and safety matters? List any health and safety posters or leaflets in your area and state how you make staff aware of these and their meaning.
2. What is the advice/training given to staff on manual handling and moving/lifting housekeeping items? Are staff in your area allowed to use stepladders? If so, what is the advice/training given to them?
3. Produce a short explanation leaflet for staff about their own responsibilities with regard to health and safety and the Health and Safety at Work Act 1974. In the leaflet explain to staff the implications that a breach in health and safety responsibilities could have on themselves, colleagues, customers and the organisation.

2.4 Storing information about customers and staff: Data Protection Act 1988

The Data Protection Act controls how personal information is used by organisations, businesses or the government. To comply with the Act, everyone with access to personal data must follow strict rules, making sure the information is:
- used fairly and lawfully
- used for limited and specific purposes
- used in an adequate, relevant non-excessive way
- accurate
- only kept as long as absolutely necessary
- used within people's data protection rights
- kept safe and secure
- not transferred outside the UK without adequate protection.

There is stronger legal protection for more sensitive information such as information on ethnic background, political opinions, religious beliefs, health, sexual health and criminal records.

In practical terms, for housekeeping departments this means that employers cannot disclose or display personal information about staff or guests to anyone else and they must only use it for strictly relevant purposes. Any personal information held by employers must be held in a secure system. This also applies to customers/guests. Their information and details must be kept secure and not passed on to anyone else without their permission. Also any information given to you verbally or overheard from guests must not be disclosed or repeated (unless for legal reasons).

2.6 2.8 The organisation's standards

Standards to be adopted throughout the organisation will probably be established by management or in a large organisation set centrally. Once standards are set, these must then be communicated to staff throughout the organisation and this can be done at induction, training, re-training briefings and formal courses.

The levels of training that staff need depends on their previous knowledge and experience, the capabilities of individuals and the standards the organisation wants to achieve. All staff need guidance and training on what is expected from them, the systems that are in place and the equipment and chemicals they will be using. They will also need instruction on the policy regarding expected behaviour with customers/guests, including politeness, greetings, entering guest rooms, and dealing with queries and complaints. They must understand the need to be respectful to guests and colleagues and also understand the position of trust in which they are placed by being present in guest rooms.

Personal standards

From the time an employee starts work (or even before this at interview), employees need to be given strict instructions about the personal standards required during their employment. This will include:
- personal hygiene
- correct wearing of uniform and shoes
- hair (and shaving for men)
- policy on cosmetics and jewellery
- hands and nails.

Customer care

Increasingly, the need for high standards of customer care is becoming apparent. Hospitality is a 'people industry' and looking after the customer/guest to make their stay enjoyable is very important. As well as the services provided for the guest by housekeeping, professional standards of politeness and greeting are also essential, as well as showing the guest that you are keen to do what you can to make their stay a memorable one. Make sure that staff can communicate well with guests and answer their questions when asked. They should, of course, always be tidy and with a clean and smart appearance. Hospitality is an increasingly competitive industry and customers tend to return to and recommend places where there is a commitment to customer care.

Figure 9.5 Housekeeping staff should think about their contribution to good customer care

2.9 2.10 Reviewing procedures

A business that constantly seeks to develop and improve their services is likely to remain a successful business. This is certainly true when considering housekeeping services because, as already stated, customer feedback and surveys rate good standards of housekeeping and general cleanliness as very important. Policies for improvement and development are likely to be made at a central or management level, but these must be communicated regularly and effectively to supervisors and to housekeeping operatives.

To remain effective, policies need to be reviewed regularly. Feedback from customers/guests is vitally important when doing this. There is no point in providing a service that no one wants or likes, so take feedback comments seriously and discuss ways to improve areas that cause dissatisfaction or build on areas that customers say they like and appreciate. If individual members of staff are praised in feedback, make sure it is passed on to the individuals and consider ways to share this good practice with other team members. If someone is named in a less positive way, discuss this with the individual; further or refresher training may be needed. When setting or reviewing policy, the supervisor provides a very important link between management levels and those working as part of the practical housekeeping team. Procedures may be suggested by management but the supervisor will have the practical knowledge of the likely success.

Understanding how to supervise housekeeping operations

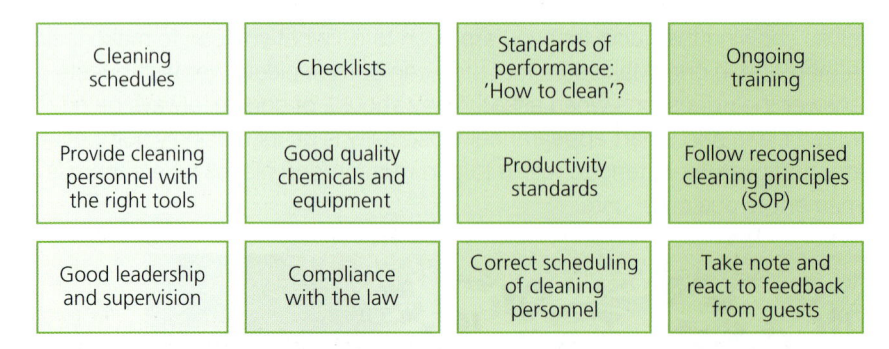

Cleaning schedules	Checklists	Standards of performance: 'How to clean'?	Ongoing training
Provide cleaning personnel with the right tools	Good quality chemicals and equipment	Productivity standards	Follow recognised cleaning principles (SOP)
Good leadership and supervision	Compliance with the law	Correct scheduling of cleaning personnel	Take note and react to feedback from guests

Figure 9.6 Tools for achieving high standards of housekeeping

3.2 3.3 Materials, equipment, machinery and tools

Most premises will have a range of surfaces and finishes that need to be cleaned and looked after by housekeeping teams. They could be loosely described as:

- **Hard surfaces** such as stainless steel, wood, various plastic finishes, marble, stone, ceramics. There are various ways of cleaning such surfaces and each must be planned and fully recorded on cleaning schedules. For example, a large ceramic floor in an entrance lobby may be cleaned at night using a large cleaning machine with rotating cleaning pads. Specialist cleaning fluids would be used with the machine. However, a marble counter would probably need wiping with a damp cloth and very dilute detergent, then drying with a dry cloth or paper roll.
- **Painted surfaces** would be dusted or damp-dusted every day but more thorough cleaning done periodically.
- **Soft surfaces** would include carpets, mats and rugs. Generally, a daily vacuum clean is all that is needed, but occasionally stain removal will be required, with a thorough carpet clean completed every six months or annually.
- **Furnishings** such as upholstered furniture, cushions, chair covers and curtains also benefit from vacuum cleaning to remove dust, grit and possibly crumbs and specialist vacuum cleaner tools may be used for this. Occasional treatment for stains may also be necessary. Once again, a more thorough clean should be completed periodically by shampooing, steaming, dry cleaning or laundering.

A wide range of cleaning materials and tools will be used throughout the housekeeping department and their selection will depend on:
- the size of the premises
- standards to be achieved
- the decision to contract out certain tasks such as interior window cleaning
- types of fixtures, fittings and furnishings to be cleaned
- skills of staff
- budgets available
- purchasing contracts (in a large group, these may be purchased on a central contract).

Cleaning agents

It is very important to use the correct cleaning chemicals for the work to be carried out. Be certain that all staff are trained in the correct use of cleaning materials and the surfaces on which they should be used. They are often all purchased from the same supplier, which may offer the greatest discounts, but it is still a good idea to investigate what other suppliers can offer occasionally. Remember that the cheapest option is not necessarily the most economic as more materials may need to be used to get the same effect as the more expensive product. Cleaning chemicals often arrive in bulk containers to be decanted into smaller containers or spray bottles. Make sure these are clearly marked with the product name/number. Sometimes they are in a concentrated form and need to be diluted with water. Make sure staff have had the necessary training to do this accurately. It is best if just one person is responsible for this; it is often done by porters on a night shift.

Make sure that all cleaning chemicals are stored correctly, preferably in a lockable cupboard with limited access. Individual items must be clearly labelled and with instructions for use, especially when they have been decanted into a small container or spray bottle from a larger container.

> **Liquid chemicals**
>
> Liquid chemicals are now often distinguished by a letter/number code, e.g. D10. This can be useful for operatives whose first language is not English. They are often different colours for easy identification.

> **Take it further**
>
> Housekeeping staff must know the importance of using the correct chemical for each job in accordance with their training. They must also use protective clothing or equipment (PPE) where recommended. All staff must be made aware (and frequently reminded) that they must not mix different chemicals. This is very dangerous and could cause harmful toxic fumes or cause skin damage.

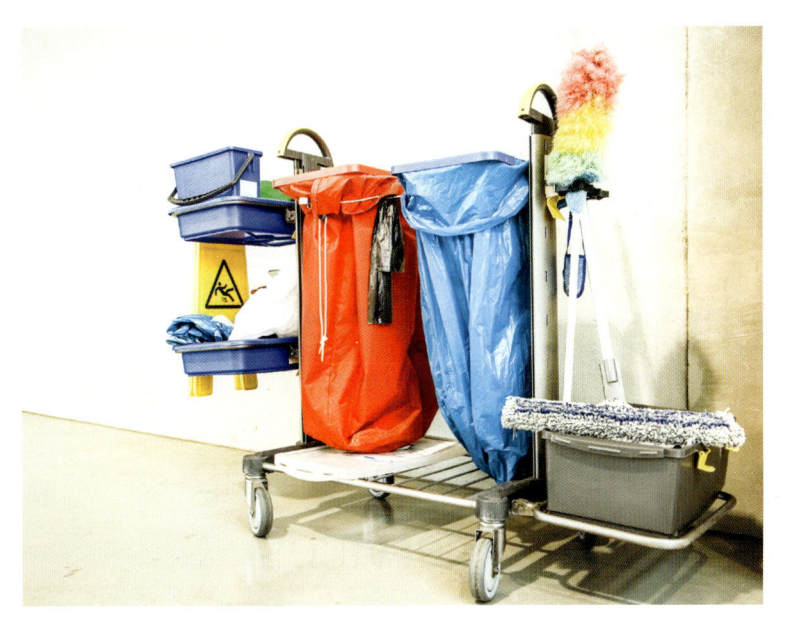

Figure 9.7 Housekeeping staff use a variety of chemicals and equipment

Cleaning chemicals will probably include:
- detergent – liquid, cream, liquid spray or powder
- toilet cleaner – liquid, gel or powder
- descaler – liquid, gel or powder
- sanitiser – usually a spray liquid
- glass and mirror cleaner – liquid or spray liquid
- disinfectant – liquid, gel, spray or powder
- stain removers – liquid, liquid spray, powder
- polishes – solid block, liquid spray.

It is essential that all staff know that they must always follow the manufacturer's instructions for use of cleaning chemicals. Even if products look the same, instructions for their safe use may be different. Do not assume that staff will read the instructions on products – correct use needs to be part of staff training and reviews. All chemicals should have the accompanying data sheets as provided by the manufacturer. Staff need to be aware of COSHH regulations and undergo the

> **Take it further**
>
> COSHH (Control of Substances Hazardous to Health) Regulations 2002 state that employers must protect employees and other persons from the hazards of substances used at work by use of risk assessments and putting safe measures in place.

necessary training to ensure safe chemical use. All chemicals must be labelled and stored properly in an appropriate place and only be accessible to those authorised to use them, in line with legislation.

Cleaning tools and equipment

A range of small equipment will include:
- brooms – hard and soft bristle
- dustpan and brush – hard and soft bristle
- mops for wet and dry use and mop buckets – could be colour coded for different areas
- cloths/dusters – likely to be colour coded for different areas
- extending dusters for higher areas.

To keep these in good condition, make sure they are cleaned after use. Cloths for wet or damp areas should be thoroughly washed and rinsed and allowed to air dry; the same for mops. Dry dusters should be washed frequently.

A range of larger equipment will include:
- vacuum cleaners
- hard floor cleaners/polishers
- steam cleaners.

> **Evidence 6**
>
> 1.4 1.5 2.1 3.2 3.3
>
> List all of the chemicals and cleaning materials used in your area and prepare a chart of the surfaces/places each could be used. Include details of the personal protective equipment (PPE) needed.

Staff must not use machinery until they have been trained in its correct use as recommended by the manufacturer. Training should include the importance of using the correct piece of equipment and attachments for the job. They should also use the appropriate PPE (personal protective equipment). Make sure that all electrical equipment is safety tested by a qualified electrician at least once a year. This is especially important when the machine uses water too. The appropriate staff should always return the machine to the correct storage area directly after use, in a clean state, ready for reuse. All water tanks and dust bags should be emptied. Make sure that all staff know the procedure for reporting faulty equipment and to do this promptly.

Monitoring and reviewing housekeeping services

Even when it is considered that a housekeeping service is successful and everything is going well, it is important to constantly strive for improvement by monitoring the current situation and deciding if there are ways to do things better. All parts of the housekeeping service need to be monitored and reviewed but special attention may be given to the areas listed below.

4.1 Monitoring use of resources

Housekeeping resources such as machinery, equipment and cleaning materials are expensive. A supervisor is in a good position to monitor their use and check there is no misuse during the everyday operation of the housekeeping service. For example, a chemical cleaner needing dilution will cost twice as much if made up twice as strong as it needs to be. Misuse of equipment can result in damage and breakdown; equipment that is not cared for properly is more likely to wear faster and need earlier replacement. Much of a monitoring procedure can be completed by observation and questioning, but keeping careful records of equipment maintenance, chemical usage and small equipment replacement will also enable monitoring.

4.2 4.3 4.4 Monitoring responsibilities and training needs

Monitoring of actual standards of work being completed is always essential to maintaining housekeeping standards. There are a number of ways that this can be done, including observation of work being completed, checking of finished work and referring to customer/guest feedback. However, this is not just about checking; housekeeping staff must understand their own responsibilities in relation to achieving high standards. This may be achieved through ongoing staff training, reviews, appraisals, briefings, updates, one-to-one discussions and team meetings. Remember that praise where it is due, along with positive feedback, comments and appraisals, can go a long way in maintaining standards and motivating staff to complete their work well. Employee recognition and awards schemes also communicate to individuals that their efforts are appreciated.

Checking rooms and areas after they have been serviced is a regular part of the supervisor's role. Checks should include: standards of cleanliness, all electrical items working, everything in good repair, towels and small room items placed correctly, complimentary products in the right place. An experienced supervisor will soon spot anything that is wrong, but an accepted way to check is to stand in the room and run the eyes slowly round the room in a clockwise direction.

4.5 4.6 Record keeping

To **monitor**, plan and **review** effectively, accurate records must be kept. These could be:

- expenditure and budget records
- staff contact details
- staff working hours, rotas and staff absence
- holiday records
- records of staff training and planned training that still needs to be completed
- maintenance records (planned and emergency maintenance)
- stock levels of materials, linen and other items
- cleaning schedules and operational procedures
- chemical data information
- periodic cleaning plans
- preferences of regular guests, e.g. non allergenic pillows.

These records need to be kept in a safe and secure way, especially where there are personal details about individuals. It will be necessary to establish who is allowed access to secure information.

Increasingly workplace records are stored on electronic systems and there will be polices for the safe and correct use of these systems. However, there is still a place for paper-based records in many situations. Records are only useful if accurate and kept up to date and this is a task frequently allocated to the supervisor. Whether the record is on paper or computer, enter the relevant information promptly and store in the correct place so it can be accessed by authorised personnel, such as other supervisors or management. Bear in mind that some individuals not familiar with using computer systems may need training to enter and use the information correctly.

Evidence 7

1.1 1.2 1.3 1.5 2.6
4.1 4.2 4.4

Design a checklist specific to your own working area that you can easily use to check that the work of your staff is meeting all of the standards required from them.

Key terms

Monitor — supervising activities in progress to ensure they are on schedule to meet the objectives and performance targets

Review — to carefully consider a procedure and perhaps make changes to it

> **Evidence 8**
>
> `1.4` `2.4` `3.10` `4.1` `4.3` `4.5` `4.6` `4.8`
>
> - What information relating to your housekeeping supervision role is kept on an electronic system? Is any of this information confidential (for example, staff contact details)? If so, how is it kept secure and who has access to it?
> - For more general electronic storage and information, make a simple list for staff, telling them how to use the system and access the files they need.
> - Is electronic feedback from customers/guests used? If so how is this retrieved and stored?
> - Prepare a list of advantages and disadvantages of a housekeeping department moving to a fully electronic recording system.

The advantages of using computer systems for records include the following:
- They can be fast to use and can be updated quickly.
- Preprogrammed systems can be used.
- They may be linked with wider computer systems in the establishment.
- They can be accessed anywhere in the building where there is a computer or other suitable electronic device.
- With required permission, can be accessed from outside the premises.
- Calculations of stock levels can be performed quickly and minimum stock levels can generate reordering procedures.
- Can eliminate cumbersome paper storage and, if properly backed up, information is less likely to get lost. Electronic systems tend to be more environmentally friendly than paper systems.

However, do remember that not all staff may be familiar with computer use so some may need additional training. Also, if total reliance is placed on computer systems, they can occasionally fail which would cause disruption.

The advantages of using paper-based systems for records include the following:
- They can be used anywhere in the building without the need for special equipment.
- Some staff may feel more familiar and comfortable with paper systems.
- Comparison of several pages at the same time is possible.
- Centrally stored files can be easy to access by different authorised people.

However, paper systems can be bulky and need significant space for storage. Loose papers can get lost. Paper systems may take longer to use and update. It may be more difficult to see the 'whole picture', for example, the stock levels of cleaning chemicals stored on every floor.

Knowledge check

1. List three different staff positions in a housekeeping team in a large establishment. What would be the expected duties of each position?
2. What is meant by scheduling? How may it be decided how much work should be allocated to each team member?
3. What are the points you would consider when allocating housekeeping staff to various tasks in your area?
4. When are the times you may need to recruit extra agency staff? What are three advantages and three disadvantages of employing staff from an agency?
5. Suggest five tasks completed routinely within housekeeping that would be covered by health and safety legislation.
6. What are the main purposes of the Data Protection Act 1988? How does this Act affect the day-to-day working of a housekeeping department?
7. What are the reasons you would present to management for transferring the paper-based records in the department to an electronic system?
8. In your own organisation, which other departments are directly linked to housekeeping? Why is good communication with these departments essential?
9. As a supervisor, suggest three procedures or information that may need to be monitored. How would you do this?
10. What are the most important points you would communicate to new staff working in your area on the personal standards required? What are the ways of checking that all staff are keeping to these standards?

Assignment

`1.1` `1.2` `1.4` `1.5` `2.1` `3.2` `4.3` `4.5`

You are in charge of equipping a new 100-bedroom city centre hotel with the required housekeeping supplies, equipment and machinery.

1. List the cleaning items and equipment needed to be in place ready for opening.
2. Make recommendations for storage of chemicals and equipment.
3. How would you record levels of stock for consumable items?
4. Suggest the training that housekeeping staff would need to use and store equipment and chemicals.
5. What are the health and safety measures that need to be in place to legally cover the use of the new machinery?

Evidence checklist

Evidence presented for this chapter must come from the candidate's work in a suitable hospitality workplace when supervising housekeeping services. There must be sufficient evidence that the candidate can achieve the learning objectives and assessment criteria on a consistent basis.

Evidence checklist		
Assessment criteria		**Possible evidence**
1.1	Schedule housekeeping procedures at suitable intervals to ensure the standards of the housekeeping service are maintained	Evidence activity 1 Evidence activity 3 Evidence activity 7
1.2	Allocate housekeeping duties to staff	Evidence activity 1 Evidence activity 3 Evidence activity 7
1.3	Brief staff on housekeeping duties including: ● procedures ● work routines ● standards of behaviour ● how to communicate with customers and other members of staff	Evidence activity 1 Evidence activity 2 Evidence activity 3 Evidence activity 7
1.4	Ensure staff have the skills, knowledge and resources needed	Evidence activity 1 Evidence activity 2 Evidence activity 3 Evidence activity 5 Evidence activity 6 Evidence activity 8
1.5	Ensure staff follow the housekeeping procedures	Evidence activity 2 Evidence activity 3 Evidence activity 5 Evidence activity 6 Evidence activity 7
1.6	Inform staff and customers about any changes that may affect the service	Activity 3

Evidence checklist		
Assessment criteria		**Possible evidence**
1.7	Manage any problems that may disrupt the housekeeping service	Evidence activity 3
1.8	Collect feedback on the services from staff and customers	Evidence activity 4 Evidence activity 8
1.9	Monitor and review procedures to ensure the housekeeping service meets the needs of customers	Evidence activity 4
1.10	Recommend ways of improving housekeeping operations following the organisation's requirements	Evidence activity 3 Evidence activity 4
2.1	Describe the health and safety standards that need to be followed with regards to the housekeeping service	Evidence activity 5 Evidence activity 6
2.2	Explain how legislation affects housekeeping procedures	Evidence activity 5
2.3	Explain the impact that a breach of health and safety standards could have on: ● customers ● staff ● the organisation	Evidence activity 2 Evidence activity 5
2.4	Describe the legal requirements in relation to storing information about customers, staff and their comments	Evidence activity 8
2.5	Explain the importance of regularly reviewing the implications of legal requirements	Evidence activity 5 Evidence activity 8
2.6	Identify the organisation's standards for ● personal presentation ● customer care ● behaviour of staff	Evidence activity 1 Evidence activity 2 Evidence activity 4 Evidence activity 7
2.7	Describe the procedures for obtaining and recording feedback from customers and staff	Evidence activity 4
2.8	Explain how the organisation's policies can affect the development of procedures for the housekeeping service	Evidence activity 2
2.9	Explain the importance of reviewing procedures	Evidence activity 4
2.10	Explain how to review procedures	Evidence activity 4
3.1	Explain the economic importance of an effective customer-focused housekeeping service to the organisation and its staff members	Evidence activity 2
3.2	Describe how different cleaning agents, materials and tools should be: ● used ● stored	Evidence activity 6
3.3	Describe how different surfaces and materials should be maintained	Evidence activity 3 Evidence activity 6
3.4	Describe the roles and responsibilities of individuals in the organisation and department relevant to the housekeeping service	Evidence activity 1
3.5	Explain how the housekeeping service integrates with other departments	Evidence activity 2 Evidence activity 3
3.6	Identify the problems that may arise with the housekeeping service	Evidence activity 2 Evidence activity 3

Evidence checklist		
Assessment criteria		**Possible evidence**
3.7	Explain how to deal with problems with the housekeeping service	Activity 2
3.8	Explain the limits of own authority when dealing with problems	Activity 1
3.9	Explain how to allocate work to staff	Evidence activity 1 Evidence activity 3
3.10	Explain how to choose appropriate methods to brief staff including: ● verbal instructions ● written instructions ● demonstrations ● diagrams	Evidence activity 3 Evidence activity 8
4.1	Explain how to monitor the use of housekeeping resources	Evidence activity 7 Evidence activity 8
4.2	Explain how to monitor responsibilities to ensure standards are maintained	Evidence activity 7
4.3	Explain how to identify training needs to ensure that staff have the skills and knowledge needed	Evidence activity 2 Evidence activity 5 Evidence activity 8
4.4	Explain how to motivate staff when giving them feedback	Evidence activity 7
4.5	Describe the different ways of completing and storing computerised and paper-based records	Evidence activity 8
4.6	Compare the advantages and disadvantages of computerised and paper-based records	
4.7	Explain the importance of collecting feedback on the service from customers and staff	Evidence activity 4
4.8	Explain the importance of confidentiality when collecting feedback on the housekeeping service	Evidence activity 4 Evidence activity 8
4.9	Explain how to alter work allocation in order to improve the service	Evidence activity 3 Evidence activity 4
4.10	Explain how to recommend ways of improving the housekeeping service	Evidence activity 4

In addition to generation of evidence suggested throughout the chapter, the following may be used as part of your evidence:
- observation of your work by someone senior to you
- products of your work – documents, letters, plans, etc.
- witness testimony
- professional discussion
- candidate statements about work completed
- observation sheets
- video clips
- housekeeping/cleaning schedules
- notes of meetings with line manager
- meeting agendas
- staff rotas
- team briefing notes

- plans for functions involving housekeeping
- housekeeping records
- witness statements
- records of professional discussion
- oral questions
- written questions
- project
- reflective account
- records of oral questioning
- question/answer sheets
- relevant photographs, plans and sketches
- forms or other information produced by you.

CHAPTER 10

Supervise reception services

This chapter is about looking at how to plan the work of your team through reviewing upcoming reservations and managing staffing levels. You need to provide your team with all the up-to-date information on the organisation's services and their prices. It must include how they must comply with the regulations outlined in relevant legislation. Also you and your team must understand how to manage customer problems effectively.

Learning objectives

On completion of this chapter, you should:
1 Be able to supervise reception services.
2 Understand the policies and procedures relating to supervising reception services.
3 Understand how to supervise reception services.

2.2 3.1 3.2 3.13 Introduction

The reception department is the first point of contact for any customer arriving at the organisation. It is in these moments that a customer's first impressions will be formed and therefore it is even more important that staff are professional in their appearance and their behaviour. The reception can be considered as the centre of a hospitality organisation as customers will normally go to the reception if they have any queries or complaints, and commonly customers will settle their bills at reception (such as in hotels). The reception team needs up-to-date knowledge on the whole organisation in order to be able to deal with these customers effectively, including:
- names and contact details of key staff in other departments
- opening hours of all outlets
- services offered by other departments and their prices
- special offers.

It is often the reception team within an organisation that will connect the customer to the service they seek and this transition needs to be as seamless as possible.

To work in reception, staff need the following qualities:
- a friendly personality
- a genuine smile
- smart grooming
- excellent spoken and written communication abilities

- confidence to deal with challenging customers
- the ability to work under pressure and prioritise workload
- IT skills.

The main activities of the reception department are as follows:
- greeting, assisting and/or directing customers and visitors
- answering incoming calls and handling enquiries
- redirecting calls and taking accurate messages, where appropriate
- answering enquiries via email
- managing a booking system
- maintaining customer records
- keeping the reception area clean and tidy.

Other activities could include:
- taking payments
- **rooming** hotel guests
- managing the visitors' book and signing-out passes
- booking transport
- cash handling.

> **Key term**
>
> **Rooming** – when a receptionist escorts a hotel guest to their room and performs a short tour of its amenities and features

Evidence 1

`1.8` `3.1` `3.2` `3.3` `3.5` `3.7` `3.11` `3.12` `3.13`

1. What are the other departments or areas that reception needs to communicate with? Who may they need to communicate with outside of the organisation? What could be the outcome if communication was not good?
2. List all the resources needed for the smooth running of your area. What are the services that you can offer to a guest? How?
3. Who needs to approve the use of additional resources?
4. How do you inform customers and staff about service changes?

More evidence

Find a telephone/contact list for those you need to communicate with. Collect leaflets or information about existing guest services.

Evidence 2

`1.1` `1.2` `1.4` `1.5` `1.6` `1.7` `1.14` `2.2`

Reception staff will deal with customers face to face on a regular basis. Prepare an information leaflet for new staff covering:
- personal presentation and behaviour standards
- greeting guests
- and the main requirements for working procedure and routine.

Mention legal requirements that affect reception areas and how to deal with problems that occur. Provide details of who to contact if there are questions they want to ask.

The role of the reception department

3.4 Service targets and standards

Every reception department will have slightly different service standards, depending on the type of organisation, but each one will aim to achieve the following targets:
- direct customer contact prioritised over other reception duties
- customers greeted promptly and without delay
- transactions completed discreetly to ensure guests' security
- customers informed of facilities and services accurately.

1.1 2.1 Reception legislation

Reception departments are required to comply with all relevant legislation and as a supervisor, you must ensure staff are trained on how to comply, including:
- **Regulatory Reform (Fire Safety) Order 2005** – plans and procedures for evacuating customers in the event of a fire. The reception team must record details of any disabled customers (who will require assistance to leave) in the building and formally hand over this information at shift change.
- **Guest register** – reception are required to maintain a register of all guests, including the passport numbers of all overseas guests.
- **Health and safety** – reception should supply clear information on who to contact in the case of an emergency, with multilingual instructions or diagram for the fire evacuation procedure.
- **Licensing** – often the night manager in a hotel reception will be a personal licence holder, as one needs to be present at all times to comply with licensing regulations.
- **Data Protection Act** – reception are responsible for storing guests' details and, to comply with Data Protection legislation, access to the information must be limited to reduce the risk of fraud or theft.
- **Consumer Protection from Unfair Trading Regulations 2008** – reception must comply with these regulations by describing accurately in any printed or verbal communication the prices and services available, including the cancellation policy.
- **Equality Act 2010** – reception staff must welcome all guests without discrimination in relation to gender, sexual orientation, disability, race, religion or belief.

Evidence 3
1.1 1.3 1.12 1.14 2.1 2.4 2.5

Complete a review of the legal requirements that affect your area and highlight any areas where you think there may not be full compliance. Recommend what should be done and, where necessary, some easy to understand instructions for staff to ensure compliance.

1.6 **1.14** **2.7** **3.11** **3.12** **3.14** **Arrival**

The reception area must be kept presentable at all times as the customer's arrival is an important part of the customer's experience with the organisation and indicates what levels of service the customer can expect throughout their stay. Any customer or visitor must be greeted promptly and not kept waiting; if there is a wait, then acknowledge them, apologise for the wait and tell them that you or your colleague will be with them as soon as possible. When you do interact with your customer (or any other type of visitor to the organisation), remember the following rules:

- Smile.
- Do not interrupt or assume you know what they are saying.
- Listen carefully.
- Use positive language.
- Be aware of and sensitive to different cultures.
- Keep the customer informed of any changes to the services they are expecting.

Records

On arrival, the customer's details should be taken and recorded using a computerised system.

The information can include the following:
- name and title
- address
- telephone number
- email address
- duration of their visit/stay
- the agreed rate for their stay
- car registration
- special requests
- signature
- **pre-authorisation** of a credit card

> **Key term**
>
> **Pre-authorisation** – a process in which a credit card is checked to ensure a certain amount of funds are available to spend

Registration card			
Name	**Nationality**		
Address			
City or town	Car registration no.		
Date of arrival	Date of departure		
Method of payment	☐ Credit card	☐ Cash	☐ Cheque
Room rate	☐ Dinner		☐ Bed & breakfast
Newspaper ordered			Checkout time: 10am
Signatur		Room no	

Figure 10.1 Hotel registration card

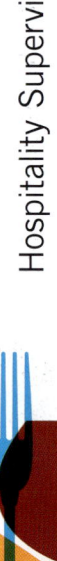

This information can be obtained through the reservation records if the customer has booked in advance. These reservations are often taken by reception but some establishments have a separate team for this. For regular customers, details of preferences can be recorded and the history used to meet the expectations of the customer in future visits. For example, if a regular guest has expressed appreciation for a particular room, then that room can be reserved for their future stays.

> **Evidence 4**
>
> **1.3** **1.5** **1.10** **1.13** **2.4** **3.5** **3.14**
>
> Collect all the records and forms used in your area including those used for performance review/appraisal. Find a feedback form or questionnaire given to customers and any analysis of these.

Promotional offers

A customer's arrival or check-in is an optimum time to explain and upsell other services in the hotel. By asking polite and probing questions at this stage, a receptionist will be better able to identify the customer's needs and promote the business. For example, the receptionist could ask, 'How was your journey?' If the customer has had a long and tiresome journey, the receptionist could suggest coffee being sent to the room or a relaxing massage in the spa. Another question could be, 'Do you have any plans while here?' If the customer is there for business and has no dinner plans, the receptionist could recommend the hotel restaurant.

Knowledge of any current promotional offers within the organisation can be used as an advantage when upselling, as the customer will enjoy feeling that they are getting value for money.

Figure 10.2 Reception staff should always after good customer service as they are the first point of contact for customers

1.10 Departure

When preparing a customer's bill, the reception team need to ensure the charges from each department are accurate. They must have clear and up-to-date information on prices and services currently offered throughout the organisation as any of the following could be included in the charges:
- accommodation
- breakfast, lunch or dinner
- drinks
- room service and/or mini bar
- telephone calls
- newspapers
- spa treatments
- laundry.

In most organisations charges are automatically added to the customer's bill from the relevant department they come from, but reception must always be mindful of the processes. For example, if a customer is leaving particularly early, a proficient receptionist might check that the food and beverage department has had time to post any charges incurred at breakfast.

When a customer's bill is presented, it must be an accurate itemised breakdown of all charges incurred and a receipt and copy of the bill must be issued to the customer.

Collecting feedback

During this transaction, the receptionist should seek feedback from the customer and encourage them to return. Any compliments or comments should be recorded in the database of guest history by the staff member.

Reception supervisor's duties

1.2 3.5 Allocating duties and estimating resource requirements

A reception supervisor must plan the work of the reception team by:
- Analysing upcoming business levels such as large groups arriving or departing.
- Checking the number of bookings for the weeks ahead.
- Scrutinising the staff levels, including any approved staff holidays.
- Writing a rota that will sufficiently cover peak periods such as check-in and check-out times.
- Initiating and supporting the handover meeting.
- Communicating all the information that the reception team members need to do their jobs successfully.
- Co-ordinating and helping to deliver any required training.

1.3 1.4 1.8 1.9 3.8 Handover

A reception supervisor should be present at the **handover** meeting to check that all key staff members are present. At this meeting the supervisor can check the grooming of the team arriving for duty and feed back any changes required for staff members to be in line with organisational grooming standards. Any issues

Key term

Handover – a meeting at shift change to communicate essential information between staff on one shift to the staff on the next shift arising from the previous shift must be explained in detail, including any follow-up action required. Any changes to normal services must be highlighted, such as maintenance issues putting rooms out of service, or changes to pricing due to promotions and special offers, so that the reception team can accurately inform the customers. Handover can also be used as a regular opportunity for refresher training to keep teams focused on targets and/or new processes. Short team-building activities can be undertaken to raise morale and feelings of belonging. Team-building activities can help to keep the tone of the handover meeting informal, which will encourage staff to feel comfortable enough to ask questions if they do not understand something.

1.5　1.7　1.13　2.3　2.4　Reception training

As with all hospitality job roles, effective training procedures are essential to ensure the reception team achieve organisational standards of performance. From the beginning of their employment within the reception team, staff must have the following clearly explained to them through training and reinforced through supporting documents:

- Reception procedures and processes.
- Procedures and processes of other relevant departments.
- Standards of presentation required.
- Standards of behaviour required.

The reception team should be provided with access to written policies and procedures such as training manuals in order to be able to refer to them if they are unsure. The information should be easily accessible to allow the staff member to be efficient for the customer. Procedures should be explained simply and clearly (such as being broken down into steps) to allow the information to be reviewed quickly. Task checklists can be used to help remind the staff member of all the duties they are required to do. Including a column for the staff member to input the time and their signature allows the supervisor to review this information and monitor the performance of the team. By reviewing the times entered by staff members, the supervisor can see how they are prioritising and managing their workloads and any potential areas for improvement can be highlighted in feedback meetings with individuals.

2.6　3.3　3.9　3.10　Dealing with problems in reception

Reception is often the point of contact for a customer when they wish to make a complaint, whether it is during their stay or on check-out/departure. It is common for the reception team to discount on services as compensation for complaints and problems that a customer has experienced. The size of discount that will be given to a customer directly correlates to the level in severity of the complaint. Reception staff can be encouraged to handle minor issues themselves by being allocated a maximum amount to spend on recovering a situation. For example, £20 allows the reception team the ability to offer complimentary tea, coffee or drinks as a gesture when a mistake has been made. A reception supervisor may be allocated £100 which could mean the ability to offer a complimentary meal. Any issue which is that severe or more should be communicated to your manager. If the customer is demanding further compensation, then a supervisor must seek authority from their manager.

> ### Evidence 5
> `1.1` `1.3` `1.11` `2.4` `2.5` `2.6` `2.7` `3.4` `3.15`
>
> Collect the establishment's:
> - policy/mission statement
> - discount policy and any recent promotions or discounts
> - complaints policy.
>
> How should promotional offers be handled?

If other departments in the organisation have not fully informed the reception team of problems or changes, then the following consequences may occur:

1. The guest will be even more frustrated at having to explain their problems repeatedly.
2. The receptionist is not equipped with the information to correctly deal with the complaint.
3. A breakdown of communication, rapport and goodwill between the departments.
4. Lowered morale in the teams.
5. A greater compensation than required may be agreed.
6. Damage to the reputation of the department and the organisation.
7. Unnecessary loss of loyalty from the customer.
8. Unnecessary loss of revenue to the organisation.

If a problem has occurred due to the mistake of a team member from another department, then the supervisor must report it to the manager of that department for them to deal with. A reception supervisor does not have the authority to correct the actions of staff from other departments and by trying to do so, will cause damage to working relationships. Similarly, when handling a complaint linked to another department, a supervisor must listen to what happened from the point of view of all the staff involved, as often customers will embellish their version of events to increase their chances of compensation. The facts must be ascertained before any discount is agreed upon.

> ### Evidence 6
> `1.9` `1.11` `2.3` `2.5` `3.3` `3.6` `3.10` `3.15`
>
> List the sorts of things that could go wrong in the day-to-day running of a reception area. Make a contingency plan to deal with the problems you have outlined. How would you advise receptionists to deal with a customer complaint?
>
> What are the limits of your authority for dealing with problems?

`1.11` `1.12` `2.5` `3.6` `3.7` Improving reception services

Monitor and record all the customer service problems that your team encounters. Use examples of issues as training topics in your handover meetings. Outline the scenarios to the group without mentioning any names and discuss possible actions that could have been taken to remedy the situation and recover customer satisfaction. Best practice is to choose three possible solutions that the group have suggested and evaluate which would be the most successful to all parties (the customer, the staff member, the department and the organisation). Your team will benefit from a raised awareness of the contingencies available when dealing with customer problems. Invite staff from other departments to collaborate in this exercise as they may bring a useful perspective that had not been considered, and involving them in the process will increase the likelihood of their approving the use of any additional resources that may be required. By using this method, you may also identify ways of improving the reception service which you can suggest to your manager for approval. If a new procedure is to be implemented, then it is important to communicate this clearly and train all staff who will be involved, including those from other departments, on the execution of the new/updated procedure to prevent confusion.

For more detail on handling customer complaints, see Chapter 14, 'Monitor and solve customer service problems'.

Assignment

1.3　1.4　1.6　1.7　1.9　1.10　1.14　2.2　2.4　2.6　2.7　3.4　3.11　3.13　3.15

You are involved in the opening of a new city centre hotel and have been given the responsibility to supervise the set up and opening of the reception area. You have been asked to investigate the needs of the new area and report back to management on the following:
- How the staff need to be trained and the topics they need to cover, including how to deal with problems and complaints.
- The overall look and appearance of the reception area and the targets/standards required from reception.
- Communication standards and greetings to be used when dealing with customers and other areas staff will need to communicate with.
- The required forms and recording documents needed in reception, including guest feedback, promotions and discounts.
- The relevant legislation that affects the reception area.

Knowledge check

1. What is the purpose of a pre-authorisation?
2. Why is the personal presentation of the reception staff important?
3. What legislation must the reception team comply with?
4. How can a reception supervisor ensure that their team is following procedures?

\multicolumn{3}{l	}{**Evidence checklist**}
\multicolumn{2}{l	}{**Assessment criteria**}	**Possible evidence**
1.1	Ensure the reception service complies with relevant legislation and organisational policy	Evidence activity 2 Evidence activity 3 Evidence activity 5 Evidence activity 6
1.2	Allocate and brief staff to reception duties including: ● personal presentation ● standards of behaviour ● relevant procedures ● work routines	Evidence activity 2
1.3	Ensure staff have the skills, knowledge and resources needed	Evidence activity 3 Evidence activity 4 Evidence activity 5
1.4	Encourage staff to ask questions	Evidence activity 2
1.5	Ensure staff follow the reception procedures	Evidence activity 2 Evidence activity 4
1.6	Ensure staff maintain the appearance of the reception area according to organisational requirements	Evidence activity 2
1.7	Ensure staff communicate with customers in a manner that promotes goodwill and understanding	Evidence activity 2
1.8	Inform staff and customers about any service changes that may affect them	Evidence activity 1
1.9	Manage problems that disrupt the reception service	Evidence activity 6
1.10	Collect feedback on the service from staff and customers	Evidence activity 4
1.11	Monitor and review procedures to ensure the service meets the needs of customers	Evidence activity 5 Evidence activity 6
1.12	Recommend ways of improving the reception service following organisation's requirements	Evidence activity 3
1.13	Report on performance and procedures as required	Evidence activity 4
1.14	Complete the required records	Evidence activity 2 Evidence activity 3
2.1	Explain how to implement the requirements of: ● health and safety ● employment legislation ● equal opportunities legislation ● other industry-specific regulations and codes of practice	Evidence activity 3
2.2	Identify organisational standards for the reception area including: ● personal presentation of staff ● behaviour of staff	Evidence activity 2
2.3	Explain how to ensure the performance of staff meets organisational standards	Evidence activity 6
2.4	Describe how procedures and work instructions should be written	Evidence activity 3 Evidence activity 4 Evidence activity 5

Evidence checklist		
Assessment criteria		**Possible evidence**
2.5	Identify the relevant channels of communication for establishing and updating procedures	Evidence activity 3 Evidence activity 5 Evidence activity 6
2.6	Describe the organisation's discount policy	Evidence activity 5
2.7	Explain how promotional offers should be handled	Evidence activity 5
3.1	Explain how the reception service integrates with other departments in the organisation	Evidence activity 1
3.2	Explain how the different roles and responsibilities of individuals within organisation and department affect reception service	Evidence activity 1
3.3	Explain the consequences of the reception service and other departments not working co-operatively	Evidence activity 1 Evidence activity 6
3.4	Identify the department's service targets and standards	Evidence activity 5
3.5	Explain how to estimate the resources required for reception activities	Evidence activity 1 Evidence activity 4
3.6	Explain how to develop a contingency plan	Evidence activity 6
3.7	Identify who in the organisation needs to approve the use of additional resources	Evidence activity 1
3.8	Describe how to build effective teams	Evidence activity xx
3.9	Describe ways staff can be encouraged to make decisions for themselves within limits of their authority	Evidence activity xx
3.10	Describe the limits of own authority when solving problems	Evidence activity 6
3.11	Explain how to communicate with customers and suppliers	Evidence activity 1
3.12	Identify customer needs and expectations	Evidence activity 1
3.13	Summarise the services that are available to customers	Evidence activity 1
3.14	Explain how to obtain information on guests including guest history where available	Evidence activity 4
3.15	Describe how customer complaints should be handled	Evidence activity 5 Evidence activity 6

CHAPTER 11

Supervise reservations and booking services

This chapter is about the competencies and knowledge that hospitality supervisors need to supervise the reservations and bookings service. It covers preparation, supervision and review of the service offered and the performance of the staff providing it.

Learning objectives

On completion of this chapter, you should:
1 Be able to supervise reservations and booking services.
2 Understand the organisation's standards and policies for reservations and booking services.
3 Understand the requirements that need to be met when supervising reservations and booking services.
4 Understand how to supervise reservations and booking services.

The reservations and booking service

4.1 Roles and responsibilities of reservation and booking supervisors

It is important to establish that all staff understand and know their roles, responsibilities and boundaries in order for a **reservation** and booking team to function smoothly. Establishing an organisational chart can be a good starting point.

In a hotel a number of services require reservations, booking and reception management, including:
- room booking management
- restaurant and room service management
- finances.

Who undertakes which roles and responsibilities is often dependent on the size of the organisation. For example, in larger, five-star plus hotels, given the scale of operations, there can be dedicated teams for reservations and bookings. For example, there may be a dedicated telephone reservation team. In contrast, in smaller operations, team members are expected to be cross-functional across different departments. For example, the hotel receptionist may take restaurant bookings along with accommodation bookings.

The General Manager will ultimately be responsible for the overall operation.

Key term

Reservation – an arrangement whereby something, especially a seat, room or an item, is reserved for a particular person or a group

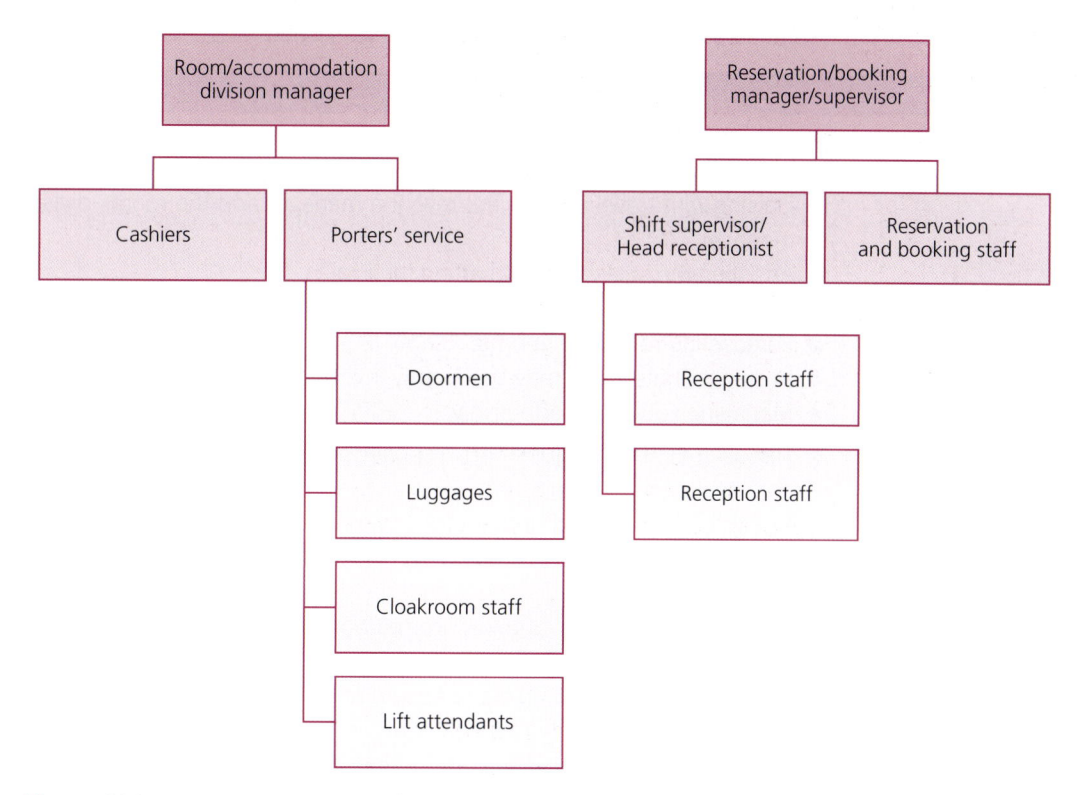

Figure 11.1 Example hierarchy of room booking management

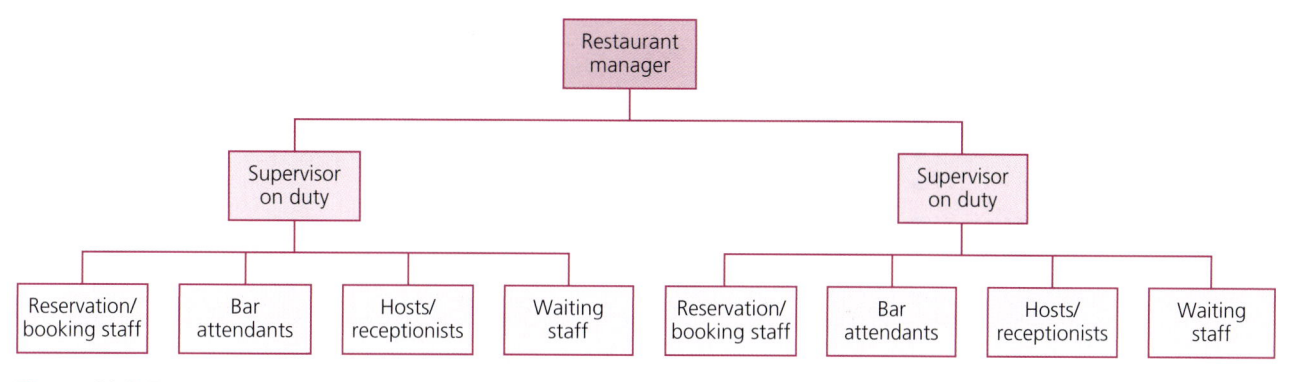

Figure 11.2 Example of an organisational chart for a restaurant

Some of the roles and responsibilities related to the reservations and bookings service are shown in the table on the following page.

Supervise reservations and booking services

167

Table 11.1 Roles and responsibilities related to the reservations and bookings service

Job role	Duties
Reservation/booking manager	<ul><li>Liaising with central reservations to communicate new rate plans and promotions</li><li>Liaising with travel agents, the revenue manager and the rooms division manager</li><li>Assisting the sales team in setting their rates</li><li>Maintaining the in-house reservations systems</li><li>Forecasting revenue streams</li><li>In smaller hotels you may be directly involved with room sales</li><li>Managing your team effectively</li></ul>
Head receptionists	<ul><li>Handling aspects of guest arrivals, check-in and departure in line with organisation's core standards</li><li>Being the first point of contact for any escalated guest queries/complaints and ensuring they are dealt with in a professional manner</li><li>Handling cash payments, float and main safe in accordance with company standards, ensuring that there are no overages or underages and whenever there are, reporting them accordingly</li><li>Overseeing the receptionists to ensure all duties are completed</li><li>Has experience in duty management</li><li>Being effective at motivating a team to achieve upselling targets</li><li>Experience in training and coaching team members</li><li>Having a flexible approach and being able to adapt quickly to changes in customers' and staff's demands</li></ul>
Receptionists (hotels)	<ul><li>Meeting and greeting clients</li><li>Booking meetings</li><li>Arranging couriers</li><li>Keeping the reception area tidy</li><li>Answering and forwarding phone calls</li><li>Screening phone calls</li><li>Sorting and distributing post</li></ul>
Hosts (restaurants)	<ul><li>Monitoring the open dining sections of the restaurant for empty and cleaned tables</li><li>Estimating wait times for guests</li><li>Monitoring the guest waiting list</li><li>Ensuring that the needs of the guests are met while they are waiting</li><li>Often responsible for answering the telephone, booking reservations and moving tables together to accommodate large parties</li></ul>

Evidence 1

4.1 **4.4** **4.5**

- Write a brief account of one of your working days to reflect your supervisor role and responsibilities.
- Draw an organisational structure of your organisation highlighting the reservation and booking staff and how they are connected with other departments.
- Identify possible impact on reservation and booking due to the lack of communication among different departments.
- List how people from other departments can help reservation and booking staff in their tasks.
- List the types of problems where your authority is limited as a supervisor, and in order to make decisions you would have to consult or refer to your senior managers.

1.7 Briefing staff

Customer-facing reception and booking staff have to observe certain professional conduct standards:
- **Behaviour:** be polite, friendly, smile, be courteous.
- **Personal presentation**: maintain excellent personal hygiene; ensure smart company uniforms are worn all the time. (Often name badges showing job title are part of the uniform.)
- **Know your responsibilities and boundaries.** You should comply with company policies and legislation at your work place; for example, when dealing with customers with disabilities and young and vulnerable adults. If you are unsure, ask your supervisors or senior managers.

1.4 1.6 Communication

Reservation and booking involves active participation of staff and customers, whether face-to-face, online or over the phone. In order for the booking process to be accurate, staff have to be trained to ask questions to the right people at the right time.

Supervisors should ensure the staff are trained and encouraged to ask questions to gather vital information. This is not only crucial for the business, but also vital for the staff to keep the customers updated about the services that your business offers.

The following approaches can be considered when asking questions.

1 Communication ground rules

Encourage your staff to communicate regularly, honestly and openly. The best place to start is that you lead by example, with the model that you want your staff to follow. Allow your junior staff to shadow you in a real-time situation.

Do not hesitate to give constructive feedback to your staff so that they can be more effective when asking questions.

2 Innovative approach to asking questions and communication

Share new ways of asking questions throughout the organisation. Organise staff development sessions, promoting communication champions within your staff base. This may help staff to break old habits while building a positive and proactive approach.

3 Reward good practices

Give staff an incentive to ask the right questions.

Rewards can vary from a simple thank you to more official recognition and responsibilities and possible cash rewards.

4 Evaluate performance of staff

Honest and impartial critique is essential for the staff to identify their area for development. The critique should be constructive with SMART targets. Conversely as supervisors, you should listen to your staff, as their suggestions may be valid and valuable for the business.

5 Build cross-department communication

Supervisors should ensure that their staff buy into the projects. If the staff across departments understand the main objectives of the organisation, the communication among them becomes meaningful. You can achieve this through team-building exercises, job role swaps, shadowing and mentoring.

Observe if the staff are speaking up, asking the right questions, demonstrating positive body language and being honest. These exercises could inform the supervisors to plan actions accordingly.

> **Evidence 2**
>
> 1.4 1.6 1.7 1.8 4.6
>
> 1 Describe a team-building activity or a social event that took place at your work which promoted communication among staff.
> 2 As a supervisor, list three strategies that you would adopt to encourage your staff to ask questions of appropriate people, especially customers, during the reservation process.
> 3 Under your supervision, one of the staff receives a call from a customer who wants to book a room for a week.
>   a) List the questions that you would expect your staff to ask this customer.
>   b) You observe that the staff member misses out on asking some vital questions. What would you do?
> 4 You expect your staff to communicate with customers in a way to promote goodwill and understanding. List tips that you would give your staff on this.
> 5 Describe briefly how you would go about informing customers, in a timely manner, about changes that may affect the services you offer.

1.3 Staff training

Staff training is an important investment to ensure your customers are being looked after according to your organisation's core values. Training will enable you to provide a superior customer experience, but will also have a potential positive impact on staff morale and loyalty. It could also help to minimise staff turnover and the additional costs of hiring, inducting and training new staff, which can be tedious and take up valuable managerial time.

When employing or deploying staff for a specific job role, supervisors may want to consider certain criteria:

- **New staff:** supervisors should ensure that new staff meet the required skills and knowledge for the position.
- **Existing staff:** supervisors should ensure the training needs are identified and development plans and training are arranged, consistent with the position in question.

Training your reservations and booking staff to make sure they have the skills and knowledge they need can be arranged in different ways, including in-house, on-the-job mentoring, or via external training providers delivered either on- or off-site.

Although staff training can affect the organisation's operating budget, the long-term benefits can be numerous.

- Minimises the health and safety risks.
- Positive staff attitude as they know how to do the job; translated into better productivity and customer experience.

- Happy staff means less absenteeism, fewer conflicts, low staff turnover and likely staff promotions and progression.
- A reliable and loyal staff force is instrumental for organisations wishing to expand.

Cross-job training should be considered in order to ensure the financial viability of your organisation. For example, a receptionist trained on telephone reservation tasks will enable the business to minimise unnecessary staff costs during down time or out-of-season periods.

However, care should be taken to ensure adequate human resources are deployed, even in down time. Failing that, over-stretched staff can be tempted to cut corners in order to tackle the extra workload and this may lead to poor customer service and experience.

> **Key term**
>
> **Core value** – this is a principle or belief that guides an organisation in internal conduct, as well as its relationship with the external world. Organisations communicate these values through their mission statement or value statement.

> **Evidence 3**
> **1.2** **1.3** **4.1**
>
> In the role of supervisor, you have been assigned to design a presentation for the new reservation and booking staff induction.
>
> Briefly list the topics you will cover in the presentation material.

4.2 4.4 Time and resources

Staff should be inducted and trained to know who to ask or where to look for any resources required to fulfil their reservation and booking activities. The resources could range from printer papers to expensive computer hardware.

Supervisors would have established through experience the time and resources required to complete a reservation and booking. This information should be clearly communicated to the staff so that they understand what is expected from them. Supervisors also communicate this through active role play in real conditions, e.g. leading by example, mentoring, timely feedback and analysing customer feedback.

Each organisation has their own system when approving investment or distribution of resources. Generally, the staff in question will raise their needs with supervisors. Supervisors will pass this to the procurement department. Once the requisition order has been authorised, the order will be placed. It can be a long process so the supervisors and staff must ensure that optimum amounts of resources are in stock for an uninterrupted operation.

> **Evidence 4**
>
> **4.2** **4.3** **4.4**
>
> - Draw a flowchart demonstrating the activities and time involved in taking a reservation from one customer on the telephone.
> - You have been processing a reservation request with one customer. The computer system went down. What are the contingency actions you would consider?
> - Explain situations where you may need additional resources. Who would you approach to request them in your company?

1.6 **1.7** **4.6** **4.7** **4.8** **4.9** Assessing customer needs and communicating with customers

The hospitality industry must meet the diverse needs of potential customers. In order to remain successful, it should be prepared to respond to the demands of customers with specific needs by offering products or services that meet their requirements. Examples of some potential requests which may arise from different customer groups in the hospitality industry include:

- special needs requirements such as disability access, special diets or access to health services
- child-friendly facilities (e.g. children's menus, play facilities)
- requests related to the nationality, language, religious or cultural beliefs of the customer – for example, money exchange and international money transfer facilities, international food offer, translated documents or online translation capabilities
- special transportation or parking-related facilities
- prayer facilities
- security services
- tour guides
- taxi services
- left luggage.

Well trained staff should be able to assess and identify customers' needs through processing reservations information gathered during the booking procedure and communicate to the correct departments in a timely manner.

Communicating effectively with customers is an art in itself. Staff can consider the following points to be especially customer-facing:

- **Beware of interrupting:** you may unintentionally do this and it can mean you are unable to understand the true situation, while frustrated customers desert your business. Patience and good listening skills help staff to overcome this issue.
- **Active listening skills:** this is as important as not interrupting. When communicating with customers, you can demonstrate that you are listening to them through your body language, e.g. attention and nodding, or making comments such as, 'I see' or 'I understand'. These actions will strengthen the communication and trust and make a better impression.
- **Communication and technical knowledge of customers:** often staff are better trained in using modern information and communication technology than an average customer. Therefore, avoid using jargon and acronyms which may confuse the customers, especially older customers. Ask if they understand and

keep your eye on the customer for signs indicating the opposite. Technology-related issues must be communicated in an unambiguous manner, as more and more hospitality businesses rely heavily on them. Learn to use simple analogies when explaining unfamiliar ideas and terms.

- **Use positive statements and avoid negative ones:** your customers are more interested in your capabilities than in your limitations. In other words, they are interested in what you can do, rather than what you can't do. The way you phrase things will influence the customer's perception of your capabilities. Using positive statements tends to minimise the negative effect. For example, in your hotel, a customer reports that the Wi-Fi is not working. You may want to avoid negatives such as, 'I don't know' or, 'I am not an IT expert'. Instead, you could apologise and offer to find out what the issue is and when the Wi-Fi will be re-established. In another scenario a negative statement can have serious consequences if misunderstood when talking to a customer on a mobile phone. Mobile phone connections can sometimes be poor, the line can break up and you may lose part of the conversation; if you are saying the word 'not', the person on the other end of the line may hear the opposite message.
- **Be proactive in informing customers:** ensure that customers are regularly updated about disruption to services and any potential technical issues. This will give the customers enough notice to organise alternatives. Likewise, it is important to inform customers when problems are resolved. Nothing is more frustrating to customers than finding out that they could have been working or using the facilities sooner if they had known.

Like any service, reservation and booking services can be disrupted. Causes may vary, but technical issues such as internet and telecommunication failure, reservation data corruption or loss, human error, miscommunication or lack of communication between departments are some common ones. The impact could be that staff are unable to process the reservation request, or unknowingly over or undersell bookings due to incorrect internal data, with a subsequent loss of customers to competitors.

Supervisors should have a contingency plan in place to address such disruption. For example, dedicated IT support including for out-of-hours operations, alternative communication points and special numbers in case of internet or telecommunication failure.

Evidence 5
1.9 1.12 4.7

Design a questionnaire which informs the hospitality staff about customer needs.

Evidence 6
1.6 4.8 4.9

Describe how you expect your reservation staff to communicate with customers:

1. Face-to-face
2. On the phone
3. Via email.

Customers have to be informed about the facilities that your business offers. As a supervisor, how would you ensure the reservation and booking staff are aware of and familiar with these. Summarise the facilities, products and services available in your organisation.

Organisational standards and policies

1.1 2.7 3.4 4.10 4.11 Taking reservations and bookings

Reservation or booking involves setting aside rooms (hotels), tables (in restaurants), conference rooms (in business centres and hotels) for a specific person or a group of people.

When customers reserve one of the above services, they enter into a contract with the provider (i.e. the hotel, restaurant, conference centre or holiday resort). Therefore, it is expected that both parties will honour their commitments towards each other. It should be recognised, however, that on some occasions these commitments cannot be fulfilled for various reasons (see Managing problems below).

In essence, the reservation process is an exchange of information between the business and its customers. This information has to be recorded, followed through and updated constantly by various departments of the business.

Each organisation tends to have their own policies and procedures, especially with regard to pricing, booking, refunds and over-booking. A hotel, for example, is likely to need to know the following information about their customers:

- customer names
- contact number/email address
- next of kin
- ages
- disability information, if any
- special dietary requirements
- date of arrival
- date of departure
- payment methods.

The customers will need to know:

- the address of the hotel
- checking in and out times
- breakfast/lunch/dinner service times, if provided
- childcare/entertainment for children facilities
- room type and floor
- booking number.

Customers should also be given the terms and conditions of the booking. These include:

- contact telephone, fax or email details
- payment methods and additional charges, if any
- cooling-off period, if any
- where to log complaints
- disclaimers on personal properties or vehicles
- deposit amount, if applicable
- reservation fee
- notice period for cancellation and refund amounts.

Evidence 7

1.2 1.3 1.5 2.7 3.4

In your position as a supervisor, you're going to be away for a day due to training. You are planning to ask one of your staff to cover for you. Write a checklist for your colleagues to ensure that they are aware of your company's reservation and booking procedures and policies.

> **Evidence 8**
>
> **3.4** **4.17**
>
> Highlight how your organisation processes a review of the above procedures.

1.13 **4.12** **4.13** Reservation and booking systems: paper-based versus computerised records

Reservation data has to be stored correctly and safely and should be easily accessible by authorised staff. This can be done manually using hard copies or stored electronically in a secure, computerised database.

Paper-based (manual) systems

Table 11.2 Pros and cons of paper-based (manual) systems

Pros	Cons
• Risk of data loss due to system failure is minimal • Provides relatively high data protection • Unlikely to be hacked and corrupted or stolen by electronic means	• Time consuming • Data will not be available readily for business analysis (e.g. sales mix, trends etc.) • Valuable data can be lost through theft, fire, flooding • Requires storage space, which can be expensive • Requires additional staff time for processing the same amount of data compared to computerised systems

Computerised systems

Table 11.3 Pros and cons of computerised systems

Pros	Cons
• Speedy processing of customer data for timely responses • High accuracy • High storage capacity • Saving on clerical staff cost • Higher productivity • Frees up staff time for more customer interaction and other duties • Data communicated instantly across all departments concerned • Back-up facilities available • Enables e-transaction, avoiding cash handling and security and safety issues	• Hard copies still have to be produced as a back-up in case of system failures or power cuts • Back-up on 'cloud' computing can incur additional costs • Vulnerable to electronic data vandalism and theft and data protection can be breached • Extra staff training cost • Regular software and hardware updates required • Can pose compatibility issues between different brands and operating systems – possibly lengthy and expensive to fix

Supervise reservations and booking services

175

Overall, computerised systems are favoured due to their speed, cost savings, efficiency and ability to respond to a globalised customer base.

2.3 2.4 3.4 Pricing policy: discounts and promotional offers

Often hotels and holiday resorts announce the full price (also known as the '**rack rate**'), but during the booking process, customers and tour operators tend to get favourable rates. Some tour operators enter into agreements with hotel groups to get exclusive discounts which will then be passed on to customers.

Prices can also fluctuate depending on seasons and special events. Hotels around large exhibition halls tend not to apply discounts, as the exhibitors will pay full price for convenience.

All hotel operators wish to have 100 per cent occupancy. When there is a low demand, they adjust their prices to attract more bookings – whether they fill up or not, their **fixed costs** are not going to change. Hotels may well sell the rooms cheaper but in return they will expect extra revenue from additional food and beverage sales.

> **Key terms**
>
> **Rack rate** – term commonly used in the hotel industry. Often customers have been charged rack rate prices when they book directly and on the day. Rack rate prices are more expensive than the rates customers could have got if they booked well ahead or through sole agents. Rack rates can vary depending on offer and demand and are generally more expensive during weekends and holiday seasons.
>
> **Fixed costs** – expenses that have to be paid by a business, regardless of the level of any business activity. For example, business rates and standing charges on electricity bills.
>
> **Gross profit** – the total revenue of a business minus the cost of the services or the goods it has sold. Gross profit does not take into account selling and admin expenses.

1.8 2.5 2.6 3.4 Overbooking and out-booking

The reasons behind **overbooked** hotels are similar to airlines (i.e. every empty seat on a flight is considered to be a loss). However, unlike airlines, hotel businesses have walk-in customers and other customers who decide to stay longer or leave earlier than planned. Usually there are no financial penalties for these customers.

On the other hand, not all bookings materialise and hotels tend to lose out on such no-show customers. As a result, every hotel sets overbooking targets (based on historical trends), with the hope that a percentage of bookings will be cancelled.

This practice can become an issue for the hotel staff and customers concerned in peak activity periods. This may affect the customer experience, often leading to complaints. Reservation and bookings staff are on the front line when it comes to dealing with overbooked guests. Supervisors should ensure the staff are briefed about what to do and how to deal with these situations.

Generally, hotels do everything they can to accommodate their guests. The hotel industry works together in such situations and will transfer guests to an alternative hotel with no extra charges (**out-booking**).

> **Key terms**
>
> **Overbooking** – when more rooms/places are booked than are actually available
>
> **Out-booking** – when a hotel moves customers to another hotel, usually because it has been overbooked

These are delicate times and reservation and booking staff and head receptionists should have direct supervision and be adequately trained to deal with such situations.

> **Evidence 9**
>
> **2.3** **2.4**
>
> Identify online discount offers for your own company or your competitors on hotel rooms, and highlight the key terms and conditions.
>
> **2.5**
>
> Investigate your company's overbooking policy and identify the extent of this practice.
>
> **2.6**
>
> List the competitor businesses that you deal with when out-booking.

Other requirements for reservations and booking services

1.1 3.1 3.2 3.3 Legislation

Hotels must be compliant with relevant legislation. It means that all senior staff and supervisors need to be aware of standards. Senior management can achieve that through training, meetings, noticeboards and staff newsletters.

Hotels and licensed premises have the obligation to ensure the safety, security and well-being of their customers and staff alike. The following legislation applies to all hospitality businesses, big or small:
- Health and Safety at Work Act 1974
- Health and Safety Information for Employees Regulations 1989
- Manual Handling Regulations 1992
- Fire Precautions Act 1971
- Fire Precautions (Workplace) Regulations 1997

> **Health and safety legislation**
>
> For more information on health and safety legislation, refer to Chapter 4, Maintain the health, hygiene, safety and security of the working environment.

The Data Protection Act

Reservations and bookings involve handling and storing of personal and sensitive data about customers. This data has to be protected.

Any company or professional that needs to store the personal data of customers for business activities is classified as a 'data controller'. Data controllers are subject to the Data Protection Act 1998.

The Data Protection Act 1998 stipulates that information:
- must be processed fairly and lawfully
- must be processed for limited purposes
- must be adequate, relevant and not excessive
- must be accurate and up to date
- must not be held for longer than is necessary
- must be processed in accordance with the individual's rights
- must be kept secure
- should not be transferred outside the European Economic Area, unless adequate levels of protection exist.

This implies that reservation staff must abide by the above requirements. Supervisors should ensure that staff who work with personal data receive adequate training and commit to the relevant code of conduct. Staff can demonstrate their suitability for the role by signing confidentiality contracts and other vetting processes; for example, stating that they do not have any criminal convictions or haven't committed similar offences in the past.

The Data Protection Act also protects staff. Their personal details must be stored securely by their employer and they should be provided with the same level of protection as customers.

Generally, data is stored electronically, making it convenient and easy for supervisors to monitor and address any breach in a timely manner.

Disability Discrimination Act 1995

The Disability Discrimination Act stipulates that:

> 'service providers include holiday accommodation, tourist attractions, restaurants and transport providers. They cannot refuse to serve you as a person with disabilities or provide a lower standard of service because of your disability, unless it can be justified. Service providers may need to make "reasonable adjustments" to any barriers that may prevent a person with disabilities using or accessing their service'.

Under this Act, service providers only need to make changes that are 'reasonable'. These might include simple changes to layout, improved signage and information, and staff training, which can improve accessibility to customers with disabilities. On the other hand, service providers are not required to make changes that are impractical or beyond their means.

This Act also protects staff in an organisation where employers are required to make reasonable adjustments to accommodate any staff with disabilities. Examples of reasonable changes that can be made include:
- using large print for registration and guest information
- ensuring that at least one copy of the fixed menu is in Braille
- providing phones with large buttons
- providing portable vibrating alarms for guests who will not be able to hear an audible fire alarm
- where a low reception desk is not available, providing an alternative low desk for wheelchair users
- sending staff on disability-awareness training courses to increase awareness of common disability-related issues.

Equality Act 2010

The Equality Act protects staff and customers against unfair treatment (discrimination) on the grounds of age, disability, gender reassignment, marriage and civil partnership, pregnancy and maternity, race, religion or belief, sex and sexual orientation. This law concerns hospitality businesses too; any breach may trigger prosecution.

Given the potential gravity of a breach in the law, staff should be trained and be made aware of the fundamentals of this legislation. They should be supervised and given guidance to deal with its consequences correctly in all situations. One of the preferred methods of training might be awareness training, and supervisors should make sure their staff attend training and are updated with any recent changes in legislation.

Other regulations and codes of practice

There are official bodies, namely the Competition and Markets Authority (CMA) and the Financial Conduct Authority, to protect consumer interests. They have powers to sanction unfair terms, for example, mis-selling, unfair competition, price fixing, misleading or fraudulent claims.

Breaches of requirements

Breach of one or more of the above legislation can lead to prosecution and can be potentially costly for organisations. Therefore, supervisors should approach this proactively rather than reactively. Combining regular awareness training, analysing customer and staff feedback with strict supervision, supervisors can minimise the risk of a breach. In the event of any breach, corrective action should be taken in order to prevent further incidents. Actions could include sanctions, arranging further training, seeking legal advice and a review of policies and procedures.

Evidence 10
3.1 4.10 4.11 4.12 4.13

- What customer information do you require to complete a reservation?
- List ways in which this data can be recorded and stored (Also refer to Chapter 17.)
- List the legislation affecting the data that you collect.
- List the advantages and disadvantages of computerised and paper-based data storage methods. (Also refer to Chapter 17.)

Evidence 11
1.1 1.2 1.3 3.1 3.2 3.3 3.4 4.1

In a staff meeting, it has been suggested that there should be a poster reminding the reservation and booking staff of their code of conduct, to be displayed in the staff room.

Produce a poster covering key topics, including:
- the chain of communication and reporting system
- health and safety good practices
- performance norms and disciplinary procedures.

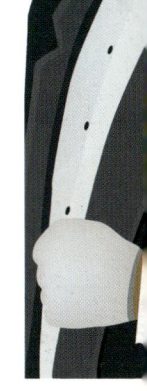

Monitoring and reviewing procedures

1.7 **1.8** **4.3** **4.5** Dealing with problems and changes affecting the service

Occasionally managers have to make changes based on unavoidable or unforeseen situations (for example, over-running refurbishment work). Staff and customers should be informed about such changes to minimise confusion and a negative customer experience.

Supervisors can achieve this with staff through pre-shift briefing, internal notes, email and text alerts, and providing staff with alternative actions.

In some situations, supervisors may not have the authority to make key decisions. In those situations, they should refer to the senior managers; for example, when dealing with law enforcement officers, head office staff, major competitors and partners or a major security breach, such as terrorism.

Supervisors must be aware of key individuals and their contacts as part of the contingency plan. In the meantime, they should try to protect customers' and staff safety and well-being with the resources available to them.

Staff should take extra care when explaining changes to customers, conducting themselves in a professional manner (see above) and being proactive; for example, if the telephone booking service is out of order, place an announcement with alternative services available.

> **Evidence 12**
> **1.8**
> List your organisational procedures when dealing with a disruption to the booking service.

1.5 **2.1** **2.2** Monitoring staff performance against organisational standards

Good managers and supervisors succeed by motivating and encouraging their staff to achieve the core values of the organisation. It is not easy, but reservation supervisors may devise different stages and schemes to incentivise their staff. For example:
- rewards/recognition for handling and managing a volume of customers in a given time period
- staff of the month/year
- data analysis of customer and mystery shopper feedback
- staff of the week for upselling
- staff of the day/week/month for exceeding customer expectations
- displaying customers' positive feedback letters and emails to demonstrate and share good practices.

An effective work performance system would normally have established guidelines on:
- within what time period a customer call will be answered
- average time spent per booking
- number of calls dealt with per hour, day, week and month
- average time spent per call/booking
- sales per member of staff or team
- number of calls versus real sales (conversion ratio)

- average additional revenue generated through upselling
- identifying upselling and other products sales opportunities
- minimum and maximum price targets to be achieved and discounts within a given period
- face-to-face communication with customers, e.g. were your staff polite, friendly, courteous, compliant with the organisation's uniform standards?

One of the important roles of the supervisor is to check that the products and services and staff performance meet the expected standards. Supervisors may want to oversee their staff in action, carry out spot checks and intervene when required, or analyse customer and staff feedback and take necessary actions accordingly. This can be a good opportunity for the supervisor to identify the strengths and areas for development for individual members of staff and consequently suggest additional responsibilities or developmental training that may be needed.

1.9 1.10 1.12 4.14 4.15 4.16 Customer and staff feedback

Staff feedback

Supervisors should listen to customer-facing staff's feedback and attempt to understand specific issues. This will promote positive working relationships among staff, which will lead to greater customer satisfaction. Feedback is critical to improving performance. Staff need to be told how they're performing. Without feedback, it's like walking blind. Staff may accidentally reach their goals/targets. At worst, they will aimlessly perform tasks which you don't expect them to do, leading to poor performance and substandard customer experience.

Getting customer feedback: monitoring and using data to improve customer satisfaction

Collecting customer feedback and suggestions is invaluable to assess the standards of products and services that your business offers. Your responsibility as a supervisor is to analyse this information and inform your colleagues and senior managers in a timely manner for review and action.

With growing e-commerce, potential customers tend to read reviews about previous customer experience with your business. Monitoring such websites and following up the negative comments are the best way to minimise any damage. This will also prevent unscrupulous competitors and customers attempting to cause trouble.

The last people customers are likely to see are receptionists, especially in hotels and holiday resorts. Supervisors can seize this opportunity to collect vital and possibly genuine verbal or written feedback.

> **Evidence 13**
>
> **4.16**
>
> As a supervisor, list the methods you use to receive feedback from the staff in your organisation (include formal and informal methods).

> **Evidence 14**
>
> **1.9 1.10 1.11 4.14 4.15**
>
> - List the methods of getting feedback from customers and staff in your organisation.
> - Explain who is responsible for processing the collected feedback data in your organisation, and how this is done.

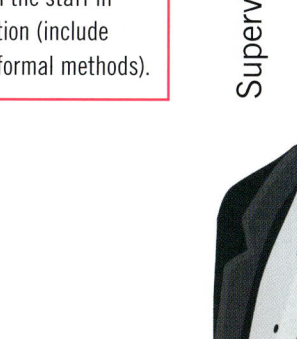

Dealing with complaints

Supervisors should ensure any complaints have been handled appropriately, in compliance with company policies and standards.

As a general rule, the dos and don'ts for dealing with complaints are shown in the table below.

Table 11.4 Dos and don'ts for dealing with complaints

Don't	Do
• Argue • Interrupt • Ignore • Get angry • Blame anyone	• Listen: focus your complete attention on the unhappy customer • Maintain eye contact • Display positive body language • Be sympathetic and positive • Apologise • Assist: offer a refund or freebies or a discount if you are authorised to do so and if appropriate • Record the complaint • Follow up

Investigate the issue and identify potential improvements in the product or service provided. Inform staff and arrange relevant training as required.

4.17 Suggesting improvements

Supervisors and managers can enable staff to discuss ways in which the current reservation and booking system can be improved. Suggestions should focus on addressing feedback gathered from customers and staff. For example:
- Customer feedback may suggest that they have experienced long delays in phones being answered. Suggestions could include introducing a call-back service or directing customers to online booking/live chat-booking services.
- In an independent hotel, staff feel that booking takes valuable time from the operations. Possible suggestions for improvements could be subscribing to a centralised or price comparison website who will handle the booking process for a fee. This can also expose the hotel to a wider customer base.
- In a popular high street independent restaurant, customers comment that they are unable to ring to make bookings between 2pm and 5pm due to closure between shifts. A possible improvement could include subscribing to one of the restaurant-booking websites.

4.18 Reviewing and updating plans, targets, objectives, activities and work performance

One of your responsibilities as a supervisor is to communicate effectively with staff and ensure that they understand the standards that you expect them to achieve in their work performance. Supervisors in reservations or booking teams will do this by analysing the process involved and establishing organisational and industry norms and monitoring their staff performance against such benchmarks (see Monitoring staff performance against organisational standards above).

Work performance management involves working together with staff and reviewing and identifying strengths and areas for improvement in their performance and how to help them to be more productive and effective workers.

Effective and timely feedback is critical for a successful performance management programme and should be used in conjunction with setting performance goals. If effective feedback is given to staff on their performance towards their goals, staff performance will improve. Staff need to know in a timely manner how they're doing and what they have to do to optimise their output.

Supervisor feedback to staff tends to work best when it relates to a specific performance; for example, time spent on processing a telephone booking. Establishing staff performance management guidelines at the very beginning provides opportunities to discuss performance and give specific feedback. Telling staff that they handled 10% more customers in a given time is more meaningful feedback than, 'You have done well today'.

Feedback should be constructive and people tend to react better when it's presented in a positive manner. However, feedback must be accurate, valid, factual and complete. Always start with reinforcing what people did right and what they have to do in future. Constant criticism eventually will have no effect.

Remember success breeds success, failure breeds failure and poor performance.

Feedback can be planned and naturally occurring. Staff will be able to gain feedback themselves following a specific target being met or not. For example, booking staff are expected to cover 100 calls per day. In this example, staff don't need feedback from others about their performance.

The second type of feedback is given through a carefully planned performance measurement system. This could include formal appraisals and informal job chats.

Feedback can be given to individuals or to a team. Effective feedback embedded in a performance management system can ensure that staff help the organisation to achieve its goals successfully.

Feedback can come from many different sources: managers and supervisors, measurement systems, peers and customers just to name a few. However feedback occurs, certain elements are needed to ensure its effectiveness.

Corrective actions and updating

Despite all efforts, supervisors may not be able to achieve the intended performance from their staff. Possible approaches include:

- **Proactive approaches:** supervisors do not wait until they have observed poor performance and received a high level of complaints, which can be detrimental to the business. Actions could include staff training and refresher training workshops, mentoring schemes and appraisals.
- **Reactive approaches:** the supervisor will have taken action when the situation becomes out of control and affects the customer experience, other staff's well-being and the business. Issues that the supervisor would address include a high level of complaints received, conflict among staff, breaches in employment contracts and the organisational code of conduct.

Corrective action could include a cause for concern meeting with staff concerned, which will normally be recorded. In these meetings, supervisors attempt to set time-bound goals and improvements to the standard of work, monitoring and suggesting appropriate training courses for the individuals concerned. As a last resort, supervisors can action disciplinary procedures with verbal or written warnings.

> **Evidence 15**
>
> **1.13** **2.1** **2.2** **4.18**
>
> 1. In your opinion, describe why it is important to complete relevant documents during performance reviews. Outline what types of information will be recorded.
> 2. You have been requested to chair a meeting to remind and inform staff about the consequences of not meeting performance targets. Produce a leaflet outlining possible actions which could be taken against staff in the event of not meeting the performance standards.
> 3. You have been promoted into a junior manager role. You have been asked to mentor one of your junior supervisors to fill in your role. Draw a flowchart representing your organisational procedures for reviewing and updating the following:
>
>   - Customer service experience during the booking and reservation process, including the complaints handling process.
>   - Performance review of your staff.

Knowledge check

1. Explain how to determine the percentage of overbooking.
2. When is a customer more likely to be charged the rack rate?
3. What are the inconveniences with out-bookings?
4. List three advantages of computerised booking systems.
5. Outline the professional conduct of staff when dealing with complaints.
6. Reservation and bookings in the hospitality industry have to comply with certain legislation. Name the organisation governing this activity.
7. What are the key responsibilities of a reservation and booking supervisor?

Evidence checklist

Evidence for Learning objective 1 must be gathered by the candidate, demonstrating competencies by doing. The candidate's performance should be observed by an assessor or an expert witness. An expert witness can be the candidate's supervisor or manager who holds a recognised assessor qualification.

Evidence checklist			
Assessment criteria		**Possible assessment methods and forms of evidence**	**Possible evidence**
1.1	Ensure the reservation and booking service complies with relevant legislation and organisational policy	Assessment methods: ● Direct observations ● Work product ● Expert witness testimony ● Professional discussions ● Question and answers ● Candidate's reflective account/ statement Forms of evidence: ● Log book ● Observation diaries ● Record of professional discussions ● Video/audio and photographic evidence ● Record of work schedules/rota ● Witness testimonies ● Statement of professional discussions ● Work rota ● Presentation materials ● Internal and external correspondence (emails/ telephone conversation notes)	Evidence activity 11
1.2	Brief staff on reservation and booking duties including: ● personal presentation ● standard of behaviour ● procedures ● work routines		Evidence activity 3 Evidence activity 7 Evidence activity 11
1.3	Ensure staff have the skills, knowledge and resources needed		Evidence activity 3 Evidence activity 7 Evidence activity 11
1.4	Encourage staff to ask questions when needed		Evidence activity 2
1.5	Ensure staff follow the reservation and booking procedures		Evidence activity 7
1.6	Ensure staff communicate with customers in a manner that promotes goodwill and understanding		Evidence activity 2 Evidence activity 6
1.7	Inform staff and customers about any changes that may affect the service		Evidence activity 2
1.8	Manage problems that may disrupt the reservation and booking service		Evidence activity 2 Evidence activity 12
1.9	Collect feedback on the service from staff and customers		Evidence activity 5 Evidence activity 14
1.10	Monitor and review procedures to ensure the service meets the needs of customers		Evidence activity 14
1.11	Recommend ways of improving the reservation and booking service following your organisation's requirements		Evidence activity 14
1.12	Report on performance and procedures as required		Evidence activity 5
1.13	Complete the required records		Evidence activity 5

Evidence checklist			
Assessment criteria		Possible assessment methods and forms of evidence	Possible evidence
2.1	Explain how to monitor staff performance against the organisation's standards	Assessment methods: • Oral questioning and written tests • Role play • Presentation • Professional discussions Forms of evidence: (All evidence can be cross-referenced to Learning objective 1) • Written exam/knowledge check (short-answer and multiple-choice questions) • Case study • Presentation materials (PowerPoints, posters, leaflets) • Staff newsletter	Evidence activity 15
2.2	Explain what to do if staff performance does not meet these standards		Evidence activity 15
2.3	Describe the organisation's discount policy		Evidence activity 9
2.4	Describe how promotional offers should be handled		Evidence activity 9
2.5	Explain the organisation's overbooking policy		Evidence activity 9
2.6	Explain the organisation's policy for out-booking guests when full		Evidence activity 9
2.7	Explain how to develop reservation and booking procedures to meet requirements		Evidence activity 7
3.1	Explain how to implement the requirements of: • health and safety • employment legislation • equal opportunities • other industry-specific regulations and codes of practice	Assessment methods: • Oral questioning and written tests • Role play • Presentation • Professional discussions Forms of evidence: (All evidence can be cross-referenced to Learning objective 1) • Written exam/knowledge check (short-answer and multiple-choice questions) • Case study • Project • Presentation • Staff newsletter	Evidence activity 10 Evidence activity 11
3.2	Explain ways of assessing whether requirements are met		Evidence activity 11
3.3	Describe the action that should be taken in response to breaches of requirements		Evidence activity 11
3.4	Identify organisational policies that apply to: • the running of the reservation and booking service • review of procedures		Evidence activity 7 Evidence activity 8 Evidence activity 11

Evidence checklist			
Assessment criteria		**Possible assessment methods and forms of evidence**	**Possible evidence**
4.1	Explain how the different roles and responsibilities of individuals in the organisation and department affect the reservation and booking service	Assessment methods: ● Oral questioning and written tests ● Role play ● Presentation ● Professional discussions Forms of evidence: (All evidence can be cross-referenced to Learning objective 1) ● Staff rota ● Written exam/knowledge check (short-answer and multiple-choice questions) ● Case study ● Presentation ● Staff newsletter	Evidence activity 1 Evidence activity 3 Evidence activity 11
4.2	Explain how to estimate the time and resources required for reservation and booking activities		Evidence activity 4
4.3	Explain how to develop a contingency plan		Evidence activity 4
4.4	Identify who in the organisation needs to approve the use of additional resources		Evidence activity 1 Evidence activity 4
4.5	Describe the limits of your own authority when solving problems		Evidence activity 1
4.6	Describe how to communicate with customers		Evidence activity 2
4.7	Explain how to assess customer needs		Evidence activity 5
4.8	Summarise the products and services that are available to customers		Evidence activity 6
4.9	Identify the guest facilities that are available in the organisation where the booking is being made		Evidence activity 6
4.10	Identify the information needed to maintain the reservation and booking service		Evidence activity 10
4.11	Explain how to collect required information on the reservation and booking service		Evidence activity 10
4.12	Describe the different ways of completing and storing computerised and paper-based records		Evidence activity 10
4.13	Compare the advantages and disadvantages of computerised and paper-based records		Evidence activity 10
4.14	Explain the importance of staff and customer feedback		Evidence activity 14
4.15	Explain how to collect and analyse feedback		Evidence activity 14
4.16	Explain how to give feedback to staff		Evidence activity 13
4.17	Explain how to present recommendations to improve the reservations and booking service		Evidence activity 8
4.18	Explain how to review and update: ● plans ● targets ● objectives ● activities ● work performance		Evidence activity 15

CHAPTER 12

Contribute to promoting hospitality services and products

This chapter covers the skills required of hospitality supervisors in order to be able to promote and increase the revenue through sales of products and services. It includes promotional activities (for example, special or themed events) and resources such as banners, posters, personal selling, web presence and loyalty schemes, among others.

> **Learning objectives**
>
> On completion of this chapter, you should
> 1. Be able to contribute to promoting hospitality services and products.
> 2. Understand how to plan the promotion of hospitality products and services promotions.
> 3. Understand how to contribute to promoting hospitality products and services.

Promotional activities

1.2 3.1 Promoting products and services

In order to maintain and develop business, organisations undertake marketing and promotional activities. These can range from simple activities, to large-scale, complex promotions. Hospitality businesses are constantly targeted by competitors and therefore promotional activities can help a business to retain customers and **market share**. The ultimate purpose of promotional activities is to influence and persuade potential customers to choose a particular brand or business and not the others, and to encourage them to make purchases.

> **Key term**
>
> **Market share** – a percentage or portion of total sales volume in a market captured or controlled by a brand, product, or company.

The first stage in planning a promotional activity is to identify what products and services you are going to promote. You need to be clear about what product or service is going to be promoted and justify your reasoning. For example, the business unit has not been operating to its maximum capacity and can take more business without additional capital expenditure (e.g. new kitchen) or variable costs (e.g. staff); or competition is increasing and you may want to persuade your customers to stay with your brand. There may have been a change in the demography in your customer base (e.g. arrival of immigrants with different needs).

1.1 1.2 3.3 Types of promotional activities

There are a range of promotional activities, some of which are more effective than others. Identifying what type of promotional activities should be undertaken, when and for how long are crucial for success. Poorly planned promotional activity can become a cost as opposed to contributing to an increase in sales and profitability.

Personal selling

Staff play a key role in this. Staff interaction with the customers can be utilised to influence the purchasing decision. This type of promotion will have an instant result. Sales can take place in face-to-face situations, on the telephone, via **Skype** or **video conferencing** or live text chat.

Advantages

The biggest advantage of personal selling is that the staff can change and/or adjust the message they are conveying to the customer as they gain feedback from the customers. If the customer didn't understand the original message, the staff can deliver it differently to answer a customer's question or concern.

Disadvantages

Personal selling ability belongs to the person who is selling. Some staff are naturally talented in doing this kind of promotion and others may have a negative impact on sales. For example, customers can be annoyed by repetitive messages or an overly aggressive sales pitch.

> **Key terms**
>
> **Skype** – an internet telephone service provider that offers free calling between computers and low-cost calling to regular telephones that aren't connected to the internet.
>
> **Video conferencing** – using computers to provide a video link between two or more people. You are able to see them during the communication.

Direct marketing

This involves sending emails or mail outs direct to the customer. This method can be cheaper than traditional advertising; the message can be tailored to suit customer profiles and can even be personalised. For a better result, direct mail promotions should be personal, creative, informal and selective, rather than targeting all customers from the mailing list.

Advantages

It is very easy to implement and relatively cheap. It can be launched within days or weeks. This is an efficient way to gain feedback and gauge customers' reactions on new offers and prices within a targeted customer sample.

Disadvantages

The biggest downfall of this method can be the junk mail effect, whether via post or email. The organisation can risk customers' hostile and unsympathetic reaction towards the company despite a genuine bargain offer.

Advertising

This method is impersonal and most often costly. It predominantly uses traditional, electronic and digital mass media.

The different outlets for advertising include TV, newspaper, magazine, internet and smart phone apps, as well as traditional outdoor displays such as billboards, posters, buses, taxis and railways.

Advantages

The main advantage of this method is that it alerts a large population who may or may not be interested in the offer. From the possible increased customer flow, companies can quickly identify the target market and understand what consumers are looking for in their products or services.

Disadvantages

Some customers may find these types of promotions intrusive and invasive and may or may not respond. It can be difficult to distinguish some advertising from others and to stand out, especially if the market is flooded with similar promotions due to increased competition.

Public relations

This practice involves creating and maintaining goodwill with the stakeholders (customers, staff, shareholders, suppliers, local community) of the organisation, usually through non-paid publicity and communication methods. It may involve, for example, getting involved in supporting sports, charity, educational and other similar community events.

Advantages

A well structured campaign undertaken by large third-party companies can result in the target customers being exposed to your company's information that they may not get from other promotions.

Disadvantages

Public relations often uses the traditional publicity mediums such as news. These types of promotions have lost their effectiveness due to more effective digital platforms such as the internet. Therefore, the intended target market may not be reached by the media coverage.

Sponsorship

This method involves the company financially supporting activities such as sports events. As a return, companies get exclusive advertising space/time and highlights during the event.

Advantages

The chance of getting greater unintended promotions, especially in live telecast or broadcast, where the company's brand and products can reach out to a wider customer base.

Disadvantages

It can be extremely costly and a gamble. For example, if in a sport event the sponsored team or individual loses, it may have negative impact on the brand or product and spread to the rest of the company.

Sales

Often include short-term promotions such as 'buy one, get one free' offers, kids eat for free, free upgrades on bedrooms, percentage discount on next visit, discount vouchers, and goody bag giveaways.

Advantages

Customers are persuaded to act quickly, disregarding alternative brands and make the purchase faster than they would have done otherwise.

Disadvantages

Price-sensitive customers may not spend in the non-promotional period and may wait for the discount offers to be announced, leaving companies with reduced cash flow and potential financial difficulties.

Other promotional activities specific to the hospitality industry

You can undertake a range of activities, including those mentioned above, to promote your business. Some specific examples are given below.

- **Open day/evening:** this is an effective method to encourage potential customers to visit your business premises to view what will they get, including amendments and upgrades that you have recently achieved or proposed. For example, wedding open days where potential customers come to visit the facilities and taste the menu.
- **Trade fair/exhibition:** you let out your premises/facilities and invite other organisations who may be presenting their products and services to the market place. It could be an event promoting local products such as dairy, fish, meat or vegetables. Hiring and exhibiting products and services your business offers in renowned trade shows, for example, can also be very effective. Here, not only will you meet potential customers, but you will also be able to compare what your potential competitors offer and review your positioning.
- **Charity events:** businesses may want to allow charities to utilise their venues as a promotion activity. This has the potential to create a positive impression of your business as it's likely to convey the message that, besides profit making, your business also cares about the local community and gives back. Such events can expose your business to potential customers who would not have been reached by other promotional activities.
- **Use of your premises for promotion of other businesses:** some companies do not necessarily have their own premises, or are not in the right location suitable for their own promotion; for example, mobile giants, internet providers, banks. Therefore running their events in your premises can open up new potential customers and corporate business deal opportunities.
- **Leaflets or pamphlets:** these types of campaign can be suitable to promote a new development, or a re-opening following refurbishment, for example. This method can also be cheaper than traditional advertising methods.
- **Email marketing**: web presence is a popular interface between customers and businesses, regardless of the size and types of business. It is more likely than ever that customers will browse websites for particular information or register to receive future offers. This can present a huge potential to businesses. Dedicated webmaster teams can profile and attempt to capture customers' interests for business growth. Personalised email has become the most popular method of communicating promotions to customers. If done well, email marketing can be lucrative to the business. It is relatively easy to implement from a desktop without major investment. It can reach out to as many customers as you like or to a specific customer base, based on different factors such as geographical area, age group, gender etc. However, businesses should be careful about which potential customers these email offers are going to. Not all offers may be suitable for all potential customers. On the downside, your email with a genuine promotional offer may be overlooked by the customers who might discard them as spam.
- **Trade discounts/loyalty scheme:** these methods allow businesses to ensure returning custom from the same customer base more often. The investment/costs can in turn pay for themselves through increased sales volume. Examples include 'buy five coffees and the sixth cup is free'; or 10 per cent discount on the accommodation bill on your next visit. Businesses can also offer discounts in the form of vouchers for customers who recommend the business to their families and friends.

Evidence 1
1.1 1.2 2.5 3.1 3.2

List the promotional activities that have been running in your organisation.
- Identify the types of promotions.
- Highlight the activities in which you are directly involved.
- Collect promotional materials which are readily available for customers (e.g. leaflets, web banners, menus, radio/TV adverts).

How have these activities helped your organisation?

Figure 12.1 Hosting conferences is one way of promoting your business to potential new customers

Preparing promotional activities

1.4 1.5 1.6 1.9 2.4 2.5 3.12 Knowing your target customers and your objectives

Knowing the target market or customers that your promotional activities have been aimed at is a fundamental requirement. This can be achieved by consulting senior managers and the strategists within your company.

The activity you may be running can be part of the company's larger marketing strategy. The purpose of the promotional activity may be to:
- expand the customer base and increase the sales targets
- win back lost market share
- prevent the loss of market share to competitors.

Identifying and planning your promotional needs involves determining the expected outcome in the short, medium or long term. As a starting point, you may want to look at historical data for the sales at a given time of year to determine the trends year on year. From this reference point, you can determine a measurable outcome.

For example:
- Increase the sales of food and beverages by n% over the next three months.
- Bring the sales levels back to year-before levels.
- Prevent the sales level from falling due to increased competition and unsatisfactory customer feedback.

Look at your local main competitors' offers and determine what your strengths are. Study your competitors' prices and determine if your offers are good value for money. Value for money can become the driving force of your marketing strategy. Planning in this way will help you to review the effectiveness of your strategy by comparing the actual outcome with intended targets.

There are numerous small- and medium-sized hospitality businesses that require promotional activities. Unlike large and corporate businesses, they will not necessarily have the resources and time. Often such operators tend to promote their activities through a relatively low-cost method. Planning, decision making and implementing are often done by the same person or a small group of people. The decision-making process can be instant thanks to the flat organisational structure. Promotional activities may include posters on the shop window, a board, leaflet distribution to passers-by, and mostly rely on returning customers and word-of-mouth promotions. Some may invest in prime locations such as corner shops, in front of tube/railway stations and high visibility locations where they are exposed to potential customers.

Figure 12.2 You should be aware of who your target customers are

1.5 1.6 2.5 2.8 Costing

As part of the planning process, you need to forecast the cost involved in the promotional activities. You may want to consider costs such as printing, media fees, consultant fees or outsourcing fees.

Forecast the anticipated increase in turnover following the promotional campaign, and evaluate the net impact against the cost. In theory any promotion should raise your profile and increase sales. However, promotional activities planned in isolation in a medium to larger business may have minimal or no effect. For example, launching a new pizza formula may be successful, but could have a negative impact on existing sales, resulting in a net zero result. Therefore it is well worth considering promotional activities to encourage additional takings/upselling without compromising existing or potentially guaranteed sales, regardless of your promotional offers.

As a guide for good practice when you plan a promotional activity:
- Consider what your like-for-like/similar competitors are offering and what alternatives there are.
- Carry out a cost–benefit analysis to determine or predict whether the return on investment in promotions would outweigh the cost in the short, medium or long term.
- Think about the costs involved and whether they could be minimised through creativity and innovation. For example, a takeaway and delivery pizza business can capitalise on the existing delivery network for promotional offers, such as new products or special offers to the customers. In this model the only additional cost to account for would be the printing of leaflets.

193

1.3 1.4 1.8 2.6 2.7 3.5 3.6 3.7 Consulting with colleagues and obtaining resources

Often medium to large companies will have an annual budget for marketing and promotional activities. Your promotional offers may have to go through the marketing department for approval and resources allocation. Therefore, you need to consult your superiors and put forward your business case in order to gain resources. In this process, you and your marketing department may consider the following points.

- Short-, medium- and long-term benefits for the business. Businesses should not underestimate the impact of loyal customers moving away from your brand. It is harder and costlier to win new customers than keep the existing customer base.
- Promotional activities can be directed at suppliers and the strategy will be different as suppliers grow their market share through your growth. For example, a supplier may help you to run certain promotional activities by offering favourable financial terms and conditions (longer or interest-free credits or competitive pricing). In return, they may benefit from your future expansion of business and surge in sales volume.
- Staff are internal customers and you could promote your business with them. For example, a hotel group may offer certain discounts to staff. The staff and their families will contribute to increased sales overall. Benefits of this type of promotion are two-fold, as not only will the business gain higher turnover, but they also develop staff loyalty and happiness. The impact of such schemes cannot be underestimated as happy staff tend to provide better customer service, promoting positive customer reviews and encouraging repeat business.
- Promotional activities should be innovative, interesting and dynamic. Otherwise your offer becomes one more offer in the marketplace and risks not being noticed. You must also be mindful of not repeating similar promotional activities.

Often operational staff (you) won't have access to financial health information and higher-level decision making on the strategic direction of the company. Therefore, it is advisable that you get adequate commitment – be it finances or human resources – from your superiors beforehand.

Supervisors and managers must ensure that the staff buy into their promotional ideas/activities. This can be achieved through clear communication of business, departmental, team or branch objectives, which should be achieved in a timely manner. Supervisors may want to introduce internal staff incentives alongside promotional activities; for example, a special bonus for achieving or exceeding business targets within a certain time frame.

Evidence 2
1.3 1.5 1.6 1.7 1.8 1.10 2.5 2.6 2.7 3.5 3.6 3.7

You have been asked to organise staff and materials for a forthcoming trade exhibition.
- What information do you require to do this task?
- Where/who would you get the required data from?

You are planning to call a meeting to discuss and exchange ideas with your colleagues about this promotional activity. Write an agenda for the meeting, indicating the topics you should cover.

Produce a script for your colleagues who will be involved during the exhibition period.
- What information would you gather during the exhibition?
- What would you recommend is done with the information you have gathered and by whom?

1.4 2.3 Social responsibility, best practice and ethical issues

For a better result, businesses must consider their corporate and **social responsibilities**. Corporate social responsibility can be defined as the efforts of an organisation that go beyond what may be required or imposed by the law or lobby groups. Committing to such initiatives can have a short-term cost to the business. However, it will help to promote positive social and environmental developments in the longer term. For example, businesses may want to convey to the public what they do to protect the environment.

Ethical consideration have to be addressed when organising big events. In essence, ethical issues can be tackled by considering alternatives after evaluating the rights (ethical) and wrongs (unethical) within the given context. For example, ensuring disability access is available; making sure the food and drink offer caters for different religions and cultures; or increased payment or additional days off for staff who work unsociable hours and during public holidays, and during promotional events/activities in particular. This may also include environmental considerations such as the need to consider increased traffic, parking space, increased noise and pollution to the local residents and public health implications.

> **Key terms**
>
> **Ethical consideration** – being in accordance with the rules or standards for right conduct or practice, especially the standards of a profession or industry.
>
> **Social responsibility** – acting with concern and sensitivity, aware of the impact of your actions on others, particularly the disadvantaged.

Figure 12.3 Trade fairs and exhibitions are forms of promotional activity

Any promotional activity should have the potential to raise the net business activity and therefore **cost–benefit** analysis is key. The promotional activity may bring huge return in monetary value, but at the same time may upset local residents and other stakeholders. If you are concerned about your promotional activities, you should alert your superiors and public relations officer (if you have one). In some cases, you will be conducting a promotional activity where there would be small or no financial difference to the business; for example, a charity event which may raise thousands of pounds for a charitable cause. The benefit for the business tends to be indirect and long term, through exposure to a wider audience and positive customer perception.

> **Key term**
>
> **Cost–benefit analysis** – the process of comparing the costs involved in doing something to the advantage or profit that it may bring in.

> **Evidence 3**
>
> **1.4** **2.3**
>
> Where do you find your company policies in general and your social responsibility statement/policy or mission statement in particular? If you cannot find one, look at your competitors' businesses and briefly summarise the content.

> **Key term**
>
> **Trading standards** – trading standards professionals act on behalf of consumers and business. They advise on and enforce laws that govern the way we buy, sell, rent and hire goods and services.

1.4 2.1 2.2 3.3 3.4 Legal requirements

Promotional activities are regulated by trading standards. There are a number of laws and legal requirements that you may need to consider when promoting hospitality products and services.

Trade Descriptions Act

The Trade Descriptions Act sanctions the trader for making false or misleading statements or claims about goods or services (i.e. certain kinds of false statement about the provision of any services, facilities or accommodation can be sanctioned). Sanctions can range from warnings to criminal penalties, depending on the severity of the offence.

It may sound trivial but it is important to pay extra attention to spelling, colours of leaflets, font sizes, addresses, correct dates of the promotional period if any, telephone numbers, emails, website addresses and opening hours or days. The consequences of a misprint or inadvertent misinformation can be a great risk for the entire promotion and, depending on the severity, may well become a trading standards issue.

Consumer Protection Act

Along with the Trade Descriptions Act, the Consumer Protection Act ensures extra protection to customers. This law gives customers protection against unfair selling practices. Consumers have basic legal rights if the product has been given a misleading description, is of an unsatisfactory quality and/or is not fit for its intended purpose.

Organisations and individuals who are undertaking responsibility for promotional activities must ensure that the intended activities are compliant with the law applicable to the nature of the industry and activities.

Copyright law

Copyright gives the creators of some types of media rights to control how they are used and distributed by others in order to promote businesses. Promotional activities are in the first line to be looked at under this law. For example, using another brand to promote your own organisational benefit, without formal agreement with the organisation in question, can incur legal action against your organisation.

Other legislation

- **Health and Safety at Work Act** – the Health and Safety at Work Act 1974 (also referred to as HSWA, the HSW Act, the 1974 Act or HASAWA) is the primary piece of legislation covering occupational health and safety in Great Britain. These laws are there to protect staff and customers from minor to potentially life-threatening hazards through in-depth risk assessments and remedial actions. The legislation extends to specific industries and the hospitality industry is subject to general and specific acts of legislation.

- **Equality/Discrimination Acts** – the Equality Act 2010 legally protects people from discrimination in the workplace and in wider society. It replaced previous anti-discrimination laws with a single Act, making the law easier to understand and strengthening protection in some situations. It sets out the different ways in which it is unlawful to treat a person or a group of people. Promotional activities should comply with these Acts, otherwise, not only is the organisation at risk of prosecution, its reputation will also suffer significantly.
- **COSHH** – this piece of legislation gives guidelines to organisations, individuals and managers on the day-to-day use of chemicals and substances that are being used in the hospitality industry. The aim of this legislation is to prevent or reduce staff and customers' exposure to hazardous substances.
- **Food hygiene** – food and drink provision is an integral part of any hospitality activity. Therefore it is essential that organisations are compliant with strict food safety management systems to ensure customer as well as staff safety. HACCP (Hazard Analysis and Critical Control Point) is a system that helps food business operators look at how they handle food and introduces procedures to make sure the food produced is safe to eat on the premises, in retail settings, takeaways and large on- and off-site events, i.e. mass catering.

Take it further

Further information of the legislation relevant to promotional activities can be found using the following sources:
- Trade Descriptions Act 1968 (www.legislation.gov.uk/ukpga/1968/29)
- Consumer Protection Act 1987 (www.legislation.gov.uk/ukpga/1987/43)
- Copyright, Designs and Patents Act 1988 (www.copyrightservice.co.uk/copyright/uk_law_summary).

Evidence 4
1.4 1.8 2.1 3.4 3.6 3.7

As part of a national promotional campaign, your company's head office has drafted a poster. You have been assigned to check this material before it goes to print. Produce a checklist to help your colleagues spot the sort of things they should be checking for in this material to ensure it meets legal requirements and organisational objectives.

Evidence 5
2.2

Your role is as a supervisor in a fine dining restaurant. As part of an ongoing promotion, your business offers a 25 per cent discount on bills to customers on certain days. However, the promotional material does not specify the days.
- Does this material comply with legislation, and why?
- Under what piece of legislation could your organisation be sanctioned?
- List the possible sanctions.

Evidence 6
1.4 1.9 2.1

Write a brief note (not more than one A4 page) on how well the promotional activities of your organisation meet legal requirements. You should consider:
- the Trade Descriptions Act 1968
- the Consumer Protection Act 1987
- the Copyright, Designs and Patents Act 1988
- any health and safety and food safety legislation relevant to your area of work.

3.8 3.9 Use of organisational logos, trademarks and branding

It is common practice nowadays to evaluate the strength of competitors and differentiate or augment your offer to attract customers to your business, or target the gap in the market. It is also usual to collaborate with already well established brands and consolidate on their existing customer base. For example, pubs, restaurants, cafés, hotel and conference centres take **franchises** with high street coffee shop brands. The biggest advantage of this is that these brands have their own specialised marketing strategies, promoting their offerings. As a result, the franchisee benefits directly for a fixed or variable fee based on the sales percentage.

> **Key term**
>
> **Franchise** – a right granted against a payment, to an individual or group, to market that company's brand, goods or services within a certain location for an agreed period.

Figure 12.4 Franchises can bring new customers to your organisation

You must ensure you have full prior agreement with the organisations concerned about the use of a recognisable logo or trademark. Unscrupulous, misleading and unlawful use of brands, logos and trademarks without relevant contracts can lead to prosecution. If you are unsure, you must seek advice from your superiors.

3.3 3.11 Disruptions to promotional activities

It is also important to take into account the impact of unpredictable factors when planning and launching promotional events. For example, weather changes, political decisions, right product but wrong targeted audience and surprisingly cheaper or better alternatives from your competitors. Organisations should think about a **contingency plan** in such situations, although some situations cannot be overcome (for example, last minute venue changes due to health and safety concerns or planning permission restrictions). Such situations are hard to predict but the impact can be minimised through comprehensive health and safety and risk assessments.

When planning promotional activities businesses must be mindful if they can cope with the surge in potential demand. Otherwise, such promotional activities can have a detrimental effect due to unsatisfied customers.

> **Key terms**
>
> **SWOT analysis** – SWOT stands for 'Strengths, Weaknesses, Opportunities and Threats'. This is a method of analysis of the business environment and the company's positioning within it.
>
> **Contingency plan** – a plan designed to take account of a possible future event or circumstance which may or may not happen.

Evidence 7

`1.3` `1.4` `1.5` `1.6` `1.10` `2.4` `2.6` `3.3` `3.8` `3.9` `3.10`

Carry out a SWOT analysis of your business.

Briefly explain how you would plan a promotional activity in order to minimise the threats and overcome weaknesses of your offer?

Evidence 8

`1.2` `1.7` `2.8` `3.5`

You have been delegated the task of improving the turnover in the forthcoming Father's Day bookings at a four-star hotel.

Your managers need to know how you would achieve this (e.g. leaflets, website promotions, emails or advertising in the local paper). Produce a PowerPoint presentation to show your managers and colleagues describing:
- what product/products you are planning to promote
- the resources required
- how you are planning the promotion
- what the possible adverse effects are and how you are planning to minimise them.

`3.11`

You have also been asked to evaluate how the above activity could potentially be disrupted and to suggest actions to minimise the impact of this.
- Consider factors such as weather, staff capabilities, resources available and errors in promotional products, delays in transport, delivery and distribution.
- Counter-promotional activity from your potential competitors.
- Recent changes in legislation.

Table 12.1 Promotional activity planning checklist

Stages		Yes/No
1	Do your promotional activities conflict with your organisation's vision and values (e.g. fair trade commitments, carbon footprint policies, equality and diversity policies, healthy eating agenda)?	
2	Have you consulted your superiors about your plans before fully committing your time and effort in formulating and planning potential promotional activities?	
3	Have you or will you inform your superiors and collaborators about the activities, timing, when and where, including contingency arrangements? Have you taken on board others opinions and ideas, which may improve your initial plans?	
4	Is your planned activity complying with local, regional and national laws (e.g. planning permission and trading standards)?	
5	Have you conducted a risk assessment (e.g. impact on staff and customers' health and well-being, potential noise pollution and possible traffic disturbance)?	
6	Have your identified the SMART targets for your promotional activity? • **Specific:** what product/service, to who and when? • **Measurable:** how are you going to evaluate the impact: daily/weekly/monthly sales, number of customers or number of enquiries/bookings about your product? • **Achievable:** can you deliver what you are promising while meeting organisational requirements? • **Realistic:** do your staff have the skills and capabilities to deliver what you are promising? • **Timely:** can your logistics (supply, production, delivery of service and products) cope with the increased demand?	

Supervising promotional activities

1.8 Instructing colleagues

As agreed with your superiors and staff, once the particular promotional activity has been launched, you must keep your managers and staff informed about how well it is progressing. Regular staff briefings and reporting to managers are both crucial in order to avoid or overcome unforeseen issues. Remember: others may see or question things that you do not. You should give clear instructions to the staff and delegate the right staff to the right duties.

1.9 1.10 Monitoring the promotion

Monitoring promotional activities is important to ensure that you get value for money. It is crucial to collect customer reaction/feedback to your promotions and to inform your managers in order to improve future campaigns.

Some classic examples of reasons to monitor your promotion would be:
- You hire staff to distribute hundreds of thousands of leaflets. Unless you monitor the distribution, there is no guarantee that those leaflets reached your target market.
- A web campaign creates an unexpected surge in enquiries. You should be able to respond to this by making some quick adjustments.
- A charity event will be taking place at your premises and you want to make sure that the target audience has been reached with information on your products and services.

1.11 3.12 3.13 Reviewing the effectiveness of the promotion

Once promotional activities are finished, you must evaluate the true impact. These results can tell you about the effectiveness of the campaign.

This could be done by analysing:
- the like-for-like sales
- average spend per head
- number of bookings in the given week or month
- number of enquiries about products and services
- time and money spent versus net benefit
- analysis of potential and actual customers' feedback data.

Armed with the review data, you should inform your managers about the full impact of the promotions. Evaluation will enable you and your managers to make decisions on future promotions. This involves measuring the extent of success or failure, and evaluating what went well and what could be improved for next time. Depending on the types of activities and impact in real terms, businesses may choose to increase, decrease or even abandon such activities.

Your own and your managers' evaluation should be communicated to all staff involved in the activity. Remember, the success of promotional activities relies heavily on to what extent all involving parties buy into the idea.

Key term

Sales mix – the breakdown of the variety of services or products sold by a company. A company's sales mix can also be looked at as percentage of sales for each type of service or products over the total sales volume.

Evidence 9
1.9 1.11 3.12

List how you would evaluate and measure the success of a promotional activity.

For example, you could consider the following:
- Look for the variation in takings following the event.
- Ask customers if your promotional offer reached them.
- Consider customer feedback on the promotional activity.
- Look at the sales mix to establish if the total profit has progressed.

Knowledge check

1. Name four methods of promotional activities in the hospitality industry.
2. What are the benefits of organising events for charities in your hospitality premises?
3. What is the fundamental purpose of promotional activities?
4. What could be the possible benefits of personal selling?
5. What information would you expect to find out through a SWOT analysis?
6. What is the main disadvantage of promotional offers in the hospitality industry?
7. Name three things that you would look at when evaluating the success of promotional activities.

Evidence checklist

Assessment criteria		Assessment methods and forms of evidence	Possible evidence
1.1	Identify possible activities to promote the services and products in own area of responsibility	Assessment methods: • Direct observations • Work products • Expert witness testimony • Professional discussions • Question and answers • Candidate's reflective account/ statement Forms of evidence: • Log book • Observation diaries • Record of professional discussions • Video/audio and photographic evidence • Record of promotional activities • Witness testimonies • Statement of professional discussions • Work rota • Presentation materials • Internal and external correspondence (emails/telephone conversation notes)	Evidence activity 1
1.2	Identify the sales improvements promotional activities could generate		Evidence activity 1 Evidence activity 7
1.3	Consult with relevant colleagues about own ideas for promotional activities		Evidence activity 2 Evidence activity 6
1.4	Ensure promotional activities are consistent with: • targets • the organisation's objectives and values • social responsibility practices • legal requirements		Evidence activity 3 Evidence activity 4 Evidence activity 5 Evidence activity 6
1.5	Collect relevant information to support ideas for promotional activities		Evidence activity 2 Evidence activity 6
1.6	Organise relevant information to support ideas for promotional activities		Evidence activity 2 Evidence activity 6
1.7	Contribute to the development and implementation of plans		Evidence activity 2 Evidence activity 7
1.8	Instruct colleagues on planned activities as appropriate		Evidence activity 2 Evidence activity 4
1.9	Monitor activities to ensure that: • targeted customers are being reached • promotional activities are run according to agreed plans and standards		Evidence activity 5 Evidence activity 8
1.10	Collect information about the promotional activities		Evidence activity 2 Evidence activity 6
1.11	Evaluate the effectiveness of promotional activities		Evidence activity 8

Evidence checklist			
Assessment criteria		**Assessment methods and forms of evidence**	**Possible evidence**
2.1	Outline the legal requirements that should be taken into account when developing and implementing promotional activities including: ● Trades Descriptions Act ● Health and Safety at Work Act ● Discrimination Acts ● Copyright law ● COSHH ● Food hygiene	Assessment methods: ● Oral questions and written tests ● Role play ● Presentation ● Professional discussions Forms of evidence: (All evidence can be cross-referenced to Learning objective 1) ● Written exam/knowledge check (short-answer and multiple-choice questions) ● Case study ● Project ● Presentation materials (PowerPoint, posters, leaflets) ● Staff newsletter	Evidence activity 4 Evidence activity 5
2.2	Explain the consequences of promotional activities not meeting legal requirements		Evidence activity 4
2.3	Describe social responsibility practices, 'Best Practice' principles and ethical considerations that need to be considered when promoting hospitality services and products		Evidence activity 3
2.4	Identify the organisation's target markets, sales targets and main competitors that are relevant to own area of responsibility		Evidence activity 6
2.5	Identify what information is needed to support suggested promotional activities		Evidence activity 1 Evidence activity 2
2.6	Identify the resources that are available for promotional activities		Evidence activity 2 Evidence activity 6
2.7	Explain how to obtain additional resources		Evidence activity 2
2.8	Explain how to cost promotional activities to ensure profitability is maintained and improved		Evidence activity 7

Evidence checklist			
Assessment criteria		**Assessment methods and forms of evidence**	**Possible evidence**
3.1	Describe the nature of the product being promoted and any other materials that feature in the promotion	Assessment methods: ● Oral questions and written tests ● Role play ● Presentation ● Professional discussions Forms of evidence: (All evidence can be cross-referenced to Learning objective 1) ● Written exam/knowledge check (short-answer and multiple-choice questions) ● Case study ● Project ● Presentation ● Staff newsletter	Evidence activity 1
3.2	Outline any other promotional plans within the organisation that are relevant		Evidence activity 1
3.3	Describe the possible adverse results that the promotion, products and other materials may have and how to avoid these		Evidence activity 6
3.4	Identify the terms and conditions that need to be included in promotions and how these should be written		Evidence activity 4
3.5	Describe how to present promotional ideas to other people in the organisation		Evidence activity 2 Evidence activity 7
3.6	Identify which colleagues need to be briefed in relation to different types of promotional plans		Evidence activity 2 Evidence activity 4
3.7	Outline the information that colleagues should be given about promotional activities		Evidence activity 2 Evidence activity 4
3.8	Explain when to use product and organisational logos, trademarks and branding to support promotional activities		Evidence activity 6
3.9	Describe how to use product and organisational logos, trademarks and branding to support promotional activities		Evidence activity 6
3.10	Outline the organisation's procedures for implementing promotional activities		Evidence activity 6
3.11	Explain how promotional activities could become disrupted and how to deal with this		Evidence activity 7
3.12	Describe how to measure the effectiveness of promotional activities		Evidence activity 8
3.13	State who to make recommendations for improving promotional activities to		Evidence activity 8

CHAPTER 13

Supervise linen services

This chapter covers the competence that hospitality supervisors need to maintain and improve the linen service. It deals with the preparation, supervision and review of the service, involving the planning of equipment and supplies, preparing staff rotas and briefing staff and collecting customer feedback.

Learning objectives

On completion of this chapter, you should:
1. Be able to supervise linen services.
2. Understand how to plan the linen service.
3. Understand the importance of supervising the linen service.
4. Understand how to supervise linen services.

Linen services are an important part of any housekeeping operation and a room providing good quality, freshly laundered linen, utilised and arranged correctly will enhance the room and help to give a welcome to the guest.

The linen service

3.1 3.2 3.3 Roles and responsibilities related to the running of the linen service

Key term

Linen – the generic term used for such items as sheets, pillowcases and towels. Nowadays, these items are only occasionally actually made from linen. They are more likely to be made from cotton or even a cotton/synthetic fibre mixture such as polyester/cotton.

It is obvious that an efficient and well run **linen** service is essential to a successful housekeeping department. In the majority of establishments, linen services will be part of wider housekeeping operations and the day-to-day procedures and planning will be carried out by head housekeepers and housekeeping supervisors. The roles and responsibilities of those dealing with linen relate completely to those of the housekeeping department as a whole (see Chapter 9: Supervise housekeeping operations). Providing a linen service may be the role of one person within the housekeeping team, or could be a shared role.

Everyone working within the housekeeping department will have some contact and involvement with linen and the services provided. However, the impact of well run linen services will have a positive outcome throughout the establishment, especially in guest rooms, public areas, coffee shops, bars and restaurants. Good communication between departments using linen will be essential to provide an integrated service and ensure that the required amounts of linen are available when and where needed.

Other departments must ensure that the linen room knows:
- exactly what type of linen is required
- if linen is required earlier than usual or at specific times
- of any increase in the usual requirements such as for special events
- of special requirements such as items needed flat rather than folded
- if any linen is lost or damaged.

It is also essential that other departments return used linen promptly after use so it can be sent for laundry and there is no hold up in clean linen returns.

If other departments who require linen do not integrate and communicate well, it is likely that linen will not be available when needed, wrong items could be supplied and expensive losses could occur.

Planning and supervising the service

1.1 2.3 2.4 Allocating duties and briefing staff

An efficient and well run linen service is essential to the smooth running of any hospitality establishment. The linen provided for guests needs to be of good quality, in good repair, well laundered and presented and replaced with the required regularity.

Figure 13.1 It is important to carefully plan the working procedure for those providing a linen service

Relevant procedures

Like the rest of the housekeeping provision, it will be necessary to plan actual working procedure and instruction for those providing a linen service. A proper planned procedure will ensure that staff are absolutely sure about what is expected of them and how to actually complete their work. Planned procedure also ensures that standards throughout the establishment remain consistently high. Linen provision procedures will be established by head housekeepers or others at management level. These in turn may be implemented and maintained by housekeeping supervisors. Procedure may involve:
- collection of linen from the right area at the relevant times
- transporting linen to the work area efficiently and safely, without causing disruption

- preparing used linen for laundry
- receiving and checking linen returned from the laundry
- storing clean linen correctly
- using the linen according to procedure
- reporting any quality problems or faults with the linen.

When writing procedures and work instructions, firstly consider the process that each member of staff will need to complete and list each procedure. For example:

Table 13.1

Task	Also consider
Check the working rota to establish which rooms you are going to service.	Note how many twin, double or king-sized beds.
Collect the required linen, record it in the linen record book and load it safely onto a housekeeping trolley.	Make sure the load is not too heavy, is safe and will not topple when you move it. Ensure you do not stack the linen too high so you can see where you are going.
Enter each room using the standard procedure for entering a guest room.	If occupied, leave and return to the room later unless the guest asks you to service the room.
Select the linen needed for the room and bathroom.	Make sure you select the required sizes.
Remove the towels and other linen items from the bathroom and bag ready for the laundry. Record on laundry sheet.	If the guest has placed the 're-use' card, fold and place the towels in the correct place. Note any damaged or missing items.
Remove the linen from the bed and bag ready for the laundry. Record the numbers and types of items on the laundry sheets.	If the guest has placed the 're-use' card, remake the bed to operational procedure.
Make the bed or beds following operational procedure. Operational procedure covered at initial training session.	Note any damaged or missing items.
Place any extra linen items such as bathrobes and slippers.	These are placed in the wardrobe.
Return all used linen along with the laundry sheets to the linen room.	
The above linen tasks will be integrated with the other housekeeping requirements.	

Once the procedure has been broken down into individual tasks, check it with the head housekeeper or line manager to see if there is anything they would like to change or add.

The procedure then needs to be tested with someone actually carrying it out to establish that it works in the real situation. Adjustments and changes may need to be made.

Work routines

Use of linen, stripping used bed linen, making beds and removing used bathroom linen and correctly placing fresh linen is part of the general housekeeping service. Training for these tasks and the allocation of duties will be part of the overall housekeeping training and task allocation.

Housekeeping staff will usually collect the linen they require to service their areas at the start of their shift. This will usually be in the morning, so it is essential that there is enough clean linen available to do this. If there are long delays in waiting for clean linen to be delivered from a laundry, it could result in staff not being able to complete their work and ultimately vacated rooms cannot be re-let, resulting in loss of sales and revenue. Not having enough clean linen available to service the rooms of guests in residence may result in complaints and loss of return business. It is also essential for staff to return used linen to the relevant place promptly so the items can be sent for laundry and returned for use as quickly as possible.

1.2 2.1 Ensuring staff have the skills, knowledge and resources needed

Staff training and briefing

Once a procedure for carrying out a linen service has been established, staff will need to be trained and briefed on its use and implementation. All staff need to be trained in the correct procedures, ensuring that they have the knowledge and skills required to complete tasks to provide linen services to the required standards. Initial and ongoing staff training will ensure that all staff have the required skills to complete their job effectively. Planned training sessions, recap sessions, handover meetings and briefing sessions, and good supervision and mentoring will all help to ensure that staff are equipped with the knowledge they need. Training leaflets, videos and posters may also be used.

Estimating time and resources needed

As with all housekeeping tasks, a quality service can only be maintained if the full range of resources are available, for example, adequate supplies of clean, good quality linen in the required sizes. Provision of linen can prove to be a significant financial outlay for any establishment and purchase of linen can include:
- sheets of various sizes
- pillow cases
- bed **valances**
- duvet covers
- towels of various sizes, bathmats and facecloths
- guest bathrobes.

Other items such as pillows, duvets, bedspreads, curtains and cushions may also be the responsibility of the linen area. They could be involved in the purchase and care of restaurant linen, such as tablecloths and napkins, and kitchen linen, such as tea-towels and staff uniforms, though these may be dealt with specifically within the relevant working areas.

Many establishments also offer guests a personal laundry service during their stay. The collection, recording, laundering and return of these personal items will be dealt with by housekeeping/linen room staff.

As a general guide, the numbers of linen items purchased would allow for each room a minimum of: one of each linen item in use, one of each at the laundry and one of each in storage. This would obviously need a reliable and prompt laundry return. Most establishments would carry extra stock for **contingency**.

> **Key terms**
>
> **Valance** – a piece of plain or decorative fabric that is placed between the mattress and the bed base to provide a neat or ornate finish.
>
> **Contingency** – planning ahead for something that could happen that was not planned.

Linen sizes

The sizes of various pieces of bed linen do vary slightly, but tend to be similar to the sizes stated below:

Table 13.2 Types of bed linen and their sizes

Bed linen type	Size
Flat bed sheet – single	178 cm × 290 cm
Flat bed sheet – double	230 cm × 290 cm
Flat bed sheet – king size	280 cm × 315 cm
Pillowcase – UK housewife style	51 cm × 76 cm
Pillowcase – UK Oxford style	62 cm × 90 cm but can vary
Duvet cover – single	160 cm × 260 cm
Duvet cover – double	220 cm × 260 cm
Duvet cover – king size	250 cm × 260 cm
Face cloth	30 cm × 30 cm
Hand towel	50 cm × 100 cm
Bath towel	70 cm × 135 cm
Bath sheet	100 cm × 170 cm
Bath mat	60 cm × 80 cm

Restaurant linen includes tablecloths, placemats, slip-cloths, tray-cloths, napkins, doilies and coasters.

Tablecloths are available in a wide variety of sizes to suit different table arrangements and may be square, rectangular, round or oval. Other restaurant items also come in a range of designs and sizes to suit the individual establishment.

Pillow cases

A housewife pillowcase is similar in size to the pillow with the seams on the inside. There is an overlapping pocket of fabric on the inside to hold the pillow in place. The Oxford pillowcase has the same seamed stitching and pocket for the pillow but extends by about 6cm all around the outside to give an extra fabric edge.

Figure 13.2 Housewife pillow cases (in front) and Oxford pillow cases (behind)

In most establishments, linen services come under the direct management of the head housekeeper. Housekeeping would certainly have responsibility for linen used in guest rooms and bathrooms, as well as in public areas. They may also have responsibility for restaurant/kitchen linen, as well as staff uniforms, though these are often dealt with by the individual areas themselves.

The time and resources needed for linen provision will depend on a number of factors around ownership and care of the linen. One of the following procedures is likely to be used:
- The establishment purchases, stores and replaces its own linen and laundry is completed on the premises, maybe along with minor repairs.
- As above, but an off-site laundry is used. They would collect used linen and return it when laundered.
- A linen company would supply (hire) all linen to the establishment and provide a full laundry service.

Whichever of the above procedures is used, time will still need to be allocated for:
- preparation and recording of items being sent to the laundry
- recording and storage of linen returning from the laundry
- organising and storage of linen
- stocktaking
- issue of linen items and uniforms.

Linen provision

Combinations of the above may apply. For example, sheets, pillowcases and bathroom linen may be owned by the establishment and laundered in-house, but restaurant linen rented and laundered by an outside company. Or the linen items may be owned by the establishment and sent out to a laundry, but staff are responsible for laundering their own uniforms.

Key terms

Man-made fibre – a type of fibre that is made artificially, such as polyester or rayon.

Thread count – refers to the number of horizontal and vertical threads in one square inch of fabric. A thread count of 200 is considered good quality and higher than this is called percale.

Evidence 1

2.1 2.2 2.3 2.4 2.5 2.6

Collect examples of the following:
- Plans for use of time/resources.
- Emails, letters or notes you have written asking for more resources.
- Work procedures or instructions you have written.
- Contingency plans for different situations.

2.2 Getting approval for additional resources

When it is identified that additional resources are needed or would be beneficial to the linen service, provision approval will be needed from the right person or department. Write or list your reasons for why the additional resources are needed and what the benefits will be. Actual facts and figures to support your ideas will always be useful. These could be concerned with more efficient working procedures, better or safer working conditions for staff, financial savings or a range of other matters. Take your list or send by email to your head housekeeper or line manager and maybe also explain your reasoning verbally.

1.3 4.4 Effective communication

It is important to maintain effective communication with others, irrespective of whether they are those you supervise, people in other departments, your head housekeeper or managers, or outside contractors and suppliers. Communication may be face to face, written messages and letters, by telephone, internal paging systems and electronic systems including email or text messages. It is likely that you will use a selection of these methods to communicate with others.

Throughout the housekeeping and linen areas, good communication between staff at all levels is essential if an efficient and high quality service is to be maintained. Part of this communication will be to encourage staff to ask questions about their work and achieving the required standards. It is likely that questions will frequently be asked of the supervisor as this is the person in direct contact with the member of staff providing the service. Listen to questions, answer them promptly and when the answer is not immediately known, find out and communicate it back as soon as possible.

3.4 Organisational objectives and policies

There will be certain objectives and policies within the organisation that may influence the running of a linen service. These could include:
- budgets available for purchase, care and replacement of linen
- quality of linen required
- storage facilities available for linen
- provision of in-house laundry or laundry sent to an external laundry
- tablecloths used in restaurants and other dining areas or plain table tops used, linen or disposable napkins
- colour schemes and themes to be reflected in some or all of the linen
- logo or signature markings on linen
- the required 'look' of guest rooms, e.g. beds with just a white duvet cover or finished with a bedspread, types of pillow cases and decorative items on the bed.

Evidence 2
3.1 3.2 3.4

Find:
- A chart showing the positions and responsibilities of different people in your establishment.
- Forms/record sheets used when sending linen to other departments.
- A printed policy related to linen.

4.1 4.2 4.3 Legal requirements

The requirements of health and safety legislation are covered in Chapter 4: Maintain the health, hygiene, safety and security of the working environment and in Chapter 9: Supervise housekeeping services.

Health and safety requirements that are specific to providing a linen service are likely to be those around fire risk assessment and fire prevention. It is also important to comply with legislation to protect employees' health and well-being when lifting and transporting heavy linen and moving heavy items such as beds when bed making.

It is of the utmost importance in an area dealing with guests and employees that legal requirements are understood and complied with at all times. Where there are concerns that legal requirements are not being met, immediate action is needed. Record your concerns and discuss with your head housekeeper or line manager immediately. In a serious case, it may be more appropriate to voice your concerns in writing, on paper or electronically.

Legislation

Further information about legislation affecting housekeeping areas, including those relating to employment and equal opportunities, can be found in Chapter 9: Supervise housekeeping services.

Evidence 3
4.1 4.2 4.3

Collect:
- Leaflets, photographs of posters, information sheets, codes of practice on relevant legislation.
- Notes, emails, messages to staff about the importance of legislation and the consequences of non-compliance.
- Training or briefing notes on legal requirements.
- Performance/progress records used for staff.

Evidence 4
1.8 3.4 4.2 4.6 4.7

To ensure that your department is meeting its legal requirements, you have been asked to check the implementation of health and safety, employment and equal opportunities legislation and other regulations and codes of practice relevant to the department and make recommendations.

Find out what the company's objectives and policies are on these matters. Prepare a presentation with this information. Who would you present it to? Include where the limits of your own authority are on these matters.

1.4 Staff conduct and presentation

Those providing a linen service will probably be part of the overall housekeeping services and, as such, are likely to have contact with guests during the completion of their day-to-day work and in moving around the premises. For this reason, staff will need to wear their uniform correctly and must be clean, tidy and well presented, in line with company organisational policy at all times. It will be part of the supervision role to ensure that all staff fully understand the rules and procedures of the establishment and comply with them.

Evidence 5
1.1 1.2 1.3 1.4 1.6 1.8 1.9 1.10 2.3 2.4

Produce a leaflet for new staff that could be used as part of a training session. Include:
- The organisational policy for collecting linen and transporting it safely and correctly to the work area.
- Greeting and addressing guests.
- Giving a good impression to guests.
- Who to approach if any problems occur with the linen service and who can answer questions arising.

Also include the types/sizes of linen needed for a twin room and a double room, and the records that need to be kept when collecting linen and returning used linen to the linen room.

Evidence 6
1.1 1.2 1.3 1.4 1.10

Find the following resources for your organisation:
- staff rotas
- task/working procedures
- training booklets and instructions
- training and team briefings, notes and plans
- procedures and requirements for staff conduct and appearance.

Policy and procedures will also include how to communicate with guests, both when in their accommodation and when encountering them in corridors or public areas. Polite greetings and helpful responses to guests will present and promote the establishment well, building the required goodwill and understanding.

Staff will also need to fully understand the legal requirements and limitations of their contact with guests, especially around matters of security and data protection.

4.3 Monitoring staff performance against organisational standards

Once staff are trained and are fully aware of procedure, it will be necessary to monitor their performance to check that it consistently reaches the standards required. The supervisor will usually monitor standards by observing work being completed and checking standards of finished work. To maintain standards and consistency, some of the training procedures listed above may need to be revisited as necessary.

Key terms

Feedback – offering a helpful response to someone's work, performance or ideas

Monitoring – observing and checking progress or quality of something being completed

Reviewing – to examine a situation to find out if changes or improvements need to be made

Stock levels – amounts of specific items available for use or in storage

1.5 Informing staff and customers about service changes

Occasionally there may be changes to services that may affect staff and/or customers. These could include a wide range of changes such as:
- late or early guest arrivals or departures
- repair or maintenance work affecting normal linen services
- changes to the service over weekends and bank holidays
- special requests such as special pillows or cots for babies
- changes to storage procedures for linen
- laundry collection/delivery times
- staff shortages resulting in a change in normal procedure.

When changes occur, it is important that the supervisor communicates the necessary information quickly so high standards of service can be maintained.

1.6 2.5 2.6 4.5 4.6 4.7 Managing problems

As with all housekeeping services, there will occasionally be problems that could disrupt the service provided. Where possible, anticipate any likely problems that may occur and have contingency plans in place to deal with them. Contingency means considering and anticipating any possible problems and having plans in place to solve the problem and prevent disruption. Production of contingency plans may involve a number of different people such as the hotel manager, head housekeeper, supervisors and maybe some of the relevant contractors. Possible problems that could occur need to be discussed, along with suggested actions and who would be responsible for carrying them out. Names and contact details of individuals or agencies who may help with the situation could also be included (keep these details in a secure place). Contingency plans need to be revisited and updated regularly to check that they remain relevant and are likely to work in given situations.

Support staff to overcome problems in their area and, if appropriate, introduce measures that could prevent a specific problem from occurring again. Depending on the actual problem, it may be necessary to seek help from your line manager, from another area or seek help from outside of the organisation where appropriate. Concerns about problems disrupting the service or any recurring problems should be discussed in team or management meetings in order to seek a long-term solution.

Some problems you will be able to solve by yourself using your knowledge of the area, previous experience and the establishment's requirements. However, some problems will arise which are beyond the limits of your authority. When this situation occurs, it is necessary to seek help and this is likely to be from the head housekeeper, line manager, human resources or possibly occupational health or a counselling service.

Evidence 7
1.5 1.6 1.7

Find printed copies of:
- Fire evacuation procedures and any contingency plans.
- Notices sent to staff and customers about such things as maintenance work at the weekend.
- Questionnaires used for staff and surveys/questionnaires used with customers.
- Outcomes of telephone or email surveys.

Evidence 8
`1.6` `3.1` `3.2` `3.3` `4.5`

The coffee shop/afternoon tea area have reported shortages of their linen and the problem seems to be that losses are occurring and linen is not being returned for laundry. The manager of the area states that more linen needs to be purchased but you do not think this is the solution to the problem. Plan in steps/bullet points the actions you would take to address the problem.

Find out what the company's objectives and policies are on these matters.

Key terms

Organisational policy – the policies, practices and set procedures of an establishment

Human resources – the part of a company concerned with matters relating to employees such as recruitment, induction and training, employee benefits and retention

Occupational health – an area or department concerned with the health and well-being of employees

Contractors – a separate company contracted to provide goods and services

Evidence 9
`1.1` `1.2` `1.6` `2.1` `2.5` `2.5` `2.6` `4.5` `4.7`

A problem has occurred. You have been informed of two days of strike action by staff at the laundry you use. You will have no collections or deliveries from tomorrow for 48 hours.
- What could you do to overcome this problem and keep services running as smoothly as possible?
- How could you re-allocate some of the tasks to staff and brief them on changes in procedure?
- What extra time and resources will be needed?

`1.10` `4.8` Completing the required records

Purchase and upkeep of the necessary linen for an establishment can be very expensive so it is essential to keep careful records of purchase, stock levels and movement of linen to and from the laundry.

Linen records can be paper-based or kept on an electronic system. There are advantages and disadvantages to both ways of completing and storing records, and there is more information about this in Chapter 9, 'Supervise housekeeping services'.

Records kept will include:
- Purchase of new linen including date, supplier, amounts, sizes, cost of each item, date of issue for use.
- Total stock amounts of each item.
- Items sent to and returned from the laundry; any discrepancies will need to be investigated and any problems investigated and solved.
- Amounts of linen items sent to floor level linen rooms.
- Issue of items to staff.

- Guests' personal items sent for laundry or dry cleaning.
- Missing items from guest rooms and other areas.
- Damaged or worn-out items to be taken from use.

It is usual to see a card or notice in guest rooms asking guests to consider not having their linen changed every day but reusing it. Reuse saves on resources and energy, as well as reducing expensive laundry costs.

Figure 13.3 Hotel guests can be asked to consider reusing their linen

Evidence 10
`1.1` `1.2` `1.3` `1.9` `1.10` `2.1` `2.3` `2.4` `4.5` `4.8`

You have noted that improvements could be made to the linen service. Too much time is being spent by staff recording the linen they collect for use and the linen they send to the laundry. The forms they use are over-complicated and difficult to use, especially for staff whose first language is not English.

Produce a new form that is simple and easy to understand and use. How will you instruct staff in its use and save time but still provide the necessary information?

`1.7` `1.8` `4.9` `4.10` Monitoring and reviewing procedures and collecting feedback

Collecting feedback from staff and customers and how this is achieved is discussed in Chapter 9, 'Supervise housekeeping services'. Inevitably some of this feedback will refer to linen and the linen service. Feedback comments are very important and can provide valuable information for how the service can be improved in the future. Collecting feedback comments is important because this will show the main concerns over a given time and also highlight recurring complaints and concerns. Once the necessary information is available, it can be discussed and relevant remedial action taken.

Evidence 11
`1.8` `1.9` `1.10` `4.1`

Find:
- Any printed occupational standards or procedure.
- Leaflets, booklets and photographs of posters relating to health and safety that are used in your establishment.
- Letters, notes and emails you may have used to recommend improvements.

1.9 4.11 4.12 4.13 Recommending improvements

The supervisor will be in close day-to-day contact with the staff providing the linen and housekeeping service, so is in a good position to hear from them of any improvements that may be needed. Observing and monitoring the work completed may result in recommendations for improvement. Small improvements within the requirements of the organisational policy could possibly be implemented immediately. However, where the need for more major improvements are identified, representation and discussion with a head housekeeper or line manager may be required.

Using information gained from staff and customer feedback will give supervisors and managers valuable insight into the issues considered important to customers and how their requirements can be met to improve the overall service. Recommendations can then be made and changes implemented that could also make the service given more efficient.

When recommendations for improvements are made, you will need to support your recommendations with suitable evidence. Provide as much information as possible to support your case, outlining the advantages and improvements that could be made. Evidence may include written explanation, photographs, comparisons, magazine, newspaper or internet articles, recommendations from another establishment, financial comparisons, statements from staff and physical items such as fabric samples.

Initially your recommendations are likely to be to your head housekeeper or line manager but you may be required to present your findings to others such as the general manager or food and beverage manager.

Evidence 12
4.8 4.9 4.10

Collect:
- any computer-based or paper-based records relevant to the purchase, allocation, laundary or care of linen
- feedback forms and questionnaires
- questionnaire outcomes and findings.

Evidence 13
1.5 1.6 1.7 1.8 1.9 4.4 4.6 4.7 4.9 4.10 4.11 4.12 4.13

In recent guest surveys some issues around the linen service have been raised on a number of occasions. The issues are:
- Some of the towels appear to be worn and frayed at the edges.
- Although no request was made to reuse bed linen and towels, the linen was not changed.
- Linen change is completed late in the day.
- The wrong selection of towels were placed in the bathroom; too many hand towels and no bath sheet or face cloths.

1. How could you find out why these problems are occurring?
2. What recommendations you could make to management to prevent these problems recurring and who could you approach for extra resources?
3. How much of this could you deal with yourself and what would you need to refer to someone else? Who would you refer it to?
4. How can you communicate the agreed improvements to staff?
5. How will you monitor and review the improvements?

Knowledge check

1. What is meant by thread count?
2. What are three types of records you may need to keep in relation to linen services?
3. What are the ways you could collect feedback from guests on linen services provided?
4. What is meant by a contingency plan and why is it needed?
5. What are the health and safety issues specifically relevant to running a linen service?
6. What are the ways that you could communicate with others when providing a linen service and why is good communication essential?
7. What are the advantages of using an off-site laundry?
8. When supplying linen for another area or department, suggest four questions you may ask them about their requirements.
9. Suggest four ways that you could inform/brief staff on the procedures needed for linen supply.
10. What are the ways that employees can give a good impression of themselves and the establishment to guests? How could you communicate this to the staff you supervise?

Evidence checklist		
Assessment criteria		**Possible evidence**
1.1	Allocate and brief staff to linen duties including: Relevant procedures and work routines	Evidence activity 5 Evidence activity 6 Evidence activity 9 Evidence activity 10
1.2	Ensure that staff have the skills, knowledge and resources needed	Evidence activity 5 Evidence activity 6 Evidence activity 9 Evidence activity 10
1.3	Encourage staff to ask questions when needed	Evidence activity 5 Evidence activity 6 Evidence activity 10
1.4	Ensure conduct and presentation of staff	Evidence activity 5 Evidence activity 6
1.5	Inform staff and customers about service changes that may affect them	Evidence activity 7 Evidence activity 13
1.6	Manage problems that disrupt the linen service	Evidence activity 5 Evidence activity 7 Evidence activity 8 Evidence activity 9 Evidence activity 13
1.7	Collect feedback on the service from staff and customers	Evidence activity 7 Evidence activity 13
1.8	Monitor and review procedures to ensure the service meets the needs of customers and complies with relevant legislation and organisational policy	Evidence activity 4 Evidence activity 5 Evidence activity 11 Evidence activity 13

Evidence checklist		
Assessment criteria		**Possible evidence**
1.9	Recommend ways of improving linen service following organisational requirements	Evidence activity 5 Evidence activity 10 Evidence activity 11 Evidence activity 13
1.10	Complete the required records according to organisation's procedures	Evidence activity 5 Evidence activity 6 Evidence activity 10 Evidence activity 11
2.1	Explain how to estimate the time and resources needed for the linen service	Evidence activity 1 Evidence activity 9 Evidence activity 10
2.2	Identify who to approach to get approval for the use of additional resources	Evidence activity 1
2.3	Explain how to write procedures and work instructions	Evidence activity 1 Evidence activity 5 Evidence activity 10
2.4	Explain how to brief staff on procedures relevant to running of the linen service	Evidence activity 1 Evidence activity 5 Evidence activity 10
2.5	Explain the importance of contingency plans	Evidence activity 1 Evidence activity 9
2.6	Explain how to develop contingency plans	Evidence activity 1 Evidence activity 9
3.1	Explain the different roles and responsibilities of individuals within the organisation	Evidence activity 2 Evidence activity 8
3.2	Explain how the linen service integrates with other departments in the organisation	Evidence activity 2 Evidence activity 8
3.3	Explain the consequences of the linen service and other departments not working together	Evidence activity 8
3.4	Describe the organisation's objectives and policies that are relevant to running the linen service	Evidence activity 2 Evidence activity 4
4.1	Explain how to implement the requirements of: ● Health and safety ● Employment legislation ● Equal opportunities legislation ● Other industry-specific regulations and codes of practice	Evidence activity 3 Evidence activity 11
4.2	Describe the actions to take when legal requirements are not met	Evidence activity 3 Evidence activity 4
4.3	Explain how to monitor staff performance against the organisation's standards	Evidence activity 3
4.4	Explain how to communicate effectively with others	Evidence activity 13
4.5	Explain how to deal with problems that are likely to occur when running a linen service	Evidence activity 8 Evidence activity 9 Evidence activity 10

Evidence checklist		
Assessment criteria		**Possible evidence**
4.6	Describe the limits of own authority when dealing with problems	Evidence activity 4
		Evidence activity 13
4.7	Identify who to approach when a solution to a problem is beyond the limits of own authority	Evidence activity 4
		Evidence activity 9
		Evidence activity 13
4.8	Compare the advantages and disadvantages of completing and storing computer-based and paper-based records	Evidence activity 10
		Evidence activity 12
4.9	Explain the importance of feedback from staff and customers	Evidence activity 12
		Evidence activity 13
4.10	Describe how to collect and analyse feedback from staff and customers	Evidence activity 12
		Evidence activity 13
4.11	Identify the types of recommendations that could be made to meet customer needs and improve efficiency	Evidence activity 13
4.12	Identify who to present recommendations to	Evidence activity 13
4.13	Explain how to support recommendations with appropriate evidence	Evidence activity 13

Evidence presented for this unit must come from the candidate's work in a suitable hospitality workplace when supervising housekeeping services. There must be sufficient evidence that the candidate can achieve the learning objectives and assessment criteria on a consistent basis.

In addition to the generation of evidence suggested throughout the chapter, the following may be used as part of your evidence:
- observation of your work in linen areas by someone senior to you
- products of your work – documents, letters, plans etc.
- witness testimony of professional discussion
- candidate statements about work completed
- observation sheets
- video clips
- linen allocation charts
- notes of meetings with line manager
- meeting agendas
- staff rotas
- team briefing notes
- plans for functions and events involving linen allocation
- linen records
- witness statements
- records of professional discussion
- oral questions/written questions
- project related to provision of a linen service
- reflective account
- records of oral questioning
- question/answer sheets
- relevant photographs, plans and sketches
- forms, charts or other information produced by you.

CHAPTER 14

Monitor and solve customer service problems

This chapter is about looking at both your organisation and your staffing resources and bringing these together in a constructive way to improve overall customer service. You need to give support and guidance to your team to encourage them to improve their customer service delivery. It is about having a passion for customer service and sharing this enthusiasm with your colleagues and staff team. It is about leading by example.

Learning objectives

On completion of this chapter, you should:
1 Be able to solve immediate customer service problems.
2 Be able to identify repeated customer service problems and options for solving them.
3 Be able to take action to avoid the repetition of customer service problems.
4 Understand how to monitor and solve customer service problems.

How to resolve immediate customer service problems

1.1 Responding positively to problems following organisational guidelines

You and all your team must follow organisational practices and procedures relevant to your customer service work and always check with someone in authority when unsure. This includes following all in-house rules and guidelines and external legislation.

Customer service charter

A customer service charter is an organisation's promise to the customer, outlining what any customer can expect. It is the organisation's duty to provide all the resources required to staff to allow them to fulfil that promise. For example, any customer would be frustrated when they order their favourite cocktail from the menu, only to be told by staff that the ingredients are not in stock. The menu is a promise of a product that can be provided and breaking this promise can hurt the emotional relationship that the customer is building with the organisation and damage future loyalty.

The customer service charter is also a guide to what is expected from the organisation's employees in terms of customer service. As supervisor, you need to ensure that new employees are trained in all of this information and work in line with the organisation's rules and guidelines. Failure to do so can result in mistakes, customer complaints and the employee may feel despondent and leave the organisation sooner. The hospitality industry often has high levels of turnover so this process can be challenging. A consistent, structured and well supported training plan is essential for success.

Customer service charter

- Ensure that customer expectations are understood
- 24-hour reception service
- Provide polite and friendly service to customers at all times
- Provide a professional service at all times
- Respond quickly to customer requirements
- Provide customers with honest information and advice
- Respond quickly and appropriately to feedback and complaints

Figure 14.1 Sample of a customer service charter

Evidence 1
4.1

Collect samples of customer service charters from three different hospitality organisations.

Consumer regulations

Consumer regulations relevant to dealing with customer service problems include the following:
- Consumer Contracts Regulations – give rights to customers when buying online, at a distance or away from a trader's premises.
- Unfair Terms in Consumer Contracts Regulations 1999 – explains why a contract term might be unfair.
- Consumer Protection from Unfair Trading Regulations 2008 – protect consumers from unfair or misleading trading practices and ban misleading omissions and aggressive sales tactics.
- Payment Services Regulations 2009 – protects customers and organisations against card fraud.
- Sale of Goods Act 1979 – states that goods must be as described, of satisfactory quality and fit for purpose.
- Misrepresentation Act 1967 – protects customers from false or fraudulent claims that might encourage you to enter into a contract.
- Financial Services Regulations 2004 – regulates the sale of financial services.
- Supply of Goods and Services Act 1982 – ensures that customers can expect goods and services to be supplied with reasonable care and skill.

For other legislation that affects your customer service work, see Chapter 4: Maintain the health, hygiene, safety and security of the working environment.

Always view customer service problems as an opportunity to learn and improve your service, your team's service, your customer relationship and your personal skills. Problem solving is an essential skill in the workplace (and in your personal life) and, with practice, you will become better at it. Approach a customer complaint in a positive frame of mind: assume that they are speaking truthfully and follow the steps below to find resolution.

1.2 1.3 1.4 1.5 1.7 4.1 Solving customer service problems

Five simple steps for complaint handling

This section explains the five key steps for handling complaints.

1 Listen

Listen actively to the customer while they talk; do not interrupt and do use appropriate eye contact. Never assume that you know what the problem is before listening to the customer. By taking notes while they are talking, you are showing the customer that you are taking what they are saying seriously. In the case of a serious complaint, the guest may feel extremely frustrated and feel the need to 'rant' – allow them to without being emotional. Don't take it personally. If they become verbally abusive at any point, calmly tell them that it is not acceptable and politely request they stop at once or you will need to contact security or the police. Only once the guest has finished what they are saying should you ask any questions that you need to, in order to clarify your understanding. Then paraphrase what the customer has told you in your own words to confirm the situation.

2 Acknowledge

If a mistake has been made, acknowledge it and apologise. Apologise only for the relevant problem and nothing further. Use language that reflects the customer's feelings so you sound like you are on their side, such as, 'It upsets me to hear this has happened'. Don't be afraid to tell the guest if you need time to investigate the problem to ensure that you have all the facts. Just ensure that you inform them clearly on the steps you intend to take, how much time you will need and stick to it.

3 Act quickly

Leaving an upset customer without speedy resolution will only serve to make the situation worse. With the customer, decide on what action should be taken whilst ensuring you're not rushing too quickly to compensation; often a solution to the problem is enough. Get authorisation from the appropriate management, keeping them fully informed of the situation, and implement your chosen action. By discussing your plans with your peers, and your team as well, you can secure their approval too; they may be able to offer expertise that can enhance your solution. Considering their point of view shows respect and then they are more likely to reciprocate in the future.

4 Follow up

Check that the solution went smoothly and ask the customer if there is anything else that you can assist them with. The worst complaints happen when continuous mistakes are made and, by following up in this way, you can work to prevent them happening in future; also the customer's last interaction with you will be one that made them feel valued.

5 Review

Record the details of what happened and review them with colleagues and managers to ensure future mistakes are avoided. Use each complaint as a learning opportunity.

> **Evidence 2**
> 1.1 1.2 1.3 1.4 1.5 1.7 4.1
>
> Collect some records of previous complaints, or write some common complaint scenarios, and role play with your teams how the issues could be resolved. At the end of the session write a written review and discuss the team's performance.

Empowering your team to be able to make decisions, deliver personalised service and bend the policies of the organisation in your absence is a great way to make your customers feel special and valued. The added benefit is that staff will feel motivated and trusted with this **autonomy**. For example, you may allow staff to extend a check-out time or provide complimentary coffee when an order has taken a bit too long. Clear boundaries on what decisions employees do not need permission for must be set in advance and clearly communicated. One restaurant authorised employees to spend up to £50 to correct mistakes or encourage customer loyalty; they only needed to complete a form with details of the reason. The result meant that if customers were celebrating a special anniversary or birthday, then staff could offer a complimentary aperitif; or if there was a complaint about a dish, they were able to remove the food from the bill without calling the manager or supervisor. The success of the strategy depends on trusting the team to make decisions; employees should not be reprimanded for making poor decisions, but should be taught to make a better decision next time.

> **Key terms**
>
> **Empowering** – provide the authority to do something
>
> **Autonomy** – the opportunity to be self-governing in the workplace

> **Evidence 3**
> 1.1 1.2 1.3
>
> With your team, create a list of examples of customer problems, increasing in severity. In the column next to your examples, list actions employees are authorised to take without permission in order to rectify the problem. Display the final table in back of house areas for employees to refer to.
>
> Repeat the exercise for opportunities to 'wow' guests, e.g. birthday celebrations.

1.6 Solving problems before customers become aware of them

The customer service provision needs to be reviewed and refreshed regularly and continual improvement strived for, not just when a customer complains. Competitors will keep evolving so don't let your team become complacent. Keep setting specific achievement goals which are measurable.

Touchpoints are the times when a customer encounters customer service from the beginning to the end. Touchpoints can be mapped into a customer journey and used to identify areas for improvement.

> **Key term**
>
> **Touchpoints** – any point of contact between a customer and a member of staff

---

Evidence 4

1.3 1.6 2.1 3.4

The following activity can be carried out with your teams to start the process of evaluating the customer touchpoints:
- Step 1: Interview customers to ascertain any needs not being met; use a variety of methods (e.g. in person, email, focus groups) and target a variety of customers.
- Step 2: Create a list of your customer's points of contact with your team using flow charts from the customer perspective. What happens to them from the moment they arrive to the moment they leave?
- Step 3: Make a list of customer service needs and rate your organisation on how well they are met. Clearly outline what you already excel at, and where improvement is needed.
- Step 4: Generate a list of ideas to tackle the areas for improvement.
- Step 5: Implement the chosen ideas; allow some time to pass and repeat your survey.
- Step 6: Interview the same groups and seek some new additional views.
- Step 7: Ask your team members what has changed for them. Have the new systems for improvement affected their job satisfaction and morale?
- Step 8: Repeat regularly to ensure your team consistently delivers customer service excellence.

How to prevent repeated customer service problems

2.1 4.1 4.2 Monitoring and identifying problems

Have a formal system in place to record all customer service problems and report all problems to the manager on duty. The manager should write the day's events into a logbook that can be reviewed. Records need to be detailed and thorough, including the following points:
- date
- time
- name of staff who dealt with the problem
- names of anyone else involved, such as security
- details of the issue
- action that was taken
- any follow-up that occurred or is required
- whether the issue is open, pending or closed
- guest's details, if secure.

Customer name	
Company name	
Phone number	Mobile
Correspondence address	
Email	
Date compliment/complaint received	
Nature of compliment/complaint	
How was the compliment/complaint communicated	In person ❏ Written ❏
	Telephone ❏ Other ❏

Figure 14.2 Example of a compliment or complaint record

Ensure customers have an easy way to contact you if they have had a bad experience, as it gives you the chance to correct problems before they tell other people. Monitor all forms of feedback, including social media and independent review sites such as TripAdvisor. Even better practice is to seek feedback through surveys in-house or in an email after the customer's visit. Create a forum for staff to provide feedback too, as they are continually working with your customers and will want the organisation to be successful.

Meet with your manager and team at least once a week to review the feedback you have received and use the information to identify any repeated problems. Ensure that you gather all the facts and contributing factors; give everyone a chance to express their point of view. You will always encounter people who say your service is too expensive or who are looking to get something for free and they should be largely ignored. But if you repeatedly receive letters outlining connection problems with the Wi-Fi signal in your hotel, for example, then action needs to be taken.

2.2 2.3 4.2 Selecting options for solving repeated problems

As a group, brainstorm solutions to repeating customer problems. Some solutions are a simple matter of whether to make a change such as replacing something. For a more complex problem, with varying factors and options, you could use the 'pros and cons' and the 'weighted' decision-making methods.

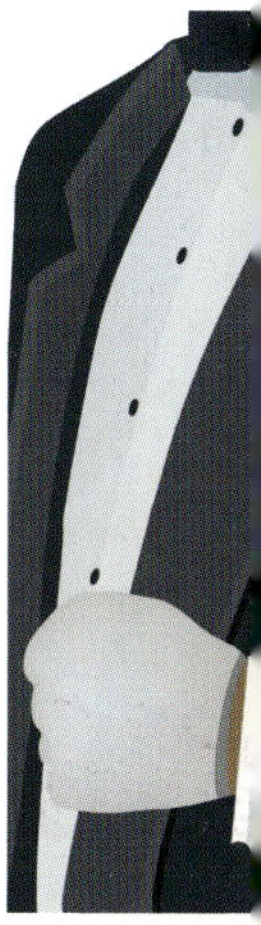

Identify which criteria of a potential solution are most important to the organisation and rate them from 1 for 'low importance' to 5 for 'most important'. In order to balance the needs of the customer with those of the organisation, repeat the process from the customer's perspective.

For example:

Table 14.1 Criteria and ratings of a potential solution

Criteria for solution	Weight
Low cost	5
Reputation	4
Customer satisfaction	3
Speed it can be implemented	2
Disruption to daily activities	1

Create a table as below and give each factor a score against the criteria from 1 (low) to 5 (high). If the factor completes the criteria, then it may score a five; if the factor provides no support at all for the criteria, it may score zero. Repeat the process for each potential solution. The resulting scores will provide some objective clarity and measurement.

Table 14.2 caption to follow

Option – Install better Wi-Fi							
Organisation pros & cons				Customer pros & cons			
Pro	Score	Con	Score	Pro	Score	Con	Score
Total		Total		Total		Total	

If there are too many options to start with, the table can be adapted to help narrow them down.

Table 14.3 Caption to follow

Criteria	Weight	Option1 Wi-Fi provider A	Option2 Wi-Fi provider B	Option3 Wi-Fi provider C	Option4 Repair current Wi-Fi
Low cost	5				
Reputation	4				
Satisfaction	3				
Speed	2				
Disruption	1				
Total					

For more complex decisions, you can weight the criteria from 1–10, from 1–20 or even 1–100.

3.1 3.2 3.3 3.4 Taking action to avoid repetition of the problem

Make certain that the solution, agreed by somebody with sufficient authority, is implemented and keep the change on the agenda of subsequent meetings, so that the results can be monitored for improvement. Always remember to adjust the new process if needed.

Try to respond to all feedback that you receive from customers and not just with 'thank you for your feedback'. Instead, tell your customer what action you are taking to improve things; they will feel that their opinion is valued and respected. They may even become loyal to the organisation after helping.

4.3 The benefits of successful resolution of customer service problems

Any organisation that offers services is certain to experience complaints; they are inevitable. Each complaint is an opportunity for service recovery and to strengthen loyalty. By taking steps to correct a customer's problem, you are showing them that they are important to you; and when the resolution experience exceeds a customer's expectations, an organisation can build loyalty with them.

Any member of staff will prefer to work for an organisation which can resolve customer problems and create loyalty, compared to working for an organisation where the staff member has to deal continually with unhappy, unsatisfied or irate customers. They may transfer these skills when dealing with service partners, who would then go on to believe that the organisation must be good to work for as its staff are so happy. All of these stakeholders will contribute to the organisation's elevated reputation.

> **Evidence 5**
> 1.3 2.2 2.3 3.1 3.2 3.3 4.2
>
> Collect a copy of a completed 'weighted' decision matrix.

> **Evidence 6**
> 4.3 4.4
>
> Through your experience, or that of an expert witness, describe in detail one complaint that was resolved by a solution that exceeded the expectations of the customer. Explain the stages of solving the problem and the benefits to the organisation, individual and team.

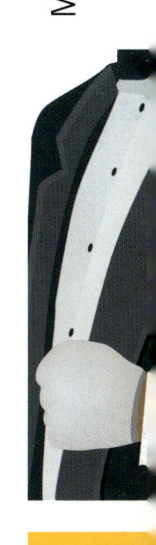

Knowledge check

1. How could an organisation prevent a customer service problem?
2. What method can an organisation use to monitor customer problems?
3. What are the five steps when dealing with a complaint?
4. What information should be recorded when a customer problem occurs?
5. How should an organisation deal with a repeating customer service problem?

Evidence checklist		
Assessment criteria		**Possible evidence**
1.1	Respond positively to customer service problems following organisational guidelines	Evidence activity 2
		Evidence activity 3
1.2	Solve customer service problems when they have sufficient authority	Evidence activity 2
		Evidence activity 3
1.3	Work with others to solve customer service problems	Evidence activity 2
		Evidence activity 3
		Evidence activity 4
		Evidence activity 5
1.4	Keep customers informed of the actions being taken	Evidence activity 2
1.5	Check with customers that they are comfortable with the actions being taken	Evidence activity 2
1.6	Solve problems with service systems and procedures that might affect customers before customers become aware of them	Evidence activity 4
1.7	Inform managers and colleagues of the steps taken to solve specific problems	Evidence activity 2
2.1	Identify repeated customer service problems	Evidence activity 4
2.2	Identify the options for dealing with a repeated customer service problem and consider the advantages and disadvantages of each option	Evidence activity 5
2.3	Work with others to select the best option for solving a repeated customer service problem, balancing customer expectations with the needs of the organisation	Evidence activity 5
3.1	Obtain the approval of somebody with sufficient authority to change organisational guidelines in order to reduce the chance of a problem being repeated	Evidence activity 5
3.2	Action their agreed solution	Evidence activity 5
3.3	Keep their customers informed in a positive and clear manner of steps being taken to solve any service problems	Evidence activity 5
3.4	Monitor the changes they have made and adjust them if appropriate	Evidence activity 4
4.1	Describe organisational procedures and systems for dealing with customer service problems	Evidence activity 1
		Evidence activity 2
4.2	Describe organisational procedures and systems for identifying repeated customer service problems	Evidence activity 5
4.3	Explain how the successful resolution of customer service problems contributes to customer loyalty with the external customer and improved working relationships with service partners or internal customers	Evidence activity 6
4.4	Explain how to negotiate with and reassure customer while their problems are being solved	Evidence activity 6

In addition to the generation of evidence suggested throughout the chapter, the following may be used as part of your evidence:

- TripAdvisor reviews, with responses from the organisation
- complaint and compliment letters and subsequent correspondence
- manager on-duty logs
- agendas from feedback review meetings
- minutes from feedback review meetings
- staff training records and materials
- a copy of your own performance development review.

CHAPTER 15

Improve the customer relationship

This chapter is about looking at both your organisation and your staffing resources and bringing them together in a constructive way to improve overall customer service. You need to give support and guidance to your team to encourage them to improve their customer service delivery. It is about having a passion for customer service and sharing this enthusiasm with your colleagues and staff team. It is about leading by example.

Learning objectives

On completion of this chapter, you should:
1. Be able to improve communication with your customers.
2. Be able to balance the needs of your customers and your organisation.
3. Be able to exceed customer expectations to develop the relationship.
4. Understand how to improve the customer relationship.

Communication

1.1 4.1 Communication with customers

Communication skills are a huge part of our lives. Every day you pass information and messages back and forth through verbal, non-verbal and written forms of communication. Successful communication is when the receiver completely understands the information from the sender. Being capable of expressing yourself effectively and conveying your message accurately is a valuable ability in your professional and personal life and will help you to achieve your goals.

Communication goes through stages, and barriers to the successful transference of the information can occur at any time.

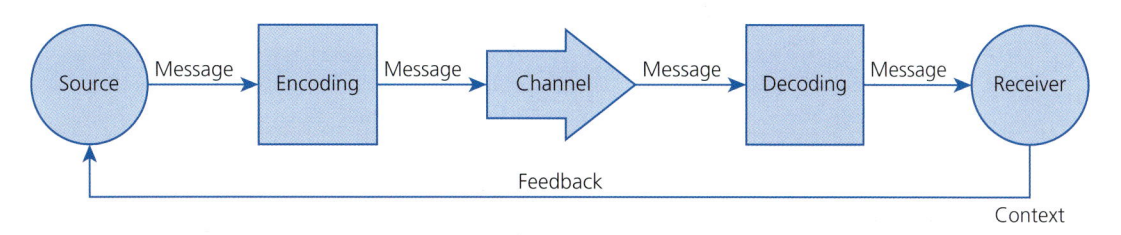

Source → Message → Encoding → Message → Channel → Message → Decoding → Message → Receiver

Feedback

Context

Figure 15.1 The stages of communication

> ### The stages of communication
>
> **Stage One:** Sender – Who is sending the message and why.
>
> **Stage Two:** Message – What you want to communicate.
>
> **Stage Three:** Encoding – How the message is phrased and whether the information is clear and simple.
>
> **Stage Four:** Channel – Which method of communication is chosen? For example, face to face, telephone, letter, email etc.
>
> **Stage Five:** Decoding – How the receiver understands the message.
>
> **Stage Six:** Feedback – How the receiver reacts to the information (verbal or non-verbal).

With planning and practice, barriers to communication can be removed. When the message you want to send is important, ask yourself the following ten questions before acting:

1. What do you want to communicate?
2. Is it accurate?
3. Is there any information missing?
4. Is the language used comprehensible?
5. Is it useful to the sender?
6. Is all the information relevant and required?
7. Which method of communication would be best?
8. How urgent is it that the receiver gets the information?
9. Which method of communication is the receiver most likely to like and understand?
10. Can any of the information be misinterpreted?

Effective communication is about choosing the best form of communication for the specific purpose. All have advantages and disadvantages. See the tables below for some examples.

Table 15.1 Advantages of face-to-face communication

Face-to-face communication	
Advantages	**Disadvantages**
Body language can be used to help	It can take time to arrange a meeting
Questions resolved quickly	Difficult to practise in large organisations
Immediate responses and feedback	Ineffective in large groups
Feelings can be expressed	No record of communication to refer to
Opportunities to adjust style	Harder to hide negative responses

Table 15.2 Advantages of telephone communication

Telephone	
Advantages	**Disadvantages**
Tone of voice can be used to help	No record of communication (except voicemail)
Questions resolved quickly	Facial expressions cannot be read
Immediate responses and feedback	There is some financial cost involved
Geographical barriers resolved	Phone calls can disrupt activities

Table 15.3 Advantages of email communication

Email	
Advantages	**Disadvantages**
Messages can be sent instantly	The tone can be misinterpreted
Geographical barriers resolved	There is some financial cost involved
Large groups can receive same message	Emails can be forwarded and so less secure
Messages can be stored to refer to	It may take time to receive a response

Carefully selecting your method of communicating by considering the advantages and disadvantages and the situation will help you to meet customer expectations.

Evidence 1
1.1 1.3 4.1

Consider the advantages and disadvantages of using an online form as a communication method and complete the box below.

Online form	
Advantages	Disadvantages

Meeting expectations

2.1 Meeting customer expectations

Communicate honestly with your customers and never over-promise. Make sure that the perceived expectation of service that you are communicating meets the service levels that you are able to deliver. Failure to do so can result in unsatisfied customers, complaints, cancellations and a poor reputation. Everybody makes mistakes and as hospitality is led by humans, there is no doubt at some point human error will occur. When it does, be honest about what happened, apologise and work to rectify the issue.

If a problem occurs always take the initiative to contact the customer in advance to keep them fully informed. Explain what has happened and why then offer possible courses of action. Most customers will understand that things don't always go as planned and will appreciate being kept informed.

1.3 2.2 2.3 2.4 2.5 2.6 4.2 4.3 Negotiating with customers

Effective communication skills are most beneficial to supervisors when a customer is unhappy. If a customer is unhappy because the organisation cannot deliver the service that the customer was expecting, then you may need to negotiate.

1. Consider the context and what you want to achieve. The situation may change the way you engage with the customer or the way that they interpret your message.
2. Know who you are talking to. If you are interacting with an angry customer, your tone and language need to be calm and formal, whereas if the customer is emotional and upset, your tone needs to reflect that and be soothing and reassuring.
3. Carefully select your method of communicating by considering the advantages and disadvantages. For example, if a customer emails you with an urgent query, you might choose to call them to answer their questions, but if your day is extremely busy already, you may email them to be quicker.
4. Be genuine. Use eye contact where possible. Show the customer that they are important to you using positive words and body language.
5. Actively listen, not only to what the customer is saying, but also to their body language and responses to what you say.
6. Analyse the situation and identify where the disagreement is.
7. Look for an option that you will be willing to trade on; seek advice from your manager, colleagues and other departments to explore what can be offered.
8. Consider the cost to the organisation of each option against the benefits to the organisation.
9. When negotiating with the customer, keep your emotions out of the conversation.
10. You will need to be decisive and quick to move during the negotiation as it may be necessary to compromise.
11. Maintain a positive attitude through negotiating and be patient with the customer.
12. Any promises made to the customer must be fulfilled if the customer's trust and loyalty is to be kept.

Scenario

Consider the following example.

A receptionist worked at an organisation consisting of two five-star hotels. A regular guest booked a room at the hotel that the receptionist worked at through a third-party provider. Unfortunately, due to a mistake on the part of the third-party provider, the reservation never reached the hotel and when the guest arrived after a long journey, he was informed that the hotel was fully booked. The receptionist said, 'Sorry we are full, there is nothing I can do.' The guest got very aggravated and left.

The costs were as follows:
1. The guest was upset.
2. The guest was a regular customer of the hotel but after the incident did not return.
3. The guest told his business colleagues at work of his bad experience.
4. The receptionist was upset when the guest was angry at her and lost motivation.
5. The hotel lost the income from this guest.

The receptionist could have contacted the sister hotel to check if they had availability before aggravating the guest. If a room was available, then it would have been unlikely to sell at that late stage and the receptionist could have negotiated a referral.

The receptionist would have needed to negotiate with the guest by pointing out that the benefit to the guest was that he would have a room for a night at the level of hospitality he was expecting. If the guest was unhappy about having to travel further, the receptionist could have compromised by discounting the room rate and by arranging a taxi to the sister hotel. The guest could have been offered a cup of coffee while they waited for their taxi.

The benefits of this negotiation are:
1. The sister hotel would gain revenue.
2. In the future the sister hotel may have returned the favour.
3. The guest was happy and satisfied.
4. The hotel benefited financially from his return business.
5. The hotel's reputation was not tarnished.
6. The receptionist's performance was commended by her manager.

The costs of this negotiation are:
1. A telephone call.
2. A cup of coffee.
3. Initiative from the receptionist.

> **Evidence 2**
>
> `1.2` `2.2` `2.3` `2.4` `2.5` `2.6` `4.2` `4.3` `4.4`
>
> Consider a scenario from your own experience where something has not gone to plan and you have helped a member of your team to resolve the problem.
>
> 1. Describe how they communicated the problem to the customer
> 2. Describe what options they used to negotiate with the customer
> 3. Describe the cost and benefits of their solution to the organisation
> 4. Write a witness statement describing how they resolved the problem effectively
> 5. Describe any involvement required from colleagues of other departments and how their help and support was secured
> 6. Explain how customer loyalty or internal relationships where affected

- On average, loyal customers are worth up to ten times as much as their first purchase.
- There is a 5–20% probability of selling to a new prospect.
- There is a 60–70% probability of selling to an existing customer.
- It takes 12 positive experiences to make up for one unresolved negative experience.

`3.1` `3.2` `3.3` `3.4` How to exceed expectations

Exceeding expectations should not be a 'one off'; it should be something to strive for every day. It is unusual for expectations to be exceeded by accident; it normally takes thought and initiative to seek out opportunities to achieve it. Success also depends on elements of surprise and being different – a product or service which is new and exciting now will be expected and normal tomorrow. An example of this is kettles in hotel rooms – not so long ago they were a luxury and now they are expected.

Remember and use the customer's name, their needs and preferences and seek opportunities to ask questions to gather more information. Using a customer's name shows recognition and that they are not just another customer to you, they are important enough to be remembered. Reach out to your customers as frequently as possible to remind them that you exist. Try feedback request forms/emails, news of special offers and promotions, send Christmas cards to your regular clientele, or remember their birthdays. Anything to make them feel individual, special and valued.

Once you have learned about your customer, you can find ways to add value to their experience and exceed their expectations. For example, one waitress was working at a restaurant with a live band playing when she noticed a lady dining alone. The waitress decided to start a polite conversation with the lady and she revealed that she was a widow having dinner to celebrate her wedding anniversary. From the information that the waitress was able to learn through this short interaction, she was able to arrange for the band to play the favourite song of the widow and her late husband. This small gesture cost the organisation nothing but that customer would remember it for a long time to come and tell her friends and family.

Continuously learning about your customer every time you meet them will extend your relationship beyond 'Hello, how are you today?' and provide the tools you need to keep them coming back. The more knowledge you procure, the more you can anticipate what the customer will want and then you have the tools to deliver an effortless, personalised service unique to the customer. Consider the questions most commonly asked by customers and seek ways to ensure they no longer need to ask.

In one historical hotel, a common question the staff were frequently asked was, 'Do you know anything about the history of the building?', so the hotel created a team of staff who were history enthusiasts and gave them time to investigate the building's past. They were able to put together a timeline, including stories, which was put on display to guests.

Try assessing the range of options available to your customers by considering competitors that offer similar services in your area. Is there anything that they do that your organisation could adapt? What does your organisation do to differentiate itself from these competitors? Be objective, don't just look for answers that fit with what your organisation offers already and dismiss other aspects. Your unique selling point will be what keeps people talking about your business.

It is vital to ensure that any action taken to exceed customer expectations is done in an appropriate way and adheres to organisational policies and procedures. A supervisor must not give away complimentary products and services without authorisation from a manager and a good reason why it is required. Although providing such gestures will secure the customers satisfaction in the short term, too much will result in the customer coming to expect 'freebies' which will impact profitability. If you are unsure what measures to exceed expectations of customers are appropriate seek advice, help and support from your manager.

Evidence 3

2.1 3.1 3.2 3.4

Try it from the customer's point of view. Many businesses use mystery shoppers or inspectors to test the customer service of their organisations. This does not always need to be someone external. Experience your organisation as a customer and see if the quality of service is how you would expect it to be. Identify areas where customer interactions could be enhanced – there are always opportunities to improve. Write a summary of your experience including positive and constructive feedback and present it to your manager. Include answers to the following questions:

1. Did the service meet your expectations? If not, why?
2. Were you able to identify any areas where the customer experience could be improved?
3. What would be the cost of these improvements to the organisation?
4. What would the benefits be to the organisation?
5. What would the benefits be to the customer?
6. Whose authority is required to implement the improvements?
7. Who would need to work to achieve them?

> **Key terms**
>
> **Unique selling point** – a feature of the organisation that competitors do not have
>
> **Sister hotel** – a hotel affiliated with your organisation through having the same owner or brand
>
> **Referral** – recommending another organisation when the required products and services are not available
>
> **Revenue** – the organisations income from business activities before costs are deducted

Knowledge check

1. What are the six stages of communication?
2. What are the advantages of face-to-face communication?
3. What are the disadvantages of face-to-face communication?
4. Give an example of how you can exceed expectations in an appropriate way

Evidence checklist		
Assessment criteria		**Possible evidence**
1.1	Select and use the best method of communication to meet customers' expectations	Evidence activity 1
1.2	Take the initiative to contact customers to update them when things are not going to plan or when they require further information	Evidence activity 2
1.3	Adapt communication to respond to individual customers' feelings	Evidence activity 3
2.1	Meet customer expectations with the organisation's service offer	Evidence activity 3
2.2	Explain the reasons to customers sensitively and positively when customer expectations cannot be met	Evidence activity 2
2.3	Identify alternative solutions for customers either within or outside the organisation	Evidence activity 2
2.4	Identify the costs and benefits of these solutions to the organisation and to customers	Evidence activity 2
2.5	Negotiate and agree solutions with customers which satisfy them and are acceptable to the organisation	Evidence activity 2
2.6	Take action to satisfy customers with the agreed solution when balancing customer needs with those of the organisation	Evidence activity 2
3.1	Make extra efforts to improve your relationship with customers	Evidence activity 3
3.2	Recognise opportunities to exceed customers' expectations	Evidence activity 3
3.3	Take action to exceed customers' expectations within the limits of your authority	Evidence activity 3
3.4	Gain the help and support of others to exceed customers' expectations	Evidence activity 3
4.1	Describe how to make best use of the method of communication chosen for dealing with customers	Evidence activity 1
4.2	Explain how to negotiate effectively with customers	Evidence activity 2
4.3	Explain how to assess the costs and benefits to customers and the organisation of any unusual agreement you make	Evidence activity 2
4.4	Explain the importance of customer loyalty and/or improved internal customer relationships to the organisation	Evidence activity 2

CHAPTER 16

Support learning and development within own area of responsibility

This chapter is about looking at how to support your team in their development. You need to seek accurate information about the details of training sessions and who is eligible to attend. This information needs to be communicated to your team and you need to allocate time for them to achieve their goals.

> **Learning objectives**
>
> On completion of this chapter, you should:
> 1 Be able to identify the learning needs of your colleagues in your area of responsibility.
> 2 Understand how to develop a learning environment.
> 3 Be able to support colleagues in learning and its application.
> 4 Be able to evaluate learning outcomes and future learning and development of colleagues.

Learning and development

2.1 Benefits of learning and development

An excuse often heard throughout the hospitality industry for not training and developing their teams is that they are just *too busy*: 'They cannot send team members to a training session as the restaurant is full and such and such has called in sick.' A supervisor must prioritise the development of their team or they will continually feel the consequences. If staff are not given the opportunity to improve on their skills, then their performance cannot improve and neither can the teams. This is illustrated in Figure 16.1.

Figure 16.1 Reasons why staff might leave

Training can improve staff morale and boost the profitability of your department in the following ways:
- By training your team in carefully chosen new skills, you can meet customer expectations of future trends, such as latte art or tea sommeliers.
- Training shows your staff that you value them and are willing to invest in them; this will raise morale.
- Staff who are learning through courses and qualifications, for example, are more likely to work for their organisation for longer.
- The more experience that your staff have, the better the service for customers.
- By developing your staff for the next level in their careers, you can form a **succession plan** before it is even required, to reduce the cost of recruitment.

Providing advice

3.1 3.3 Information, advice and guidance

A supervisor is the link between staff and management; they must know what training opportunities are available for their teams. This information can be found through your Human Resources department, the Learning and Development Manager, departmental trainers or your manager. There are also many independent external training providers which may be useful. Some organisations have sponsorship schemes in place to help staff members pay for relevant courses.

Use briefings and monthly departmental meetings to highlight upcoming training sessions that are available to the team and answer any questions they might have on the details.

> **Evidence 1**
> 2.1 2.2 3.1 3.3
> - Collect a learning and development policy and a training calendar from your workplace.
> - Collect a witness statement from a member of your team outlining how they access information on training opportunities.
> - Explain why learning and development are important.

1.1 1.2 Performance gap analysis

A performance gap is the gap between a team member's current performance and the performance level they need to achieve.

> **Key term**
>
> **Succession plan** – thinking ahead about which team members could be ready for a position before the person currently doing it leaves the organisation

> **Key terms**
>
> **Departmental trainers** – a member of staff nominated to be responsible for the co-ordination and recording of the team's learning and development activities
>
> **Training calendar** – a calendar normally circulated by the Human Resources department, outlining upcoming training opportunities

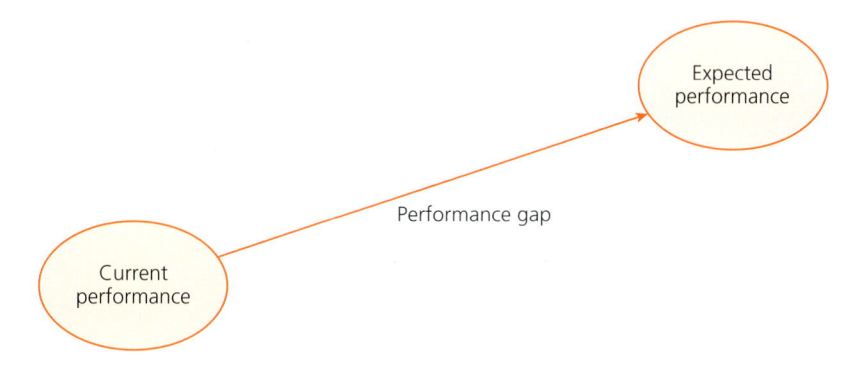

Figure 16.2 The performance gap

To identify performance gaps, consider the job description and personal specification of the role. Think of individuals in the same job that you consider to be excellent and ask yourself what they do that this staff member does not and write it down. Be sure to identify the activities/actions and consequences that are wrong, and not the personality characteristics of the individual. Do not make it personal. For example, if a staff member is negative and continually complains about everything, tell them that their views are affecting the morale of the team; if they have a complaint, they can talk to you about it directly. Don't say that they are negative as this will only offend them and make them defensive.

Newer team members will naturally have performance gaps while they are learning their roles, whilst more experienced team members may be working towards their next role and wish to close the gaps between their current role and the next level up.

It is important that the staff member is informed if a gap exists as they may not realise there is a problem. This conversation must be approached delicately in order to maintain the working relationship. Be as specific as possible in what they must do to improve. It may not be the fault of the staff member if they have not received the right training to do their job.

When considering the individual's needs for learning and development, it is important to look at them in relation to the needs of the organisation. Filling immediate skills gaps that allow team members to perform their role more effectively can contribute to the success of the organisation. Helping individuals to close skills gaps so that they can move up to the next level can also be advantageous (increasing staff morale, reducing staff turnover and possible recruitment and training costs), but filling immediate skills gaps may need to be prioritised.

1.3 2.2 3.2 4.2 How to close the gap

The next step is to identify what action needs to be taken to get the staff member's performance where it needs to be. This could be something that the staff member, the supervisor, or the organisation needs to do:

1. The staff member may only need to apply themselves more now they are aware of what needs to be achieved.
2. The supervisor may need to arrange or deliver one-to-one training for this area, such as a staff member 'shadowing' someone in the role they aspire to.
3. Your manager may need to book the staff member onto a relevant training session.

Any actions that are decided on should be recorded in the staff member's performance review and their progress monitored in the regular meetings that you have with them. You and the staff member must stay focused on their goals and not just mention it once a year in a review.

A personal development plan will help to identify targets and set timescales to improve skills. These targets could be short or longer term. It can be used to record feedback from a mentor, supervisor, manager or trainer, and help to improve performance. Keeping a record of skills and personal development plans will help you to refer back to your targets and check progress towards achieving goals.

It is important to realise that development takes self-motivation from the staff member; you can arrange all the training but it is useless unless the staff member wants to learn. Explain to them that they need to take responsibility for their own progression and this may take investment of their time. Once actions have been agreed, watch to see if the staff member delivers on the promises they make. Did they attend the training session you arranged for them? If not, are they making excuses for not going? You must also stick to what was agreed and not, for example, cancel their training if the department is too busy.

Evidence 2
1.1 1.2 1.3 3.2 4.2

1. Consider your own performance and identify any gaps between your current performance and the performance level you want to achieve. Write down the steps that you could take to achieve this, including any support you may need. Add this information to your personal development plan and request to discuss it at your next meeting.
2. Repeat for each member of your team.
3. Collect a witness statement from a member of your team outlining how the organisation has supported them through training (e.g. time allocated on the rota).

3.4 | 4.1 Follow up

Meet with team members straight after their learning to gather their feedback. You can record this information in a simple form for their personal development record. Include the following questions:

1. Did the training achieve its objectives?
2. Did you enjoy the training session?
3. Was the trainer effective?
4. What did the trainer do well?
5. How could the training be improved?
6. How will you apply this training to your job?
7. What further training do you require?

Monitor the progress through observations and remember to keep your manager fully informed. Be sure to provide the staff member time and opportunity where possible for practising the new skills. If progress is not taking place, further training may be required.

Key terms

Shadowing – when a member of staff follows the work of a person in another role for a set period of time

Personal development plan – to follow

Evidence 3

3.4 | 4.1

Create a training evaluation form and ask a member of your team to complete it after a training session you have delivered.

Knowledge check

1. What are the benefits of learning and development in the workplace?
2. Where can information on learning and development opportunities be found in your workplace?
3. How do you ensure that your team has access to this information?
4. Who is responsible for the learning and development of your team?

Evidence checklist		
Assessment criteria		**Possible evidence**
1.1	Identify gaps between requirements of colleagues' current or future work roles and their existing knowledge, understanding and skills	Evidence activity 2
1.2	Prioritise learning needs of colleagues	Evidence activity 2
1.3	Produce personal development plans for colleagues in your own area of responsibility	Evidence activity 2
2.1	Explain the benefits of continual learning and development	Evidence activity 1
2.2	Explain how learning opportunities can be provided for your own area of responsibility	Evidence activity 1
3.1	Identify information, advice and guidance to support learning	Evidence activity 1
3.2	Communicate to colleagues to take responsibility for their own learning	Evidence activity 2
3.3	Explain to colleagues how to gain access to learning resources	Evidence activity 1
3.4	Support colleagues in practising and reflecting on what they have learned	Evidence activity 3
4.1	Examine with each colleague whether the learning activities undertaken have achieved the desired outcomes	Evidence activity 3
4.2	Support colleagues when updating their personal development plan	Evidence activity 2

CHAPTER 17

Supervise the use of technological equipment in hospitality services

This chapter covers the competence that hospitality supervisors need to support the use of technology in your area of responsibility.

> ### Learning objectives
> On completion of this chapter, you should:
> 1. Be able to supervise the use of technological equipment in hospitality services.
> 2. Understand the requirements that need to be met when using technological equipment in hospitality services.
> 3. Understand how to supervise the use of technological equipment in hospitality services.

The aim of this chapter is to expose supervisors to the competencies they need in order to complete their own tasks and to ensure that their colleagues are able to use technological equipment to the maximum capacity. While recognising the advantages of the use of modern technology, it also considers the drawbacks, contingency options in the event of system failures, staff training requirements, potential health, safety and data protection issues and possible solutions.

Modernising hospitality operations with modern in-house and mobile technology enables organisations of all sizes to compete and meet customers around the world, overcoming time, language and geographical barriers. Computer technology is not very recent. However, with the expansion of internet technology, more and more businesses have opted to computerise their operational procedures for real-time communication and faster data processing.

> ### Key terms
> **Website** – virtual location containing information about company or individuals; webpages and data files accessible through internet connection
>
> **URL (uniform or universal resource locator)** – the letters and symbols (such as https://www.hoddereducation.co.uk/) that make up the website address

3.1 3.4 Types of technology

Hospitality businesses deal with huge amounts of data every day, which must be stored safely with easy access. The following **hardware** and **software** are commonly used in the hospitality industry in order to achieve that.

> ### Key terms
> **Software** – software is a general term for logically organised collections of computer data and instructions. There are two types: system software: provides non-task-specific functions of the computer, e.g. booting, and application software: specific functions to execute specific task, e.g. Microsoft Word
>
> **Hardware** – the physical components that make up a computer system

Staff–computer interface

Input and output devices

- **Keyboards**: a complete set of keys including alp. Usually hand operated.
- **Mouse**: a hand-held device used to control the cursor movement and select computing functions without keying.
- **Touch screen**: a visual display unit screen that allows the user to give commands to the computer by touching part of the screen instead of using the keyboard.
- **Computer screens**: the display that is electronically created on the surface of the large end of a cathode-ray tube or thin film transistor (TFT).
- **Central processing unit (CPU)**: the part of a computer that performs logical and arithmetical operations on the data, as specified in the instructions.
- **Printers**: an output device that prints on paper. This includes text documents, images, photos or a combination of these. The two most common types of printers are inkjet and laser printers. Laser printers are also called page printers due to their high-speed output. Dot matrix printers are now used rarely due to their low speed and limited image quality.
- **Scanners**: an input device that scans documents. It converts text and images into digital format and creates an electronic backup version of the original document.
- **Barcodes and quick response (QR) codes**: a QR code (quick response code) is a type of two-dimensional barcode that is used to provide easy access to information through a range of optical reading devices (e.g. smartphones, tablets, electronic point of sale (EPOS)).
- **Card and fingerprint readers**: devices which can read data from cards with magnetic storage mediums and fingerprints respectively.
- **Interactive television**: television connected online which can be used as a computer screen.
- **Contactless payment systems**: this system allows payments by credit/debitcard, smartphones and other specific smart cards through radio-frequency identification. The means of payment can be scanned over the specific reader without physical contact. For security, the maximum amount of any transaction tends to be capped to small amounts as they do not require a personal identification number (PIN).
- **Credit card terminals**: a payment device connected on a telephone network where the credit or debit card will be authorised for payment with a PIN and/or customer signature.
- **Tills/EPOS**: all-in-one computerised device that can perform a number of functions including processing payments, sales mix, stock limits, sales and refund reports.
- **Photocopiers**: an instrument using light-sensitive photographic materials to reproduce written, printed, or graphic work.

Figure 17.1 A keyboard is an example of an input device

> **Key terms**
>
> **Server** – a computer or sets of computers that acts as the database to other computers
>
> **Wi-Fi** – stands for wireless fidelity; this technology allows computers and other devices to communicate over a wireless signal

Temporary and mass data storage

- **RAM** (random access memory) is a temporary memory in a computer where the operating system, application programs and data in current use are kept so that they can be quickly accessed by the computer processor. Data from RAM is much faster to read and write than the other storage in the computer, e.g. the hard disk, floppy disk, and CD-ROM. However, the data is temporary as it stays in the RAM only when the computer is running. When a computer is switched on again, the necessary data will be loaded into RAM from the computer hard drive.
- **Cloud computing:** use of networked remote servers, hosted on the internet, to store, manage and process data, instead of relying on local servers or personal computers. An internet connection is vital for cloud computing.

Internal hard drives

There are two types: **hard disk drives** (HDD) and **solid-state drives** (SDD).

- **Hard disk drives (HDD):** the hard drive is a device where computer operating software and all the data files created and used have been stored. It is a permanent storage and, unlike RAM, switching off the computer will not affect the data. Data is stored on magnetised thin discs, which can be accessed by a moving mechanism called a head.
- **Solid-state drives (SDD):** these are newer alternatives to hard disk drives. Unlike hard drives, solid-state drives do not have a moving head; the data is stored electrically. Since there are no moving parts, data stored on SDD is less vulnerable to physical damage.

Mobile technology

- **Tablet:** a small hand-held computer with a touch screen to input and visualise data, which does not require an external keyboard or mouse. The internet connection is achieved via Wi-Fi or a mobile data connection similar to smartphones.
- **Laptop**: a portable compact personal computer ideal for travelling and working off-site. It has an integrated keyboard, mouse pad and can connect wirelessly to the internet. Some modern laptops come with an integrated touch screen.
- **Smart phone:** a mobile phone that is capable of executing many standard computer functions. Modern smartphones come with a touch screen interface, internet access and powerful operating systems capable of complex and simultaneous data processing.
- **Satnav (satellite navigation):** a system of computing device, using satellite for tracking the position or travel of a person or an object and guiding the user to get from A to B.

Figure 17.2 The use of tablets is becoming increasingly common in the hospitality industry

Software

Microsoft Windows

The operating system (OS) designed and made by Microsoft Corporation. It is a user-friendly, computer–human interface providing a colourful display. This operating system is capable of complex operations performed by computers. It is probably the most commonly used OS in the world. Similar systems which are well known worldwide include iOS, developed by Apple exclusively for their hardware, and by Google, for Android mobile phones and tablet computers.

Microsoft Office

A desktop computer application including word-processing, data-processing, publishing and presentation.

Other software

There are different types of specialist software that have been developed for specific purposes, for example: Micros stock and ordering, payments, and Sage for accounting.

Similarly, other software systems exist to manage hospitality operations such as booking, reservation and reception activities.

Sources of information and best practice

In essence, a range of technologies and hardware have been used to enhance and automate the information processing and communication among customers and staff. Managers and directors will also use the information and data generated and stored by organisations for statutory financial reporting, marketing and business trend analysis purposes. The latter will generally include confidential data and only authorised individuals can have access to it. Likewise, the personal data of customers and staff must be stored and handled safely. It is a statutory obligation for organisations to comply with data protection legislation (see Chapter 11).

Supervisors must ensure that staff are aware of their responsibilities and boundaries when using technology. In general, organisations have policies and procedures that have to be followed by all staff. Supervisors will ensure that these policies are updated and communicated with staff in a timely manner, and that staff are aware of where to go and who to approach for information.

Staff who will be using the technology must be trained and competent, otherwise the consequences can be costly; for example, loss of data, breaches in data protection legislation and health and safety related incidences. (See below for information on staff training.)

> **Key term**
>
> **Morale** – the ability of a group to maintain a positive attitude and motivation

> **Evidence 1**
>
> **3.4**
>
> List the sources of information and best practice guidelines that your staff could refer to when using technologies.

Introducing new technologies

3.2 Advantages and disadvantages of introducing new technologies

Computerised technology and innovations have helped organisations to increase productivity, receive timely reports and analysis, project sales and underpin marketing activities. Other departments where computers and technology play an integral role include human resources, payroll, finance, forecasting, purchasing, marketing and accounting.

Key advantages of computerised systems
- Demonstrates professionalism and modernity.
- Increases speed of customer service and business data processing.
- Accurate data/record keeping.
- Random and remote access is possible for staff at different levels for effective customer service, financial management, strategic business planning/projection, without unnecessary delays.
- Security: thanks to encrypted data transfer and storage, combined with anti-virus and firewall data protection systems, confidential data is relatively secure. Internal servers and cloud back-up systems increase the reliability of data recovery in case of mishaps such as power failure or cyber-attacks.
- Given the speed of evolution of technology, it could be argued that hiring a comprehensive modern computing system, including hardware and software and maintenance, may translate into better value for money for the organisation.

Disadvantages of technology
Using technology and an over-reliance on it can have disadvantages too:
- High cost of initial investment on hardware, software and staff training.
- Additional layer of protection required for sensitive data storage, in line with the Data Protection Act 1998.
- Ongoing maintenance, training and license fees: computer technology is fast evolving and at some stage, software and hardware must be upgraded for better efficiency and to avoid non-compatibility issues with customers and stakeholders. This has an additional cost, including staff training.
- Costly disposal of obsolete hardware due to the toxicity and danger to public health.

1.1 3.3 3.5 3.6 3.8 Minimising the negative impact of disadvantages linked to new technology or changes: staff training

Progressive introduction, as opposed to sudden and large-scale implementation of technology, will minimise the negative impact on staff competence and confidence. With appropriate training, they will have time to familiarise themselves with and learn how to use the new technology effectively.

Proactive and timely staff training
Supervisors could identify specific staff training needs during appraisals and performance reviews, using colleagues' feedback and by analysing data on the degree of customer satisfaction.

Supervisors' responsibilities include:
- Planning and implementing a comprehensive induction programme for new staff.
- Assessing and determining training needs (in terms of effective operational procedures, data protection, health and safety when using technology) of all staff that are likely to be involved with using technology.
- Ensuring staff are well aware of where to go and who to approach for required information and best practice protocols when using technology.

Levels of staff competence can be directly linked to their levels of confidence and performance. Therefore, it is logical that well trained staff are key for a great customer experience and successful and sustainable business activities. It is always good practice to adopt a proactive approach that assesses staff training needs and need for support, and allow the time required for staff to develop.

The opposite can result in low staff morale, substandard customer experience and eventually loss of profitability and business.

Some best practices could be adopted by supervisors to overcome potential issues when using technology:
- Pre-shift, daily or weekly staff briefing and updates on changes and expectations.
- Specific training on new features added to the technology.
- Appoint technology champions; these individuals can mentor other staff when required.
- Announce well in advance any changes in operational procedures and arrange appropriate training sessions.

Remember the purpose of using technology is to improve business and the same technology must not hinder the day-to-day operation of a business.

Figure 17.3 Technology, such as a laptop, should improve business

Encourage good practices, sharing knowledge among colleagues

Some individuals are more knowledgeable than others. By encouraging knowledge sharing, customer service can be provided with minimum interruption.

Ensure effective communication of maintenance work or new procedures to all staff, especially when staff change shifts.

> **Evidence 2**
>
> `1.1` `2.2` `3.5` `3.6`
>
> - Describe the staff training activities in relation to the use of technology in your organisation.
> - If you were leading a refresher-training day for staff in order to emphasis the good practices linked with technological equipment usage what topics would you include in the training agenda?
> - Briefly describe how you asses and evaluate the training needs of your staff in using technology.

> **Evidence 3**
>
> `3.2` `3.3` `3.8` `3.9`
>
> - Produce a table to show the advantages and disadvantages of introducing new technology. Suggest what steps could be taken to minimise the negative impact. Your table could reflect your own organisational procedures in dealing with the above.
> - What are your organisation's monitoring processes in using the technological equipment?

`1.2` `1.3` `1.4` `2.2` `2.4` `3.7` `3.9` `3.11` `3.12` Dealing with problems

Customers and staff can encounter problems when using technologies. Supervisors could minimise or prevent such problems through risk assessment, monitoring and reviewing the process on a regular basis.

Some common problems and suggested solutions that supervisors can implement among their staff are shown in the table below.

Table 17.1 Common problems and possible solutions when using technology

Problems	Possible solutions
Power cut	Follow company procedures: - Alert maintenance/facilities - Emergency power supply - Use of offline computer system - Manual record keeping
Computer doesn't start Slow/frozen computers	- Use another computer - Alert IT department - Ask colleagues to help - Apologise to customers
Temporary data loss	- Apologise to customers and process manually - Alert IT services and attempt to access backed-up data - Inform supervisors for further investigation and review
Added new functions on the system New staff	- Ask colleagues for help - New staff work with a mentor/supervisor - Create written steps to implement the new procedures - Create a bank of frequently asked questions available for all staff - Trainee staff wear a badge for customers' understanding
Online payment system down	- Apologise to customers - Suggest alternative payment methods: cash or cheques - Take payment details manually for processing later
Wi-Fi not working	- Apologise - Alert IT maintenance - Offer users alternative connections – e.g. ethernet/wired connection where possible

Table 17.2 Potential issues encountered by back office staff

Issue	Possible solutions
Server down	Follow company's contingency procedures: ● Activate back-up data access ● Communicate the issue with front-of-house staff so they can proceed with manual process ● Supervisors to contact service providers for re-establishment of the system ● Take preventive actions to avoid future incidents
Telephone system down	● Supervisors contact service providers or maintenance for repair ● Use emails for communication

Staff can be encouraged to take ownership of their actions in the use of technology. A personal identification number (PIN) allocation for each staff member, and providing different levels of data accessibility, not only makes the individual staff member accountable for their performance, but also empowers them to deal with technological issues within their control and expertise. In addition, supervisors and managers can nominate staff who demonstrate a better understanding and use of technology as 'technology champions'. These individuals can mentor other staff in using the technology more effectively.

1.7 3.7 Reporting procedures and suggesting improvements

Reporting procedures are important to operational success. Supervisors must enable and encourage their staff to report any issues, and give their opinions and views. By doing so, supervisors can reduce their direct supervision tasks and spend time in better planning and administrative tasks. Staff could actively participate in reporting issues, suggestions for good practice or even new ways of doing things when using technology. From this, supervisors can update all staff and relevant individuals about any issues – for example, hardware that needs repairing, software updates, or supplies that have reached the minimum level (e.g. toner for printers).

Some of the ways which the staff could report are:
● face-to-face
● email
● a written note
● during team briefing and meetings
● during staff training sessions.

Customer-facing staff can give vital clues to supervisors and managers about required changes and updates to technology, as they deal directly with emerging technologies that customers are familiar with. Supervisors should not overlook such suggestions for improvements.

1.5 2.3 Maintenance

All technological equipment requires maintenance. There are four main types of maintenance:

> **Evidence 4**
>
> **1.7 3.7**
>
> ● How do your staff report any improvements that could be applied to the use of technology?
> ● Reporting improvements to technology or its use can enhance staff performance and customer service. List strategies that you use to empower the staff and encourage them to do this.

1. **Corrective maintenance:** maintenance required following the detection of a fault which aims to restore normal functioning. This type of maintenance requirement is highly unpredictable, and a clear and robust communication system should be put in place by supervisors (i.e. who to report the fault to and how; how to ensure customer service with minimal disruption). If not, the operations will suffer delays and malfunctions and this will consequently have a negative impact on the customer experience.
2. **Preventive maintenance:** this maintenance has been carried out at planned intervals or according to the manufacturers' recommendations. It aims to reduce the amount of corrective maintenance and maintain the performance of the equipment or software.
3. **Risk-based maintenance:** this maintenance is carried out by analysing and measuring the data collected during the above two types of maintenance. The data analysis will be looked at in the context of the environmental and operational process. This maintenance helps to determine the timing and frequency of preventive maintenance and guarantees the high-level performance and reliability of the technological system.
4. **Condition-based maintenance:** this maintenance is based on the equipment performance monitoring and the control of the corrective actions taken as a result. The condition of the hardware in particular is monitored by the maintenance team and replacement or upgrades are carried out to minimise the occurrence of any major failures. For example, replacing an older PC with a new one with a new generation of processors, or upgrading an ordinary *broadband* network to fibre optic.

Key term

Broadband – high-speed data transmission in which a single cable can carry a large amount of data simultaneously

Evidence 5

`1.3` `1.4` `1.5` `1.6` `2.3` `2.4` `3.1` `3.11` `3.12` `3.13`

- List the information and communication technology used in your organisation.
- Explain the procedure for routine maintenance of this equipment.
- Explain your organisational procedures when any of the technological equipment fails – e.g. who would you report it to? What is the record-keeping process and contingency plan while the repair takes place?

Evidence 6

`2.3` `3.13`

Describe your organisational procedures on record keeping for maintenance activity for the technological equipment (i.e. computers, servers, antivirus software updates, telephone and mobile devices) that your staff use.

1.2 2.1 Health and safety

Computer devices can cause injuries to the user. For example:
- Prolonged exposure to computer screens can affect the eyes. Supervisors must ensure the staff are provided with adequate personal protective equipment (PPE) and that they follow the good practices.
- Repetitive use of keyboards and mouse can cause injury. Providing ergonomically designed alternatives can minimise such injuries.
- PAT (portable appliance testing) has to be carried out to all computer and portable devices in order to prevent any accidents such as electric shock, burns or fire hazards.

1.6 3.13 3.14 Data protection and record keeping

Supervisors should work with relevant departments (i.e. IT services and finance) to ensure added layers of security are in place when staff have access to data. For example, ensure the use of an authorised person password, data access history checks, and internal policies for staff, including restriction on remote access, use of external storage devices and digital copying of sensitive data.

Supervisors should ensure that comprehensive risk assessments have been carried out in all aspects of the use of computer and communication technology.

These records, along with other health and safety maintenance checks such as portable appliance testing (PAT) records, have to be maintained and reviewed according to the company policies and health and safety legislation.

3.10 Technology and environmental issues

Like all businesses, hospitality businesses have a moral and ethical responsibility to do everything within their power to minimise the negative impact of the use of technology on the environment.

Manufacturing and disposing of technological equipment can have many negative impacts on the environment. Hospitality businesses have no control over these procedures but can take decisions to minimise the negative impact at policy levels. For example, the business can choose to purchase computers made from recycled materials and to do business with suppliers who are committed to and demonstrate a proactive attitude towards minimising the impact on the environment.

Furthermore, the growth in the use of smartphones and tablet computers with mobile internet usage and cloud computing means many hard copy documents are no longer required. For example, you may not need a printout of your booking confirmation, as just a code or a reference number should be sufficient for the staff to access full customer details from a secure database. This will have a positive impact on the environment as reduction in printing leads to reduced use of natural resources such as paper, and reduced transportation, waste management and recycling costs and processes.

Evidence 7
1.2 2.1 3.14
- Explain why it is important to maintain an accurate record-keeping system concerning technological equipment maintenance and training.
- List any relevant legislation and health and safety requirements that you have to comply with when using technological equipment.

Evidence 8
3.10
- Does your organisation have recycling facilities?
- Briefly explain how technological equipment waste have been recycled.

Knowledge check

1. What are the key advantages of technological equipment usage in the hospitality industry?
2. Explain how cloud computing works.
3. Other than chip and pin, how else can customers pay using credit or debit cards?
4. How can staff training needs in technology be identified?
5. What are the possible impacts of untrained staff on the use of technological equipment and systems?
6. What action should you take if a PC fails while serving customers?
7. What are the likely risks that you might come across during a risk assessment process?
8. Why is risk assessment important?
9. You may not be allowed to use portable external storage devices such as memory sticks and external hard drives on the computer system at work. Why is that?
10. Name four main types of maintenance, with examples.

Evidence checklist			
Assessment criteria		**Assessment methods and forms of evidence**	**Possible evidence**
1.1	Ensure that staff are competent in the operation of equipment that they have to use in own area of responsibility	Assessment methods: • Direct observations • Work product • Expert witness testimony • Professional discussions • Questions and answers • Candidate's reflective account/statement Forms of evidence: • Log book • Observation diaries • Record of professional discussions • Video/audio and photographic evidence • Record of IT maintenance records • Witness testimonies • Statement of professional discussions • Work rota • Presentation materials • Internal and external correspondence (emails/telephone conversation notes)	Evidence activity 2
1.2	Monitor the use of the equipment to ensure it is being used: • safely and efficiently • to the benefit of customers • to the benefit of the organisation • in line with the organisation's and manufacturer's guidelines		Evidence activity 7
1.3	Deal with problems promptly and effectively within the limits of own authority		Evidence activity 5
1.4	Seek help and guidance from the relevant people if unable to deal with problems		Evidence activity 5
1.5	Ensure that maintenance activities are carried out correctly		Evidence activity 5
1.6	Ensure records are completed accurately		Evidence activity 5
1.7	Identify and report ways in which use of technology could be improved		Evidence activity 4
2.1	Describe the health and safety requirements and precautions in relation to the use of technology in own area of responsibility	Assessment methods: • Oral questioning and written tests • Role play • Presentation • Professional discussions Forms of evidence: (All evidence can be cross-referenced to Learning objective 1) • Written exam/knowledge check (short-answer and multiple-choice questions) • Case study • Project • Presentation materials (PowerPoints, posters, leaflets) • Staff training manuals	Evidence activity 7
2.2	Describe the operational procedures that staff in own area of responsibility should follow when using technology		Evidence activity 2
2.3	Describe maintenance procedures for the technology in own area of responsibility		Evidence activity 2
2.4	Describe organisational procedures and contingency arrangements in the event of the failure of the technology in own area of responsibility		Evidence activity 5

Evidence checklist			
Assessment criteria		**Assessment methods and forms of evidence**	**Possible evidence**
3.1	List existing technology that supports activities in own field of work	Assessment methods: ● Oral questioning and written tests ● Role play ● Presentation ● Professional discussions Forms of evidence: (All evidence can be cross-referenced to Learning objective 1) ● Written exam/knowledge check (short-answer and multiple-choice questions) ● Presentation ● Staff training materials	Evidence activity 5
3.2	Compare the possible benefits and disadvantages of introducing new technologies in organisations		Evidence activity 3
3.3	Explain how to overcome or minimise the disadvantages of introducing new technologies		Evidence activity 3
3.4	Identify sources of information and best practice in relation to various types of technology used in the industry		Evidence activity 1
3.5	Explain how to ensure that self and staff are competent in the operation of the technology		Evidence activity 2
3.6	Explain how to identify and address training needs in connection with the use of technologies		Evidence activity 2
3.7	Explain how to empower staff members to deal with technological problems that are within their control and expertise		Evidence activity 4
3.8	Explain how to manage change during the introduction of new technology		Evidence activity 3
3.9	Explain how to monitor the use of equipment		Evidence activity 3
3.10	Explain how to minimise negative effects on the environment when using new technology		Evidence activity 8
3.11	Explain how to deal with a range of problems that might occur with the technology in own area of responsibility		Evidence activity 5
3.12	Explain how to deal with customers when equipment failure causes disruption		Evidence activity 5
3.13	Describe the systems used to record information on the maintenance of technology in own area of responsibility		Evidence activity 5 Evidence activity 6
3.14	Explain the importance of maintaining accurate records		Evidence activity 7

CHAPTER 18

Supervise practices for handling payments

This chapter is about monitoring and controlling the handling of payments, collecting takings and processing payment information. This chapter also covers maintaining security and dealing with difficulties that may arise in connection with payments and takings.

Learning objectives

On completion of this chapter, you should:
1. Be able to supervise practices for handling payments.
2. Understand how payments should be handled.
3. Understand how to supervise practices for handling payments.

1.1 2.1 3.1 3.2 Supervisor's daily responsibilities and resources needed for taking payments

As with all businesses, it is essential that payments for products and services are taken efficiently. It is the organisation's and the supervisor's responsibility to ensure that their staff have the equipment, resources and training to understand their responsibilities and those of their team members when handling and collecting payments and takings.

As a supervisor, it may be your responsibility to oversee the day-to-day running of a cash register. This may also mean that you will have the responsibility to carry out or oversee the following procedures:
- Pre-opening of business – checking the opening float.
- Checking that the organisation's procedures and guidelines are being carried out by staff.
- Monitoring the day's business.
- Checking that the resources needed for the day's business are available to ensure your staff can work efficiently; for example, till rolls, pads, pens and card vouchers. In the case of EPOS systems, the resources linked to other departments such as the restaurant, bar or kitchen may also have to be checked. It may be necessary to get the authority of a manager if additional resources are needed.
- Solving any problems with the cash register and payment issues
- Carrying out or overseeing the closing period. This may involve checking the cash balance, cashing up, completing relevant paperwork and resolving discrepancies.

Evidence 1
2.1
List the payment-handling responsibilities of a supervisor and a staff member in your organisation.

> **Evidence 3**
> **3.1** **3.2**
> Produce a brief spreadsheet of the resources your tills and payment points need during the course of one trading day. Identify the person you need to authorise additional resources when they run out.

> **Evidence 2**
> **1.1** **2.2**
> What are the skills and resources needed to carry out these responsibilities? List any tasks that may be out of your responsibility.

Handling payments

1.1 **1.3** **1.9** **2.4** **2.5** **3.3** **3.4** Organisational guidelines for collecting and handling payments

Different payment handling systems will be used, depending on the organisation and department within the business. The organisation will have specific policies and guidelines on all aspects of handling and processing financial **transactions**. Training should be given to all staff handling financial transactions. The training should include individual policies and responsibilities, and how the payments systems are used. All staff handling payments should know which forms to use and how the organisation accepts and processes payments quickly to avoid embarrassment and delays when processing cash via the cashier till, debit/credit cards, cashiers' cheques, smart cards and electronic payments.

These procedures could include:
- handling cash, including £20 and £50 notes
- checking for counterfeit bank notes and coins
- checking credit cards and credit card payments, including the transaction limits on cards
- dealing with vouchers, traveller's and cashier's cheques
- placing payments on accumulated bills, such as bar tabs and payments placed on a guest's room.

As a supervisor, it is your responsibility that the organisation's payment handling policies and guidelines are followed and maintained. This can be done on a regular or even daily basis using team meetings, on-the-job training sessions and shift briefings to highlight important and specific policies, which can reinforce the importance of these procedures for the safe and efficient handling of payments.

> **Key terms**
> **Transaction** – when something is exchanged, for example, a product for money
> **Fraudulent** – dishonest act of behaviour

Processing and collecting payments

As a supervisor, it is essential that you know and understand the organisation's policies and guidelines for collecting payments. This will include the use of cash registers and EPOS systems used in the business, the opening and closing of the tills and how to recognise and deal with cash security and fraudulent activity. Depending on the business, these policies and guidelines may be found in the business quality manual.

As a supervisor, it is essential that your staff are able to operate the payment point systems efficiently. You must ensure:
- They know how to operate the tills, till procedures and how to deal with any security issues that may occur.
- They are trained on the till and payments systems.
- They know how to change the paper rolls, make minor adjustments and identify when the till needs repair.

> **Evidence 4**
> **1.9** **2.4** **3.3** **3.4**
>
> With your manager, identify all of the documentation and guidelines your organisation has on collecting and handling payments. When you have identified these documents, add additional guidelines that you and you manager feel are important.

1.6 2.3 2.4 2.6 2.7 Systems for taking payment

There are three main methods for handling payments in the hospitality business. These systems will differ depending on the department using them. A supervisor would be expected to know how to use and resolve issues with all of the payment systems in their department.

Electronic point of sale (EPOS) systems

These systems are generally used in busy, high turnover businesses such as bars, restaurants, coffee shops and hotels. They often have touchscreens and allow the staff to input the products and items by name and quantity. The system can be used like a cash machine for individual purchases, or it can hold orders and billing information by table or part, to be paid at the end of the meal or event. The system can also be linked to other departments, such as the kitchen and bar, where the order will be printed out. This speeds up service, centralises the order and allows the order to be amended and additions made to the bill. This helps to prevent mistakes and orders getting lost, which can happen when using paper-based orders. Training is essential when using these systems. This ensures they are used correctly and that staff understand how to rectify any problems that may occur when using them. Training can be given in-house by the organisation or supplier. On-the-job training can also be given to staff members to rectify any problems with the system and remind them of organisational policies.

Cash tills and cash registers

Cash tills and cash registers are often used in smaller businesses. These systems are often simpler and quicker to use. They do not usually have the ability to save orders and bills. The operator inputs the prices of the product or service and gives an instant total and receipt for that transaction. It is essential that a supervisor ensures that the payments paid through this system are accurate and records are kept of the transactions made. These systems require greater security as they operate with cash floats. These **cash floats** can be a temptation and cause some staff to be dishonest. Some more modern cash tills are operated using a key or card system, which shows the transactions carried out by each member of staff. This can be used to highlight incorrectly rung items, poor performance and dishonest behaviour.

Cash tills and cash registers can also be linked to chip and pin devices. Debit cards and credit cards are often targeted by criminals. They can be stolen or cloned from the original card. Due to this, it is essential that all staff are trained how to recognise cards that may not be genuine. When processing these cards, organisations will have rules, guidelines and checks that must be followed to reduce the risk of processing fraudulent cards. The check may include the following procedures:

- Is it of a type that is accepted by the organisation – for example, Visa, Maestro, MasterCard, Solo and Switch?
- Check to see if it is a legitimate card. Does it look tampered with?
- Check if it is on a warning list of fraudulent cards.
- Are all of the details and prices being put into the card reader correctly?
- If in doubt, can the signature on the card be verified by another card or document, e.g., driving licence?
- Get an additional signature on the till receipt to verify and accept the charge.
- If the payment exceeds the organisation's floor limit or single transaction limit, get additional authorisation from a superior.

> **Key term**
>
> **Cash float** – money of different denominations put into the till at the beginning of the day to allow the cashier to give customers change

> **Evidence 5**
> **1.6** **2.3** **2.4** **2.6** **2.7**
>
> Produce a PowerPoint presentation showing the tills and payment point equipment used in your department and your organisation's procedures when collecting payments.

Payment security

1.4 3.14 3.15 3.16 Security of payment and dealing with emergencies

When handling money, it is important to follow guidance and procedures to keep customers' payment details safe and identify and protect against any security issues, theft and other suspicious activities. All the money being handled belongs to the organisation you work for, so it is essential that supervisors follow strict security measures to plan, monitor and manage any financial transactions within their department. Security issues may include:

- Cashing up, locking up and securing payments.
- Handling cash and giving change to customers – in a busy department mistakes can be made when ringing up and returning change. This can cause problems for both the business and the customers.
- Handling cash and card payments in the restaurant and bar. Distractions could prevent accurate payments and card transactions being made.
- Cash registers and electronic point of sale (EPOS) systems may require passwords and keys to open and close the till. All transactions are linked to the member of staff via a keycard, so it is important that these are kept safe and out of the reach of unauthorised staff and the public.
- Cash registers and EPOS systems can be opened and closed hundreds of time during the day. Due to this, staff should not leave the till open when it is unattended. It should be emptied at the end of the day and only left open to show the till is empty.
- In the case of a fire or robbery, it is important that all staff put their safety first.
  - In the case of fire, the till should be locked and secured before exiting the building in a calm manner to reassure the customers.
  - In the case of a robbery, the robbers' demands should be carried out to the letter and no attempt should be made to prevent the robbery. Call the police immediately after the incident.

> **Evidence 6**
> 3.14 3.15 3.16
>
> Create a leaflet identifying security issues with payments that may occur in your department. Include details of your organisation's procedures and how these should be dealt with. Give the names and numbers of key people who should be contacted to gain security advice.

1.2 1.5 3.6 3.7 Dealing with payment problems

Organisations will have policies and procedures on how to deal with payment problems in a calm and professional manner, which is essential when these issues may involve customers and members of the public. Payment problems may include inputting or receiving an incorrect order or payment. Receiving incorrect payments or giving the wrong change can also be an issue. When these problems do occur, all staff should be able to follow the organisation's guidelines and act in a way that does not jeopardise the organisation's reputation, leading to ill-feeling from customers. If these issues are resolved quickly and in a professional manner, they can help to enhance the organisation's reputation, which could lead to more business.

Good customer care when dealing with payment issues could include the following:
- Being calm and polite at all times.
- Listening to the customer's issues to avoid mistakes.

- Reassuring the customer that you will deal with the problem immediately.
- Keeping the customer informed on what you are doing and how the issue will be resolved.
- If you are unable to help, contacting someone immediately who *can* help.

1.2 1.3 3.10 3.11 How to recognise and deal with fraudulent acts during the payment process

As a supervisor, you and your staff may come across fraudulent acts within your department. These acts may be by carried out by a customer or by a member of your own team. Ways in which fraud can be carried out include receiving forged bank notes, forged or expired vouchers or cashiers' cheques, and using cloned, stolen and unverified credit and debit cards.

Members of staff may also steal money from the payment point, or be involved in other fraudulent activities such as giving incorrect change, not putting the money in the till from a transaction and swiping card details and pin numbers for cloning. They may also take money from the business in other ways, such as helping themselves to food and drink on duty and over-diluting drinks and keeping the cash difference for themselves.

Ways to deal with problems could include those listed in the table below.

Table 18.1 Dealing with fraudulent acts

Issue	Check	Reaction
Forged notes	Ultraviolet light or counterfeit detector pen	Inform the customer of your concerns. Check and inform a manager. Keep the note.
Cards that have expired or without a signature	Without signature – check against another card or driving licence	If unsure about any card, ask for another card or cash to be used. If still in doubt, ask a manager to intervene.
Credit or debit card declined – insufficient funds or unusual activity	Without embarrassing the customer, check if they know why it may have been declined	Ask for another form of payment and/or get the customer to contact their bank or provider
Possibility of the wrong change being given or being overcharged	Check against the order and the receipt	If the customer is correct, apologise for the mistake. Give them the correct change and take note of the issue and the staff member involved. More training may be needed.

The majority of issues with payments will be a simple mistake or human error and not criminal activity. In a busy department, these issues may occur on a regular basis, so it is essential that a supervisor and their staff are vigilant and able to act quickly and professionally to ensure that there is no financial risk to the business.

Evidence 7
1.2 1.3 2.5 3.10 3.11

Linked to your leaflet in Evidence activity 6, produce a policy linked to training on how staff should communicate with customers and staff when dealing with general payments, dishonest behaviour and fraudulent payments.

`1.7` `1.9` `1.10` `2.9` `3.5` `3.12` `3.13` Recording information – till readings at the point of payment

It is essential that all purchases go through the till accurately so that the till reading and printout can be used to give an accurate picture of the day's trading against the money and other payments put through the till. Each system used will give the information at the end of the day in a slightly different way. It can be broken down showing a number of different forms of information, including:

- cash/credit sales
- sales history by item and price
- times of cash register usage
- staff operator information
- cancellations
- refunds.

All organisations will have procedures and records that need to be kept on each day's trading. As a supervisor, it may be your responsibility to manage or monitor and co-ordinate the closing-down of any tills and payment systems in your department. This would include collecting all till data and reconciling the takings against it. This can be a long process; however it is essential to calculate the business's profits and any discrepancies or losses for that day's trading.

The organisation will expect all the cash registers to have their takings totalled and recorded according to their organisational policy. This would include an income and expenditure sheet. It will record accurately:

- the cash taken that day
- non-cash takings including cheques, vouchers and card transactions
- the balance between the cash register and the cash takings.

All payment documentation and reconciliation sheets must be kept secured for financial and tax records and audits.

Evidence 8
`1.7` `1.9` `1.10` `2.9` `3.5` `3.12` `3.13`

With your supervisor or manager, help in the recording of all information relating to your payment points and fill out all of the necessary documentation linked to this process. Collect a completed copy of all of the documentation as evidence, with a written statement from your manager saying you have taken part in this. If your company will not let you have completed forms, use blank forms and fill in the relevant information yourself hypothetically.

Identify all the people involved in collecting and completing payment information in your department and organisation.

`1.5` `1.8` `2.2` `2.8` `3.6` `3.7` `3.8` `3.9` `3.10` Dealing with payment and financial discrepancies

As a supervisor, it is your responsibility to ensure that the takings or cash values in the till at the end of the day match the total payment information from the cash register or EPOS. Any differences or discrepancies between the two figures need to be dealt with using the organisation's procedures.

Discrepancies between the takings shown at the end of the day and the actual money in the till are often due to human error. At busy times, mistakes can happen when inputting items or price, giving incorrect change or changing and rectifying orders and cancellations. When this happens, it will show a loss on the till and it is essential that you know the correct procedures to resolve these problems. With electronic tills, staff members often use keys and pass cards and controls to use the till, and this gives the supervisor the ability to identify any issues and trends individual staff may have had during the day. It is for this reason that staff should log in and out accurately during their shifts. Some cash tills do not have the facility for staff to log in and out when making transactions, which makes it difficult to identify when a member of staff may have made a mistake.

It will be the responsibility of the supervisor or manager to deal with any discrepancies in the takings and to make anyone working on that till aware of any issues, so they can possibly explain where the error may have occurred. If staff members are not able to explain what may have caused the error, further action may have to be taken in line with the organisation's policies. Organisational policies do not usually include deducting any shortages from staff salaries. It is important that, as a supervisor, you are able to deal with any issues and discrepancies and your immediate manager is also made aware of these, in case further investigation is necessary or advice is needed on how to proceed.

Any unresolved discrepancies may have to be documented on the day's income and expenditure documentation, or there may be a direct **discrepancy** report document for these issues. As with any financial documentation, it is essential that it is completed accurately and kept secure, with all other financial records and documentation.

Key terms

Discrepancy – a difference or issue between things; for example, if the money at the end of the day is short because an item was not put through the till, this would be a discrepancy in the figures

Audit – the checking and verification of accounts and often stock to check they are accurate and correct

Reconcile – to compare and check that one account is compatible or consistent with another; for example, the cash register's end-of-day report matches the money in the till

Evidence 9

`1.5` `1.8` `2.2` `2.8` `3.6` `3.7` `3.8` `3.9` `3.10`

Produce a flow chart showing how discrepancies are dealt with in your organisation. This should include:
- How staff performance is monitored
- The actions taken when performance falls below expected standards or when staff are suspected of dishonesty.

Identify the areas you are responsible for and the areas that are beyond your limits of responsibility.

Evidence 10

`3.8`

Discuss and record with your line manager how staff performance is measured in your organisation.

Knowledge check

1 Name two types of till or system used to record and take payments and orders.
2 Identify three forms of fraud that can occur at the payment point.
3 What should you do if your business is being robbed?
4 List any actions that should be taken at the payment point in the case of a fire.
5 What should you do if a customer's credit or debit card is declined?
6 What is the name of the money put in a till before opening to be used for change?
7 How do you deal with staff if there is a discrepancy with the takings in their till?

Evidence checklist		
Assessment criteria		**Possible evidence**
1.1	Ensure staff have the resources, information and skills needed to carry out their responsibilities	Evidence activity 1
1.2	Ensure that staff communicate with customers in a way that is likely to promote goodwill and understanding	Evidence activity 1 Evidence activity 7
1.3	Ensure staff handle payments and refunds according to the organisation's procedures	Evidence activity 7
1.4	Ensure staff follow payment point safety and security procedures	Evidence activity 6
1.5	Deal effectively with any problems which occur at payment points	Evidence activity 9
1.6	Collect payment point contents in line with the organisation's procedures	Evidence activity 5
1.7	Reconcile actual takings against recorded takings	Evidence activity 8
1.8	Deal with discrepancies between takings following the organisation's procedures and legal requirements	Evidence activity 8
1.9	Complete documents relating to takings and process in line with the organisation's procedures	Evidence activity 4
1.10	Process documents relating to takings and process in line with the organisation's procedures	Evidence activity 8
2.1	Describe the different roles and responsibilities of individuals in own area of responsibility in relation to handling payments and collecting takings	Evidence activity 1
2.2	Explain limits of own authority when controlling payments	Evidence activity 9
2.3	Identify the methods of payment that are ● accepted in the organisation ● used in the hospitality industry	Evidence activity 5
2.4	Identify the organisational guidelines and procedures that should be followed when ● handling payments ● processing payments ● processing payment information ● collecting takings	Evidence activity 4 Evidence activity 5

Evidence checklist		
Assessment criteria		**Possible evidence**
2.5	Describe how to present information relating to payment procedures to staff	Evidence activity 7
2.6	Describe the confirmation systems that should be used when authorising payments	Evidence activity 5
2.7	Identify the electronic point of sale systems (EPOS) used within own area of responsibility	Evidence activity 5
2.8	Explain how to identify and deal with discrepancies	Evidence activity 9
2.9	Explain how to complete documentation that is needed	Evidence activity 8
3.1	Explain how to estimate the till items needed for handling payments	Evidence activity 3
3.2	Identify who to gain approval from when additional till items are required	Evidence activity 3
3.3	Describe how to control the issue and use of till items	Evidence activity 4
3.4	Explain how to operate the payment points and equipment used in own organisation	Evidence activity 4
3.5	Explain how to obtain till readings	Evidence activity 8
3.6	Identify the types of problems that may occur when controlling payment practices	Evidence activity 9
3.7	Explain how to deal with payment practice problems	Evidence activity 9
3.8	Explain how to monitor staff performance against organisational standards	Evidence activity 9 Evidence activity 10
3.9	Describe what action to take when staff performance falls below standards	Evidence activity 9
3.10	Explain how to deal with suspected dishonesty in the organisation	Evidence activity 7
3.11	Explain how to deal with fraudulent payments	Evidence activity 6 Evidence activity 7
3.12	Describe how to record information about payments	Evidence activity 8
3.13	Identify who information on payment handling should be passed on to	Evidence activity 8
3.14	Explain how to plan and implement the organisation's security procedures to protect staff and takings	Evidence activity 6
3.15	Identify who to gain security advice from	Evidence activity 6
3.16	Explain how to deal with emergency situations including robbery and threats to safety	Evidence activity 6

CHAPTER 19

Contribute to the selection of staff for activities

This chapter covers the competence that hospitality supervisors need to identify personnel needs for their team and assist in the selection of appropriate personnel.

> **Learning objectives**
>
> On completion of this chapter, you should:
> 1 Be able to contribute to the selection of staff for activities.
> 2 Understand how to contribute to the selection of staff for activities.

The NVQ Level 3 in Hospitality Supervision and Leadership is based on what you do in your working area and working day. It is therefore necessary for you to provide evidence of what you do and how you do it. Throughout the chapter there are suggestions showing the assessment criteria for your qualification, and the types of evidence you could supply related to each criterion. These are also summarised in the Evidence Checklist at the end of the chapter. Use these as a guide; you will probably be able to find more examples of evidence within your workplace.

Identifying staffing needs and planning

To run a successful business, you must employ the best people possible to work within your organisation to ensure it runs efficiently and remains profitable. Employing staff who have the skills, experience and qualifications required to enhance your team can also ensure that your organisation has the ability to adapt and lead the market it is in. The hospitality industry is constantly adapting and reinventing itself to meet the needs of its customers and it also has a reputation for a high turnover of staff. These issues make it essential that all recruitment is backed up by a well planned and professional process of identifying staffing needs through job descriptions, essential skills and experience required for the role. Understanding the labour market and where to advertise the position to attract the right people is also an essential part of the recruitment process. The final stage of the process is shortlisting and interviewing to identify the applicant who most suits the needs of the business.

1.1 1.2 Identifying staffing requirements

All departments within a hospitality business have an optimum number of staff required to operate effectively. These numbers are governed by organisational and departmental budgets. Staffing costs are usually the largest expense for any

> **Evidence 1**
>
> **1.1** **1.2**
>
> Identify a staffing requirement you feel needs filling and justify why this position should be authorised and filled. Give at least five reasons why this new person is needed.

business and due to this staffing levels are tightly managed. Depending on the business needs, staff may be employed on part-time or short-term contracts, which can fulfill seasonal and short-term increases in business. Permanent staff are generally recruited when a member of staff leaves and needs replacing, or there is an increase or change in the business itself that needs an increase in staff numbers or new skills to meet the needs of the business. When a position is identified, it is the role of the supervisor and manager to identify the skills and experience required to fill and enhance their team's needs.

Recruitment and selection process

1.4 Human resource management and planning

Firstly a position needs to be available within the organisation. Then the recruitment and selection process can take place. This would involve the following steps:

- **Job analysis** – this would include writing a job description and the personal specifications needed for the job.
- **Authorisation** – seek authorisation from senior management to recruit.
- **Selection methods** – choose the selection methods most suitable for the role. This could include interviews, trial days, skills tests and exams.
- **Advertising** – specialist papers, magazines, websites and recruitment agencies may be used to target the best applicants for the job.
- **Applications** – all of the applications will be analysed and shortlisted to identify the candidates most suitable for the role.
- **Interview and assessment** – all applicants interviewed and assessed. If there is more than one applicant who suits the role, further interviews and assessment may be carried out.
- **Making an offer** – the applicant will be made an official offer stating the details of the role and the terms of employment.
- **Acceptance** – after the applicant accepts the position, their qualifications and references will be checked. Then after they start, they will begin their induction, training and probation period before gaining their permanent or part-time contract.

> **Evidence 2**
>
> **1.4**
>
> With your line manager, identify any organisational procedures to assess and select staff in your department. Use any documentation your organisation may have to illustrate this. If your organisation does not have a detailed policy, implement five new policies with your line manager.

> **Key terms**
>
> **Assessment** – a method of judging how a person performs a task, skill or test
>
> **Recruitment** – the process of identifying, finding and hiring the person most qualified and suitable for a job
>
> **Procedures and processes** – pre-organised or step-by-step activities or methods
>
> **Objectives** – goals or realistic things that need to be achieved
>
> **Policies** – a statement or ruling of how an organisation, government or society should conduct itself

2.2 2.6 2.8 Organisational needs and job analysis

When a department feels that there is a job vacancy or a member of staff leaves, it is not always the case that the organisation will recruit and fill this position. It is the human resources' role to assess the needs of the department against the business needs and the organisation's business and financial plans. The job would be analysed to see if there is a need for this particular role or if the role needs to be changed. There may also be an opportunity to recruit a less experienced member of staff on less money and train them in-house to perform the role.

Analysis of the vacant position

Key questions that may be asked.

The current job:
- What is the job and what does it involve?
- How is the job carried out?
- What experience, qualifications and skills are needed to do the job?

Possible changes to the role:
- Change of hours or shifts.
- Changes in the skills, experience and qualifications required.
- Add more responsibilities or duties to the role. Make it more productive.
- Change the rate of pay to suit the new role or meet the financial targets.

1.3 2.3 2.5 2.9 Authority to recruit staff

In most businesses, staff are the greatest cost and resource the business has. It is essential that when a person leaves or a manager feels they need additional staff in their department, they seek the authority to recruit new members of staff. This authority must be sought so the management team can look at the demand and the level of business to assess the need for new members of staff. The authority to recruit may be sought in some organisations through the human resources department. However, it may sometimes be necessary for a manager or supervisor to present their suggestions for the selection procedure to the management team using a report or PowerPoint presentation. Financial restraints, new technologies and departmental restructuring may also eliminate the need to replace or recruit additional staff. The recruitment process can also be very expensive and time-consuming for the staff involved. This makes it even more important that the management evaluate the need for any future positions.

> **Evidence 3**
>
> 1.5 1.6 2.2 2.8
>
> Use the position you have identified in Evidence activity 1 and compare your reasons for employing this person against your organisation's selection criteria and any constraints it may have. If you cannot obtain this information, ask your line manager to list their selection criteria and any issues or constraints they may have.

> **Key terms**
>
> **Analysis** – the careful evaluation and study of something
>
> **Criteria** – the list of requirements used to measure a person or an assessment against

Figure 19.1 Managers and supervisors need to consider and discuss any potential recruitment requirements

> **Evidence 4**
>
> **1.3 2.3 2.5 2.9**
>
> Using the information you have gathered in Evidence activities 1, 2 and 3, produce a PowerPoint presentation that you would use to make a case to the HR department and senior management team.

Staffing requirements and selection procedures

Job descriptions

A job description is a brief overview of the job and the duties and responsibilities that come with it. In most organisations, every job has a standard job description that staff can check to see what their duties and responsibilities are. These standard job descriptions can change over time as new technology and departmental changes may alter some responsibilities. When an organisation writes a job description for new members of staff, they often include the key duties and responsibilities of the job and end with a clause that states that their hours and days off may change and they may be expected to carry out other duties after discussion with their line manager. These clauses have been added to help to make their staff's hours and conditions more flexible and make it easier for them to adapt to change.

JOB DESCRIPTION

Title of job: Restaurant waiter
Purpose of job: To provide a quality food and beverage service to meet our customers' expectations and to enhance and maintain the reputation of the company.
Reporting to: Restaurant supervisor

Skills, experience and qualifications required:
- Good communication, presentation, time management and social skills
- One year's similar experience
- Wine knowledge useful but not essential as training will be given
- Current Food Handler's Certificate desirable but full training will be provided

Main duties:
- Preparation of the restaurant area ready for service in accordance with the establishment daily duties list.
- Service of food and beverages to customers in accordance with the service specification.
- Ensuring correct charges are made and payment received.
- Clearing of restaurant area in accordance with service specification.
- Ensuring compliance with control procedures for equipment and other stock.
- Following correct health and safety procedures to ensure welfare of both staff and customers.
- Explaining to customers the content, preparation and presentation of all menu and beverage items, and promoting sales through positive selling techniques.
- Additional food and beverage service duties as required in order to meet business demands.

Training requirements
- Induction and company policy as contained in the Staff Handbook
- Menu and beverage list content and updates as required
- Customer care programme
- Basic food hygiene
- Basic fire training at induction and further training every six months
- Basic health and safety at induction and full COSHH every six months
- Manual handling at induction

Performance measures
- Customer feedback
- Management feedback
- Regular knowledge test on foods, wine and other services offered
- Six-monthly appraisals with restaurant supervisor

Figure 19.2 Job descriptions provide an overview of the key responsibilities of the role

Person specifications

Where the job description outlines the duties and responsibilities of the job, the person specification will list the other skills, experience and qualifications that are **essential** for the candidate to do the job. A potential applicant must be able to meet all of the essential specifications for the job. This helps the candidate to assess their suitability for the job and prevent people from applying who are not qualified for the role. The person specification will also list additional or **desirable** skills, experience and qualifications that the employer would like the candidates to have. A better applicant will be able to fulfill most or all of these desirable specifications, which highlight the applicants who may have additional qualities to offer the employer and therefore may help in the shortlisting process before the interviews. Tests and assessments may also be used to confirm they have the qualities asked for.

2.1 2.4 Legal and organisational recruitment needs

When any organisation is recruiting staff, it is important that, as well as meeting the organisation's requirements, they should also follow employment law to ensure a fair and non-discriminatory recruitment process. The best candidate for the job should be identified on the basis of the job description and person specification. Employment law ensures that no other bias such as age, race, colour or sexual orientation has prevented them from getting the job.

Legal requirements
The laws that need to be adhered to when recruiting staff are listed below:
- The Equal Pay Act 1970 – equal pay and contracts for men and women.
- The Sex Discrimination Act 1975 – law preventing people being treated less favourably on the grounds of sex, marital status and gender reassignment.
- The Race Relations Act 1976 – law preventing people being treated less favourably on the grounds of ethnic origin, nationality, race and colour.
- Trade Union and Labour Relations (Consolidation) Act 1992 – makes it unlawful to discriminate against people on the grounds of union membership.
- Disability Discrimination Act 1995 – makes it unlawful to discriminate against people on the grounds of any form of disability.
- Part-Time Workers Regulations 2000 – prevents part-time workers being treated less favourably than full-time workers.
- Fixed-Term Employees Regulations 2000 – prevents fixed-term workers being treated less favourably than full-time workers.
- Employment Equality Regulations 2003 (Sexual Orientation) – protects people against discrimination on the grounds of sexual orientation of any kind.
- Employment Equality Regulations 2003 (Religion or Belief) – protects people against discrimination on the grounds of religion or belief.
- Employment Equality Regulations 2006 (Age) – prevents people being discriminated against on the basis of age in relation to employment and vocational training.

Understanding the labour market
After completing all of the planning procedures, such as seeking the authority to recruit, analysing the job and writing the job description and specifications, you will have identified the type of person you need to fill the position. Now you have to decide how and where you can find this person. Some jobs will first be advertised internally. This can be beneficial to both employers and employees, as it can help in promoting staff or allow them to move departments and gain new skills. Staff already working for the company may also know someone who they feel would be a suitable candidate for the position. In addition, recruiting from your internal pool of staff can save the company money in advertising and the recruitment process.

When recruiting externally there are many things to take into consideration. This includes how many people within commuting distance have the skills and knowledge required to do the job and how to make contact and attract these people to apply for the job. You could look at the local labour profile for your area to see how many people have the qualifications you require. If you have very specific professional qualifications, skills and experience that are required, you may need to target professional organisations and colleagues in that field to see if there are any potential candidates before advertising the position.

Evidence 5
2.1 2.4

From the list of laws above, identify any laws you would have to observe for your position and highlight the three you feel would be the ones that need to be observed the most.

Key term
Discrimination – the treatment of someone differently on the basis of colour, age, religion, sex or nationality

Advertising jobs

It may be necessary to advertise some positions if you are not able to recruit from within the business or identify anyone in your local area. Advertising can be very expensive depending on the size of the advertisement and where it is advertised. Some newspapers have specific days for various professions and industries to advertise for staff. However, the internet is being used more and more to advertise jobs as it can narrow down the people most suitable for the job and allow them to apply for the position instantly if they wish, with minimal costs to the applicant. When writing an advert, it is important that it stands out and is written using the minimum amount of words to explain exactly what the job is and the skills and attributes needed in order to attract as many potential applicants as possible.

These could include:
- job title, name of the business and salary
- brief description of the job
- introduction to the company and the vision
- type of person they need – e.g. dynamic, flexible, highly motivated
- additional benefits – bonus, club membership or staff accommodation
- application details – reference number, closing date and address
- equal opportunities statement
- further information – company website.

1.5 1.6 The interviewing and recruitment process

> **Evidence 6**
>
> **2.6** **2.7**
>
> Write a list of additional questions you would like to put on the application form to ensure you have all the information necessary to check the validity of the people applying for the job.

2.14 Job applications

Once you have decided how to target your potential recruits, you need to decide how you would like them to apply and what documents and information you need from them in order to shortlist and identify the best candidates for the job. Depending on the organisation's preference, applications and supporting documents can be sent via email or through the post. Application forms are the most efficient way to shortlist the applicants. Application forms can limit the questions to the essential aspects of the job. Some jobs attract high numbers of applicants, so some organisations may only accept standard application forms, as they are easier to process and manage. However, some senior positions may need to be backed up by curriculum vitae, supporting letters or statements. It is essential that all applications remain confidential throughout the application and interview process. This is to meet with the Data Protection Act 2014 and to ensure that the organisation can hold the applicant's data, so they can be contacted if another position becomes available.

Job application forms may require the following information:
- the position being applied for
- the name and address of the applicant
- current or most recent employer, position and duties
- previous employment – starting with the most recent first
- education and training – starting with the most recent first
- membership of professional bodies and associations
- a brief statement stating why they should be offered the job may be requested
- references or supporting statements from previous employers may be asked for
- declaration that all of the information given is the truth, by signing and dating the application
- equal opportunities statement may be attached for the applicant to read and keep.

> **Evidence 7**
>
> **2.14** **2.15**
>
> Explain in 300 words why you think it is important to make the selection process confidential. Then list the information that could be shared with the department's manager.

1.5 2.13 2.15 Shortlisting

When shortlisting your candidates, it is important that they are fairly judged on their skills, experience and qualifications. Some organisations have all of the personal information like name, address, date of birth and sex on the first page and work experience and further professional information on the other pages. To prevent any discrimination in the shortlisting process, the first page with the personal information would be removed and applications would be judged on their professional experience and ability to do the job. The candidates would then be shortlisted on all of the criteria set out in the job specification.

Interviewing

Interviewing candidates is still the most common and cheapest way to select a candidate. If there are a lot of potential candidates shortlisted, a telephone or Skype online interview may take place before inviting them to a formal face-to-face interview. Depending on the position, there may only be one person interviewing or in some cases there may be a panel of people interviewing in order to ask more directed questions and gain a more objective opinion of the candidate's ability to fill the position.

Interviews can be very productive; however, it is the interviewer's responsibility to ask the right questions and get some idea of the applicant's personality, reliability and ability to do the job. An interviewer may use a mix of closed questions to quickly find out basic information such as the number of years' experience the applicant has, or what their highest professional qualification is. They would then ask open questions, probing and challenging questions to find out more about the person and to get a feeling about them personally.

Figure 19.3 Interviewers should think carefully about the types of questions they ask

Examples of different question types

- **Closed question** – How long have you worked for your current employer?
- **Open question** – Why do you feel it is time to leave your current employer?
- **Probing question** – Why do you feel I should offer you this job and what can you offer us that none of the other candidates can?

If more than one candidate is suitable for the job, they may be invited back to meet with a senior manager, so they can make a final decision. This may not be in the form of another interview. The previous interview would have confirmed they all have the ability to do the job. Due to this, the meeting with the senior manager may only be an informal meeting, so they can decide who they would like to have working for their company.

2.10 Job-related tests and assessment activities

For some jobs, it may be necessary to assess the candidate's ability to do the job. Some tests may assess their personality type and how they would react in certain situations when dealing with the public. These tests can be carried out online during the application process to help in the shortlisting process. They can also be used to assess the candidate's literacy and numeracy, as required, along with their practical skills and computer literacy if these are needed for the job. It is now becoming common for prospective staff in some departments, such as the kitchen, to come in and work with the team for a pre-arranged time to assess their skills and see how they interact with the team.

Evidence 8

2.13

Write three closed, three open and three probing questions you feel would help you make a fair and objective assessment of your candidates.

2.11 Assessment methods – advantages and disadvantages

There are a number of ways to assess a candidate's ability to do a job. The table below lists the advantages and disadvantages of some of these methods.

Assessment method	Advantages	Disadvantages
Skills test – a short test to demonstrate the skills needed for the role.	Allows the employer to assess the applicant and the candidate to demonstrate their ability, organisational and practical skills.	Can be time-consuming and expensive, depending on the skills being demonstrated.
Trial day – a period of time working with the team on a normal working day.	Gives the employer the opportunity to assess the candidate's attitude, skills and ability to work with their team. It also gives the applicant the opportunity to see if they would like to work in this environment.	Can be time-consuming and difficult to organise. It can also prevent other members of the team performing their duties while working with and assessing the candidate.
Group activities – working in a group to meet an objective set by the assessor.	Gives the employer an opportunity to assess the applicant's ability to work with others and solve problems.	Can be time-consuming and difficult to organise and manage.
In-tray/e-tray exercises – to analyse, assess and perform a number of tasks within the job-holder's everyday role.	Like the skills test, it gives the applicant an opportunity to demonstrate their ability to do the job.	Can be time-consuming and difficult to organise and manage.
Presentations – to present a topic given to the candidate, usually a few days before.	Not expensive and easy to set up. Gives the candidate the opportunity to demonstrate their knowledge and presentation skills.	Would only be suitable for some roles, including management, training and sales.
Case studies – an issue or situation you need to resolve. Could be discussed, role-played or written.	Gives the employer and employee the opportunity to demonstrate how they would deal with important issues that may occur within the role.	Can be time-consuming and difficult to organise and manage
Psychometric testing – questions to assess a candidate's ability, personality, aptitude and motivation.	Can be easy to carry out, often as part of the application process. Online tests can generate the results instantly, making it easy to manage and assess.	The software can be expensive. Can dismiss good candidates for the role if the results are misinterpreted.

Making an offer

After the selection process, all of the applicants should be contacted as soon as possible to inform them if they were successful or unsuccessful. This will put the candidates' minds at rest and leave them with a positive impression of the business. If there are a lot of applicants, a brief letter or email may be sent to thank them for their application and inform them they were not successful on this occasion. If there were only a few candidates shortlisted, some form of feedback may be given to them on their application and the interview process. As discussed in the section on job applications, it is important that application forms, interview notes and results on assessments for the position are kept securely so they can be used to identify candidates unsuccessful on this occasion but who may be suitable for future positions, and to record your contribution to the selection process should there be any issues in the future. This is called 'due diligence' – proof you have done everything in your power to ensure the process is fair and unbiased.

Evidence 9
2.10 2.11 2.12

From the list of assessment methods, chose the methods you would use for the job you identified in Evidence activities 1, 2 and 3. Then justify your reasons for using these methods. What are their advantages and disadvantages?

> **Evidence 10**
>
> **2.16**
>
> Record in a brief statement why you feel it is important to accurately record and save your own contribution to the selection process.

The successful applicant would normally be called or sent an offer letter to inform them they have been successful. This letter may also give them further information on the proposed start date and may confirm the details of the job, salary, holiday entitlements and further benefits. When the successful applicant accepts the position, their references would then be checked. When the new member of staff starts their job, it is important that they receive a thorough induction and training. Most organisations have a probation period of three months to a year, depending on the position. During this time, their performance would be monitored and at the end of this period, they would receive their permanent contract. After this it is important that the new member of staff is developed further to motivate and retain them.

Knowledge check

1. Why is it important that an organisation has a good and thorough recruitment process?
2. What is the process of assessing whether a position is needed and what responsibilities that role might have?
3. What do you call the document with all of the details about a job and a person's responsibilities?
4. Name the people who would give the authority to recruit?
5. Give examples of five questions an application form may include.
6. What happens with the applications when they are received?
7. Name the three styles of questions that may be used during an interview.
8. What assessment method might be used when recruiting a chef?

Evidence checklist		
Assessment criteria		**Possible evidence**
1.1	Identify staffing requirements, taking account of work objectives and constraints	Evidence activity 1
1.2	Ensure that identified staffing requirements are based on valid and reliable information	Evidence activity 1
1.3	Present staffing requirements to the relevant people following organisational procedures	Evidence activity 4
1.4	Follow organisational procedures when assessing and selecting staff	Evidence activity 2
1.5	Ensure the selection of staff is based on an objective assessment of the information available against agreed selection criteria	Evidence activity 3
1.6	Ensure records of own contribution to the selection process meet organisational requirements	Evidence activity 3
2.1	Describe the legal organisational requirements for identifying personnel needs	Evidence activity 5
2.2	Explain how to interpret the work objectives and constraints which are relevant to identifying own personnel needs	Evidence activity 3
2.3	Explain how to make a case for additional staffing requirements	Evidence activity 4
2.4	Describe the legal requirements that need to be followed when selecting staff	Evidence activity 5
2.5	Identify the organisational and industry requirements for the selection of personnel	Evidence activity 4
2.6	Explain how to collect the information necessary to contribute to identifying staffing requirements	Evidence activity 6
2.7	Explain how to check the validity of information for staffing requirements	Evidence activity 6

Evidence checklist		
Assessment criteria		**Possible evidence**
2.8	Explain the type of work objectives and constraints that may influence personnel considerations	Evidence activity 3
2.9	Explain how to present suggestions for selection procedures	Evidence activity 4
2.10	Describe the range of methods which may be used for the assessment and selection of staff	Evidence activity 9
2.11	Compare the advantages and disadvantages of different selection methods for own team	Evidence activity 9
2.12	Outline how own contribution can be made to the assessment and selection of staff	Evidence activity 9
2.13	Explain how to make fair and objective assessments against criteria during the selection process	Evidence activity 8
2.14	Explain the importance of confidentiality during selection processes	Evidence activity 7
2.15	Outline the type of information that may be shared with specific staff	Evidence activity 7
2.16	Explain the importance of keeping accurate records of own contributions to the selection process	Evidence activity 10

CHAPTER 20

Lead and manage meetings

This chapter is about leading meetings in order to achieve the meeting's objectives, which may be to solve a problem, take decisions, consult with people or to exchange information and knowledge.

Learning objectives

On completion of this chapter, you should:
1. Be able to prepare to lead a meeting.
2. Be able to manage meeting procedures.
3. Be able to chair a meeting.
4. Be able to undertake post-meeting tasks.

Introduction

In any large or small organisation **communication** is essential to ensure that everyone is aware of the day-to-day needs of the business and any future business plans. Depending on the information being passed on, there are a number of forms of communication that can be used. **Informal** methods of communication can be used to pass on information to individuals and small groups of people. Informal communication can include brief discussions, telephone calls, or notes written in a diary or hand-over book for the next shift. A record is not always needed to show that this information has been passed on.

Formal communication is used when the information being passed on is of an important nature to the organisation and this communication is often recorded. Formal communication can be in the form of reports, memos or emails, which can be considered both formal or informal, depending on their content and tone.

Meetings are one of the most vital forms of communication. Properly run meetings can bring together all of the relevant people needed to discuss and solve problems and formulate plans to improve any issues a business may have. This can save time, increase the productivity of the business and improve staff motivation.

It is essential that meetings are well planned, well run, and documented, with actions and issues delegated and followed up.

A meeting should always have three common elements:
1. It has a specific aim or purpose.
2. It brings together the key people in order to have an effective discussion and good communication.
3. It is carried out in a designated and controlled situation.

> **Key terms**
>
> **Communication** – method of passing on information. Some forms can be verbal, email, memos and meetings
>
> **Formal** – official communication, usually documented or minuted
>
> **Informal** – casual or general communication about a topic that does not need to be documented

1.1 Preparing to lead the meeting

It is the organiser's or chairperson's responsibility to ensure that a meeting is well planned, to lead the meeting, organise minutes to be taken and follow up any actions identified during the meeting.

Before the meeting

You must have a reason to call the meeting. Reasons for holding a meeting could be to inform, solve problems, consult and then make collective decisions.

Preparing for a meeting

- Identify the people who need to be invited to the meeting.
- Give a time and place for the meeting.
- Give the reason for the meeting and the topics to be covered, identifying any responsibilities for people to bring or introduce information at the meeting.
- Attach all of the relevant paperwork for the meeting. This could include minutes of previous meetings, the agenda and documents and reports linked to the topic of the meeting (invitations to the meeting are usually sent via email).
- Give attendees an approximate time for the meeting to close.

> **Evidence 1**
>
> **1.1** **1.2**
>
> Take on the position of the chairperson of a meeting and identify a reason for a meeting and the people needed to attend. Use the table below.
>
> **Table 20.1** Initial information required for a meeting
>
> | | |
> |---|---|
> | Identify people needed at the meeting | |
> | Time and place for the meeting | |
> | Reason for the meeting and topic | |
> | List relevant documents and paperwork needed at the meeting | •
 •
 • |
> | Give approximate time for the meeting to close | |

Carrying out the meeting

1.2 Documents needed to support the meeting

The **agenda** is the key document used for a meeting. It shows the reason for the meeting, the people attending the meeting, the time and place of the meeting and exactly what is going to be covered during the meeting. The agenda is also used to form the key headings for the minutes of the meeting. The agenda must identify all key items that realistically need to be covered in the specified time.

Heading: meeting topic

Date, time and place of meeting
- Attendees –
- Apologies for absence –
- Minutes of last meeting –
- Matters arising (from minutes of last meeting)
- Items for discussion –
    - Items 1 – Training issues
    - Item 2 – Funding
    - Item 3 – Implementation
    - Item 4 – Location and equipment
- A.O.B. (Any Other Business)
- Time and date of next meeting – If needed

Action plan
Actions linked to a delegated person responsible for each action listed with date to be completed by. Update given at next meeting.

Figure 20.1 An example of a meeting agenda

Other supporting documents that can be attached include:
- **minutes** of previous meetings
- reports
- actions from previous meetings
- linked internal and external supporting documents.

Evidence 2
1.1 1.2 3.1

In groups of four to five people, use the initial meeting information provided in Evidence activity 1 to write an agenda for a 30–40 minute meeting with the people you have invited, at the time and place you have arranged.

Key terms

Agenda – plan for the meeting and list of attendees and topics being covered in meeting

Minutes – accurate and complete overview of topics discussed during the meeting

2.1 Managing meeting procedures

Organisations may have slightly differing formal procedures. However, there are key things to be followed when chairing a meeting to ensure all the aims of the meeting are met (see below).

> **Evidence 3**
>
> 2.1
>
> Ask your manager and use a table to show any formal procedures your organisation may have for meetings. If they do not have formal procedures, make a brief list of procedures you would implement.

3.1 3.2 Chairing the meeting

The chairperson is often the person who called the meeting, or the most senior person attending may be asked to take the chair. It is the chairperson's responsibility to ensure that the meeting runs smoothly, that everyone has the opportunity to speak without disruption and that everything on the agenda is discussed, with an agreed decision where possible.

Figure 20.2 Every meeting should have a chairperson, who makes such that the meeting runs smoothly

275

The chair's responsibilities

- Make sure that you give everyone invited enough time to make arrangements to attend the meeting.
- Send all attendees the agenda and the key items to be covered.
- Check the minutes of the previous meeting with attendees and again before the meeting for accuracy and errors.
- Ensure you have someone to take accurate minutes of the meeting. This is normally someone external or who is not directly involved in the meeting.
- Keep time – start the meeting on time and make sure that all of the items and issues will be covered in the allotted time.
- Manage the items on the agenda.
- Facilitate the discussion – ensure that everyone has the opportunity to talk and round up each item when it has been discussed.
- Maintain professionalism and order during the meeting.
- Finalise each item on the agenda and, if needed, put it to the vote.
- Declare the result of each item on the agenda.
- Identify what has been achieved and ensure that everyone understands the decisions made.
- Make an action plan, where needed, and identify the individuals responsible for each action, with a date for it to be completed by.
- Declare the meeting closed and set a date for the next meeting if needed.

Evidence 4

3.4 **4.1**

- Choose one person from the group to be the chairperson and one to be a minute taker.
- Use the list of the chair's responsibilities to ensure that all of the correct organisational responsibilities have been met.
- Identify any responsibilities that were missed and use the minutes of the meeting as evidence that this was achieved.

After the meeting

4.1 The minutes of the meeting

The minutes of a meeting should be an accurate, written representation of the meeting. It should show the people who attended the meeting and the people who could not attend and who sent their apologies. The attendees' initials are sometimes put after their name. This is so the minute-taker can use the initials to identify individuals when they make a specific point or comment during the meeting.

The minutes should provide an accurate record of each individual item on the agenda and the decisions made on each point. The minutes should only highlight the key points in the meeting and do not have to record every word spoken. It is the chairperson's responsibility to identify anything that should not appear on the minutes and that they are an accurate and true representation of what was said at the meeting.

The minutes should be typed up, checked by the chair and sent to the attendees as soon as possible after the meeting. The minutes should then be sent to all of the relevant people so they can read the decisions made during the meeting and actions can be taken where needed.

> **Monthly meeting**
>
> Monday 13th April 2015
>
> 10:00 AM
>
> **Attendees**: Megan Price, Matthew Sullivan, Sebastian Rydberg, Sundus Pasha, Elizabeth Wright, Stephen Halder, Jane Adams, Gemma Parsons
>
> **Absent**: Emily Frost
>
> **Minutes**:
> - Megan Price discussed the new Spring menu. Matthew Sullivan agreed to research suitable drinks to match the new items on the menu.
> - Elizabeth Wright reminded the team of the importance of arriving at work early/on time to allow time for handovers. All agreed to arrive 5 minutes early when possible.
> - Jane Adams explained the new shifts for waiting staff. All staff will work a minimum of one weekend and one evening shift per week.
> - Elizabeth Wright explained the new cleaning rota and how it matches new regulations.
>
> **Actions**:
> - Matthew Sullivan to research the new menu and will advise on suitable drinks matches.

Figure 20.3 An example of what the minutes of a meeting could look like

Evidence 5
3.2 **4.1** **4.2**

Type up the minutes of the meeting. Use the agenda to identify the items being minuted and identify any individual's points using their initials.

For example, Gregg Smith is 'GS'; Nathan Butcher, 'NB'.

> GS explained that the financial implications of this would have an impact on the business.
>
> NB argued that this was already part of this month's budget.

When the minutes are complete, send them to all the people involved in the meeting.

4.2 4.3 Following up the meeting's outcomes

During the meeting, decisions may have been made that need to be implemented or acted on. In some cases, action plans may be used to identify individual responsibilities to implement these decisions. These action plans highlight the objective or activity being actioned. They will identify the individual responsible, the date it should be completed by and the results and evidence or measure of success.

Action Plan					
Meeting goal:					
Measure of success:					
Individual responsible (To ensure actions are achieved):					
Date for completion:					
Action/Activity	Individual responsible	Dates	Action Results	Measure of success	Completion date

Figure 20.4 An example of a simple action plan

Evidence 6
3.2 **4.3**

Using the minutes of your meeting (Evidence 5), identify any actions that can be transferred onto the action plan (Figure 20.4) and evaluate if the meeting's objectives were met.

Communicate and follow up meeting outcomes to relevant individuals

When the minutes of the meeting and any supporting actions and documentation are completed, they should be sent as soon as possible to all of the people involved in the meeting, with an overview of the meeting's **objectives**, decisions made during the meeting and any potential improvements that can be made. This is usually sent via email and the elements of the meeting may be passed on to others involved in the decisions, if needed.

Key term

Objectives – goals or realistic things that need to be achieved

Knowledge check

1. Who would be responsible for calling and organising a meeting?
2. Give two reasons why a meeting may be called.
3. Who would be invited to the meeting?
4. What is the most important document that should be sent to the people who are invited to the meeting?
5. What is the name of the person who leads the meeting?
6. What do you call the notes taken during and after the meeting?
7. Who is responsible for sending the findings and relevant documents to the people invited after the meeting?
8. What is the name of the plan that lists anything that needs to be done after the meeting with a person and date for it to be completed?

Evidence checklist		
Assessment criteria		**Possible evidence**
1.1	Perform activities needed to be carried out in preparation for leading a meeting	Evidence activity 1
		Evidence activity 2
		Evidence activity 5
1.2	Produce documentation in support of activities	Evidence activity 1
		Evidence activity 2
		Evidence activity 5
2.1	Identify any formal procedures that apply in own organisation	Evidence activity 3
3.1	Manage the agenda in co-operation with participants to ensure meeting objectives are met	Evidence activity 2
3.2	Produce minutes of the meeting and allocate action points after discussions	Evidence activity 4
		Evidence activity 5
		Evidence activity 6
4.1	Explain that the minutes of the meeting provide an accurate record of proceedings	Evidence activity 4
		Evidence activity 5
4.2	Communicate and follow up meeting outcomes to relevant individuals	Evidence activity 5
4.3	Evaluate whether the meeting's objectives were met and identify potential improvements	Evidence activity 6

CHAPTER 21

Employment rights and responsibilities in the hospitality, leisure, travel and tourism sector

This chapter will provide information about achieving the national occupational standards and understanding the issues around employment rights and responsibilities within the hospitality, leisure, travel and tourism sectors.

Learning objectives

On completion of this chapter, you should:
1. Know employer and employee rights and responsibilities and your own organisational procedures.
2. Know factors that affect your organisation and occupation.

Employer and employee rights and responsibilities and organisational procedures

1.1 1.2 Employer and employee rights and responsibilities under employment law

It is important for employees and employers to understand their rights and responsibilities so that working procedure can be carried out correctly and everyone concerned will be working within the relevant legal requirements.

An understanding of employment rights will assist you in protecting yourself and helping you to understand what you are entitled to from your employment. It is important to ensure fair pay, conditions of work and treatment by both colleagues and employers. It is, however, equally important for you to know and understand your employment responsibilities for yourself and your colleagues, so you act appropriately and legally. Employees have to work together and have responsibilities to each other and can expect their rights to be upheld.

For employers it is essential to know their rights and responsibilities in relation to employment so they can provide the best possible working conditions and procedures for their employees and to avoid possible fines and lawsuits for non-compliance.

There are significant amounts of legislation affecting employment in the sector and employers as well as employees have both rights and responsibilities. The legislation making most impact on the sector is listed and explained in Chapter 4: Maintain health, hygiene, safety, and security in the working environment.

Examples of employment rights and responsibilities applying to both employer and employee are outlined in Table 21.1 below.

Table 21.1 Employers' and employees' rights and responsibilities at work

Health and Safety at Work Act 1974

Employers' responsibilities	Employers' rights	Employees' responsibilities	Employees' rights
Where there are more than five employees, a risk assessment of all areas that includes fire risk assessment must be conducted and procedures to ensure safe ways of working must be introduced. This must be fully recorded, updated and available for inspection. Premises and equipment must be kept in safe working order and personal protective equipment (PPE) made available and maintained for employees.	Employers can expect their employees to co-operate with the health and safety measures put in place, including the use of protective clothing and equipment, and attend relevant information and training sessions. They expect employees to work in a safe way that will not endanger themselves or anyone else.	Employees' responsibilities include co-operating fully with their employers on health and safety matters. This includes attendance at briefings and training sessions or relevant courses. They must use the clothing and equipment provided to keep them safe and report to their employers anything they think may be unsafe or a hazard. They must work in a safe way that will not cause illness or injury to themselves or to anyone else.	Employees have the right to expect a workplace and working procedures where all reasonable precautions have been taken to keep them safe and prevent illness or injury. Employees can expect their employers to have completed risk assessments and produced a Health and Safety policy that they can have access to. Employees can expect training and instruction in safety procedures where appropriate, including fire evacuation and to be provided with suitable PPE.

Disability Discrimination Act (DDA) 1995

Employers' responsibilities	Employers' rights	Employees' responsibilities	Employees' rights
It is against the law for an employer to discriminate against a disabled person by refusing employment, denying promotion, training or transfer opportunities and they cannot dismiss them because of their disability. The employer has a duty to make *reasonable* adjustments in order for a disabled person to carry out their duties. Some of these adjustments may include reallocating work or relocation of work as appropriate such as: • Making adjustments to the buildings including ramps and automatic doors. • Being flexible about working hours, especially for assessment, treatment and rehabilitation. • Providing specific training or retraining. • Providing modified equipment and making instructions and manuals more accessible. • Providing a reader or interpreter.	The employer needs to be in full possession of the facts of an individual's disability in relation to their employment or potential employment so consideration of reasonable adjustments can be made. Considerations may include: • How effective will changes be? • Is it practical for the building, work area and procedures? • Will changes seriously disadvantage other employees? • Will changes cause too much disruption? • Will it help other people? • Is the cost prohibitive? • The extent of the employer's financial and other resources.	Employees could discuss possible adjustments with their employers, bearing in mind that they need to be *reasonable*. They could ask if the employer is aware of the *Access to Work Programme*. Through this, employers can get advice on appropriate adjustments and maybe some financial help towards the cost of the adjustments. Employees might also want to encourage the employer to speak to someone with expertise in providing work-related help for people with disabilities, such as an occupational health adviser.	Under the DDA, it is unlawful for employers to discriminate against anyone with disabilities in relation to their employment, unless it can be justified. DDA covers matters such as recruitment, selection, application forms, job descriptions, person specifications, recruitment advertising, the application process, shortlisting, interviewing, selection testing arrangements, medical questionnaires/assessments, references, job offers, terms of employment, harassment, pregnancy, promotion, transfer or training opportunities.

> **Take it further**
>
> For more information on employment legislation, see the following websites:
> - Disability Discrimination Act: www.nidirect.gov.uk/employment-rights-and-the-disability-discrimination-act
> - Health and Safety at Work: www.hse.gov.uk
> - Citizens Advice Bureau (Rights at Work): www.adviceguide.org.uk/england/work_e/work_rights_at_work_e
> - UK working, jobs and pensions: www.gov.uk/browse/employing-people/contracts
> - Equality and diversity: www.gov.uk/government/organisations/home-office/about/equality-and-diversity and www.acas.org.uk/media/pdf/a/c/Delivering-equality-and-diversity-advisory-booklet.pdf

1.3 Organisational procedures for health and safety

Employees have the right to be provided with a safe workplace and procedures that will not injure or harm them in any way in the course of their work.

All employers must show due regard and compliance with the Health and Safety at Work Act 1975 and ensure that all buildings, processes and procedures within the business comply with the current legislation. (See Chapter 4, 'Maintain health, hygiene, safety and security in the working environment'.)

Unless there are fewer than five employees, the regulations require employers to conduct risk assessments including fire risk assessment of all areas and procedures and ensure safe ways of working. The outcomes of risk assessments must be fully recorded and available for inspection. Employers will need to keep premises and equipment in safe working order and provide/maintain personal protective equipment where needed for employees. All of this must be recorded and updated within the risk assessment records. However, even if there are fewer than five employees, the employer still has a responsibility for their health, safety and welfare.

Compliance with health and safety law is inspected and enforced by:
- Health and safety inspectors from the Health and Safety Executive – the HSE.
- Environmental health officers (EHOs) and technical officers from local authorities.
- Fire officers: in the majority of premises, local fire and rescue authorities are responsible for enforcing fire safety.
- For factories, farms and hospitals, the enforcing officer is a health and safety inspector from the HSE.
- For shops, restaurants and leisure centres, the enforcing officer is the local EHO. Fire officers can visit all these premises for the purposes of enforcing the law on fire safety and fire precautions.

Most documentation concerned with health and safety will be kept and updated as part of the health and safety policy. A wide range of documents will need to be kept to ensure compliance with health and safety legislation and will include such items as risk assessments, PAT records, security checks and reports, records of chemicals used including the data sheets, records of new equipment and equipment maintenance, staff training records and many more items that may be relevant to specific work areas.

1.4 Organisational procedures for equality and diversity

Issues concerning equality and **diversity** now play a major role within workplaces and should form part of the operational procedure for each working area. Equality and diversity matters are also covered by legislation in the Equality Act 2010.

Equality is about treating people fairly and ensuring everyone is given a fair chance within their employment. Equality and diversity procedures are not about treating everyone in exactly the same way but are about acknowledging people's differences and their specific needs, which could have an impact on how they are feeling and the work they complete.

An equality and diversity policy will contain a policy statement of the company's aim to encourage, value and manage a diverse workforce. It will state the company's commitment to providing equality for all, and their wish to have a workforce that is representative of the group of people from which it is selected, to secure the widest range of skills and abilities possible. Wherever possible, the policy should reflect the organisational procedures of the area or workplace.

Documentation in the equality and diversity policy should have four distinct parts:
1. A statement of intent to challenge discrimination and to encourage employee participation.
2. A list of objectives showing the desired achievements.
3. Procedures to put the policy's aims and objectives into action in specific working areas.
4. Processes for monitoring, evaluating and reviewing the policy.

The policy should deal with addressing the following types of discrimination:
- gender (explicitly including transgender and transsexual identity)
- race or ethnicity
- sexual identity or orientation (lesbian, gay, bisexual and heterosexual)
- age
- relationship or marital status
- disability
- background
- faith or religious belief
- physical appearance
- political opinions
- disciplinary and grievance policy
- disability policy
- harassment and bullying policy
- race equality policy.

> **Key term**
>
> **Diversity** – acceptance and respect of others, understanding that each individual is unique, and recognising individual differences.

1.5 Sources of information and advice

Employers and employees may need to seek advice on employment rights and responsibilities from time to time and it is important to be aware that legislation may be changed or adapted occasionally; workplace policy and procedure must remain up to date to reflect this.

Some of the other chapters in this book will outline sources of information relating to employment rights and responsibilities; the websites above are also good sources of information. Also consider information available in libraries, job centres and industry-specific magazines and trade journals.

Within the workplace, advice can be sought from line managers, senior managers or human resources departments. They can also advise on additional learning support for employees and help with this can also be found at libraries, job centres, local colleges and adult education centres.

> ### Evidence 1
> **1.1** **1.2** **1.5**
>
> Find out which employment legislation affects your working area and list the relevant Acts. Select the three most important for your area and point out the main features affecting the rights and responsibilities of both employers and employees.

> ### Evidence 2
> **1.4**
>
> How could equality and diversity within your area be ensured when wording an advertisement for a job in your team?
>
> What would you include in an induction session for new staff to inform them about equality and diversity within the organisation?

> ### Evidence 3
> **1.1** **1.2** **1.3** **1.4** **1.5**
>
> Find the information that your organisation gives to new employees about employment rights and responsibilities. These could include health and safety policies, risk assessments, leaflets, induction booklets, data protection policy, equal opportunities policy etc.

Factors affecting your organisation and occupation

2.1 2.2 The hospitality industry, your occupation and career pathways

In order to fully understand and to be able to apply good practice concerning employment rights and responsibilities, it is essential to have a good understanding of the hospitality, leisure, travel and tourism industry, and where your organisation fits into the relevant industry sector.

The industry is large and remains a fast-growing area, with considerable importance for the UK and its economy. The leisure sector, including hospitality, travel and tourism, is large and employs over two million people. Around seven per cent of all jobs in the UK are in the leisure sector and this accounts for about one in every fourteen UK jobs; the sector is predicted to grow even more.

There are approximately 181,500 hospitality, leisure, travel and tourism businesses in the UK. The UK leisure industry (tourism and hospitality) is estimated to be worth around £90 billion or more. It is estimated that UK accommodation alone contributes £7.5 billion to the total leisure market.

> ### Size of the industry
>
> The hospitality industry has:
> - 2 million + people employed
> - £90 billion annual turnover, worth £40.6 billion to the UK economy
> - £7.5 billion on accommodation

As can be seen, hospitality is a fast-growing industry sector offering good opportunities for career progression and promotion. There is also good opportunity for movement in different parts of the industry; for example, a food service supervisor could work in hotels, restaurants, airlines, cruise ships, events, resorts, yachts and many more establishments.

All employees are important to the continuing success of this industry and career progression can happen quickly for committed, enthusiastic and well-qualified employees. Be aware of how your own role contributes to the organisation as a whole, look at the organisation's structure and consider the further opportunities that may exist for you. Also consider the measures you may take to assist you with progression and career development.

2.3 Representative bodies

Sector Skills Council

The relevant Sector Skills Council for the industry is called **People 1st**. It is a skills and workforce development organisation for employers in the hospitality, tourism, leisure, travel, passenger transport and retail industries, focusing on developing skills through effective recruitment, training and people management. It aims to enable employers in the sector to compete in a rapidly changing global market and to improve the quality and accessibility of career and professional development within the industry.

State of the nation is a report produced by **Sector Skills Council** - People 1st. State of the Nation 2013 Hospitality and Tourism is the fourth report to examine skills and labour market trends across the hospitality and tourism sector. It looks at the on-going issues around retention in the industry and how this is contributing to skill gaps and skill shortages. The report also offers insights into the trends that will influence the sector in coming years, and includes a special report on the London 2012 Olympic and Paralympic Games.

There are a number of professional and representative bodies supporting the hospitality, leisure, travel and tourism sectors. They have been formed for a number of reasons:
- To provide a recognisable, professional organisation for the industry sector.
- To maintain the professional standards of a specific sector.
- To offer membership; this could be through application, recommendation, examination, interviews or be linked with employment.
- To provide training, support and qualifications advice.
- To provide members with up-to-date information on a number of current issues including changes within the industry and legislation.

There are a large number of these industry-linked **representative bodies**, including:
- British Hospitality Association: www.bha.org.uk
- Academy of Food and Wine Service: www.afws.co.uk
- Institute of Travel and Tourism: www.itt.co.uk
- Institute of Hospitality: www.instituteofhospitality.org
- Hospitality Guild: www.hospitalityguild.co.uk
- Craft Guild of Chefs: http://craftguildofchefs.org
- Royal Academy of Culinary Arts: www.royalacademyofculinaryarts.org.uk
- Air Travel Organisers Licencing: www.atol.org.uk
- Association of British Travel Agents: http://abta.com
- UK Sommelier Association: www.uksommelierassociation.com
- British Institute of Innkeeping: www.bii.org/home

Take it further

For further information, please see the following websites:
- British Hospitality Association: www.bha.org.uk
- Hotel Industry Magazine: www.hotel-industry.co.uk
- Big Hospitality: www.bighospitality.co.uk Trends-Reports
- State of the nation – hospitality and tourism: www.people1st.co.uk
- Britain's tourism industry: www.visitbritain.com
- Institute of Travel and Tourism: www.itt.co.uk
- PwC UK travel and tourism: www.pwc.co.uk/hospitality-leisure/issues/travel-and-tourism.jhtml

Key terms

Sector Skills Council – employer-led organisation covering specific industries. The goals are to support employers with apprenticeship standards, to reduce skills shortages and improve productivity.

Representative or professional body – an organisation that has a common goal for the members or interested parties. It often represents an industry sector such as hospitality or travel and may campaign for or publicise current industry issues.

- The Society of the Golden Keys: www.thegoldenkeys.co.uk
- National Concierge Association: www.ncakey.org
- Professional Association of UK Housekeepers: www.ukha.co.uk

2.4 Sources of information and advice on the industry, occupations, training and careers

To find information and advice on your particular industry sector, your employment/career or training, consider the following:
- trade and professional associations as listed above
- industry and trade journals/magazines
- various websites and online materials
- senior colleagues, line managers, training managers, human resources departments
- libraries
- TV advertising, radio, social networking sites
- trade exhibitions and promotional events.

Specifically for career development, education and training:
- career and employment fairs
- in-house and work-based trainers
- industry exhibitions and shows
- colleges, universities and adult education centres
- training and apprenticeship providers
- online training programmes.

2.5 Principles, policies and codes of practice

There are a large number of principles, policies and codes of practice used in the hospitality, leisure, travel and tourism industries. Some of these may apply generally when employing people, such as data protection, equality and diversity and minimum wage regulations. Others may be more relevant to specific industries and the work being carried out, for example, handling of food and COSHH regulations and practices.

However, some policies, procedures and codes may be more specific and will be recorded in **standard operational procedures (SOPs)**. These policies, procedures and codes could have similarities across industries but could just apply to one or a group of establishments. Examples of these could be:
- The procedure to be followed when entering an occupied guest room.
- How the telephone should be answered and greetings to be used.
- How to deal with complaints.
- Specific codes of practice on guest/customer confidentiality.
- The way uniform is worn, for example, the company logo badge always on the left lapel.
- The procedure for taking a booking.

There are likely to be many more examples of specific **codes of practice** in workplaces.

2.6 Issues of public concern

Those employed within the hospitality, leisure, travel and tourism industries become familiar with the relevant policies, procedures and how the various practices work. However, these service industries provide for a wide range of people of different ages, from different backgrounds and with varying experiences of the industry that you may be familiar with. Worldwide travel is now commonplace so those working

> **Key terms**
>
> **Standard operational procedure (SOP)** – recorded, regularly recurring tasks describing a procedure and how something should be done. The purpose is to carry out the tasks correctly and always in the same manner.
>
> **Codes of practice** – a set of written regulations issued by a professional or official body that explains how people working in a particular professional area should behave.

in the industry encounter people of many different nationalities and from a diverse range of cultures. Not surprisingly, such a diverse range of people could have a variety of concerns about what is being provided for them, how it is delivered and the standards they should expect.

The main areas for concern might include:
- food safety and health and safety issues
- unfamiliar foods and ingredients
- allergen concerns
- security and personal safety
- data protection issues
- credit card and passport security
- ease of access to premises and movement around interiors
- language barriers
- sight and hearing difficulties
- loss of luggage and belongings.

Evidence 4
2.1 2.2 2.4

If you are keen to be promoted or want to progress within your organisation, what are the specific measures you may need to take? (Consider more experience in other areas, education/training, building a portfolio of experience and achievement.) Draw up a timeline of how you may achieve your goals, starting with a description of your current role.

Evidence 5
2.2 2.3 2.4 2.5

Make a chart for someone completely new to the industry and your work area, showing some of the codes of practice and policies in place, professional representative organisations dealing with your area and some suggestions to help them find out more about the industry and organisation.

Evidence 6
2.6

People may sometimes have concerns about various aspects of the hospitality, leisure, travel and tourism industries. Find some of these concerns. They may be in customer feedback or questionnaires, newspaper or internet articles, on consumer websites such as TripAdvisor or something you have been told verbally. Select the three concerns that seem to occur most frequently, especially if they concern health and safety issues, and suggest how the concerns could be addressed.

Knowledge check

1. Suggest three advantages for employees in having some knowledge of their employment rights and responsibilities.
2. What are the advantages to employers of understanding the requirements of employment rights and responsibilities?
3. How does the Disability Discrimination Act affect an employer? What must they do for disabled employees?
4. Who inspects and enforces compliance with the Health and Safety at Work Act?
5. What is meant by equality and diversity?
6. Suggest four topics that should appear on an equality and diversity policy.
7. Approximately how many people are employed in the UK hospitality, travel and tourism industries and approximately how many businesses are there?
8. Name three industry representative bodies and what can they offer to employees in the industry.
9. How could you find out about career progression in your industry?
10. Suggest some codes of practice or policies that are used at your workplace.

Evidence checklist		
Assessment criteria		**Possible evidence**
1.1	State employee and employer rights and responsibilities under employment law including the Disability Discrimination Act, health and safety and other relevant legislation	Evidence activity 1 Evidence activity 3
1.2	State the importance of having employment rights and responsibilities	Evidence activity 1 Evidence activity 3
1.3	Describe organisational procedures for health and safety including documentation	Evidence activity 3
1.4	Describe organisational procedures for equality and diversity including documentation	Evidence activity 2 Evidence activity 3
1.5	Identify sources of information and advice on employment rights and responsibilities including access to work and additional learning support	Evidence activity 1 Evidence activity 3
2.1	Describe the role played by your own occupation within the organisation and industry	Evidence activity 4
2.2	Describe career pathways available to	Evidence activity 4 Evidence activity 5
2.3	Describe the types of representative body related to the hospitality industry, their main roles and responsibilities and their relevance to the industry	Evidence activity 5
2.4	Identify sources of information and advice in own industry, occupation training and career	Evidence activity 4 Evidence activity 5
2.5	Describe principles, policies and codes of practice used by own organisation and industry	Evidence activity 5
2.6	Describe any issues of public concern that affect own organisation and industry	Evidence activity 6

GLOSSARY

Age verification policy – the organisational procedures set out to ensure that staff check the age of those that they serve alcohol to ensure they are over 18

Agenda – plan for the meeting and list of attendees and topics being covered in meeting

Analysis – the careful evaluation and study of something

Assessment – a method of judging how a person performs a task, skill or test

Audit – a complete and careful inspection and examination of how a system or business is operating.

Audit – the checking and verification of accounts and often stock to check they are accurate and correct

Autonomy – the opportunity to be self-governing in the workplace

Broadband – high-speed data transmission in which a single cable can carry a large amount of data simultaneously

Budget – an estimate of the amount of money, resources or revenue that can be used over a set period of time

Calibration – the setting or correcting of a measuring device, usually by matching it to a set standard. For example, testing a food temperature probe by placing in boiling water.

Cash float – money of different denominations put into the till at the beginning of the day to allow the cashier to give customers change

Chronological order: a record of events starting with the earliest and following the order in which they occurred

Codes of practice – a set of written regulations issued by a professional or official body that explains how people working in a particular professional area should behave.

Communication – method of passing on information. Some forms can be verbal, email, memos and meetings

Contingency – planning ahead for something that could happen that was not planned.

Contingency plan – a plan designed to take account of a possible future event or circumstance which may or may not happen.

Contractors – a separate company contracted to provide goods and services

Contravention – violation or failure to comply with requirements.

Core value – this is a principle or belief that guides an organisation in internal conduct, as well as its relationship with the external world. Organisations communicate these values through their mission statement or value statement.

Corrosive – something that causes the deterioration or eating away, usually of metal. Acid is an example of something that would be described as corrosive.

Cost–benefit analysis – the process of comparing the costs involved in doing something to the advantage or profit that it may bring in.

Criteria – the list of requirements used to measure a person or an assessment against

Critical control points – the stages in food production where any possible hazards need to becontrolled.

Critical limits – the actual limits within a process to keep food safe. They must be absolute and measurable. For example, food being kept not for service must never fall below 63°C.

Customer service charter – a promise on what kind of service an organisation delivers so that a customer knows what to expect

Customer/guest surveys – a way of getting feedback from guests about their opinions of the service they received. They could be verbal questions at reception, a questionnaire in the room or a telephone/email survey.

Departmental trainers – a member of staff nominated to be responsible for the coordination and recording of the team's learning and development activities

Discrepancy – a difference or issue between things; for example, if the money at the end of the day is short, because an item was not put through the till, this would be a discrepancy in the figures

Discrimination – the treatment of someone differently on the basis of colour, age, religion, sex or nationality

Dispense bar – an area that dispenses beverages to staff to be served in another outlet

Diversity – acceptance and respect of others, understanding that each individual is unique, and recognising individual differences.

Due diligence – the reasonable steps taken to avoid committing an offence

Due diligence – when a person or organisation who may be subject to legal proceedings can establish a defence to show that they have taken 'all reasonable precautions and exercised due diligence' to proceed in the correct way to avoid committing an offence.

Employee cycle – the stages that every employee goes through, from the time they start working for an organisation to the time they leave

Empowering – provide the authority to do something

Entrapment – getting trapped, for example, clothing or hair trapped in machinery, or a person completely trapped in an area or equipment.

Ethical consideration – being in accordance with the rules or standards for right conduct or practice, especially the standards of a profession or industry.

Evaluate – find or judge the value

Feedback – offering a helpful response to someone's work, performance or ideas

Fixed cost – expenses that have to be paid by a business, regardless of the level of any business activity. For example, business rates and standing charges on electricity bills.

Food safety management system – having this in place is a requirement for all food businesses. The system must be based on the principles of HACCP and be available for inspection.

Formal – official communication, usually documented or minuted

Franchise – a right granted against a payment, to an individual or group, to market that company's brand, goods or services within a certain location for an agreed period.

Fraudulent – dishonest act of behaviour

Function sheet – A sheet recording all of the customer requirements for a specific functions

Gross profit – the total revenue of a business minus the cost of the services or the goods it has sold. Gross profit does not take into account selling and admin expenses.

Group coherence – a shared mental and/or emotional state of mind that allows a group to work well together

HACCP – an internationally recognised food safety management system that identifies stages in any process and identifies hazards that could occur, i.e. what could go wrong, when, where, how.

Handover – a meeting at shift change to communicate essential information between staff on one shift to the staff on the next shift

Handover session – this usually refers to areas where staff work shifts to cover the required hours; for example, 6am–2.30 pm and 2.30 pm–10pm. Time would be allocated in the middle for a team meeting all together so one shift can fully hand over to the next.

Hardware – the physical components that make up a computer system

Health and Safety Executive (HSE) – the national independent 'watchdog' for work-related health, safety and illness. It acts in the public interest to reduce work-related death and serious injury across Great Britain's workplaces; www.hse.gov.uk.

Human resources – the part of a company concerned with matters relating to employees such as recruitment, induction and training, employee benefits and retention

Improvement notice – issued by an inspector if he/she thinks there is a contravention of legislation. It states the details of the contravention and requires the person responsible to remedy it within a fixed time.

Induction – a procedure for welcoming new employees and preparing them for their roles

Informal – casual or general communication about a topic that does not need to be documented

In-house training – any training that is happening at the organisation and could be delivered by the employees themselves

Internet – a global computer network providing a variety of information and communication facilities, via interconnected networks using internet protocols

Intoxication – to lose control of behaviour or faculties, especially through alcohol or drugs

Legislation – as required by law.

Linen – the generic term used for such items as sheets, pillowcases and towels. Nowadays, these items are only occasionally actually made from linen. They are more likely to be made from cotton or even a cotton/synthetic fibre mixture such as polyester/cotton.

Maintain – to keep something at the same level and keep it there

Man-made fibre – a type of fibre that is made artificially, such as polyester or rayon.

Market share – a percentage or portion of total sales volume in a market captured or controlled by a brand, product, or company.

Mentoring – an experienced person assists another in developing specific skills and knowledge, and provides support while learning the job.

Minutes – accurate and complete overview of topics discussed during the meeting

Mise en place – translates from French as 'put in place' and is a term used in the hospitality industry to describe the preparations needed for service

Monitor – observing and supervising activities in progress to ensure they are on schedule to meet the objectives and performance targets and that the procedure is working properly

Morale – the ability of a group to maintain a positive attitude and motivation

Objectives – goals or realistic things that need to be achieved

Occupational health – an area or department concerned with the health and well-being of employees

Operations manual – a document that describes in detail the procedures that an organisation uses to deliver services

Organisational policy – the policies, practices and set procedures of an establishment

Out-booking – when a hotel moves customers to another hotel, usually because it has been overbooked

Overbooking – when more rooms/places are booked than are actually available

Par level – the minimum quantity of a stock item that an organisation must have stored on the premises

PAT testing – portable appliance testing; yearly testing of electrical equipment by a qualified electrician.

Performance measures – the process of collecting, reviewing and taking action on information regarding the performance of an individual

Personal development plan – to follow

Policies – a statement or ruling of how an organisation, government or society should conduct itself

Portable appliance testing (PAT) – yearly testing of electrical equipment by a qualified electrician.

Pre-authorisation – a process in which a credit card is checked to ensure a certain amount of funds are available to spend

Procedures and processes – a pre-organised or step-by-step activity or method

Prohibition notice – issued if an inspector believes that work activities involve a serious risk of 'personal injury'. This will prevent further work being carried out in the premises or area deemed to be dangerous.

Rack rate – term commonly used in the hotel industry. Often customers have been charged rack rate prices when they book directly and on the day. Rack rate prices are more expensive than the rates customers could have got if they booked well ahead or through sole agents. Rack rates can vary depending on offer and demand and are generally more expensive during weekends and holiday seasons.

Reconcile – to compare and check that one account is compatible or consistent with another; for example, the cash register's end-of-day report matches the money in the till

Recruitment – the process of identifying, finding and hiring the person most qualified and suitable for a job

Recycling – to re-use old or waste products and turn them into other products

Referral – to follow

Refresher training – training intended to certify recall and reinforcement of previously acquired knowledge and skills (such as fire training procedures or food hygiene)

Representative or professional body – an organisation that has a common goal for the members or interested parties. It often represents an industry sector such as hospitality or travel and may campaign for or publicise current industry issues.

Reservation – an arrangement whereby something, especially a seat, room or an item, is reserved for a particular person or a group

Resource – a product, person, money or an item used in an organisation or individual to function efficiently

Revenue – income

Reviewing – to examine a situation to find out if changes or improvements need to be made

Risk assessments – these require the employer to evaluate risks to employees' health and safety from any workplace hazards. The employer needs to consider what in the working area could cause injury or harm and if the hazards could be eliminated; and if not, which preventive or protective measures can be put in place to control the risks.

Rooming – when a receptionist escorts a hotel guest to their room and performs a short tour of its amenities and features

Sales mix – the breakdown of the variety of services or products sold by a company. A company's sales mix can also be looked at as percentage of sales for each type of service or products over the total sales volume.

Scheduling – this is a plan of procedure, usually written, to establish time allowed for each item or process.

Sector Skills Council – employer-led organisation covering specific industries. The goals are to support employers with apprenticeship standards, to reduce skills shortages and improve productivity.

Server – a computer or sets of computers that acts as the database to other computers

Shadowing – when a member of staff follows the work of a person in another role for a set period of time

Sister hotel – a hotel affiliated with your organisation through having the same owner or brand

Skype – an internet telephony service provider that offers free calling between computers and low-cost calling to regular telephones that aren't connected to the internet.

SMART objective – objectives that are Specific, Measureable, Achievable, Realistic and Time-bound

Social responsibility – acting with concern and sensitivity, aware of the impact of your actions on others, particularly the disadvantaged.

Software – software is a general term for logically organised collections of computer data and instructions. There two types: system software: provides non-task-specific functions of the computer, e.g. booting, and application software: specific functions to execute specific task, e.g. Word

Staff turnover – the rate at which employees join and leave an organisation

Standard operational procedure (SOP) – recorded, regularly recurring tasks describing a procedure and how something should be done. The purpose is to carry out the tasks correctly and always in the same manner.

Standards – a set level of attainment, quality and service

Stock – purchased products and items being stored on the premises before being used

Stock control – the process of managing products and items stored on the premises to ensure there are enough to meet the demands of the business and stay within the budget

Stock levels – amounts of specific items available for use or in storage

Succession plan – thinking ahead about which team members could be ready for a position before the person currently doing it leaves the organisation

SWOT analysis – SWOT stands for 'Strengths, Weaknesses, Opportunities and Threats'. This is a method of analysis of the business environment and the company's positioning within it.

Thread count – refers to the number of horizontal and vertical threads in one square inch of fabric. A thread count of 200 is considered good quality and higher than this is called percale.

Touchpoints – any point of contact between a customer and a member of staff

Traceability – having information and records to be able to trace something back to its source. For example, being able to trace eggs back to the farm where they were laid.

Trading standards – trading standards professionals act on behalf of consumers and business. They advise on and enforce laws that govern the way we buy, sell, rent and hire goods and services.

Training calendar – a calendar normally circulated by the Human Resources department, outlining upcoming training opportunities

Transaction – when something is exchanged, for example, a product for money

Unique selling point – to follow

URL (uniform or universal resource locator) – the letters and symbols (such as https://www.hodder.co.uk/) that make up the website address

Valance – a piece of plain or decorative fabric that is placed between the mattress and the bed base to provide a neat or ornate finish.

Video conferencing – using computers to provide a video link between two or more people. You are able to see them during the communication.

Website – virtual location containing several information about company or individuals; webpages and data files accessible through internet connection

Wi-Fi – stands for wireless fidelity; this technology allows computers and other devices to communicate over a wireless signal

INDEX

A
accident book 33
accidents 54–5, 64, 65
achievements, recognising 8
administrative duties 13–14
advertising 189–90
alcohol
 legislation 121–3
 misuse 123
 weights and measures 122
allocating tasks 16, 80–1, 108–9, 132–3, 160, 205–6
Approved Codes of Practice 48
assault 60
atmosphere 93
authority, limits of 70–1
autonomy 223

B
back pain 34
banquet 88
 see also functions
bed linen *see* linen service
beverages *see* alcohol; drinks service
bookings *see* reservations and booking service
Braille 178
brainstorming 4
briefings 52, 81, 112, 133, 281
 see also debriefing; meetings
budgets 27

C
career pathways 284–7
cash-and-carry 26
cash float 254
cash registers 241, 254
charity events 191
chemicals 45, 53
chilled storage 31
cleaning 138, 146–8
 equipment 148
 materials 34, 45, 147–8
 see also housekeeping service
collective decisions 4
communication 20, 52
 breakdowns in 20
 clarifying 21
 with customers 172–3, 229–34
 effective 3–4, 20–1, 134
 email 231
 face-to-face 230
 formal 272
 informal 272
 negotiation 231–3
 questions 169–70
 stages of 229–30
 telephone 230
 verbal 21
complaints 141, 182, 222–3, 225
 see also customer service

computerised systems 244
 booking systems 175–6
 contactless payments 241
 electronic point of sale (EPOS) 254
 failure of 33
 see also technology
confidentiality 19
 see also data protection; record keeping
conflict 21–2
consumer regulations 221
contactless payment systems 241
contingency planning 71, 113–15
Control of Substances Hazardous to Health (COSHH) Regulations 2002 45
credit notes 29–30
customer satisfaction 32, 181
customer service 77–82
 charter 77, 220
 complaints 141, 182, 222–3, 225
 consumer regulations 221–2
 exceeding expectations 233–4
 failures 78
 feedback 98, 141, 145, 181
 meeting expectations 231
 negotiation 231–3
 problems 220–7
 skills 80
 see also communication

D
data protection 40, 46, 144, 177–8
Data Protection Act 1998 46, 144, 177–8
data storage 242
deadlines 7
 see also objectives
debriefing 81
 see also briefings
decisions, collective 4
 see also leadership
deep fat fryer fires 58–9
delegation 16
deliveries 61, 29–30
delivery note 29–30
departmental trainers 237
dermatitis 34
designated premises supervisor (DPS) 121
difficulties, resolving 22
direct marketing 189
 see also marketing
Disability Discrimination Act 1995 178, 281
disciplinary procedures 86
discounts 190, 191
discrimination 178, 281
distributors 26
diversity 283
drinks service 117–25
 alcohol misuse 123–5
 contingency plan 124
 job roles 118–19

licensing 121–2
refusal of service 125
specifications 120–1
weights and measures 122
legislation 121–3
drunk customers 123–5
due diligence 68

E
Electricity at Work Regulations 1989 46
electronic ID cards 61
electronic point of sale (EPOS) systems 254
 see also computerised systems
email 231
email marketing 191
emergency procedures 53–9
Emergency Prohibition Order 41
emergency signs 53
employee
 cycle 77
 induction 78–9, 135
 responsibilities 51, 281–3
 rights 281–3
 see also job roles; recruitment; staff
employer responsibilities 43, 49–50, 281–3
employment legislation 281–3
energy, managing 25, 32, 33
Environmental Health 40
environmental impact 35
equality 18–19, 283
Equality Act 2010 179
equipment 25
 cleaning 148
 faults 71
 functions 91
 inventory 26
 legislation 44, 46
 monitoring use of 33
 portable appliance testing (PAT) 46
 protective 44
 see also technology
ethical considerations 18–19, 195
evacuation procedures 61–2

F
fairness 18–19
feedback
 constructive 84–5
 customer 98, 141, 145, 181
 see also briefings
financial management 25, 27, 32, 36
fines, non-compliance 41
Fire Precautions (Workplace) Regulations 1997 45–6
fire safety 57–9
 evacuation procedures 61–2
 extinguisher colour codes 58
 fire-fighting signs 53
first aid 53, 55–6
first impressions 128

293

food
    allergens 47
    legislation 47
    monitoring use of 32, 36
    safety 47, 69–70
Food Safety Act 1990 47
Food Safety (General Food Hygiene) Regulations 1995 47
food service 103–15
    checklists 110–11, 113
    contingency plan 113–15
    job roles 106–9
    legislation 47, 104–6
    maintenance report 109–10
    methods 103
    preparation 112
    stock check 111
formal communication 272
fraud 60, 61, 256
frozen storage 30
functions 88–98
    atmosphere 93
    customer care 95
    equipment and resources 91–3
    health and safety 96–7
    marketing 89
    problems and complaints 98
    record keeping 90–1
    risk assessment 97
    seating plans 91
    special requirements 96
    staffing 93–4
    table layout 91–2
    table plans 91
    timing 92
H
handover sessions 52
    see also briefings; debriefing
Hazard Analysis Critical Control Point (HACCP) 69–70
hazard warning signs 53
hazardous substances 45
hazards 34, 53, 64–5, 67
health and safety 34, 39–71
    contingency planning 71
    enforcement 40–1
    food service 47, 69–70
    for functions 96–7
    hazards 34, 53, 64–5, 67
    housekeeping service 142–3
    legislation 43–7, 281–2
    non-compliance 42
    organisational procedures 282
    risk assessment 34, 43, 66–70, 97
    sources of support 48
    staff training 51, 52
    technology 249
Health and Safety Executive (HSE) 34, 40
Health and Safety at Work Act 1974 43, 281, 282
housekeeping service 128–50
    allocating duties 132–3
    briefing staff 133–4
    cleaning 138, 146–8
    complaints 141
    health and safety 142–3
    job roles 130–1

legislation 142–4
problems with 139–40
procedures 136–8, 145
record keeping 149–50
resources 148
scheduling 131–2, 137
staff training 135–6
human resources *see* recruitment; staff
I
ID cards 61
improvement notice 41
in-house training 77
incentives 18
induction 78–9, 135
informal communication 272
injury 60
interviewing 267–8
invoices 29
J
jargon 4
job description 14–15, 264
job roles 12–15
    drinks service 118–19
    food service 106–9
    housekeeping service 130–1
    reservations and booking service 166–8
    see also supervisor
job satisfaction 17
Johari Window 84–5
L
leadership
    qualities 17–18
    styles 18
leaflets 191
learning and development 236
    see also training
legislation
    aims of 42–3
    Approved Codes of Practice 48
    breaches of 179
    consumer regulations 221–2
    data protection 46, 144, 177–8
    drinks service 121–3
    employment 281–3
    food service 47, 104–6
    health and safety 43–7, 281–2
    housekeeping service 142–4
    promotional activities 196–7
    reception duties 157
    recruitment 265–6
    reservations and booking service 177–9
Licensing Act 2003 121–2
lifting 34, 44
linen service 204–16
    linen sizes 208
    problems 213
    procedures 205–9, 212
listening skills 172
lost items 61
loyalty schemes 191
M
maintenance issues, reporting 59
Management of Health and Safety at Work Regulations 1999 43
mandatory signs 53
manual handling 34, 44

Manual Handling Operations Regulations 1992 44
manufacturers 26
market share 188
marketing 89, 189, 191
meetings 273–8
    agenda 274
    chairing 275–6
    minutes 276–7
    team meetings 81–2
mobile technology 242
motivating others 13, 16–17, 18, 80
N
negotiation 231–3
O
objectives 2–5, 7–8, 77
open days 191
organisational procedures 49
organisational standards 144–5
P
paper-based booking systems 175
payments 252–8
    cash registers 254
    daily responsibilities 252
    discrepancies 257–8
    electronic point of sale (EPOS) systems 254
    emergencies 255
    fraudulent 256
    problems 255–6
    recording information 257
    security of 255
penalties, non-compliance 41
performance gap analysis 237–9
performance management 83–6, 180–1
person specification 264
personal injury 60
Personal Protective Equipment at Work Regulations 1992 44
personal selling 189
portable appliance testing (PAT) 46
pre-service briefings 81
pricing policies 176
professional behaviour 17–19
prohibition notice 41
prohibition signs 53
promotional activities 159, 188–200
    costing 193
    legislation 196–7
protective equipment 44
Provision and Use of Work Equipment Regulations 1998 44
public relations (PR) 190
Q
questions 169–70
R
reception 155–63
    allocating duties 160
    arrival 158–9
    departure 160
    handovers 160–1
    legislation 157
    problems 161–3
    training 161
    upselling 159
record keeping 62–3, 90–1, 149–50
    see also data protection

recruitment
    advertising jobs 266
    assessment activities 268–9
    interviewing 267–8
    job analysis 262–3
    job applications 266–7
    job description 264
    legislation 265–6
    making an offer 269–70
    person specification 264
    selection process 262
    shortlisting 267
    staffing requirements 261–2
recycling 35
relationships *see* working relationships
Reporting of Injuries, Diseases and Dangerous Occurrences Regulations (RIDDOR) 1995 45
representative bodies 285–6
reservations and booking service 166–84
    complaints 182
    computerised systems 175–6
    job roles 166–8
    legislation 177–9
    out-booking 176
    overbooking 176–7
    paper-based systems 175
    pricing policies 176
    problems 180, 182
    training 170–1
resources
    availability of 26
    energy 25, 32, 33
    environmental impact 35
    equipment 25, 26, 33
    financial 25, 27, 32
    functions 92
    housekeeping service 148
    identifying 24–6
    monitoring use of 32–3, 36
    ordering 29
    problems obtaining 31
    security of 31
    staff 24, 26
    stock checks 26, 111
    storing 28–9, 30–1
    suitability of 28
    supplies 24, 26–7
    time 25
    see also staff
retail outlets 26
rewards 18
risk assessment 34, 43, 66–70, 97
S
safety signs 53–4
seating plans 91
Sector Skills Council 285
security
    payments 255
    resources 31
    workplace 59–61
self-awareness 84–5
selling *see* personal selling
Skype 189
SMART objectives 2, 5, 7–8
    see also objectives
social responsibilities 195

software 243
specialist suppliers 26
sponsorship 190
staff 24
    allocating tasks 16, 80–1, 108–9, 132–3, 160, 205–6
    assessment 32, 84, 268–9
    feedback 181
    performance 83–6, 180–1, 237–9
    requirements 261–2
    retention 236
    rotas 26
    structures 12–13
    turnover 19, 78
    see also job roles; recruitment; teams
standard operational procedures (SOPs) 286
stock
    checks 26, 111
    control 32, 36
    see also resources
storage
    temperatures 30–1
    resources 28–9, 30–1
strength and weaknesses 16
succession plan 237
supervisor
    leadership styles 18
    limits of authority 70–1
    role of 13–20, 39, 41, 50–2, 60, 63
supplies 24, 26–7
support, providing 6, 81
T
table
    layout 91–2
    plans 91
target market 192–3
teams
    allocating tasks 16, 80–1, 108–9, 132–3, 160, 205–6
    briefings 52, 81, 112, 133, 281
    characteristics of 11
    debriefing 81
    empowering 223
    meetings 81–2
    morale 80
    motivating 13, 16–17, 18, 80
    objectives 2–5, 7–8, 77
    performance management 83–6, 180–1, 237–9
    purpose of 1
    recognising achievements 8
    roles and responsibilities 78
    strengths and weaknesses 16
    supporting team members 6, 81
    working relationships 10–12
    see also staff
technology
    computerised systems 244
    data storage 242
    environmental issues 249
    health and safety 249
    introducing 243–5
    maintenance 247–8
    mobile 242
    problems 246–7
    software 243
    staff-computer interface 241

staff training 244–5
types of 240–3
temperatures, storage 30–1
terrorism 60
theft 60, 61
tills *see* cash registers; payments
time management 25
trade discounts 191
trade fairs 191
Trading Standards 40
training
    calendar 237
    health and safety 51, 52
    importance of 170–1, 236–7
    induction 78–9, 135
    in-house 77
    performance gap analysis 237–9
    reception 161
    record sheet 135–6
    technology 244–5
turnover, of staff 19, 78
U
unsafe acts 65
upselling 159
URL (universal resource locator) 240
V
vandalism 60
verbal communication 21
video conferencing 189
W
warning signs 53
waste management 32, 35
website 240
welfare, of workforce 19
wholesalers 26
Wi-Fi 242
working environment 19
    see also health and safety
working relationships
    colleagues 12–13
    teams 10–12
Workplace (Health, Safety and Welfare) Regulations 1992 43
workplace security 59–61

PICTURE CREDITS

Every effort has been made to tract the copyright holders of material reproduced here. The authors and publishers would like to thank the following for permission to reproduce copyright illustrations:

p.3 © WavebreakMediaMicro – Fotolia.com; p.8 © Lynne Carpenter – Fotolia.com; p.11 © Andrew Callaghan / Hodder Education; p.20 © CandyBox Images – Fotolia.com; p.25 © Lucky Dragon – Fotolia.com; p.28 © starekase – Fotolia.com; p.35 © Pixavril – Fotolia.com; p.44 Contains public sector information published by the Health and Safety Executive and licensed under the Open Government Licence; p.52 © KatarzynaBialasiewicz – iStock via Thinkstock; p.78 © JackF – Fotolia.com; p.82 © Nick Freund – Fotolia.com; p.89 © ilfotokunst – Fotolia.com; p.119 © © Hero Images/Corbis; p.120 (l) © Henrik Winther Ander (r) © Henrik Winther Ander (b) © VRD – Fotolia.com; p.129 © william87 – Fotolia.com; p.134 © Wavebreakmedia Ltd via Thinkstock; p.145 © Monkey Business – Fotolia.com; p. 147 © fottoo – Fotolia.com; p.159 © Robert Kneschke – Fotolia.com; p.192 © Pavel Losevsky – Fotolia.com; p.193 © DragonImages – Fotolia.com; p.195 (c) © Dmitriy Danilenko; p.198 © Art Directors & TRIP / Alamy; p.205 © contrastwerkstatt – Fotolia.com; p.208 (c) "© Chuck Franklin / Alamy; p.215 © Pete Titmuss / Alamy; p.241 © MR – Fotolia.com; p.242 © Tyler Olson – Fotolia.com; p.245 © contrastwerkstatt – Fotolia.com; p.263 © Photographee.eu – Fotolia.com; p.268 © Adam Gregor – Fotolia.com; p. 275 © Monkey Business – Fotolia.com